AF477323

CARO

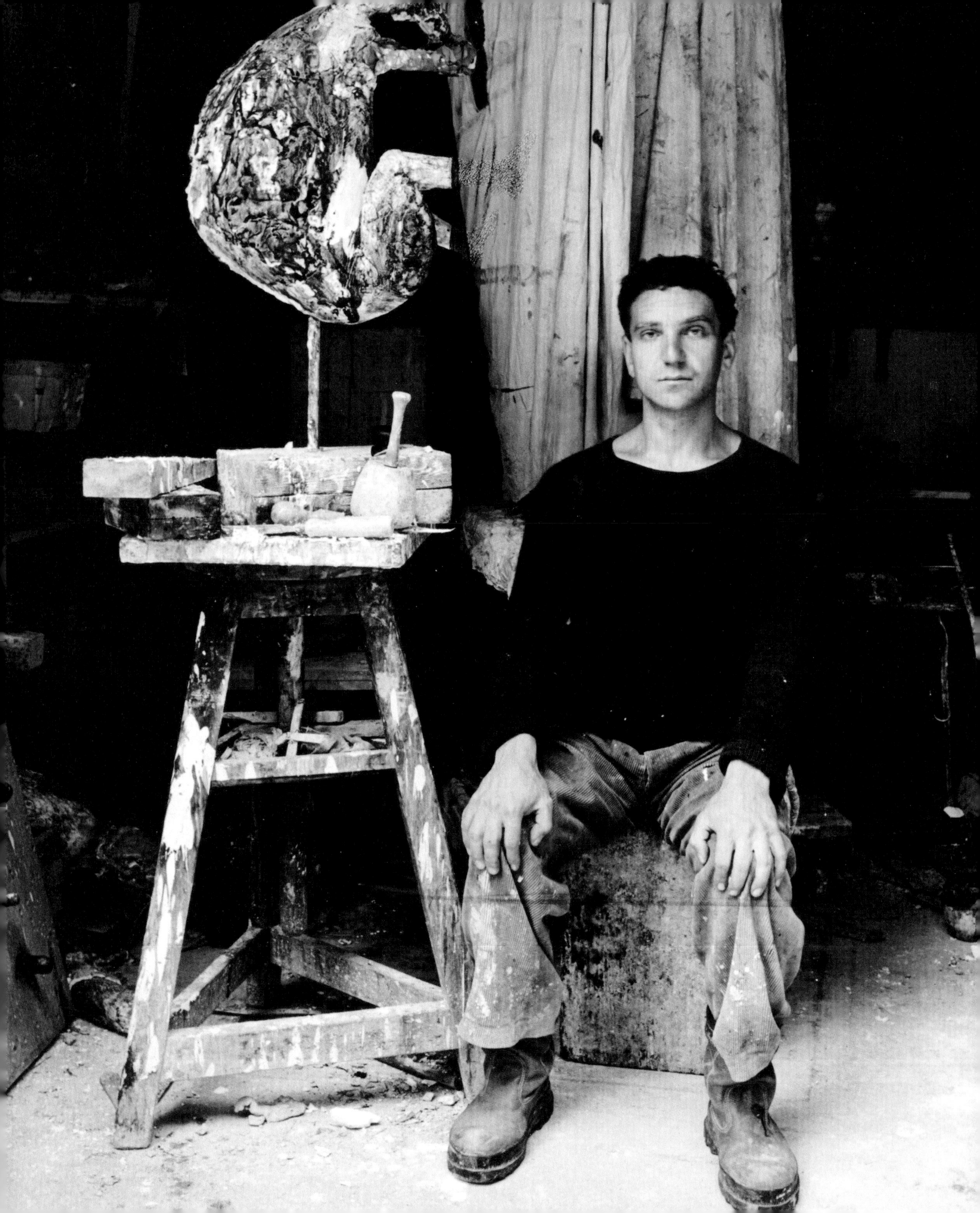

CARO
CLOSE UP

Julius Bryant and Martina Droth
with an essay by Robert Storr

Yale Center for British Art
Yale University Press / New Haven and London

This publication accompanies the exhibition *Caro: Close Up*, organized by the Yale Center for British Art, New Haven, and on view from October 18 to December 30, 2012.

Exhibition curated by Julius Bryant and Martina Droth.

Library of Congress Cataloging-in-Publication Data

Bryant, Julius.
Caro : close up / Julius Bryant, Martina Droth, Robert Storr.
pages cm
Issued in connection with an exhibition held October 18–December 30, 2012, Yale Center for British Art, New Haven, Connecticut.
ISBN 978-0-300-17603-2 (hardback)
1. Caro, Anthony, 1924—Exhibitions. I. Droth, Martina. II. Storr, Robert. III. Caro, Anthony, 1924– Works. Selections. IV. Yale Center for British Art. V. Title.
NB497.C35A4 2012
730.92—dc23
2012030896

A catalogue record for this book is available from the British Library.

Front jacket: *Table Piece XCVII* (cat. 30)
Back jacket: *Little Book of Opera* (cat. 41)
Frontispiece: Portrait of Caro by Nigel Henderson, 1957

Designed by Miko McGinty
Set in Ideal Sans by Tina Henderson
Copyedited by Mary Yakush
Printed and bound in Italy by Conti Tipocolor SpA, Florence

CONTENTS

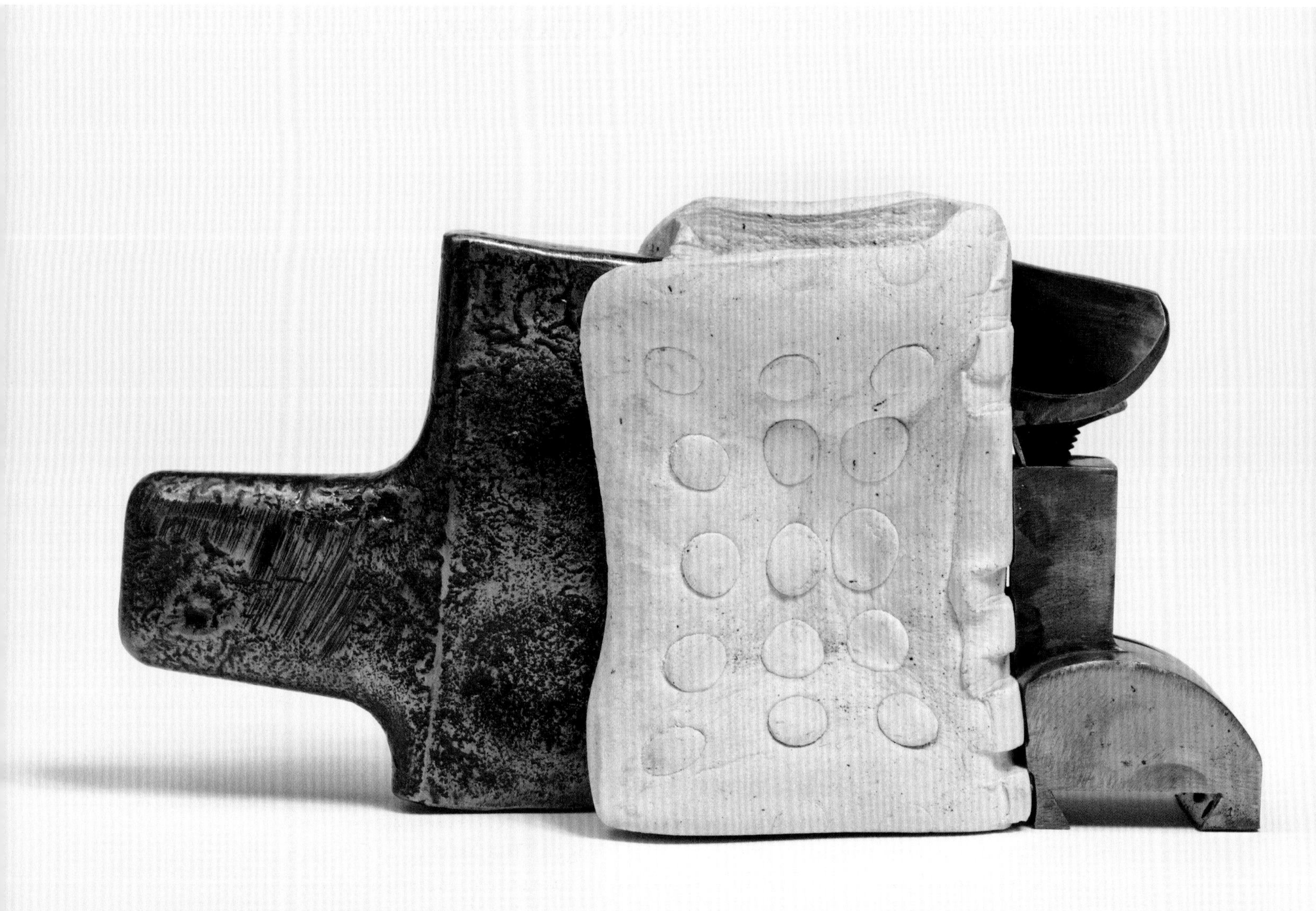

Small Wedge Book (cat. 40)

Director's Foreword and Acknowledgments

As Britain's most acclaimed and prolific sculptor, Sir Anthony Caro needs no introduction. Best known for his brilliant sculptures in museums and galleries around the world, from Seattle to Tokyo, he has inspired generations of artists to explore the potential of three-dimensional collage in his characteristic material, industrial steel. Encouraged by the best-known American art critic of the twentieth century, Clement Greenberg, Caro stepped out of the shadows of his mentor Henry Moore, and of the American Abstract Expressionist sculptor David Smith, in the 1960s. He took sculpture off the pedestal and let it speak more directly to the viewer, with all the psychological presence of a living person. Now eighty-eight, Caro is as busy as ever with international exhibitions and commissions. *Caro: Close Up* explores the artist's more private sculptures—through works made on an intimate scale in a variety of materials, from steel, bronze, and silver, to stoneware, porcelain, and paper, ranging from his earliest student drawings annotated by Henry Moore to sculptures made only months ago.

Remarkably, this is the first exhibition of Caro's work to be organized by a North American museum since his mid-career retrospective at the Museum of Modern Art in 1975. Some viewers will be familiar with his large-scale sculptures from the installation series "on the Roof" at the Metropolitan Museum of Art in 1988 and 2011. His work also has been shown in the United States at Boston's Christian Science Center (1980); the Storm King Art Center, in New York State (1981); the Frederik Meijer Sculpture Park, in Grand Rapids, Michigan (2003); and in the galleries of distinguished collectors, such as David Mirvish, and of notable dealers, including André Emmerich, Annely and David Juda, and Mitchell-Innes and Nash. The Yale Center for British Art is proud to organize this examination of Caro's career as a sculptor, long overdue in the United States.

Caro's connections with Yale span half a century. When seeking a Ford Foundation English-Speaking Union grant to visit the United States for the first time, in 1959, he included in his application his wish to visit "Yale University School of Design, where Albers is using Bauhaus methods of teaching art." The first book on Caro (after exhibition catalogues), by Richard Whelan (1974), began as a bachelors-degree essay at Yale in 1969, when the writer was a student of Kermit Champa. Paul Mellon was President of the Board of Trustees of the National Gallery of Art, Washington, DC, when Anthony Caro was commissioned to create a sculpture for the atrium of the East Building, designed by I. M. Pei and opened in 1978. Mr. Mellon's personal adviser on British art, Basil Taylor, had been (with David Sylvester) the first critic to single out Caro for praise, for his contribution to a group exhibition at London's Institute of Contemporary Art in 1955. The Yale University Art Gallery acquired two major sculptures by Caro (*Table Piece CII*, 1970, purchased in 1983 with the Katharine Ordway Fund, and *Ocean*, 1982–83, donated in 2006 as part of the Charles B. Benenson, BA, 1933, Collection), and in 1989 the university awarded him an Honorary Doctor of Fine Arts degree.

Caro has a particular affection for both of Louis Kahn's buildings, on either side of Chapel Street in New Haven: the Yale University Art Gallery and the Yale Center for British Art. Indeed, the origins of *Caro: Close Up* lie in the building itself. The special qualities of daylight playing over a subtle range of materials cast a spell over our guest curator, Julius Bryant, Keeper of Word & Image, Victoria and Albert Museum, when he came to the Center as a Visiting Scholar in 2009, as part of the curatorial exchange program between the Center and the Victoria and Albert Museum, London. We are indebted to Julius for proposing the exhibition to us, and for developing it with such sensitivity to its display, a key facet of any approach to Caro's work. As Julius recognized, the Center offers an environment particularly suited to an intimate experience of sculpture. This experience is not what is felt in great public spaces, sculpture parks, and "white cube" galleries; rather, it is more akin to the sensation of savoring sculpture in the domestic setting of a great private collection. Julius made the selection, in consultation with Sir Anthony and his studio, and in collaboration with Martina Droth, the Center's Head of Research and Curator of Sculpture. Many of the sculptures in this exhibition have been lent by private owners for the first time, allowing us to bring together works that have led a private existence, cherished as special possessions without circulating through the art market. We are immensely grateful to our private lenders for sharing with the public these works of art, which they enjoy as the finer fabric of daily domestic life. Our thanks are owed to Mr. and Mrs. Phillip King, David and Audrey Mirvish, Clifford Ross, and Karen Wilkin, as well as those lenders who wish to remain anonymous. In addition, a number of key loans come from museums: we are extremely grateful to the Museum of Fine Arts, Houston, for generously allowing us to borrow the newly acquired *Orangerie*; the Museum of Modern Art for the loan of *Deluge*; and, for *Minoan*, the Metropolitan Museum of Art, where Anne Strauss, Associate Curator, also helpfully assisted with questions concerning works in the collection. Together, these loans allow us to represent important works across the diverse range of Caro's oeuvre.

The largest single group of loans comes from the collection of the artist himself and his family. We are deeply grateful to Sir Anthony for generously sharing his work, as well as allowing liberal access to his personal archive of correspondence and photographs, which have greatly enriched the scholarly project and visual presentation of the catalogue. Work on the exhibition and research for the book were greatly facilitated by Anthony Caro's assistants, working at his studio, Barford Sculptures, in Camden Town: Pat Cunningham, who has worked with Caro for more than forty years, generously spent time showing works to the curators, and shared his expertise on handling and installation; Jackie Honsig-Erlenburg, who mediated among all parties to facilitate photography and patiently helped answer questions on the complex logistics of the exhibition and book; and Siri Fischer Hansen and Olivia Bax. We are especially grateful to Sheila Girling and to Paul Caro, for help with the selection of loans from the studio collection.

We are delighted that the Yale University Art Gallery's two masterly works by Caro will be on view: the splendid *Table Piece CII* mentioned previously is included in the exhibition, while *Ocean* was recently installed on Chapel Street, opposite the Center. The preparations for the Caro exhibition coincided with the Gallery's magnificent expansion into beautifully refurbished buildings, and we are deeply grateful to our colleagues for accommodating our requests at an exceptionally busy time. Special thanks are owed to Jock Reynolds, Henry J. Heinz II Director, and Jennifer Gross, the Seymour H. Knox, Jr., Curator of Modern and Contemporary Art, for their support of our project, as well as Karen Serres, Nina and Lee Griggs Associate Curator of Early European Art; Cathleen Chaffee, the Horace W. Goldsmith Curator of Modern and Contemporary Art; and John ffrench, Manager, Department of Digital Media.

The exhibition and its accompanying publication would not have been possible without the generous help of many individuals at Yale and beyond. Robert Storr, Dean of the School of Art at Yale University, has written an illuminating essay on the intergenerational influences that Caro absorbed and exerted. We are immensely indebted to Dean Storr for his contribution, which, together with the essays by Julius Bryant and Martina Droth, offers a springboard for the reassessment of Caro's oeuvre. This beautifully illustrated book includes documents and archival photographs of the artist, his circle, and past installations of his work—some never before published. New photography was commissioned for as many of the sculptures as possible, offering readers different views and close details that will allow a fresh examination of the material qualities of the work. We are indebted to the photographer John Hammond for his expert work; to the photographers Maris Hutchinson, of EPW Studio, and Mitro Hood, who provided additional photography of objects in private collections outside the UK; and to Richard Caspole at the Center for his photography of *Table Piece CII*. We owe thanks to Cultureshock Media and Federico Urdaneta for the accompanying filmed conversation between Sir Anthony Caro and Julius Bryant. We also are grateful to Mary Yakush for copyediting the book, Miko McGinty for her elegant design, and Rita Jules for her assistance during the production process.

The production of the book was superbly handled by Sally Salvesen and Sophie Sheldrake at Yale University Press, working in close collaboration with Eleanor Hughes, Associate Curator and Head of Exhibitions and Publications at the Center, and her colleagues in the department of Exhibitions and Publications, who also were responsible for overseeing all logistical details relating to the exhibition: Imogen Hart, Assistant Curator; Craig Canfield, former Publications Assistant; Sarah Rapuano, temporary Publications Assistant; Christina Smylitopolous, former Postdoctoral Research Associate in the department; and Ava Suntoke, Editor. Many other colleagues at the Center have supported the project ably. We are grateful to Theresa Fairbanks-Harris, Senior Conservator of Paper, and Mary Regan-Yttre, Conservation Assistant, for their expert advice and treatment of the drawings. Particular thanks are due to Timothy Goodhue, the Center's Registrar, and his colleagues, notably Corey Myers, Assistant Registrar, who handled the details of the loans, and Melissa Fournier, Associate Museum Registrar and Manager of Imaging Services, who helped to coordinate photography. We are especially thankful to Richard Johnson, Installation Manager, and his team—Kevin Derken, Rachel Hellerich, Abraham Omonte, Greg Shea, and Dylan Vitale—who not only installed the exhibition in the most expert way but were instrumental in the many decisions that had to be made in bringing the project to fruition. We also wish to extend our thanks to Beth Miller, Associate Director for Advancement and External Affairs, and her colleagues

Amelia Ewan, Senior Administrative Assistant; Julienne Richardson, Special Events and Advancement Coordinator; Amy McDonald, Senior Manager of Communications and Marketing; Kaci Baez, Communications Coordinator; and Lyn Rose, Senior Graphic Designer, and Elena Grossman, Graphic Designer, for their myriad contributions to the success of this exhibition, including the beautifully designed panels and brochure. Martina Droth and her colleagues in the Department of Research and Education have organized many events relating to the exhibition: we are grateful to Jane Nowosadko, Senior Manager of Programs; Linda Friedlaender, Curator of Education, and her colleagues Cyra Levenson, Associate Curator, and Jaime Ursic, Assistant Curator; as well as the administrative assistants to the department, for their imaginative educational and scholarly programs.

We are grateful to the many individuals who shared their expertise and lent collegial support to the project, and wish to acknowledge the help of Ian Barker, David Juda, and Lucy Mitchell-Innes. Julius Bryant wishes to extend particular thanks to Jules Prown, Professor Emeritus, with whom he first discussed the idea for the exhibition, for his encouragement and advice; Professor Michael Fried; and Barbara Bryant. Martina Droth also would like to acknowledge her gratitude to Rosie Ibbotson, Postdoctoral Research Associate in the Department of Prints and Drawings, who collaborated on a display of twentieth-century works alongside the Caro exhibition, and Juliana Biondo (ES '13), who in her capacity as Nancy Horton Bartels intern assisted on the same project; Jay Curley, who with Martina conceived a study day examining new perspectives on Caro's work, and Robert Slifkin, Sarah K. Rich, and Matthew Abrams for participating in this event; Penelope Curtis, Alex Potts, and Karen Wilkin for contributing to a workshop about the exhibition; and Nick Mead and Anne Wagner for their helpful and stimulating discussions of Caro's work.

Our greatest thanks are owed to Sir Anthony Caro himself, for his generous embrace of the project. Together with his collegial Studio Manager Pat Cunningham, Sir Anthony has allowed the curators the freedom to conceive the project in the way they saw best, to present his work in an innovative way that encourages a close, intimate reading.

Amy Meyers
Director, Yale Center for British Art

Caro: Close Up

Julius Bryant

Caro is best known for the large abstract sculptures that represent him in museums. His smaller works can be more like whispers, soliciting a contemplative response from the viewer, rather than public statements. They retain the scale of the artist's hands; they are made from a greater variety of materials and in a spirit of personal experiment. Many were begun away from Caro's studio in London, either at home in Hampstead or at his isolated coastal cottage in Dorset. As intimate forms, they have less impact as images when seen from afar, and they invite close study. In a gallery or museum only one or two viewers can look at them at once. As with master drawings, the experience is solitary and private, almost as if one owns the object.

The majority of Caro's smaller-scale sculptures belong to private collectors. In selecting such sculptures for this exhibition, visits were made to many private homes, where Caro's works are encountered in very different ways (fig. 1.1). Some private owners present their sculptures on white, museum-style plinths and seem to wish to live in a modernist art gallery. For others, the sculptures have to fit in with the clutter of domestic life. In the home, sculptures are encountered on bookcases, windowsills, antique sideboards, and on the walls, often alongside other art that may, at first

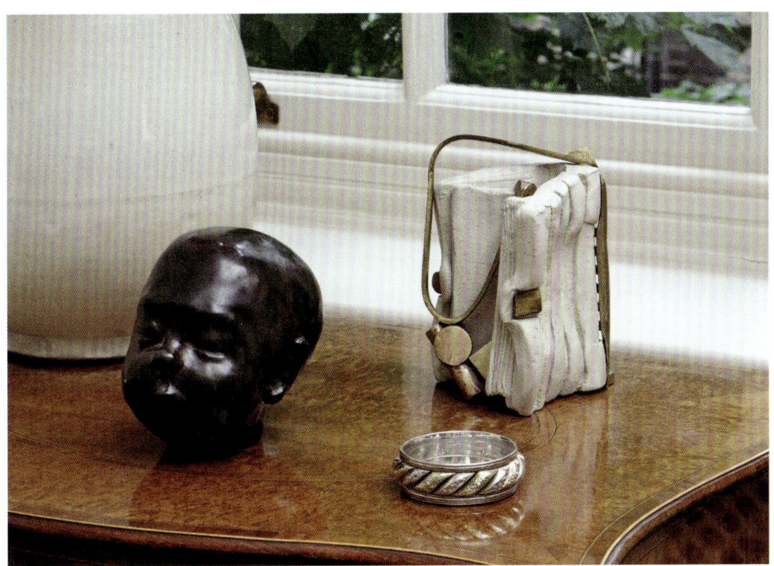

FIG. 1.1 *Little Book of Opera* (cat. 41) as shown in a London private collection, 2012

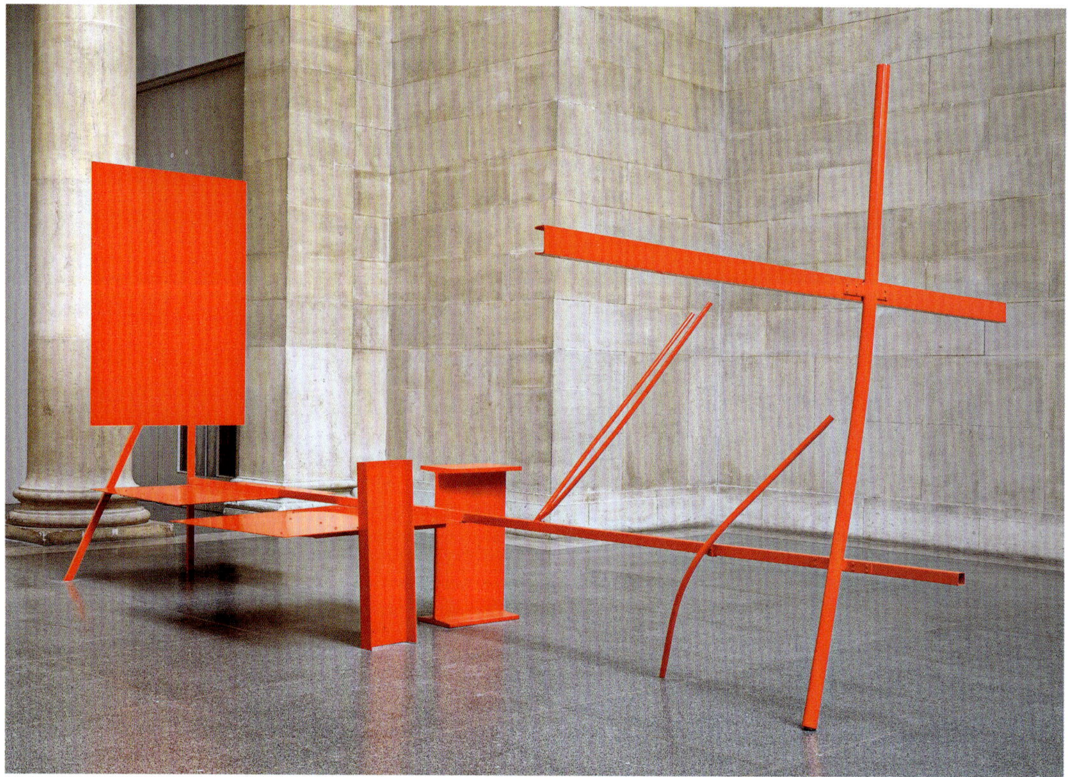

FIG. 1.2 *Early One Morning,* 1962, painted steel and aluminum, 114 x 244 x 132 in. (289.6 x 619.8 x 335.3 cm). Tate, London. © Tate, London, 2012

sight, seem to be of a very different character. Private owners get to play with their sculptures in a way that museum curators rarely can.

The Yale Center for British Art provides an ideal space in which to capture something of the private experience of Caro's sculptures in a public exhibition. In contrast to most public galleries of the late twentieth century, Louis Kahn's building offers domestic-scale interiors, subtle differentiations of materials, textures and surfaces, and varying levels of natural light, whether from the well of the atrium, top-lighting, or through large semi-shuttered windows (see fig. 5.1). The Center "experience" also differs from a conventional trip to a museum as it has a walk-in audience of local residents and university students who (partly thanks to free admission) can make regular visits. The relatively informal atmosphere is further due to the floor-length glass entrance. With no grand flight of steps up from the street to remove the visitor from everyday life, it provides the opportunity to place one of Caro's larger sculptures in the entrance hall, visible at ground level to passersby.

When asked about the different rapport that one enjoys with his smaller-scale sculpture, Caro replied "all my work is intimate."[1] The formal qualities one can explore through silent study, one-to-one, are there to be found, he believes, just as much in the public-scale sculptures of brightly painted or varnished steel. The psychological relationship between viewer and sculpture is inevitably different with larger works, as one has to look up, rather than down, to see more of them, admiring from a respectful distance and perhaps discussing with companions. Looking at a breathtaking sculpture like *Early One Morning* (fig. 1.2), the first reaction is of exhilaration and fascination rather than of secretly coveting something one wants to take home and cherish. Caro's belief that "all my work is intimate" suggests that qualities lie locked up in his classic gallery-scale works that await discovery by the patient observer. His statement challenges us, in effect, to understand how we experience smaller-scale sculpture and then to transfer that awareness and approach to the more public works that we think we know already.

The familiar photographs of Caro do not at first suggest a quiet, solitary artist. Several photographers have captured him in the workshop (fig. 1.3). Whether in the former piano factory that serves as his north London studio (fig. 1.4), at the York Steel Company in Toronto, the Ripamonte factory near Veduggio in Italy, or at his former studio at Ancram, New York, he appears as a worldly man of action with loyal assistants, commanding steel into art. There has always been, however, a private side to his work, one shared with the artist Sheila Girling, whom he married in 1949. Not many major artists have made their home in the same house for sixty years. Caro moved back to London in 1954 to teach at St. Martin's School of Art after two years as an assistant to Henry Moore. His home, a former stable and coach house up a quiet lane behind the center of Hampstead, was converted by his architect friends Peter and Alison Smithson, initially to provide five rooms. The one-car garage became his studio and is now part of the house, as his study. He took on his present studio in Camden Town in 1969, where his business, Barford Sculptures, employs a changing team of recent art school graduates. Meanwhile, he continues to work alone during evenings at home and at weekends at his studio in Dorset, a former coastguard's cottage with almost 360-degree views of the sea.

Caro's working practice has not been to make maquettes for enlargement by assistants and casting in bronze (as became customary for Henry Moore), but rather to work directly, at full-scale, hands-on to the finish. However, he has used cardboard, wood, wax, and other ephemeral materials as starting points for some of his small works. For his major commissions his team creates scale models of the sculptures and of the settings into which they will be installed, and here we see him working more like an exhibition designer (see figs. 5.4 and 5.5).

Caro likes to work close-up. The spatial limitations of his former garage studio had a positive side. In 1972 he recalled the benefits of making

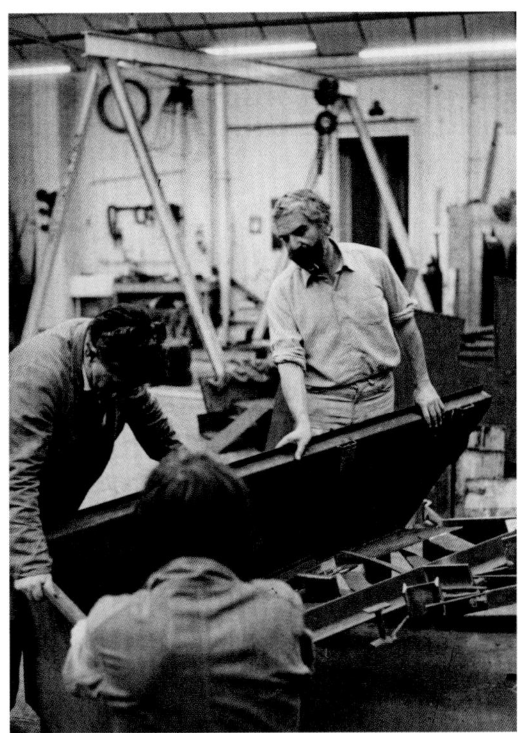

FIG. 1.3 **Caro and assistants working in his Camden Town studio, 1974**

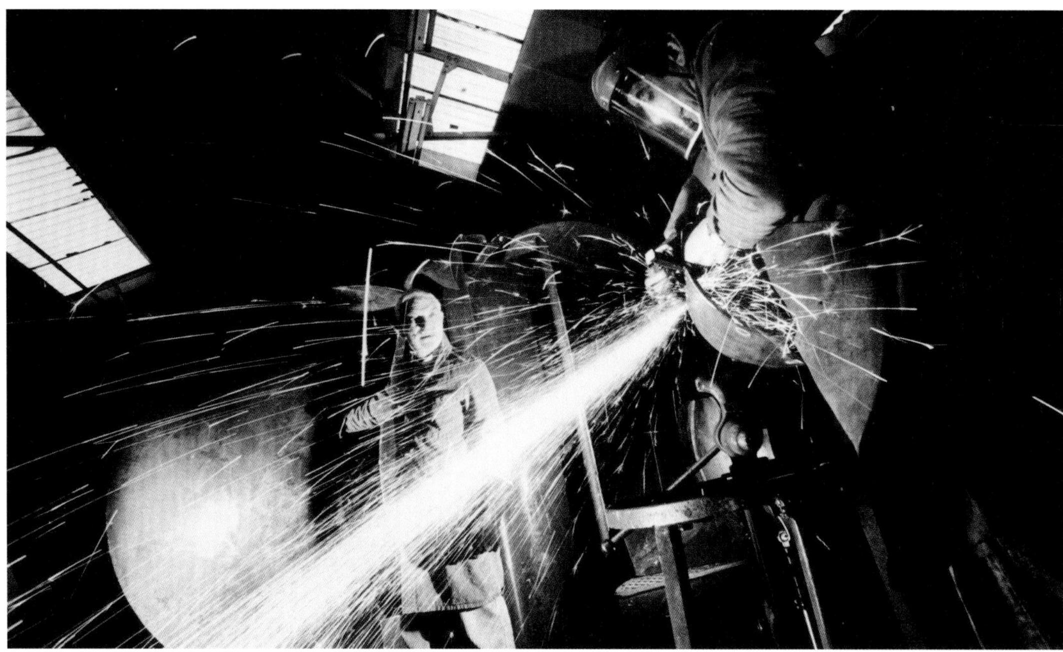

FIG. 1.4 Caro working in his Camden studio with assistants, 2004

sculpture in a confined area: "the advantage of making them where I couldn't stand back from them was that I used this limitation to prevent my falling back on my previous knowledge of balance and composition. That's not new. Kenneth Noland told me in 1959 how he painted on the floor and on sawhorses for the same reason. Working in a one-car garage as I used to do was a way of trying to force my mind to accept a new sort of rightness that I wanted—I had to refrain from backing away and editing the work prematurely."[2] Once one realizes that *Early One Morning* was made in this confined space it can be read very differently, almost like two sculptures conjoined. The vertical sheet and I-beams form the anchoring base, their proportions set by the available floor space and height of the garage, their 90-degree alignment by the side walls that supported the work in progress. In contrast, the projecting axis and poles seem to accelerate and fly out, as if the garage doors had just been opened to greet the dawn.

Caro met the American color field painter Kenneth Noland on his first visit to the United States in 1959, and they became lifelong friends. The idea of working in close-up, to resist the instinct to compose in traditional ways, had been fundamental to Jackson Pollock. In 1950, when his champion, the critic Clement Greenberg, discussed Pollock in a seminar at Black Mountain College in North Carolina, Noland was in the audience. He learned how the painter took the canvas off the easel and onto the floor in order to stop him stepping back and reviewing his composition before it felt finished. Pollock worked in close-up so that his art would not seem "fussy" or "overdone."[3] Pollock's paintings possess a similar double life to that of Caro's larger sculptures. Hung on the walls of modern galleries, some can seem as grand as history paintings, as if they are impassioned public statements about the energy and turmoil of modern life in New York. But when one visits Pollock's small garden-studio, yards away from his house on Long Island, and sees the floor on which the paintings were made, one can imagine viewing them from above and alone, making one want to look at them again close-up.[4]

Caro is no abstract expressionist, of course, and neither was Noland, but they shared a determination to make art from a fresh physical perspective, so as to escape academic conventions of composition. Pollock took paintings off the easel, but they hang on walls. Caro famously took sculpture off the pedestal, and in museums and galleries this principle is still honored. For Caro's smaller sculptures made for the "table," the sense of intimacy is there to be found by meeting them one to one. For example, through scrutiny of a small sculpture like *Table Piece XLII* (fig. 1.5) one may recognize the "intimate" qualities of *Early One Morning*, even if one did not know that Caro's most famous sculpture had been composed in a closed, confined space. The compositional theme, of balancing unity with disparity, is similar. The two blocks anchor the sculpture, positioned like the first principles of composition in a still life by Cézanne or an abstract painting by Mondrian. Parallel and at right angles are set two further rectilinear elements, firm as rulers in a geometrical equation. From each block runs a linking line that curves up to meet and support the crossbeam. Like a flow of energy from batteries, the linear progression leads to a precise springing arc that is tensed by the load it holds from one corner. Below, this rectangular sheet plunges like a diver or waterfall, frozen in midair. Like *Early One Morning*, the *Table Piece* sculpture is a play between two parts, the slow stable side heightening by contrast the more dynamic form.

Unlocking the qualities of Caro's smaller sculptures through such scrutiny enables us to see more than the intimate character of his large gallery works. Through this quiet and private pleasure we soon realize how little we really look at our own worlds in close-up.

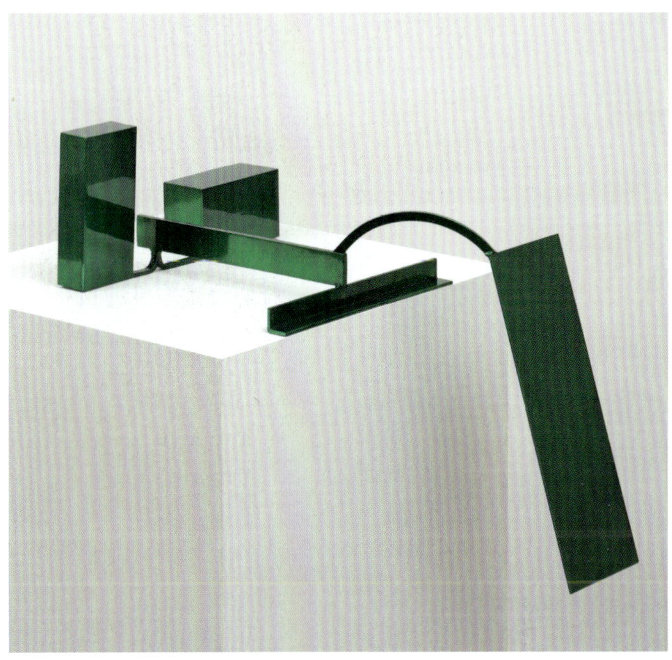

FIG. 1.5 *Table Piece XLII* (cat. 26)

NOTES

1. Caro in conversation with the author, 2011.
2. Phyllis Tuchman, "An Interview with Anthony Caro," *Artforum* 10 (June 1972): 56–58. In 1974 Caro compared his working method to that of David Smith who "often worked on the floor. . . . it gave him a freedom, but it also flattened the sculpture somewhat." Caro quoted Ian Barker, *Anthony Caro: Quest for the New Sculpture* (Künzelsau: Swiridoff Verlag, 2004), 92.
3. Florence Rubenfeld, *Clement Greenberg: A Life* (Minneapolis: University of Minnesota Press, 1997): 145-46.
4. Jackson Pollock's former home, 830 Fireplace Road, East Hampton, New York, is opened to the public by the Stony Brook Foundation. Caro first admired Pollock's work in 1953. After studying one of his paintings Caro wrote in 1965, "Pollock it seems to me wanted his paintings to float and shimmer as if they were scarcely there at all." Caro quoted in Ian Barker, *Anthony Caro: Quest for the New Sculpture* (Künzelsau: Swiridoff Verlag, 2004), 152.

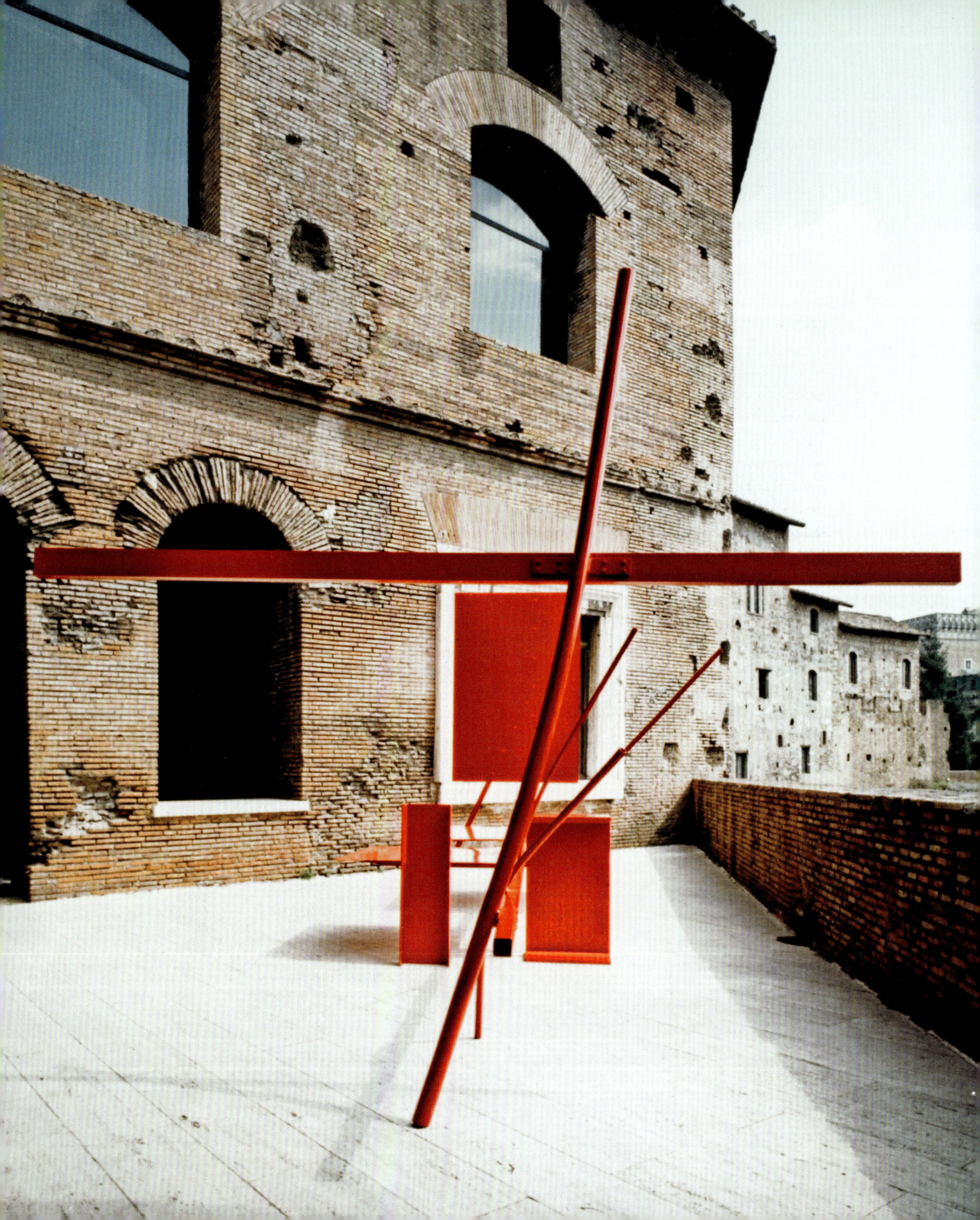

Caro and the Critics
Expanding the Vocabulary of Sculpture

Julius Bryant

Finding the Right Words

Sculptures by Anthony Caro ask to be experienced one-to-one, and close-up. This exhibition explores the rewards of close looking. To do so we need to examine not only the sculptures but also the way critics have come to write, read, talk, and think about them. The process of understanding sculpture, from the visual encounter and experience to the articulation of emotion and thought into language, is both aided and clouded by the words and images we bring. Over the half-century spanned by Caro's career, a rich transatlantic language of art appreciation has evolved. Certain words are now so well-established in the language of appreciation that they can leap to mind before a viewer has begun to look slowly. It may seem paradoxical, but the challenge of attaining a genuine one-to-one response to a sculpture requires that we recognize how words can both help and get in the way.

Many of Caro's larger sculptures are so familiar—through exhibitions and illustrations in books and in the press—that they are now celebrity objects. One gets a simple thrill from being in the same space as an acknowledged masterpiece that one last saw in a book illustration or in another international museum exhibition. One way to get back to that clarity of thought and emotional directness of response, to facilitate a close reading of the sculpture, is to look at the smaller, rarely seen works. Those assembled in this exhibition, many from the private collections of Caro's family and friends, seem the freshest. As well as new exhibitions and new photographs, new readings of the now classic writings and criticisms are essential to the appreciation of his work. This exhibition offers an opportunity not only to revisit works not often seen, but also to reappraise the responses they have drawn over the past six decades.

Despite Caro's famous friendship with Clement Greenberg (fig. 2.2), America's best-known art critic of the twentieth century, the latter did not wholly invent the vocabulary used to discuss

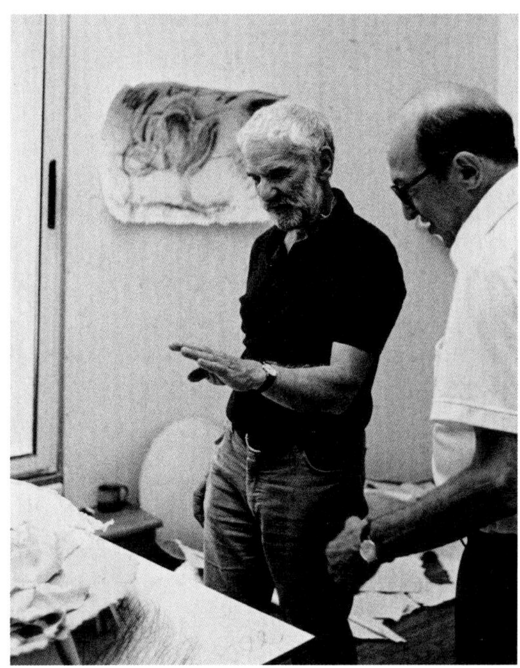

FIG. 2.1 *Early One Morning*, 1962, installed at the Trajan Markets, Rome (1992)

FIG. 2.2 Caro with Clement Greenberg working on paper sculptures, 1987

the sculptor's work. Much of it derives from the writings of Michael Fried published between 1963 and 1977, and from the intimate analysis and interpretation of new works by British critics in the 1950s (and later), such as David Sylvester, Lawrence Alloway, Andrew Forge, and Basil Taylor, who wrote exhibition reviews in *The Listener, New Statesman,* and *The Spectator.* The themes and metaphors they brought to bear continue to influence not only the choice of words used to describe modern sculpture, but also the choice of artistic ideas and formal qualities that we look for when admiring a work.

Much of the current literature about Caro is based on new interviews with the artist. His statements, which are usually retrospective, are adopted and quoted as if they were his original words from the time the sculptures were made, in some cases more than a half-century before. Comparison with earlier criticism reveals that much of Caro's own vocabulary has evolved out of that of the early writers. By tracing the over-familiar language to its first appearances, we may hope to find the original meaning of key thematic terms such as "gesture," "syntax," "pictorial," "optical," "weightlessness," "groundedness," "sprawl," "axiality," or "presence." We could try to see the art in the language of its own time.

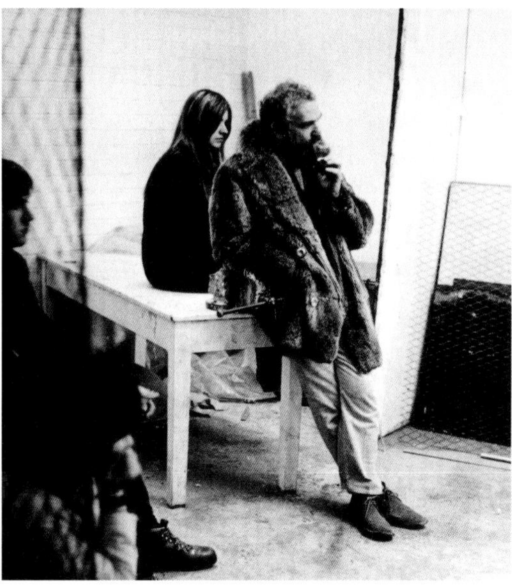

FIG. 2.3 **Caro teaching at St. Martin's School of Art, London, pipe in hand, 1960**

Bruce McLean, a former student at St. Martin's, vividly summed up the dilemma of sculpture criticism in the 1960s, despairing at how "the St. Martin's sculpture forum would avoid every broader issue, discussing for hours the position of one piece of metal in relation to another. Twelve adult men with pipes would walk for hours around sculpture and mumble."[1] McLean's sharply humorous comment evokes a quasi-religious act of witness by twelve apostles, or of worship around a holy relic, or a children's game played by "adult men." The pipes indicate their status as men of thought, detecting like Sherlock Holmes, reflecting like contemplative professors (fig. 2.3). Their mumbling "for hours" implies a private language, a reluctance to communicate with others beyond themselves, and a lack of emotion. It also suggests a language in its infancy, still evolving appropriate verbs and metaphors. McLean was a student at St. Martin's in the Advanced Sculpture course between 1963 and 1966, when Caro taught there.

For an idea of how "mumblings" evolved into language, one may read reviews from the later 1960s and early 1970s in journals such as *Artforum* and *Studio International,* where critics try to parse, to translate abstract sculptures into words. But when some formalist reviewers describe how a work actually operates, their earnest texts can be a cold read, for descriptions alone cannot convey the impact and character of a sculpture. From the 1970s art historians increasingly took up the role of art critics, and while the identification of sources and influences on sculptures is helpful, sometimes the same process of verbal rationalization can mask the encounter with the work.

Two published group discussions document the challenge of finding a language for abstract sculpture, one with Caro, for the British Broadcasting Corporation (BBC) in 1967, and one about Caro, for *Studio International* in January 1969. The vocabulary now familiar from more recent writings on Caro, and from interviews with him, is conspicuously absent. The BBC recording reveals how Caro too could be short on words. The occasion, a discussion with the American art historian and curator Robert Rosenblum "chaired" by David Sylvester (who did most of the talking), coincided with the Tate's exhibition *The Sculpture of Picasso.*[2] Caro contributes only when directly questioned. Even then, his responses are terse. Sylvester's language is peppered with French terms, italicized in print: "the whole idea of *personnage*," "the *surréalisant* side," "*jeu d'esprit*," and (one that made it into English, without italics) "Tony Caro's kind of assemblage." There is a sense of cultural crossroads: Sylvester still speaking from the school of Paris, Caro not yet deploying his growing transatlantic terminology informed by the school of New York. Caro's one use of Sylvester's language reads like a rebuttal: "The *personnage* part of it is not an interesting part for me."[3]

The second example occurs two years later, when four sculptors were asked to respond to Caro's mid-career retrospective at the Hayward Gallery in London: David Annesley, Roelof Louw, Tim Scott, and William Tucker. The discussion turns to the topic of verbalization when Tucker refers to "the Greenberg-Fried thing" and Caro's deference to them. Annesley regrets that Caro then shared "the delusion that most sculptors suffer from . . . that they are not articulate with words."

> *Tucker:* I think he did a lot to break down this image of a sculptor as a great thick, hairy sort of a guy, but he still approximates to this in many ways.
>
> *Annesley:* What he does is to talk about what he considers to be the important causes—the cause of sculpture, the cause of modern art, the way we want our sculpture seen, what the British Council and people are up to, what's the best art in the world. He'll talk about these causes. He won't talk about what is essential to him of real importance, which is how sculpture is thought of and made, and what other sculptors are up to, and what they're thinking and what he's thinking. He doesn't talk about that. He used to have a clear idea about what art is about. He sure as hell doesn't any more.[4]

These two recorded discussions illustrate how the language that is now familiar and habitual to us first had to evolve, and so must be used with caution.

Henry Moore

To step back from dependence on the rich verbal language that has evolved to explain Caro's sculptures, to avoid relying on over-familiar terminology, one can begin by looking at Henry Moore's visual criticism of Caro's early life-drawings. While working as Moore's assistant, Caro trained at the Royal Academy, ambitious to become a sculptor of public monuments and portrait busts (fig. 2.4). Analytical observation in the life-drawing class was the foundation of his art, setting many enduring themes for his sculpture. Most of it relates in scale to the human body and is concerned with the composition of mass and space, tension and balance, open gestures and tentative points of contact. Moore's marginalia, his evening annotations to the drawings that Caro had made each day at the Academy, taught the younger artist

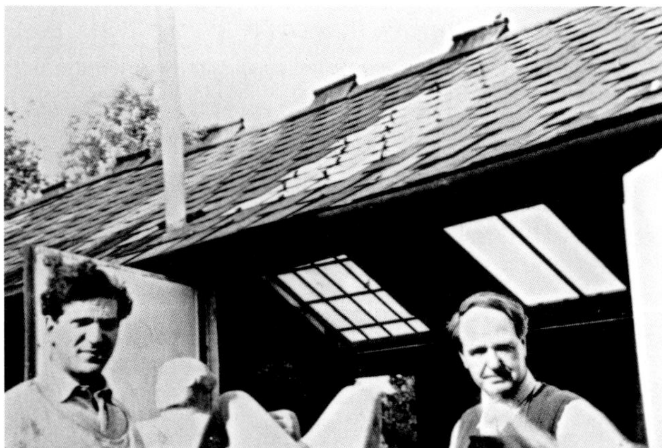

FIG. 2.4 Caro with Henry Moore at Much Hadham, Hertfordshire, ca. 1952

how to see as a sculptor (cats 1–6). In the figure drawings Moore found themes that interested him. For example, his notes include the similarities between breasts and stomach as relaxed volumes, how to express the contours of a thigh receding in perspective, how to convey the essential forms of a standing figure in profile with its center of gravity and lines of strength, and the void defined between the chest, arms, and lap of a man seated bolt upright.

Moore's spoken comments to Caro are not recorded, but his thoughts on the human figure are published. For example, in 1951, Moore told David Sylvester: "long and intense study of the human figure is the necessary foundation for a sculptor. The human figure is most complex and subtle and difficult to grasp in form and construction, and so it makes the most exacting form for study and comprehension."[5] In 1962 Moore told readers of Boston's *Atlantic Monthly:* "We make the kind of sculpture we make because we are the shape we are, because we have the proportions we have."[6] Similar ideas are echoed in Caro's own later remarks.[7]

In 1914 the vorticist sculptor Henri Gaudier-Brzeska published a manifesto in the journal *Blast* that informed Moore's verbal vocabulary. Ezra Pound correctly foresaw that this would become "the first text-book of sculpture in many academies before our generation has passed."[8] From Gaudier-Brzeska, Moore took the need for "direct energy," the conviction, as he said in 1934, that "a work must first have a vitality of its own . . . not a decoration to life, but an expression of the significance of life, a stimulation to greater effect in living."[9] Moore reconciled the formal values of the life-class with the vorticist's need for energy, through vortices and vectors, both of which are fundamental to Caro's sculpture and the way it is discussed.

Caro did not arrive at Moore's ideas and influences only at the life-class. He had a substantial library from which Caro borrowed freely, and he left his impression on the younger sculptor in many other ways, such as the importance of drawing throughout his life, of the example of Picasso, even Caro's decision to make his home in Hampstead, where Moore and other artists, including Barbara Hepworth, Ben Nicholson, and European exiles such as Naum Gabo, Piet Mondrian, and Fred Uhlman, had come to live in the 1930s. In the context of the vocabulary that facilitates and confines discussion of Caro's sculpture, Moore provides the link between the radical artistic values of the 1930s and the language of 1960s formalism.

Early British Critics and Greenberg

David Sylvester and Basil Taylor made the first mentions in print of Caro's sculpture in their September 1955 reviews in *The Listener* and the *Spectator* of a group exhibition, *New Painters and Painter-Sculptors,* at the Institute of Contemporary Arts (ICA), London. There Caro showed *Man Holding His Foot* (cat. 21) and other figurative works for the first time in London. Sylvester noted, briefly, that they "reveal, besides the influence of Picasso and Henry Moore, a sheer sculptural power indicative of rare promise."[10] Sylvester had known Jean Dubuffet and Alberto Giacometti when he lived in Paris in the late 1940s, and in 1949 he translated Daniel-Henry Kahnweiler's influential book on Picasso's sculpture into English.[11] In a review in *The Listener,* published the day after Sylvester's, Taylor also singled out Caro, noting: "only in the case of Anthony Caro is the forcefulness of method matched by a similar violence of form."[12]

In 1956, in an essay titled "Caro and Gravity" in the catalogue for the sculptor's first solo exhibition (Galleria del Naviglio, Milan), Lawrence Alloway explained that around 1950 the style of the generation after Moore was "linear in form and technological in materials."[13] Artists such as Victor Pasmore, Kenneth Martin, and Robert Adams, the first British exponents of abstract sculpture, made what Caro saw as "empty cold things"; he had no wish to pursue their constructivist idiom.[14] The values Alloway found in Caro's expressionistic figurative sculptures came from the life-class and echo Moore's concerns. He saw "the heroic combat, unnoticed but un-ending, between the body and gravity." The idea of defying gravity (even of making sculpture that might seem to float) would become a frequently stated ambition for Caro,[15] but in 1956 Alloway identifies it with the older generation, writing, "Sculptors in iron oppose it in their fears of suspension."[16]

When Caro showed the same group of sculptures and drawings in London, at the Gimpel Fils gallery in January 1957, Andrew Forge noted in *The Listener* how they formed a "dramatic ensemble" in a "small room" filled with "black snowmen" of "monstrous vitality."[17] Over the next two years Caro showed these sculptures internationally and sold one to the Tate Gallery (cat. 24). In 1959, at a party given by William Turnbull, he first met Clement Greenberg. When the critic told him "British sculpture is not all it's cracked up to be," Caro invited Greenberg to his studio.[18]

So much has been written about the intellectual partnership of Caro and Greenberg that it is surprising just how little the critic actually wrote about his British protégé. After the early deaths of Jackson Pollock (in 1956, aged forty-four) and David Smith (in 1965, aged fifty-nine), Greenberg announced in 1965 that Caro was "the only new sculptor whose sustained quality can bear comparison with Smith's."[19] Despite Caro's many tributes to Greenberg's ability to see and write "straight," and to the impact he made on him in the studio, Greenberg published only one article about him, and not a single book. Greenberg's *Art and Culture* (1961) became the bible of modern art at St. Martin's, where Caro taught (part-time, 1953–79), but it does not mention him.[20] The familiar vocabulary of formalism that is used to discuss Caro's sculptures is not all thanks to Greenberg, nor is it the "straight" response that Caro so valued in the studio.

Although not recorded, the terms of Greenberg's first critique, made in Caro's garage studio, are often retold as recollections in interviews. Caro recalls that "he told me my art wasn't up to the mark . . . said a lot of things that I had not heard before."[21] Months later, in New York, the critic gave Caro his single, oft-quoted piece of advice, "if you want to change your art, change your habits."[22] For all his status as America's most famous art critic since Bernard Berenson, Greenberg was more at home in an artist's studio than at his writing desk. His most valued opinions were given one-to-one, more as a fellow artist or an art school teacher than as a writer or critic. Caro later recalled of Greenberg's studio visits: "He did not want artists' talk about theory, he simply addressed what he saw in front of him. . . . He knew how art is made, what the process involves—how a real artist thinks and works, that the process is very practical, not literary or theoretical."[23] According to Caro, "in front of art it was as if he was listening to the angels. . . . He always said, 'Let me see it.' It was no good to talk about theory or ideas. He would make pronouncements only in the face of the art."[24]

Some idea of Greenberg's actual language and what he first said to Caro about British sculpture can be gained by reading his article "David Smith" (1956). Smith is set against the critic's disappointment with "Butler, Chadwick and the other exponents of Britain's 'sculptural renaissance'"[25] and what he saw as their adverse influence on American sculpture. Greenberg must have been reacting to their success at the Venice Biennale in 1952, to Reg Butler winning the international competition for the monument to *The Unknown Political Prisoner* (1952–53), and to the purchase in 1954 by the Museum of Modern Art, New York, of sculptures by Butler, Chadwick, and Armitage that had been exhibited in Venice.[26] Greenberg found in their work an "expected, nervous yet nerveless elegance," and "a Cubist or *art brut* artiness" that amounts to "the ultimate insipidity of their art." He lamented that "modernist sculpture in America" (presumably the work of Seymour Lipton, Herbert Ferber, and Theodore Roszak) had "succumbed so epidemically to 'biomorphism'" and such "a spinning of wires, twisting of cords, and a general fashioning of cages."[27]

A fundamental tenet of Greenberg's approach to art was that each medium must focus on its own material qualities, shunning the "literary" character of narrative and the representation of, or allusion to, the visual world. Greenberg would cite Immanuel Kant's *Critique of Judgement* (1790) in which the German philosopher observed that an individual's judgment of beauty in art is based on personal feeling, not on concepts and subject matter. In his essay "Modernist Painting" (1960), he maintained that in the Enlightenment "each art had to determine . . . the effects exclusive to itself . . . all that was unique in the nature of its medium. . . . Thus would each art be rendered."[28] This comparison between modernism and the Enlightenment built on Greenberg's essay "The New Sculpture" (first written in 1948 but revised in 1958, the year before he met Caro), in which he cited Gotthold Lessing, who "pushed against the confusion of the arts." Now that modern painting had been reduced to the "purity" of two dimensions, to the "flatness" of unprimed canvas stretched and stained with paint, Greenberg felt that sculpture offered "a greater range of expression for modern sensibility than painting now has."[29] In sculpture, the options for materials were more plentiful. In "The New Sculpture" Greenberg predicted that the future of modern art lay in "the new construction-sculpture" indebted to Picasso, Jacques Lipchitz, Julio González, and the earlier Giacometti. He found their art characterized by "linearism and linear intricacies, by its openness and transparency and weightlessness, and by its preoccupation with surface as skin alone which it expresses in blade or sheet-like forms. Space is there to be shaped, divided, enclosed, but not filled." In David Smith, Greenberg found a sculptor with "his own vision and his own originality" and the "capacity for heroic sculpture." These must have been the phrases that inspired Caro, months before his first visit to America.[30]

When Caro traveled in the United States between October and December 1959, Greenberg's words must have been ringing in his ears as he met artists across the country. He visited New York, Chicago, San Francisco, and New Mexico. The charge to "change your habits" is usually interpreted as Caro's change in choice of materials, from cast bronze in the workshop tradition of Henry Moore to assembled recycled steel following the example of Smith. But the "habits" he changed the most were his way of thinking about art. In London, discussion among artists had followed existentialist themes, which Caro had pursued in making sculpture about "what it's like to be inside the body."[31] In the studios of the American painters of the "Greenberg family," notably Kenneth Noland, Jules Olitski, and Helen Frankenthaler (fig. 2.5), he found a form of intelligence that was less philosophical and more visual, based on trusting their own eyes. Noland, in particular, talked without pretension, as Caro recalls: "he was not 'clever,' just straight-talking. I could never do 'art speak.' English artists were often able to explain the philosophy behind their work; I could not do that. Ken was like this too: a looker not a talker, artistically intelligent but not into words. The English art world had been very Paris-orientated, to do with Existentialism, Surrealism. But it seemed to me that that stuff was not what the subject was about. I was to do with making sculpture."[32]

Noland's first wife recalled that their conversations were of their time and place, filled with postwar optimism and competitiveness. The American dream seemed within reach: "It was a bit of a macho thing, Americans versus Europeans. . . . the belief that Americans still had that everything was possible."[33] Art's new avant-garde adopted the language of America's heroic pioneers, escaping corrupt old Europe to open up new frontiers and so progress to a new age. David Smith similarly took pride in straight talking, using the language of his time on the Studebaker car-production line rather than of the literary café, as Caro recalls: "David went over the top the other way. He was actually pretty smart, intelligent. But he liked to say, 'I'm just a welder.'"[34]

This pride in straight talk, without Sylvester's Francophile adjectives, is associated with Greenberg. Caro recalls that "His eye was as clear as his prose style. He looked straight and he wrote straight."[35] Quite how "straight" Greenberg wrote

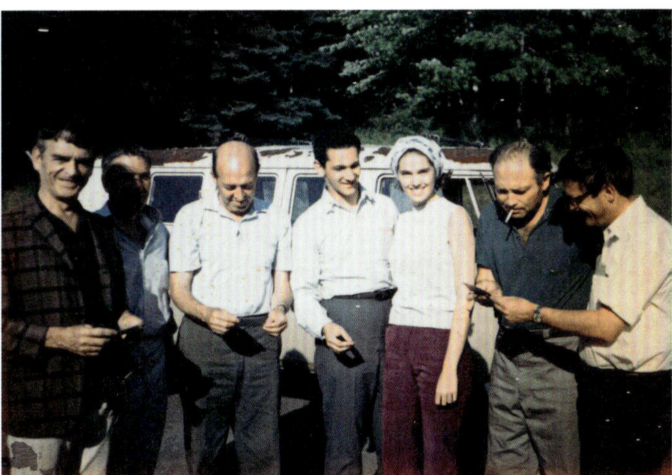

FIG. 2.5 The "Greenberg family" or "Bennington circle" at Bennington, Vermont, ca. 1964; from left to right: Paul Feeley, Caro, Clement Greenberg, David Mirvish, Stephanie Noland, Jules Olitski, and Kenneth Noland, all looking at Polaroid snaps

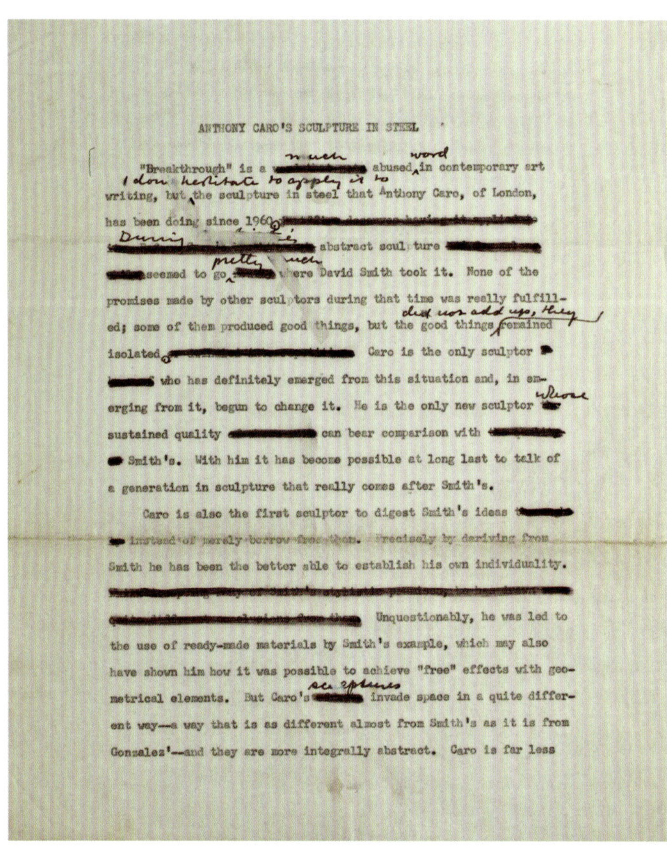

ANTHONY CARO'S SCULPTURE IN STEEL

"Breakthrough" is a abused in contemporary art writing, but the sculpture in steel that Anthony Caro, of London, has been doing since 1960 abstract sculpture seemed to go where David Smith took it. None of the promises made by other sculptors during that time was really fulfilled; some of them produced good things, but the good things remained isolated Caro is the only sculptor who has definitely emerged from this situation and, in emerging from it, begun to change it. He is the only new sculptor sustained quality can bear comparison with Smith's. With him it has become possible at long last to talk of a generation in sculpture that really comes after Smith's.

Caro is also the first sculptor to digest Smith's ideas instead of merely borrow from them. Precisely by deriving from Smith he has been the better able to establish his own individuality. Unquestionably, he was led to the use of ready-made materials by Smith's example, which may also have shown him how it was possible to achieve "free" effects with geometrical elements. But Caro's invade space in a quite different way—a way that is as different almost from Smith's as it is from Gonzalez'—and they are more integrally abstract. Caro is far less

FIG. 2.6 Clement Greenberg's "Breakthrough" essay, "Anthony Caro," published in *Arts Yearbook 8: ContemporarySculpture* (1965), as sent to Caro in draft in 1964

about Caro is evident from the manuscript for his text "Anthony Caro," which he sent to the sculptor in 1964 (fig. 2.6). Republished eight times, this classic article is usually referred to simply as the "Breakthrough" essay. This familiar title comes from the proclamation: "Breakthrough is a much abused word in contemporary art writing but I don't hesitate to apply it to the sculpture in steel Anthony Caro has been doing since 1960."[36] The sixth draft, heavily amended (as Greenberg's cover letter to Caro explains), helped to establish several themes for future observers of the sculptures. The major one is the assertion of Caro as the true heir to David Smith (in preference to Alexander Calder); his comparison of Caro's sculptures with Smith's helps to elucidate the distinctive qualities of each. He finds Caro less "pictorial" because his sculptures "ask to be looked at from many different, and dramatically different, points of view." The absence of a single ideal viewpoint, but the presence of several for the viewer to choose from (a quality of sculpture since the High Renaissance), is a theme taken up by later writers. Another difference from Smith that Greenberg notes is the way Caro's sculptures "invade space" through "vectors" (a quality that goes back to the vorticists via Moore). He describes the process of observation as one of passing from confusion to "unity in the end."

After comparing Caro to Smith, Greenberg describes familiar formalist themes, noting "the tilting, tipping and odd-angle cantilevering of his rectangular shapes" and how the "play of light against heavy is interwoven, fugally, with the play of open against closed, and of irregular against regular." While employing musical analogies (which Caro also likes to do) he also alludes to the art of calligraphy in remarking how "Caro achieves a kind of sprawling cursiveness that is all his own." Greenberg employs anthropomorphism in a way that recalls Alloway's essay on "Caro and Gravity" (1956). He writes of sculpture as if it were a living laboratory specimen whose behaviour is under observation, for in "a ground-hugging sculpture . . . the plane of the ground . . . takes its own part in the challenge to the force of gravity." Other works "search for a low centre of gravity" and form "ground-flung, wide-open enclosures." His one criticism is of Caro's choice of colors. He finds "the high-keyed off-shades that Caro favours" render his sculptures more "optical" by appealing to the intellect through the eye, rather than to the sense of touch. But he reassures readers that color "does not detract from the quality of the whole." He assumed "that the colour is aesthetically (as well as literally) provisional—that it can be changed at will without decisively affecting quality." The most significant change made by Caro to the color of a sculpture was to paint *Early One Morning* red (see fig. 1.2) on the advice of his wife, the artist Sheila Girling, having originally painted it green; that was a permanent correction. The significance of color is a point on which Caro and Greenberg differed.[37]

One theme that Greenberg identifies in Caro that is taken up by later writers is his "Englishness."[38] Finding "roots that go literally to Perpendicular Gothic" he detects how a "grand sublime manner has been a peculiarly English aspiration since the eighteenth century." He cites Benjamin Robert Haydon, John Martin, and J. M. W. Turner, noting that "Henry Moore and Francis Bacon are possessed by it in their separate ways." The pursuit of the Sublime, the overpowering disturbing alternative to the Beautiful in aesthetic theory, is not something Caro accepts as an ambition of his art. Greenberg's sudden sprinkling of cultural references to English art and art theory highlights the debt of his own ideas to nineteenth century theories. The great goal of "flatness" in Pollock's paintings, for example, is usually identified (as Greenberg had said) with late cubism. But it can be traced from the aesthetic principles of Roger Fry back via Owen Jones and Gottfried Semper to A. W. N. Pugin. At the South Kensington Schools (the future Royal College of Art and Victoria and Albert Museum) in the late nineteenth century, lectures and displays condemned floral carpets and pictorial wallpapers as illusionistic; the geometric patterns of Asian textiles were deemed more suitable to their material.[39] Greenberg's concern for the emotional impact of a work, the "gut feeling," reveals his reading of Walter Pater, whose concern for the viewer's intensity of experience of a work of art and ability to reflect on his or her own response is a central tenet of Aestheticism.[40]

Through "flatness," painting is reduced to the essential characteristic of its medium. Greenberg does not use an equivalent concept in his one article on Caro, perhaps because sculpture has no single set of materials. The temptation must have been there. Henry Moore and his champion, the leading British art historian Herbert Read, saw mass and volume as the fundamental qualities of sculpture.[41] The new sculptures shown by Caro at the Whitechapel Art Gallery, London, in 1963 were all planar and linear, offering neither actual nor implied volumes through the embrace of space. Also conspicuous by their absence from Greenberg's essay are two points that are always the first made by any reviewer today: that Caro had been Henry Moore's assistant and that he took sculpture off the pedestal.

Caro's private reply to Greenberg's article, sent in a letter, reveals how much the artist was ready to learn from the American critic about looking at his own sculptures. Caro assured him that it "helped me to understand what has been happening in the work; for instance the bit about the last 2 pieces using the ground not just as a base but as an important part of the sculpture is so perceptive, I know it'll help me to see my next piece in a new way."[42]

Another article sent by Greenberg to Caro in typescript was his earlier review of a book by Bernard Berenson: *Piero della Francesca; or, the Ineloquent in Art*.[43] In it, Greenberg quotes a passage to explain the quality of "ineloquence" that Berenson found in Piero's art, in contrast to the "over-expressive" art of our own day. It seems pertinent to the quality of Caro's smaller sculpture that is the subject of this study: "After sixty years of living on terms of intimacy with every kind of art, from every clime and every period, I am tempted to conclude that in the long run the most satisfactory creations are those which, like Piero's and Cézanne's, remain ineloquent, mute,

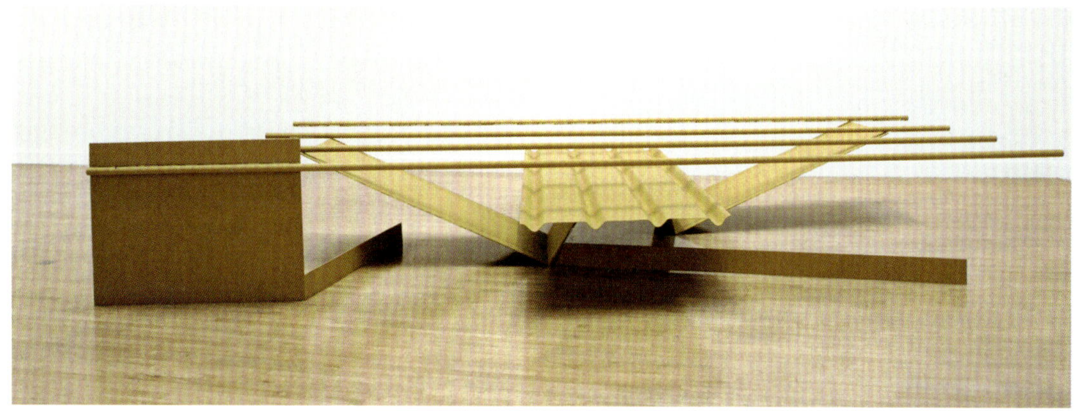

FIG. 2.7 *Prairie,* 1967, painted steel, 38 x 229⅛ x 126 in. (96.5 x 582 x 320 cm). Collection of Lois and Georges de Menil

with no urgent communication to make, and no thought of rousing us with look and gesture. If they express anything it is character, essence, rather than momentary feeling or purpose."[44]

Michael Fried

One possible reason for the absence of any further articles, or a book, by Greenberg on Caro is his respect for the opinions of Michael Fried, whom he names four times in the "Breakthrough" article. As a sculptor working in freestanding steel collage, Caro made his debut in the exhibition at the Whitechapel Art Gallery, in 1963, for which Fried wrote the introductory catalogue essay. Greenberg quotes two of Fried's points: "Everything in Caro's art which is worth looking at—except the colour—is in its syntax." Greenberg also notes "Michael Fried speaks aptly of Caro's 'achieved weightlessness.'" As noted earlier, the aspiration to defy gravity (the corollary of the concern of Caro's expressionist figure sculptures) was already a theme of the British constructivists. The most celebrated example is *Prairie* (fig. 2.7), arguably Caro's most ambitious abstract sculpture, which achieves a sense of floating planes through counter-weighting horizontal parallel poles.

With Moore, Noland, and Greenberg, Caro found practical criticism and encouragement without the Anglo-French existentialist theorising that so wearied him in London in the late 1950s. In Michael Fried, a young American art historian writing his dissertation on Manet, he found an articulate, unpretentious intellectual who married formal analysis with the ability to identify verbal tools that anyone could use. Fried first met Caro in 1961, when (as a philosophy student at University College London, and London correspondent for *Arts Magazine* in New York), he visited Caro in Hampstead (fig. 2.8).[45] There he was the first critic to see the new works made

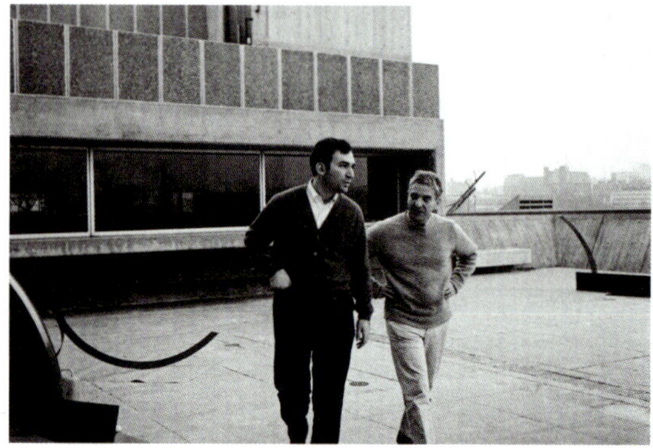

FIG. 2.8 Caro and Michael Fried installing Caro's solo exhibition at the Hayward Gallery, London, 1969

FIG. 2.9 *Twenty Four Hours,* 1960, painted steel, 54 x 88 x 33 in. (138.4 x 223.5 x 83.8 cm). © Tate, London, 2012

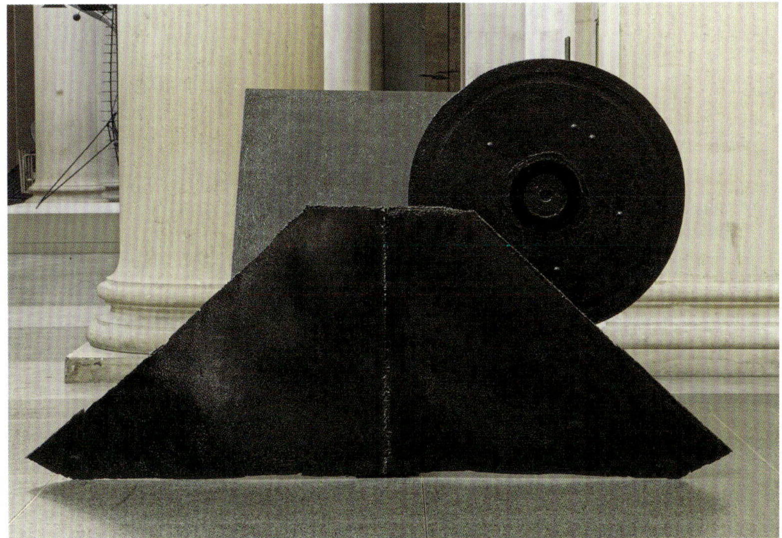

after Caro's first visit to the United States, such as *Twenty Four Hours* (fig. 2.9). Fried brought a different approach to the studio, as the artist recalled: "With Clem, you'd do it, then he'd look. Maybe he would say, 'There's something wrong with the left-hand side of the piece.' With Mike, you could talk to him about the dreams you were nursing in your head."[46] Greenberg may have had Fried in mind when he stated the lifelong dilemma of critics: "When it comes to explaining aesthetic verdicts, far better minds than mine haven't gotten anywhere near it. When something really works you're helpless."[47]

Fried's introduction to Caro's Whitechapel catalogue is twice the length of Greenberg's article. Fried went on to write five more essays on Caro, between 1967 and 1977, the last being the introduction to the traveling exhibition *Anthony Caro: Table Sculptures 1966–1977*.[48] Fried's greater influence on the appreciation of Caro's sculpture came through the inclusion of two of these essays in Richard Whelan's *Anthony Caro* (Penguin, 1974), a book that Fried had proposed to Caro and to the publisher, and which he had intended to write himself (before teaching took up his time). Recently revised for the catalogue to Caro's retrospective at Tate Britain in 2005, the Whitechapel introduction has continued to help us to see Caro's sculptures for more than a half-century. Fried articulated the qualities and significance of Caro's sculpture in a way that facilitated their discussion by historians of contemporary art.[49] Caro read it in draft and wrote to Fried: "I am constantly amazed throughout the essay how you seem to have divined my thoughts or intentions and ones of which I myself have only been intuitively aware."[50]

In this brief summary of the evolving language of the close reading of Caro's sculpture, the most enduring ideas are those launched in 1963, in the Whitechapel catalogue, to which Greenberg deferred. Seeking to be "useful to those meeting his work for the first time," Fried advises visitors to the exhibition to imagine themselves as infants, as yet incapable of recognizing speech, but able to learn by watching their parents converse.[51] He argues that the "abstract configurations in time made by the spoken words," and the "gestures" of their parents, are the "syntax" of a prelinguistic language that can also be found in Caro's sculptures. Fried expanded on this theme of gesture to distinguish Caro's art from the "objecthood" of minimalist sculpture in a seminal essay first published in 1967. He explained that Caro's sculptures are "imitating, not gestures exactly, but the *efficacy* of gesture; like certain music and poetry, they are possessed by the knowledge of the human body and how, in innumerable ways and moods, it makes meaning."[52]

This analogy with linguistics offered an alternative approach to Greenberg's use of formalist description and evaluation. Sculpture may speak another language, but it need not exclude the attentive observer. Fried puts the emphasis on the viewer, who can (if he or she wishes) learn to look. Fried also opens up the scope of appreciation beyond learning the visual language of formalism, for Caro's sculptures "cry out for something more than the appreciation of their merely formal properties, or, rather, that the cry is *in us* for something more."[53] He finds in "the making of expressive gestures" not simply "the solution of formal problems," but a release from the social conventions of modern civilization. Quoting from Greenberg's *Art and Culture,* Fried cites its insistence on the "reduction" of the visual arts to the "purity" of the flat unprimed canvas stained with paint, but finds any comparison with Caro's sculpture to be misleading: "It would be a mistake to think . . . that because one has noted the formal structure of his pieces one had fully experienced them [for they have a] nascent emotion." Unlike the extreme flatness of stained canvases (by Noland, Olitski, and Frankenthaler), sculpture lives in the third dimension, in the same "phenomenological framework in which we exist" and so has greater "potential for expression" through allusion to "our own purest and most passionate gestures." In his appreciation of modern sculpture, Fried asserts that works have a life and mood of their own that the spectator should pursue directly. Most important of all, Fried empowers the viewer above the critic or other intermediary: "the task and the responsibility of seeing belong to the spectator alone and ought not to be alienated by him or pre-empted by others."

In empowering the ordinary spectator to find human gestures, emotion, and expression in Caro's abstract sculpture, Fried challenged the conventions of formalist art criticism and, indeed, the status of art critics as preeminent authorities in the judgment of quality. The lack of a riposte from Greenberg, indeed the repeated acknowledgment of Fried in the "Breakthrough" essay, suggests that the dogmatic critic may have recognized that, in future, authoritative writing about contemporary art lay more with the new art historians than with art critics.

Herbert Read

History may have given these articles by Greenberg and Fried greater significance than they enjoyed at the time, when this new form of sculpture and writing faced well-established traditions.[54] Bryan Robertson, then director of the Whitechapel, rejoiced in proclaiming, in the catalogue of Caro's first major exhibition in 1963, the arrival of "a new sculptural vocabulary"—but the visual vocabulary had arrived ahead of its verbal counterpart.[55] In 1994, he recalled "the raw shock" and "exhilaration" caused by the exhibition, which invited a new way of looking at abstract sculpture: "Ever since the twenties, we had been taught to appreciate 'tactile values' but there was nothing here to stroke or feel with one's hand in silky-surfaced wood or stone. There was a new tactility, purely for the eye. We were all used, moreover, to sculpture preaching at us in one way or another about nobility and serenity, inhumanity and panic, ancientness and survival; and to contemplate

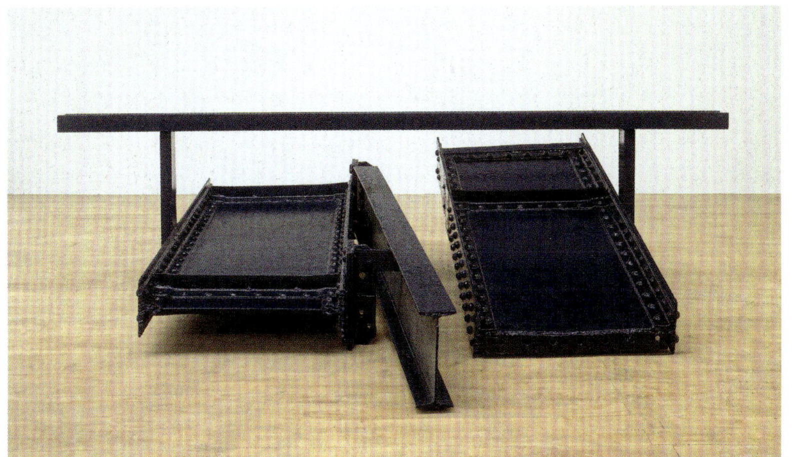

FIG. 2.10 *Lock,* 1962, painted steel, 34⅝ x 211 x 120$\frac{1}{16}$ in. (88 x 536 x 305 cm). Tate, London © Tate, London, 2012

the atavistic presence. This new sculpture didn't preach to us or exhort us, and neither did it make any kind of parade about 'truth to materials' since most of its metal was covered in paint."[56]

The standard language of experience and explanation to which Robertson referred belonged to Herbert Read, who, by the 1950s, had become the most internationally respected English writer on modern art. He is best remembered today for his text on modern British sculpture, the introduction to the catalogue of the British pavilion at the Venice Biennale of 1952—known in shorthand as the "Geometry of Fear" essay.[57] In it, Read describes this sculpture "of despair, or of defiance" through a language of evocation and allusion, and quotes from the poetry of T.S. Eliot.

Read's *Concise History of Modern Sculpture* gives a further flavor of sculpture's critical vocabulary. First published in 1964, the book came out just months after Caro's Whitechapel show, and the year before Greenberg's "Breakthrough" essay appeared in print. Read passes over abstract sculpture without mention of Pasmore, Adams, or Turnbull. David Smith is illustrated twice, but otherwise appears only in lists of names. Caro is not mentioned directly in the text, but is illustrated by *Lock* (fig. 2.10); alongside is Read's comment: "it would seem, judging from the works exhibited in commercial galleries, that almost four-fifths of all contemporary sculpture is made of metal of some kind. It is possible to speak of a 'New Iron Age.'"[58] However, Read laments "the general tendency to abandon carving and even modelling in favour of various easy methods of *assemblage*, but I cannot pretend to accept this development with complacency."[59] He asks "what has been gained and what has been lost, by this transition to *linear* sculpture? Virtually everything, one must say, has been lost that has characterized the art of sculpture in the past."[60] He sees only ugliness among the "metalworkers," an ugliness that is not "redeemed by heroism" or by any sense of "catharsis" such as one finds in the ugliness of Matthias Grünewald and Francisco de Goya.[61] Read points to the surface qualities that Moore, Giacometti, Marino Marini, and Lipchitz found in bronze to heighten sculpture's tactile appeal, but "this is not the motive of the modern sculptor in metal, who will even despise such 'finish.'"[62]

After Moore and Hepworth, he searches for hope in the next generation and concludes that "among the hundreds of sculptors who have emerged since 1945, it seems to me that there is only one who might claim to have invented a new style—Eduardo Paolozzi."[63] Read refers to him (along with David Smith) in support of his observation that "to create an *icon,* a plastic symbol of the artist's inner sense of numinosity or mystery... is the purpose of the great majority of modern sculptors."[64] Paolozzi ends Read's list of artists after Rodin who represent "the chronological development of vitalism in modern sculpture."[65]

Greenberg pulled no punches in his verdict on Read, expressed in his essay of 1955 on Wyndham Lewis (republished in *Art and Culture*): "Sir Herbert Read, supposedly an all-out champion of 'extremism" (which he is not, and it would make no difference if he were) is an incompetent art critic.... while Sir Herbert, who has no taste—not even paralysed taste—will be furtively, surreptitiously incoherent, Lewis is unabashedly so."[66] Read's *Concise History* may seem too dated—even for its own time—to be of relevance, but in the context of understanding the way in which Caro's art helped to generate a new vocabulary of appreciation, a language we now take for granted, Read's survey provides evidence of the more established ways of seeing and writing about modern sculpture at the time. Read's standing in modern art criticism was such that the publisher reprinted the book, unchanged, in 1974, and it remained a standard textbook for the history of British sculpture.[67] In championing British modernism, Read looked at sculpture as an existentialist philosopher as well as an art critic. He recognized much of the new sculpture in the 1950s as symptomatic of Cold War anxiety and yet saw artists as offering hope for society. Combining a sense of the British Romantic tradition with a Jungian belief in the collective unconscious, Read saw artists turning anxiety into creativity, inventing powerful images that could stir the viewer's spirit.

Like Bryan Robertson, some British critics were ready for a change in sculpture and how it was discussed. In 1965, John Richardson wrote in the *New Statesman* that when Caro's *Early One Morning* was included in the Tate Gallery's exhibition *British Sculpture in the Sixties,* it "wins out over the decor and makes the nearby Hepworths look as dead as dodos' eggs. Here at last is a statement which is as straightforward, uncompromising and true as an equation—refreshingly sparse after the sentimentality and mannerism of Herbert Read's angst-peddling sculptors of the Fifties.'"[68]

When Greenberg criticized Read in two articles in *Encounter* in 1962 and 1963 he saw a wider problem, that "modernist painting and sculpture have outrun the common categories of art criticism."[69] Read had celebrated the intrinsic qualities of different materials as a key to "natural beauty" and the expression of states of the human spirit through images that evoked ancient archetypes and stirred the subconscious.[70] But by 1964 such concerns could not equip the viewer confronting a new sculpture by Caro.

Greenberg, Fried, and Minimalism

Greenberg came close to discussing Caro's sculpture in print in the essay "Recentness of Sculpture," in *American Sculpture of the Sixties,* the catalogue of an exhibition at the Los Angeles County Museum of Art, which opened in April 1967. The exhibition included Caro "because of the high quality of the work he made in this country and the influence he exerted on new American sculpture."[71] Greenberg's main concern in the essay is to discredit minimalism; he makes comparisons as a way of highlighting the qualities of Caro's sculpture. Using the pop jargon of the day, he declares "the far-out as end in itself was already caught sight of, in the area of sculpture, by Anthony Caro.... who anticipated the Minimalists."[72] Greenberg's concept of the "far-out" did not enter the standard vocabulary of sculpture criticism. But his competitive tone echoes that of

Alfred Barr, founding director of the Museum of Modern Art, in valuing artists as if they are all pursuing the same belief in an avant-garde, all racing to be the first to open up new frontiers.[73] This concern to be first, for innovation as evidence of genius, persists as a value in the appreciation of contemporary art today.

Far more enduring than "far-outness" in Greenberg's essay is his use of the term "presence," deployed not to characterize Caro's sculpture but rather that of a fellow exhibitor, Anne Truitt, and the work of the minimalists (he cites Donald Judd, Robert Morris, Carl Andre, Michael Steiner, Robert Smithson, and Sol LeWitt). He does not expand on the term, but Michael Fried uses it in his essay "Art and Objecthood," first published in June 1967 in *Artforum* (while the exhibition was still in Los Angeles). Fried quotes Greenberg's discussion of "presence" and develops the argument that "the presence of literalist art, which Greenberg was the first to analyze, is basically a theatrical effect or quality—a kind of *stage* presence. . . . Something is said to have presence when it demands that the beholder take it into account, that he takes it seriously."[74] Fried's essay addresses the shortcomings he finds in minimalism, and he compares Caro, "whose work is far more specifically resistant to being seen in terms of objecthood than that of David Smith," because of the emphasis on the relationships of parts, the "syntax," rather than the "identity of each" component. The resultant sense of gesture and its effects gives meaning and "makes Caro's art a fountainhead of antiliteralist and antitheatrical sensibility." Despite its use by Greenberg and Fried in a pejorative sense to characterize the art of the minimalists, "presence" has become a quality attributed to Caro's sculpture.[75] This genealogy of the critical term underlines the need for caution when employing the familiar vocabulary of analysis and appreciation. Caro's reputation did not follow the inevitable rise that most books recount. Partly in response to criticism of minimalism by Greenberg and Fried, Donald Judd gave his opinion of Caro in *Studio International* in 1969: "by 1964 di Suvero had a tiresome number of followers and Caro's work looked like that of just another of them."[76]

"Crimble Crumble"

Catalogues for exhibitions of the work of living artists often take stock of the recent literature on their subject and consolidate their ideas and language into a new orthodoxy. In his essay for Caro's first retrospective, held at the Hayward Gallery, London, in 1969, Michael Fried echoed Lawrence Alloway's recognition of Caro's fascination with "the human body *as actually lived*,"[77] and repeated his own use of "syntax" as the key to understanding the "nuance of natural gesture" in three-dimensional compositions.[78] Fried opens his essay with an assertion that has withstood the test of time: "Caro's sculptures have always been intimately related to the human body." The "norms of Caro's art" are the same as those of our own bodies, and on the same scale: "*our* uprightness, frontality, axiality, groundedness and symmetry."[79] Intellectually, Caro had not strayed far beyond the formal values of his Royal Academy life-drawings and the graphic annotations of Henry Moore. The new development that Fried highlighted was the series of table sculptures, made since 1966 (with Fried's encouragement), which relate to the scale of the human hand (see pages 125–26).

The risk of determining continuity in Caro's sculpture from the 1950s and 1960s is that it provides too simple a way to read the work. Caro does not accept the frequent observation that a sculpture like *Midday* (fig. 2.11) resembles a reclining nude by Moore translated into steel I-beams. Indeed, the endlessly beguiling beauties

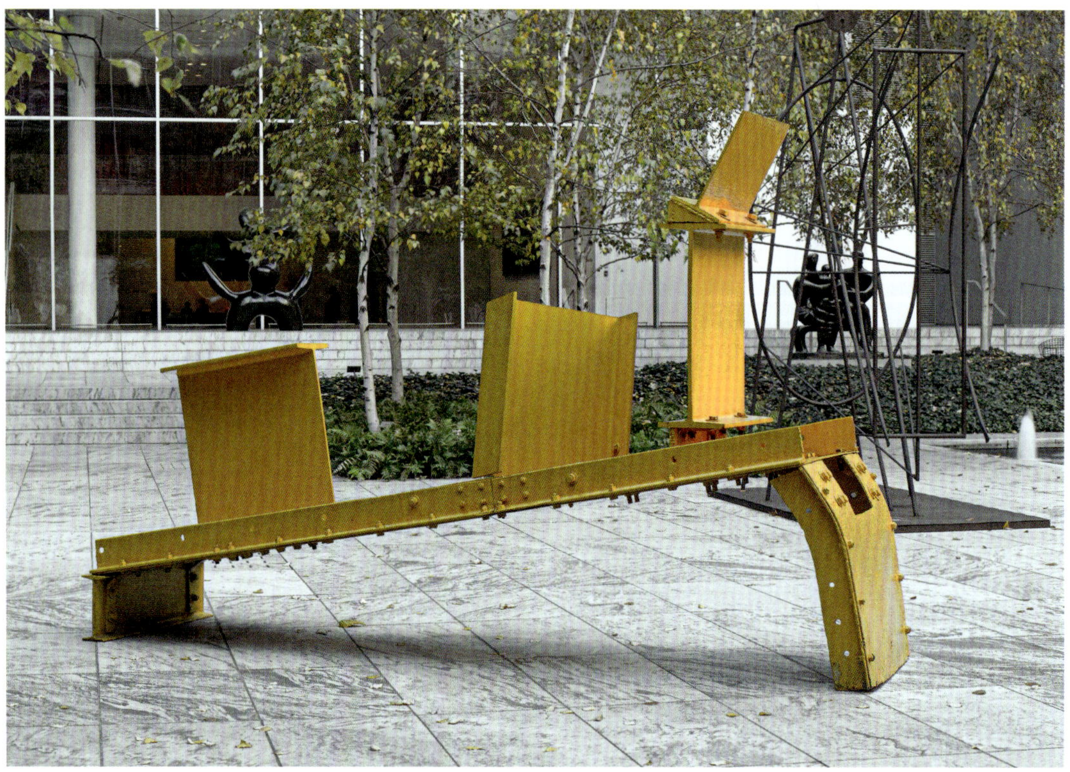

FIG. 2.11 *Midday*, 1960, painted steel, 94 x 38 x 144⅛ in. (240 x 96.5 x 366 cm). The Museum of Modern Art, New York. Mr. and Mrs. Arthur Wiesenberger Fund. © 2008 MoMA, New York

of an abstract work like *Sun Feast* (see fig. 3.15) seem lessened when described, as Fried did in 1970, as "a kind of sensuous, dishevelled, almost certainly feminine though not quite figural sprawl, as if the sculpture were displaying itself for its own delectation."[80] John Russell used a similar sexual metaphor earlier the same year, when he found in *Deep North* (1969–70, private collection) one area, "the horizontal one, in which the soft-looking spoon-or tongue-shaped forms peel away from another. . . spread-eagled" in "a kind of post-coital disarray which is quite new in Caro's work."[81] Certainly, such sexual interpretations of Caro's sculptures were quite novel in print, yet they contributed to the new vocabulary of experience and explanation. Both articles were included in the first paperback monograph on Caro (by Richard Whelan), published by Penguin in 1974.[82] The language of formalism was getting far from the analysis of "purely" abstract forms, juxtaposed and inflected around planes and axes.[83]

The language of criticism prompted by Caro's sculptures first reveals pejorative terms in response to *Sun Feast* and *Orangerie* (fig. 2.12), which, it was said, seemed too ready to please. In reviewing the 1969 Hayward exhibition, Norbert Lynton found the problem of "picturesque-ness, as though Caro were making a three-dimensional painting with metal for brushstrokes."[84] The worst, it seems, one could find in a Caro sculpture was "elegance" or "decorativeness," as if the Anglo-American mission to open up new frontiers had succumbed to worldly temptations. In 1970 Bruce McLean was ready with another humorous parody, inventing the term "crimble crumble" to describe "an attitude, ease, panache, that some people have and some people haven't."[85] Reviewing the ICA's *British Sculpture out of the Sixties* for *Studio International,* he found the only work worthy of such false praise to be Caro's *Orangerie.* McLean protested that Greenberg's circle of pioneers now seemed like a self-appointed elite: "it's all done for the few who understand and know. . . . Caro is making well-made, near crimble for Kenneth Noland. They work as if they had no problems." In the 1960s, patient looking at abstract sculpture had spread as a meaningful pursuit for all. But in the 1970s, a decade when London was no longer "swinging" but suffering from economic recession, some critics expected sculpture to embrace issues other than itself.

Rosalind Krauss articulated the risks of "decorative pictorialism" in *Passages of Modern Sculpture* (1977).[86] In a close reading of *Early One Morning,* she describes how Caro's unifying use of color could emphasize the sculpture as a "pictorial" image of shapes that appeals to the eye in contrasting ways when seen from two different viewing positions. From the "front" (by which she means from the end of the main horizontal axis, looking directly toward the vertical sheet; see fig. 2.1) it seems compressed into two dimensions, or "pictorial," while from the "side" one is more aware of it as a physical construction. To Krauss, the opportunity to find one's own viewpoint challenged the work's "meaning as image."[87] (Caro first chose the more self-explanatory, elevated three-quarter angle found in most book illustrations for his photographer John Goldblatt. The latter, working in the artist's garden in 1962, made many intriguing first photographs of now over-familiar sculptures). Seeing freestanding sculptures as unstable elements, experienced sequentially and subjectively by the viewer's whole body, may seem as old as the Renaissance, but for Krauss it raised an issue: "from its demonstration of this incompatibility of pictorial and sculptural properties . . . the emotional impact of the sculpture arises." This was Krauss the formalist, who would turn against modernism and recognize "this presumably new breed, the historian/critic" or "academic art critic," to whose "capture" of art criticism she herself had contributed.[88]

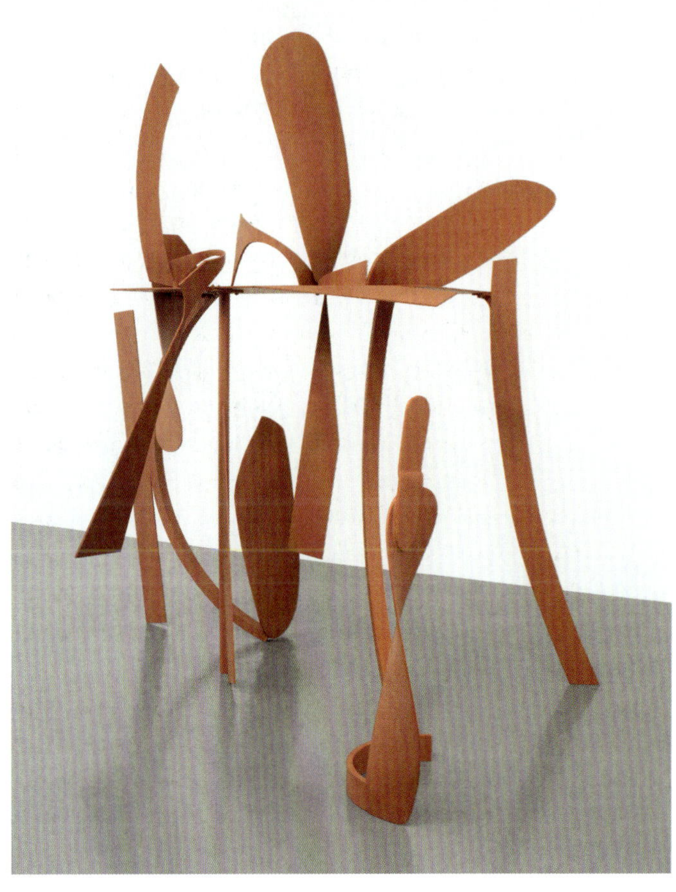

FIG. 2.12 *Orangerie* (cat. 34)

In reviewing Caro's retrospective at the Museum of Modern Art in New York in 1975 for *Art News,* Kirk Varnedoe (then an assistant professor at Columbia University) warned that an "aura of *quality* surrounds the show," at a time when other artists were questioning "quality" as a goal. He found the visitor's experience of "freshly painted and burnished" sculptures "attractively reassuring."[89] The exhibition's curator, William Rubin, explored the nationality theme in his catalogue essay: "Caro's sculpture is peculiarly English in the way it values lightness of touch, casualness and digression. . . . Its address is conversational rather than hortatory."[90] But Varnedoe, comparing David Smith's "confrontation with landscape," found Caro's need for "private space" more suited to "an English garden." Varnedoe's contribution to this language of experience and explanation was to associate the contemplation of works offering "lucid, self-contained resolution" with "tasteful . . . conservatism." To him, the process of formalist observation seemed no longer to be intellectually credible.

In his review of the same exhibition for *Studio International,* Barry Martin followed Rubin's lead in still finding plenty for formalist analysis. He felt Fried's concept of "syntax" to be less useful than an analogy with meter in poetry, "if only in that we can compare stressed and unstressed parts and their speed."[91] The analogy works equally well to emphasize the importance of the viewer following a sequence of relations, rather than the impact of a single image, as Fried had observed: "the visual initiative his pieces call for is more like *listening to* than *looking at.*"[92] However, like Fried and Russell, Martin recognized that there is more to the appeal of Caro's sculpture than the "well-tried historical and formalist path" of Rubin's catalogue text, and asked: "If Caro's art triggers in us meanings that cannot be explained in formal terms, should we dismiss these as unnecessary and subjective and not the intentions proper to the sculpture?"[93]

The popularity of the "elegant," brightly painted sculptures such as *Sun Feast* and *Orangerie* disturbed Caro and prompted him to risk making more direct, brutal works of rusted steel, which he took from an Italian scrapyard to a factory studio in Veduggio, Italy. When Barry Martin reviewed a gallery show of these works for *Studio International* in 1974 he brought the temporal element to the observation process. The sheer scale and weight of the large steel sections had prevented Caro from composing in the same way and so placed a greater emphasis on a moment of choice—on a single decision rather than several in succession. As Martin noted, in studying a sculpture we "witness a moment in time," what he termed the "event" when the artist decided it was right and stopped: "the same sculpture will always appear to be at the moment of 'becoming' each time we look at it."[94] This is a recurrent question in the published interviews with Caro ("when do you know when a work is finished?"). But if one can reinforce the temporal by imagining the sculpture being made, the "event" when the artist chooses to stop is one we can share and try to understand.

In the late 1970s, ways of writing about Caro's sculpture (echoing and informing ways of looking at it) alternated between the "purely" formalist analysis of how compositions work and a more associative response; the latter was akin to the way his works from the 1950s appealed to a shared sense of humanity. As the idea of the artist as heroic leader of the avant-garde lost credibility in the 1970s, so the need to find "content" grew. Reviews that read like solo performances in the art of formal analysis became rare; and increasingly came to represent a language that seemed private and dated.[95]

Caro's interview with Peter Fuller in 1979 is the only one where the tone is distinctly hostile.[96] Fuller had just finished a book with John Berger about a peasant sculptor (Ferdinand Cheval) and brought a Marxist perspective to the discussion of contemporary abstract sculpture. Seeking to deconstruct sculptures intellectually, to analyze them as products of their time, Fuller urged Caro to look for "the social, psychological and cultural relations" in the art he made. To Fuller, David Smith's sculptures had associative content, as celebrations of the materials and techniques used by the car production worker, a job that Smith had held. Caro felt that Fuller had been taken in by the rather defensive self-image that Smith sought to project. In Smith's sculptures Caro found qualities of "character, personal expressiveness, delicacy of touch, sculptural intelligence." Fuller pressed Caro for the "meaning" of his sculptures as images, and at this stage Caro referred him back to Greenberg's sense of meaning, that the viewer needs to cut "right through to the meaning" by asking "whether the art is true and felt, or whether the artist is performing or using his art dishonestly." Caro would not be drawn into Fuller's debate about the "social psychological and cultural influences on an artist," for Caro believed "it is his art *only* that is a pertinent subject for discussion and criticism." Fuller went on to publish a series of articles on Caro (after the exhibition of the smaller bronzes at Kenwood in 1981), criticizing him for not recognizing "the importance of the image in sculpture."[97] Another reviewer of the Kenwood exhibition noted a risk of early retirement, for at fifty-seven "Caro is at a dangerous age. Unfashionable, with no perceptible relation to a British avant-garde, he can choose to put on his carpet slippers and be Caroesque for the rest of his life . . . ."[98]

Caro says he was not aware of the backlash against Greenberg's authority at the time (known as "Clembashing"), only that the critic encouraged him not to worry about conceptual art and minimalism. He remained "Greenbergian" in his focus on making sculpture (at a prolific rate) and on finding fresh inspiration by regularly changing his "habits" by working in other countries and in other artists' studios. While art historians such as Fried and Krauss found new interests that took them away from Greenberg's circle, Caro's friendship with Greenberg continued through his studio visits and correspondence; even so, Greenberg did not write again on Caro.[99] Caro continued to produce surprises, finding original ways to work in bronze, clay, wood, and paper, and on the scale of architecture, so "expanding the vocabulary of sculpture."[100] But the language of analysis and appreciation of work by "the last Modernist" remained much the same.[101] In the 1980s Caro's public stature led to an increasing emphasis on interviews, full of biographical information and anecdotal accounts of the process of discovering fresh materials. By then the formalist language had become outmoded—but it continued to serve for Caro's art.

Caro's international adventures with different materials in artists' studios and workshops (New York, 1981 and 1982; Barcelona, 1987; Japan, 1990; France, 1993) can be understood as series of experiments within Greenberg's definition of sculpture. Paper, wrought iron, ceramic, wood, stone, even Perspex—Caro tried them all. He continued to do so long after the backlash against Greenberg's medium-specific definition of painting and sculpture, and the launch of (in Rosalind Krauss's term) the "post-medium condition" we know today, when many artists confidently work across all media.[102]

From Syntax to Content

Beyond exploring the sculptural qualities of different materials, the closest Caro came in the 1980s to moving beyond sculpture was in exploring architecture. Once again it was said (this time by Paul Moorhouse) that Caro had "expanded the vocabulary of sculpture."[103] But he also expanded the vocabulary of discussion. In a conversation between Caro and Karen Wilkin, the term "sculpitecture" was coined. Explaining how Caro's architectural sculptures need to be viewed from within, Wilkin identified "enterable" sculpture—spaces that can be entered with just the eyes or with the whole body—as a lifelong theme. This concept contrasts with the sense of shared values between Caro's sculpture and human anatomy, as identified by Alloway and Fried.[104] The first sculpitecture projects were the *Child's Tower Room* (1984), the temporary "sculptural village" made in collaboration with American architect Frank Gehry, and *Lakeside Folly* and *Pool House* (both 1988). The best-known examples of this public art of creating intimacy are *Tower of Discovery* (fig. 2.13) and the paired towers in Caro's *Chapel of Light* near Calais, France (fig. 2.14). They invite the spectator inside to ascend spiral staircases, squeeze through narrowing gaps, and emerge on radiating mezzanines that recall viewing platforms in garden follies. Like garden mazes, they force the spectator to explore and to discover space and light. Such architectural works may approach the scale of small buildings, but their "enclosure" is best experienced through total immersion, not by standing back and admiring from a safe distance as images in space.

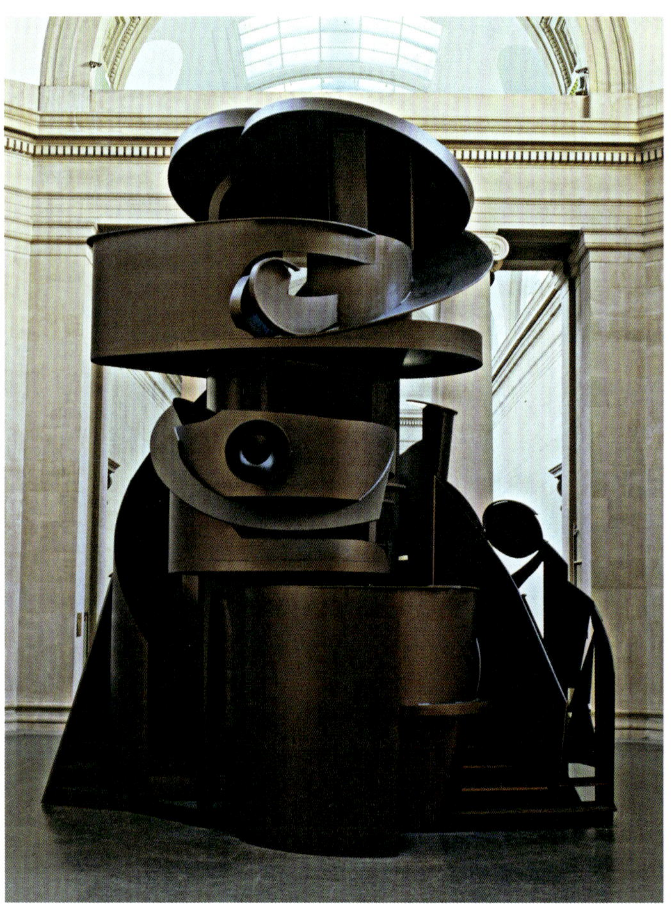

FIG. 2.13 *Tower of Discovery,* 1991, painted steel, 264.1 x 218.1 x 218.1 in. (671 x 554 x 554 cm) installed at Tate Britain. Photo: John Riddy

For all their originality, the sculpitectures still upheld modernist principles—even if it was the whole body, rather than just the eyes, that explored their formal values. Greenberg's definition of sculpture excluded any of the literary, narrative content that art has supported in the past. Caro had resisted the detection of content such as physical and sexual analogies in his abstract sculptures, dismissing evocative titles such as *Sun Feast* or *Orangerie* as simply the trade names of colors taken from the paint cans (Bruce McLean had even imagined a sculpture by Caro called "Dulux.")[105] The break with Greenberg's golden rule, when Caro invited viewers to think associatively while looking closely at his sculpture, came with *Trojan War* (fig. 2.15).

Trojan War could be seen as Caro's first postmodern sculpture, in its questioning of modernism's commitment to objective quality, its references back to sculpture's ancient history through narrative, its sense of uncertainty about both the classical past and present, and the way interpretation is as much up to the viewer as the maker. It still invites close scrutiny of sculpture, but in a very different way. It offers traditional sculptural values of composition in mass and

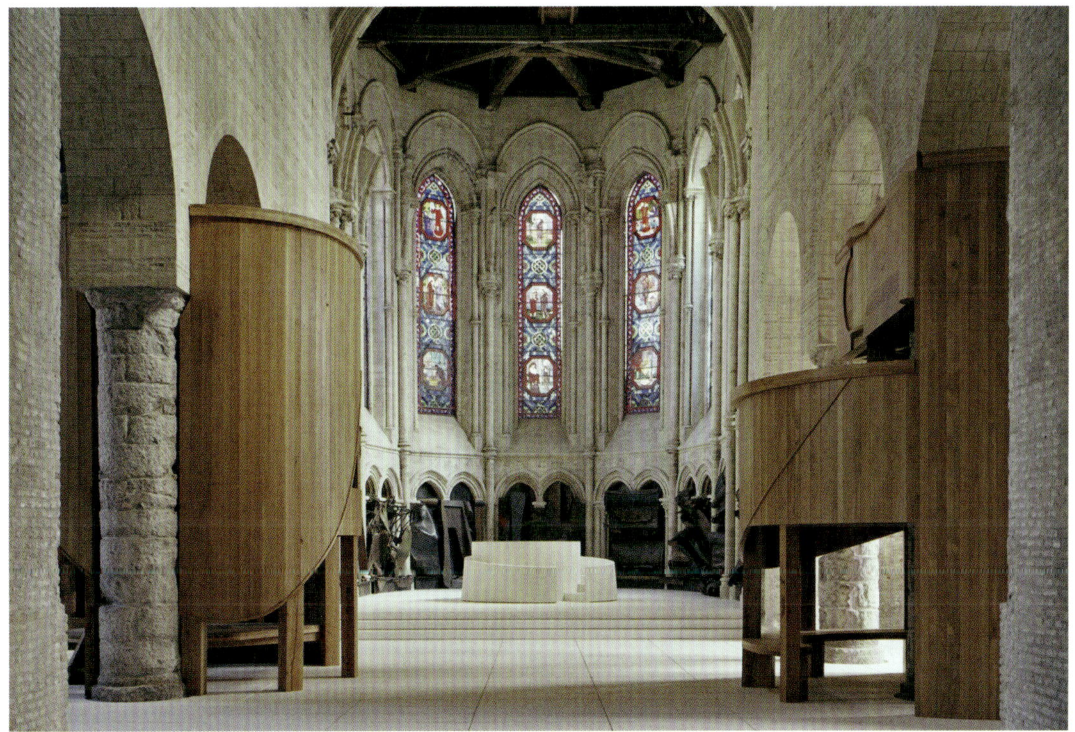

FIG. 2.14 *The Chapel of Light,* 1999–2008, stoneware, wood, steel, brass, bronze, concrete, and plaster, various dimensions. Church of Saint-Jean-Baptiste, Bourbourg, Pas-de-Calais, France

space, the use of many contrasting materials, and the experience of walking through or among sculptures. With *Trojan War,* Caro also began to use carefully chosen titles to invite an associative response. Further, he achieved a collective unity of a single work of art in forty parts. These are not independent, self-sufficient sculptures made of a single material for an anonymous, white-cube gallery space. The group developed as sculptures with a specific setting in mind: the orangery of an eighteenth-century villa (Kenwood) in a park overlooking the London skyline. He added further works, and theatrical lighting, for the second showing, in a temporary structure at Yorkshire Sculpture Park. The space between the sculptures was as critical. In effect an installation, *Trojan War* crossed the boundaries between sculpture and literature in a way that could be deemed "theatrical." In mood and atmosphere it is far from the utopian idealism of "pure" modernism in the "optical" mode and closer to the grand manner history painting in the sublime that Greenberg saw as an English artist's inescapable heritage.

Critics became fascinated by the suggestion of content. According to John McEwen, "Fashion has swung back to the figurative. . . . It results in the richest sculpture, both in materials and emotional content, of his career—the most vibrant entry into old age that any modern British artist has achieved."[106] Unlike the ambitious paintings of the grand manner, *Trojan War* forces the viewer to see the sculptures close-up; the sheer quantity all in one room ensured the sense of personal confrontation with sculptures whose ceramic "heads"

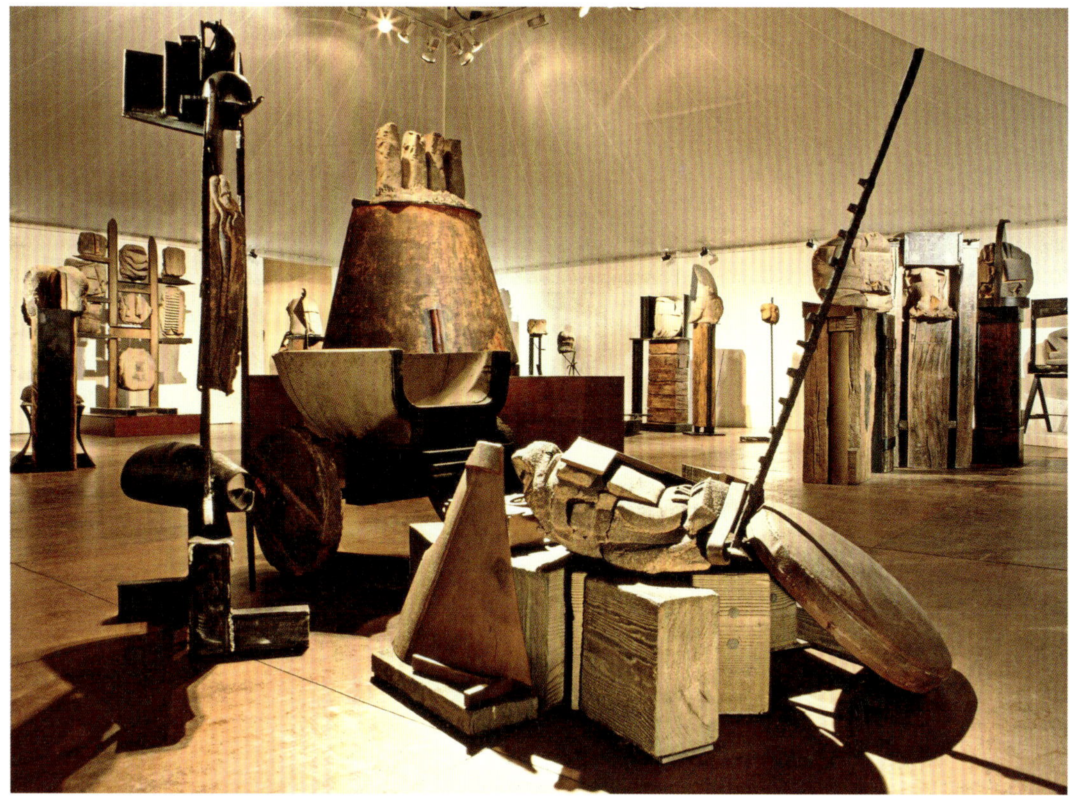

FIG. 2.15 *Trojan War,* 1993–94, installed at the Yorkshire Sculpture Park (1994), stoneware, wood, steel, brass, and bronze, various dimensions

gave them a psychological frisson. One reason why the parts seem so direct in their address is that Caro made each one himself, working alone in a small back-room studio behind his office, across the car park from his large factory studio. According to Tim Hilton, writing in 1994, they are not "figure sculpture, for they use a variety of signs and ideograms that denote rather than imitate the body. They still have the feeling of a personal presence. They do not exceed life size, and there is something like intimacy in the way they confront the spectator."[107] A few months later David Cohen noted that Caro "has more in common with the expressive figure painters of the School of London such as Bacon, Auerbach and Kitaj than with his erstwhile abstract colleagues."[108]

The potential of this new sculptural vocabulary was such that Caro made four more figurative-narrative installations, all large-scale, mixed-media, and multipartite (*Last Judgment*, 1996–99; *Barbarians*, 1999–2002; *The Kenwood Series,* 2004; *The Chapel of Light,* 2006–08). For all their scale and sense of spectacle, the relationship to the viewer is one-to-one, of individual sculptures as part of a collective whole, rather than of one great overwhelming ensemble to be admired from afar.

Few artists have been the subject of published criticism for more than fifty-five years in their lifetimes. During Caro's career the language of appreciation has had many priorities. From Herbert Read's philosophy via Greenberg and Fried's formalism, through the incoherent mumblings of "grown men" overheard by Bruce McLean, past the social perspectives of Marxism, to the relativism of postmodernism, Caro's work prompted new terms. In 1980 Caro declared his ambition to move beyond the fundamentals of visual communication: "Twenty years ago we were trying to find ways to make art with clarity and economy, to establish our grammar. Now we can write fuller sentences."[109] Statements made in interviews lack footnotes, but we can recognize here how Caro used Fried's metaphor of a prelinguistic language, a theory expounded in his introduction to the Whitechapel exhibition catalogue in 1963. From this had grown the frequent statement that Caro has "expanded the vocabulary of sculpture." Caro referred to the state of modern sculpture; however, by 1980 the issue had expanded—from visual communication through abstraction, to our actual verbal language of appreciation. In his use of the collective noun Caro spoke for modern art, drawing self-confidence from more than the state of his own sculpture. Suggesting that artists "can write fuller sentences" was not just a metaphor—and it applied equally to their more articulate admirers.

Caro's career is a long road flanked by contrasting fields of art criticism, almost art forms in themselves, framing or constraining the thoughts and eyes of the spectator encountering his sculpture. For those in need of written guidance, the "Caro literature" ranges from uncritical essays and interviews by friends and admirers to digests of anecdotes and of others' ideas by busy journalists for the popular press. In between lie the original observations of critics, curators, and art historians; each brings perspectives, themes, and terminologies to an evolving transatlantic language. The original meanings of influential texts can be well-buried, even in interviews in which the artist discusses works decades after he made them. As for all art, the challenge lies in the relationship between direct experience and articulation, between empathy and analysis.[110]

The literature around Caro is so extensive that many clichés have become part of how we "read" and understand his art. Gaining a better understanding of where these ideas originate, deconstructing them so as to rediscover their origins, removes some of the distortions that come from over-used formulas. Understanding the rich language of appreciation that evolved in response to Caro's sculpture can help us to use the words with precision and get closer to the works themselves.

NOTES

1. Quoted in Bruce McLean and Nena Dimitrijevic, *Bruce McLean* (Basel: Kunsthalle, 1981; London: Whitechapel Art Gallery, 1982), 7.

2. Roland Penrose, ed. *The Sculpture of Picasso*, New York, MoMA and London, Tate Gallery, 1967.

3. Anthony Caro, Robert Rosenblum, and David Sylvester, "On Picasso as a Sculptor," *Modern Painters* 7, no. 1 (Spring 1994): 35–39.

4. David Annesley et al., "Anthony Caro's Work: a Symposium by Four Sculptors," *Studio International* 177, no. 4 (Jan. 1969): 14–20.

5. Philip James, ed., *Henry Moore on Sculpture* (London: Macdonald, 1968), 115.

6. James, *Henry Moore on Sculpture*, 115.

7. Julius Bryant, *Anthony Caro. Figurative and Narrative Sculpture* (Farnham, Surrey: Lund Humphries, 2009), 11.

8. Ezra Pound, *Gaudier-Brzeska: A Memoir* (London: Laidlaw & Laidlaw, 1939), 119. Anne Middleton Wagner, *Mother Stone. The Vitality of Modern British Sculpture* (New Haven: Yale University Press, 2005), 18.

9. Henry Moore, "The Sculptor's Aims," cited in Wagner, *Mother Stone*, 19.

10. David Sylvester, "Round the London Galleries," *The Listener* 1 (Sept. 1955): 102.

11. Daniel-Henry Kahnweiler, *The Sculpture of Picasso* (London: R. Phillips, 1949).

12. Basil Taylor, "Art," *The Spectator* 2 (Sept. 1955): 308. He also notes, however, "the distortions are not convincingly related to the human actions from which they derive."

13. Lawrence Alloway, "Caro and Gravity," in *Anthony Caro* (Milan: Galleria del Naviglio, 1956), unpaginated.

14. Caro to Diana Eichler, quoted in Ian Barker, *Anthony Caro, Quest for the New Sculpture* (Künzelsau: Swiridoff Verlag, 2004), 22. See also Alastair Grieve, *Constructed Abstract Art in England. A Neglected Avant-Garde* (New Haven: Yale University Press, 2005).

15. For example, "All sculptors dream of defying gravity . . . of putting heavy pieces calmly up in the air and getting them to stay there," quoted in Phyllis Tuchman, "An Interview with Anthony Caro," *Artforum* 10 (June 1972): 56–58.

16. Lawrence Alloway, "Caro and Gravity," in *Anthony Caro* (Milan: Galleria del Naviglio, 1956), unpaginated.

17. Andrew Forge, "Round the Galleries," *The Listener* (Jan. 17, 1957): 102.

18. Caro quoted in Barker, *Anthony Caro*, 84.

19. Clement Greenberg, "Anthony Caro," *Arts Yearbook 8: Contemporary Sculpture* (1965): 106–09, reprinted in Clement Greenberg, *Clement Greenberg: The Collected Essays and Criticism*, John O'Brian, ed., 6 vols. (Chicago: University of Chicago Press, 1986–93), 4: 205–08. Greenberg wrote the essay in 1964 but published it in 1965.

20. Clement Greenberg, *Art and Culture: Critical Essays* (Boston: Beacon Press, 1961); republished by Thames and Hudson, 1973.

21. Quoted in Peter Fuller, "Anthony Caro: His Works and Views," *Art Monthly* 23 (Feb. 1979): 6–15.

22. Quoted in Julius Bryant, *Caro: A Life in Sculpture* (London and New York: Merrell, 2004), 47.

23. Anthony Caro, "In the Studio," in Karen Wilkin and Bruce Guenther, eds., *Clement Greenberg: A Critic's Collection* (Princeton: Portland Art Museum and Princeton University Press, 2001), 13.

24. Anthony Caro, "Obituary: Clement Greenberg," *The Independent,* May 11, 1994, 14.

25. Greenberg, "David Smith," *Greenberg*, 3: 275–79.

26. James Hall, "Clement Greenberg on English Sculpture and Englishness," *The Sculpture Journal* 4 (2000): 172–77.

27. Greenberg, "David Smith," *Greenberg*, 3: 275–79 (1956, revised 1963).

28. Greenberg, "Modernist Painting," *Greenberg*, 4: 85–93.

29. Greenberg, "The New Sculpture," *Greenberg*, 2: 313–19 (1948, revised 1958 for *Art and Culture*, 1961).

30. Another key to the unrecorded conversation between Greenberg and Caro in 1959 is Greenberg's essay, "The Pasted-Paper Revolution" (Greenberg, "The New Sculpture," *Greenberg*, 4: 61–66) first published in *Art News* 57, no. 5 (Sept. 1958): 46–49, in which he describes how Braque and Picasso sought to make their paintings "more real" (one of Caro's favorite phrases) by incorporating fragments of wallpaper or wood, an ambition that led to "the new art of 'drawing in space'" practiced by Gonzàlez.

31. Quoted in Phyllis Tuchman, "An Interview with Anthony Caro," *Artforum* 10 (Jun. 1972): 56–58; see also Bryant, *Anthony Caro. Figurative and Narrative Sculpture*, 11.

32. Quoted in Bryant, *Anthony Caro: A Life in Sculpture,* 47–48.
33. Quoted in Florence Rubenfeld, *Clement Greenberg: A Life* (New York: Scribner, 1997): 182–83.
34. Quoted in Bryant, *Anthony Caro: A Life in Sculpture,* 48.
35. Anthony Caro, "Obituary: Clement Greenberg," *The Independent,* London, May 11, 1994, 14.
36. Clement Greenberg, "Anthony Caro," in *Arts Yearbook 8: Contemporary Sculpture* (1965), 106–09, reprinted in *Studio International* 174, no. 892 (Sept. 1967): 116–17; Richard Whelan, *Anthony Caro,* (Harmondsworth, Middlesex: Penguin, 1974), 87–93, and in Greenberg, "Modernist Painting," *Greenberg,* 4:205–08.
37. On Greenberg's controversial removal of Smith's paint, see Rosalind Krauss, "Changing the Work of David Smith," *Art in America* 62 (Sep.–Oct. 1974): 30–34.
38. See, for example, James Hall, "Clement Greenberg on English Sculpture and Englishness," *The Sculpture Journal* 4 (2000): 172–77; William Rubin, *Anthony Caro* (New York: The Museum of Modern Art, 1975); Kirk Varnedoe, "Intellectual Subtlety in Constructed Steel," *Art News* 74 (Summer 1975): 38–40. Joseph Masheck, "Reflections on Caro's Englishness," *Studio International* 188 (1974): 93–96, ends "Caro's sculpture is at its best and . . . its most original when it is at its most English."
39. Harry Mallgrave, *Gottfried Semper* (New Haven: Yale University Press, 1996), 201, 203; Julius Bryant, ed., *Art and Design for All* (London: V&A: London, Publications, 2011), 144–45.
40. Elizabeth Prettejohn, "From Aestheticism to Modernism, and Back Again," *Interdisciplinary Studies in the Long Nineteenth Century* 2 (May 2006), 1–16. For an introduction to the influence on Greenberg of the literary criticism of F. R. Leavis and T. S. Eliot, see Rubenfeld, *Clement Greenberg,* 124–38.
41. Terry Friedman, "Herbert Read on Sculpture," in Benedict Read, David Thistlewood, and Robert Burstow, eds., *Herbert Read: A British Vision of World Art* (London: V&A Publications, 2011), 103–18.
42. Letter, Anthony Caro to Clement Greenberg, Aug. 5, 1964, Greenberg Papers, Special Collections, Getty Research Institute, Los Angeles.
43. Bernard Berenson, *Piero della Francesca; Or, the Ineloquent in Art* (London: Chapman and Hall, 1954).
44. Greenberg, "Review of *Piero della Francesca* and *The Arch of Constantine,* both by Bernard Berenson," *Greenberg,* 3:247–53, first published in November 1955.
45. Michael Fried, *Art and Objecthood: Essays and Reviews* (Chicago: University of Chicago Press, 1998), recounts on pages 6–7 how they met at a dinner after a gallery opening and Caro "bluntly asked when I could come and see his work."
46. Brian McAvera, "A Conversation with Sir Anthony Caro," *Sculpture* 21, no. 2 (March 2002): 25–31.
47. Anonymous, "Clement Greenberg" (obituary), *The Times,* May 26, 1994.
48. Michael Fried, *Anthony Caro: Table Sculptures 1966–1977* (London: British Council, 1977).
49. For a discussion of table sculptures see pp 125–6 in the present volume.
50. Letter from Anthony Caro to Michael Fried, July 15, 1963. Copy at Barford Sculptures.
51. Fried's introduction to the Whitechapel catalogue was revised as "Anthony Caro: Sculpture 1960–1963" for *Art and Objecthood: Essays and Reviews,* 269–73, from whence these quotes are taken.
52. Fried, *Art and Objecthood: Essays and Reviews,* 162.
53. Michael Fried, *Anthony Caro: Sculpture 1960–1963* (London: Whitechapel Art Gallery, 1963), unpaginated.
54. Caro recalled (to the present writer, 2010) that his work was not popular after his exhibition at the Whitechapel, and his dealer, Gimpel Fils Gallery, preferred his earlier expressionist figures.
55. Bryan Robertson, Preface, to Fried, *Anthony Caro: Sculpture 1960–1963* (London: Whitechapel Art Gallery, 1963), unpaginated.
56. Bryan Robertson, "Caro and the 20th Century," in Anthony Caro and Bryan Robertson, *Anthony Caro: Sculpture through Five Decades* (London: Annely Juda Fine Art, 1994), V.
57. Herbert Read, "New Aspects of British Sculpture," in *The XXVI Venice Biennale, the British Pavilion* (London: Westminster Press, 1952).
58. Herbert Read, *A Concise History of Modern Sculpture* (London: Thames and Hudson, 1964, reprinted 1974), 237–39.
59. Read, *A Concise History of Modern Sculpture,* 7.
60. Read, *A Concise History of Modern Sculpture,* 253.
61. Read, *A Concise History of Modern Sculpture,* 257.

62. Read, *A Concise History of Modern Sculpture,* 244–45.
63. Read, *A Concise History of Modern Sculpture,* 234.
64. Read, *A Concise History of Modern Sculpture,* 212.
65. Read, *A Concise History of Modern Sculpture,* 226.
66. Greenberg, "Polemic Against Modern Art: Review of *The Demon of Progress in the Arts* by Wyndham Lewis," *Greenberg,* 3:253–55. For Greenberg's exchange with Read in 1963, see Greenberg, "Modernist Painting," *Greenberg,* 4:145–49.
67. Herbert Read was known as "the Pope of Modern Art" according to Burstow in *Herbert Read,* 129.
68. John Richardson, "Early One Morning," *The New Statesman* (March 5, 1965).
69. Greenberg, "How Art Writing Earns its Bad Name," *Greenberg,* 4: 135–44; 145–49.
70. Read, Thistlewood, and Burstow, *Herbert Read,* 274.
71. Maurice Tuchman, "Introduction," in *American Sculpture of the Sixties* (Los Angeles: Los Angeles County Museum of Art, 1967), 10.
72. Greenberg, "Recentness of Sculpture," *Greenberg,* 4:250–56.
73. Sybil Gordon Kantor, *Alfred H. Barr, Jr. and the Intellectual Origins of the Museum of Modern Art* (Cambridge, Mass. and London: MIT Press, 2002), 367 illustrates Barr's "Torpedo through time diagram for the ideal permanent collection of MoMA" of 1941.
74. Fried, *Art and Objecthood,* 155.
75. Paul Moorhouse, *Anthony Caro: Presence* (Farnham, Surrey: Lund Humphries, 2010), does not mention the use of the word by Greenberg and Fried in 1967. Greenberg also used "presence" as a quality in art in his essay "Collage."
76. Quoted in Charles Harrison, "Sculpture's Recent Past," in Terry A. Neff, Graham William, and John Beal, eds., *A Quiet Revolution, British Sculpture Since 1965,* 10–33 (London and New York: Thames and Hudson, 1987), 31 n. 52. For the argument between Greenberg, Fried, and the Minimalist artists Donald Judd and Robert Morris, see Jon Thompson, "The Rise of the Object: Dispatches from the War on Form," in Penelope Curtis and Keith Wilson, eds., *Modern British Sculpture* (London: Royal Academy of Arts, 2011), 234–41.
77. Michael Fried, *Anthony Caro* (London: Hayward Gallery, 1969), 8.
78. Fried, *Anthony Caro* (1969), 9.
79. Fried, *Anthony Caro* (1969), 9.
80. Michael Fried, "Caro's Abstractness," *Artforum* 9, no. 1 (Sept. 1970) 32–34, reprinted in Richard Whelan, *Anthony Caro* (Harmondsworth, Middlesex: Penguin, 1974), 109.
81. John Russell, "Closing the Gaps," *Art News* 69 (May 1970), reprinted in Whelan, *Anthony Caro,* 113.
82. Whelan, *Anthony Caro.*
83. Alex Potts, writing in 2011 on *Early One Morning,* noted, "For all its radical abstraction, vestiges nevertheless persist of figurative reference and mimetic realism. This residual impurity gives the work some of its substance and fascination," in Penelope Curtis and Keith Wilson, eds., *Modern British Sculpture* (London: Royal Academy of Art, 2011), 184.
84. Norbert Lynton, "Sculpture on the Table," *The Guardian,* Feb. 17, 1969, reprinted in Barker, *Quest for the New Sculpture,* 182–84.
85. Bruce McLean, "Not Even Crimble Crumble," *Studio International* 180, no. 926 (Oct. 1970): 156–59.
86. Rosalind Krauss, *Passages in Modern Sculpture* (Cambridge, Mass.: MIT, 1977), 195, based on her article "How Paradigmatic is Anthony Caro?" *Art in America* (Sept.–Oct. 1975): 80–83.
87. Krauss, *Passages in Modern Sculpture,* 192.
88. Anna Lovatt, "Rosalind Krauss's *The Originality of the Avant-Garde and Other Modernist Myths,* 1985," *Burlington Magazine* 153 (Sept. 2011): 601–04.
89. Kirk Varnedoe, "Intellectual Subtlety in Constructed Steel," *Art News* 74 (Summer 1975): 38–40.
90. Rubin, *Anthony Caro,* 65.
91. Barry Martin, "On the occasion of Anthony Caro's retrospective exhibition at MoMA," *Studio International* 189 (May–June 1975): 233–35.
92. Michael Fried, *Anthony Caro* (London: Hayward Gallery, 1969), 12.
93. Martin, "On the Occasion," 233.
94. Barry Martin, "New Work: Anthony Caro," *Studio International* 187 (April 1974): 202–03.
95. See, for example, Rosalind Krauss, "Anthony Caro, André Emmerich Gallery," *Artforum* 7, no. 5 (Jan. 1969): 53–55, in which the formalist term "axis" is used ten times in two paragraphs.

96. Peter Fuller, "Anthony Caro," *Art Monthly* 23 (Feb. 1979): 6–15. Later that year Caro wrote in reply to a review by Fuller: "If this is criticism then I am a Dutchman. . . . the trite language . . . was more than I had expected." Caro, "Stockwell Depot," *Art Monthly* 32 (Dec. 1979–Jan. 1980): 27.
97. Quoted in Barker, *Quest for the New Sculpture*, 249.
98. Stuart Morgan, "Anthony Caro: Kenwood House," *Artforum* (Dec. 1981), quoted in Barker, *Quest for the New Sculpture*, 248.
99. Their last exchange was in March 1994, when Caro sent Greenberg a copy of the catalogue to his exhibition *Trojan War,* which he says the critic admired. Greenberg died May 7, 1994.
100. Marina Vaizey, "Sailing Off into a Space of His Own," *Sunday Times,* Oct. 1, 1989.
101. David Cohen, "The Last Modernist. Sir Anthony Caro," *Sculpture* 14:1 (Jan.–Feb. 1995): 20–27.
102. Rosalind Krauss, *A Voyage on the North Sea: Art in the Age of the Post-Medium Condition* (London: Thames and Hudson, 1999).
103. Paul Moorhouse, *Anthony Caro: Sculpture Towards Architecture* (London: Tate Gallery, 1991), 33.
104. Karen Wilkin, *Anthony Caro: Interior and Exterior* (Farnham, Surrey: Lund Humphries, 2009), 37.
105. McLean, "Not Even Crimble Crumble," 156. Dulux is a British brand of paint for domestic decorating.
106. John McEwen, "Tacking to the Windward of Fashion," *Sunday Telegraph*, March 20, 1994; quoted in Barker, *Quest for the New Sculpture*, 303.
107. Tim Hilton, "Still Reckless after All These Years," *The Independent*, March 13, 1994.
108. Cohen, "The Last Modernist. Sir Anthony Caro," *Sculpture* 14:1 (Jan.–Feb. 1995): 20–27. Cohen was echoing a comparison suggested by Greenberg in his essay of 1965, almost as if his prophecy had come true.
109. Quoted in Cohen, "The Last Modernist," 25.
110. Lorenz Eitner, "Art History and the Sense of Quality," *Art International* 14, no. 5 (May 1975): 75–80.

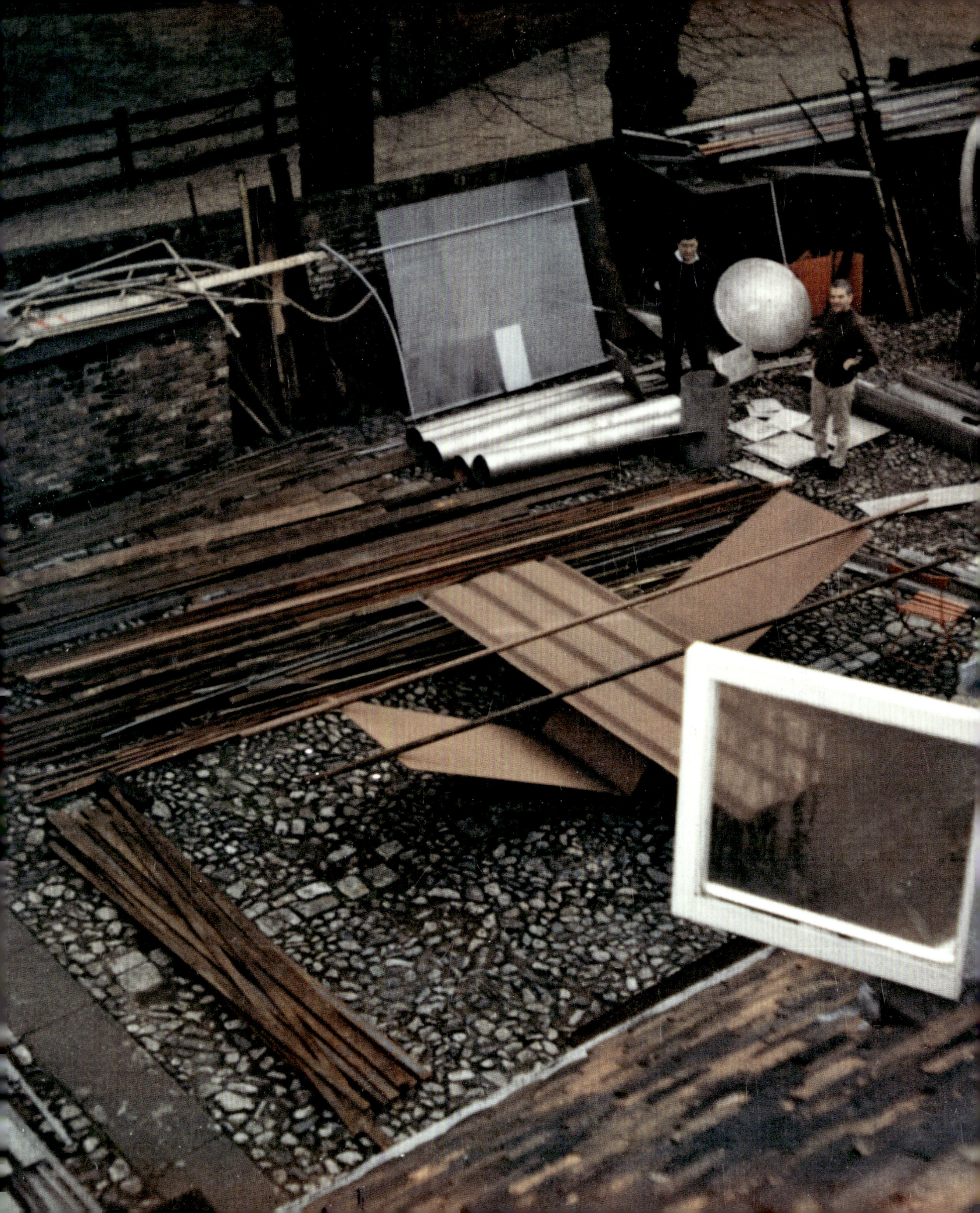

Caro and the Materials of Sculpture

Martina Droth

The copious literature that has accumulated around Anthony Caro is remarkably constant in its characterization of the sculptor's work. His dramatic shift, in 1959/60, from figurative sculpture to large-scale abstract constructions (fig. 3.1), remains the defining moment upon which an entire career—spanning some six decades and comprising thousands of works—continues to hinge.[1] The notion of a radical "breakthrough" and sudden sharpening of direction established the strong sense of chronology that remains the organizing rationale for discussions of Caro's oeuvre. Clement Greenberg and Michael Fried, Caro's most important early champions, established the critical terms for understanding the abstract sculptures.[2] The criteria that were put forward for the work then remain its most familiar associations now: the rejection of the pedestal, the emphasis on horizontality, and an object-viewer relationship of a purely visual kind, which kept the viewer strictly outside the work.

It would be hard to overstate the resilience of these ideas. Despite Caro's enormous output, the breadth and diversity of his work, and the vastly changed context of sculptural practice across his long career, the early definitions still act as the springboards for almost every discussion of his sculpture. As Alex Potts has recently noted, Caro's place in the larger picture of sculpture since the 1960s has been curiously static.[3] The notion of his "breakthrough" as a moment of field-shifting change remains undisputed, despite the brief sojourn enjoyed by the radical reputation of this form of sculpture, and despite the challenges that Caro faced almost as soon as he became established.[4] Instead, the artistic influences that were seen as crucial to his discovery of abstraction have hardened into an unshakeable framework that, if it has the appearance of placing Caro into a meaningful trajectory, has rather served to detach him from the wider art historical context.

Henry Moore (1898–1986) and David Smith (1906–1965) still loom large in the story of Caro's career, in which their respective oeuvres provide a convenient match for the established trajectory of his work's development: Moore's soft, organic, anthropomorphic forms are associated with Caro's earliest bronzes; Smith's angular, open structures and industrial idiom with Caro's abandonment of the figure and turn to abstraction. A question posed to Caro by Peter Fuller in 1988 points to the way in which the polarized ends of Caro's "breakthrough" became personified in Moore and Smith: "Isn't it true that Moore's work was English, concerned with natural form, and anthropomorphic, whereas yours became oriented towards America, urban techniques, and industrial materials, and 'radically abstract'?"[5] Presented like some essential truth about the diametrically opposed nature of sculpture in

FIG. 3.1 Caro at work on *Prairie* outside his home studio in Hampstead, 1967

Britain and the United States, Fuller's reading is, however, wholly dependent upon Caro's intersection with the two artists.[6]

Explicitly or implicitly, the common thread among the binary strands into which Caro's work and its influences have been separated, is the materials and production processes they entail. From the early twentieth century, more so than ever before, materials stood for an idea of sculpture's progression; in the timeline of Caro's development, clay, plaster, and bronze became the symbols of an outdated tradition, and steel their antithesis. Although accounts of the role that materials play in Caro's work provide an ostensibly objective assessment of the ways in which they shaped his sculptural practice, a closer look at interpretations of the sculptures suggests that materials have brought to bear a set of predetermined categorizations that are, in fact, deeply symbolic. Despite the insistently formal emphasis that frames discussions of Caro's work and the methodological descriptions it elicits, his materials have come to signify his autobiography and are inextricably bound up with the chronology established at the outset of his career.

Given that Caro is so much seen to be about "essential" qualities that originate in his commitment to a particular sculptural language, it is striking how minutely his work tends to be discussed, through the visual microcosm of the "series."[7] Indeed, there is a neatness to Caro's mode of working that lends itself to this approach. Nearly all his sculptures can be grouped into more or less discrete sets, by their shared materials, forms, and scales, as well as by places of their production and serialized titles: the *Bulls* among his figurative work of the 1950s are one such set, the *Smokers* another; the shiny, polished steel table sculptures of the late 1960s form a set apart from the rusted angular table pieces of the early 1970s; the paper reliefs made in New York State in 1981 are distinct from those made at Obama, Japan, in the early 1990s. This compartmentalized practice has invited responses that attempt to identify and track the changes of the formal characteristics from one series to the next, thereby maintaining the sense of chronological orderliness. But Caro's prolific output means that the once neat timeline along which his changing styles and interests could be traced early on has become so elongated that the logic of its sequence can now hardly be determined. The clear visual sense of a "development" and "progression," which so obviously mark his work from the 1950s into the 1970s, simply no longer seems central—or helpful—to the understanding of an oeuvre of such breadth and maturity.

Caro's long-established practice—the fluid, fast, and unencumbered way in which he goes about his work and its great diversity of scale, materials, and content—suggests that chronology and its associated connotations neither reveal the "essential" Caro nor offer the most effective means of analyzing the work. Whether made in the 1970s, '80s, '90s, or 2000s, the sculptures seem rather to elicit questions about their physical expression of Caro's material preoccupations. This essay seeks to re-examine the materials that appear most central to Caro's career—clay, bronze, and steel. It aims to consider their place in Caro's oeuvre in less anecdotal and symbolic terms, both by looking at the ways in which Caro has responded to the physical properties of materials and the sculptural opportunities inherent therein, and by taking account of the meanings, content, and historic implications they bring to the work. The different contexts in which Caro encountered these materials helpfully illuminate how their use and connotations were defined, enabling us to consider their role both in the history of Caro's sculpture and in terms of their own intrinsic material histories.

The Materials of Art Education

Caro's early figurative sculptures, made just after his student years at the Royal Academy Schools, consist of clay, plaster, and bronze, sometimes also incorporating, after the Moore manner, found objects (fig. 3.2).[8] As has been well documented, the materials and processes of these early works were corollaries of Caro's training, and of his time with Moore: thus, his later rejection of both was also a rejection of clay, plaster, and bronze. Caro's sense that he had to change his materials in order to get away from prevailing associations with historic fine art traditions ("Clay . . . has too many reminders . . . too much art history," he said),[9] is now synonymous with his progressive steps toward abstraction: in Caro's timeline, clay and bronze symbolize the morass from which the sculptor had to free himself. While the central role of materials in Caro's changing practice, and in modern sculptural practice as a whole, cannot be denied, it is nonetheless striking how seamlessly they have been absorbed into the story of Caro's artistic formation, carrying their deeply symbolic associations into the work itself. Before considering the ways in which Caro's materials have been deployed to mythologize the sculptor's artistic identity, it is worth pausing to look at their role more broadly in the context of sculptural practice at the time and at the practical conditions they brought to bear on Caro's work from his early training.

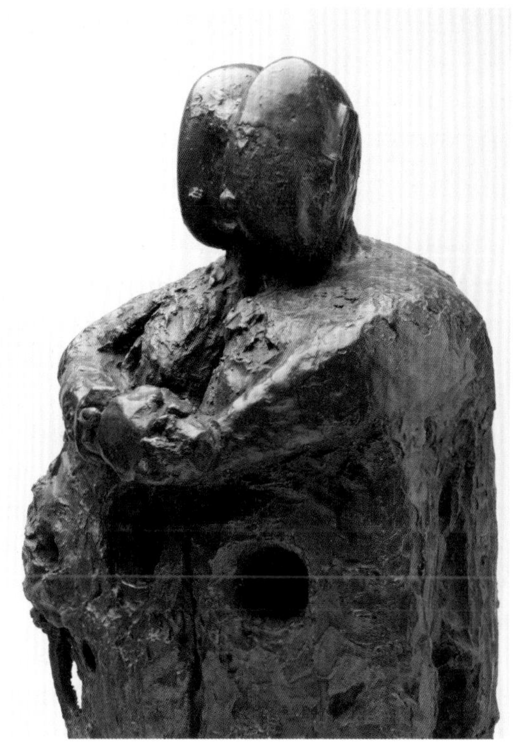

FIG. 3.2 *Baby with a Ball,* detail (cat. 23)

The importance of direct carving as a "modern" practice has been well established in the history of early twentieth-century sculpture in Britain, which entailed a rejection of the practice of modeling in pliable materials and the associated processes of mechanical transference (from model, to plaster, to bronze) that this necessitated.[10] But despite the primary status that direct carving has attained art historically, the practice of modeling was never eclipsed. On the contrary, in Britain it underpinned the sculptor's art, having been consolidated, in the mid-nineteenth century, as a state-sanctioned system of sculptural training through the National Art Training School at South Kensington, which later became the Royal College of Art. The legacy of this system and its long endurance can be tracked through generations of teachers and students as late as Caro's own student years. Henry Moore came out of the South Kensington system (and rebelled against it); however, it was not Moore who conditioned Caro's earliest experiences of sculptural practice but his art school teachers. Indeed, as Caro has often explained, in Moore he had seen an artist who stood apart from that education and who helped him break out of "that constricting thing the Royal Academy had given me."[11]

That "constricting thing" had everything to do with modeling and with the individuals who mark Caro's first exposure to sculpture. The artist who perhaps best exemplifies the endurance of modeling as a system of training during Caro's formative years is Sir Charles Wheeler (1892–1974). A highly successful sculptor of public and civic commissions, Wheeler became president of the Royal Academy in 1956, a position in which he wielded considerable authority and influence during a ten-year-long tenure. By the time of his presidency Wheeler also had come to stand for an "orthodoxy," as he himself recognized.[12] His career exemplifies the kind of long trajectory that brought forward, well into the middle of the twentieth century, a set of skills and ideas that essentially came out of a Victorian training.

The persistent influence of that training can hardly be overstated. At the Royal College, where Wheeler himself had been taught, the same Professor of Modelling—the French sculptor Edouard Lantéri (1848–1917)—had been in position for some four decades, since 1880. Generations of sculptors thus came out of a single system of instruction that barely changed over more than half a century and that spanned the lives and work of artists who today are hardly seen as related to each other.[13] Moore, just six years Wheeler's junior, attended the Royal College from 1921; although Lantéri was by then dead, his student protégés had become the teachers under whom Moore studied. Some of those same individuals crossed directly into Caro's life as visiting critics at the Royal Academy Schools where Caro studied from 1947–52. Well into the twentieth century, then, a traditional sculptors' training, with an engrained emphasis on the technical mastery of modeling, was maintained through a process of continuous generational handover.

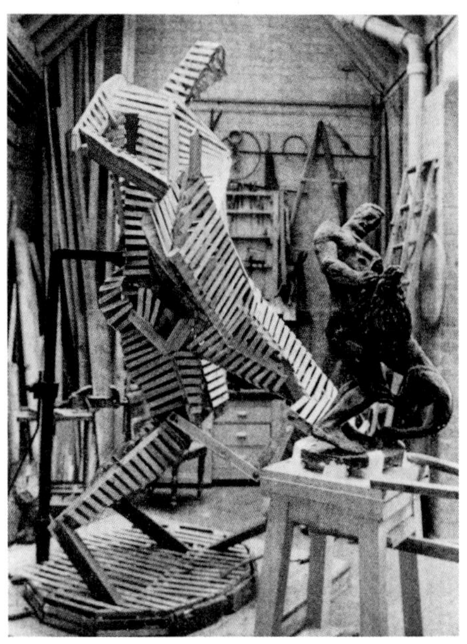

FIG. 3.3 Charles Wheeler's studio, showing the armature for the enlargement of *Hercules and the Lion* for Barclays Bank, Lombard Street, London (completed 1962)

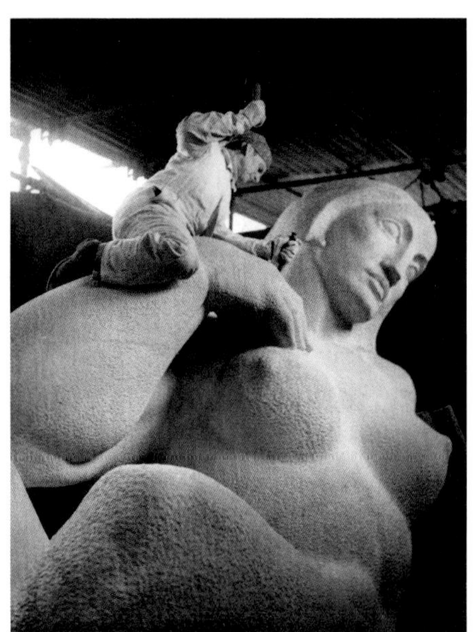

FIG. 3.4 Charles Wheeler at work on *Earth* for the Ministry of Defence, Horseguards Avenue entrance, London (completed 1953). Photo: Keystone Press

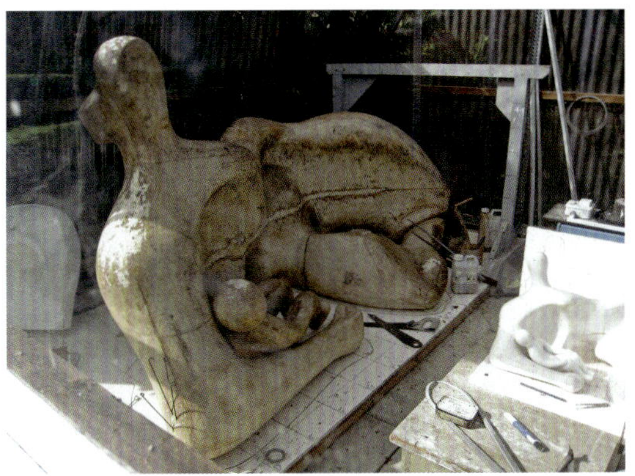

FIG. 3.5 Display illustrating Henry Moore's enlargement technique, Henry Moore Foundation, Perry Green, Hertfordshire, October 2010. Photo: Anne Wagner. © The Henry Moore Foundation. All Rights Reserved, DACS 2011

Caro had already known Wheeler as a teenager and worked for a time in his studio (fig. 3.3); it was here that he encountered, for the first and last time, a pointing machine for the scaling up of sculpture from the model, a process central to Wheeler's kind of practice.[14] Although the extraordinary cover of his autobiography—depicting the heroic master craftsman, singlehandedly sculpting his monumental figure *Earth* (fig. 3.4)—suggests an alliance to the more fashionable idiom of direct carving, Wheeler worked as frequently in bronze as in marble, and both were equally predicated on modeling. This was not untypical. Moore, too, worked in both mediums (although later increasingly in bronze), yet he had developed working methods that were more idiosyncratic and less directly handed down from his schooling. Caro recalls that Moore made up a homemade technique of transference (fig. 3.5) and that his methods and approach—if they descended from the same system as had Wheeler's—were inflected by a different set of ideas and attitudes.[15] Wheeler was among those who taught at the Royal Academy; for Caro, Moore stood as a welcome foil to his own Academy experiences.

Caro and the Expression of Materials

If Caro was deeply dissatisfied with the limitations of his training, he nonetheless did exceptionally well under the educational system, winning numerous prizes for his work.[16] Not surprisingly, his earliest works largely followed the art school methods: sculptures such as his *Bulls* began with a supporting armature, then were built up with clay, modeled in plaster, and in some cases cast into bronze (or lead). Recalling the "tyranny of materials," Caro remembers his attempts to interrupt what he was learning about proper processes and techniques: by throwing clay on the floor, or hitting it with a stick, or combining it with other materials.[17] *Baby with a Ball* (cat. 23) was made with the plaster mold of another sculpture, with additional work directly in wet plaster; the clamps that originally held the two halves of the molds together remained in the new work.[18] The introduction of shells, bones, and stones (the pebble-head of *Baby with a Ball*, see fig. 3.2), and sometimes also machine parts, reflected Moore's practice, but in retrospect also anticipated Caro's lifelong interest in discovering the sculptural potential of discarded and found materials, such as scrap metal. With this interjection of preconfigured shapes and forms, Caro made himself work under different conditions: opening up alternative choices by bringing in external factors was a way of disrupting the volitional, internally driven process of modeling formless material into an image.

Caro's avoidance, from the outset, of the usual chain of processes by which sculpture was made, such as working from preliminary drawings or scaling up from smaller models, indicates a similar departure from his schooling. Despite direct equivalents in subject matter among some of Caro's sculptures and works on paper (see, for example, the *Bulls*, figs. 3.6 and 3.7), the relationship among them is not progressive, in the sense of one stage following on from another toward the completed work, but rather of parallel expressions of the same preoccupations through different mediums. The sculptures themselves are as direct in approach as Caro could achieve without studies or models: the first conception was what went into the making of the final sculpture. Caro's practice of working in series, intently pursuing a single idea, might thus be seen as a formative strategy, deployed to help preclude the need for preliminary studies. Rather than work out an initial idea from which to realize a "finished" work, Caro runs these two ends of the process together. In a sense, the objects that make up a series suggest an open-ended project, a continual working out, the process itself standing as the work in its own right.

Yet, as is often noted, if Caro thereby challenged his learned methods, the degree to which he could do so was necessarily limited. The work was in the end still rooted in all that he was trying to get away from: as long as he continued to be wedded to clay and bronze, his work would remain wedded to the traditions they embodied. The idea that Caro was caught in a creative trap, that his artistic potential was physically choked by material conventions, is one that has become tightly knit into his biography and subsequent perceptions of the work. The early works, marking the moment before Caro's "breakthrough," seem to stand as visual evidence for the sculptor's inner artistic turmoil, a direct reflection of his frustration as he reaches the end of the road with the figure. As Terry Fenton put it, Caro's endeavors had to be "frustrated": the "lumpishness" of clay becomes "seldom more than sluggishly expressive" and, in the end, would "overwhelm" its own objects.[19] The awkwardness of the figures, the contorted positions and bodily struggle they convey, seem to cohere as a manifestation of the artist's own struggle to break free from the conventions of his training. This is a compelling notion, but it is also one that gives the work a retrospective symbolic meaning that is contingent on Caro's biography.

No doubt Caro was highly conscious of the physical restrictions within which he worked. But these restrictions are hardly unique to clay—any material brings its own demands, to which the artist adjusts accordingly. To view Caro's early sculptures in terms of limitation and frustration can only be reductive. I would suggest that a positive, even affirmative reading—one that is in some ways actually latent in these responses—

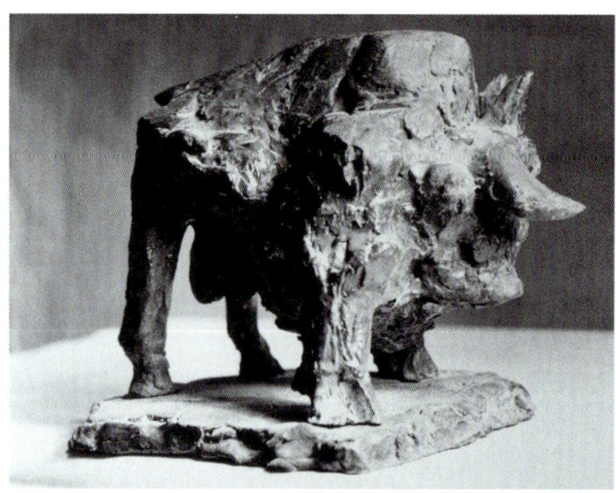

FIG. 3.6 *Bull*, 1954. Bronze, height 6½ in. (16.5 cm). Art Gallery of Ontario, Toronto

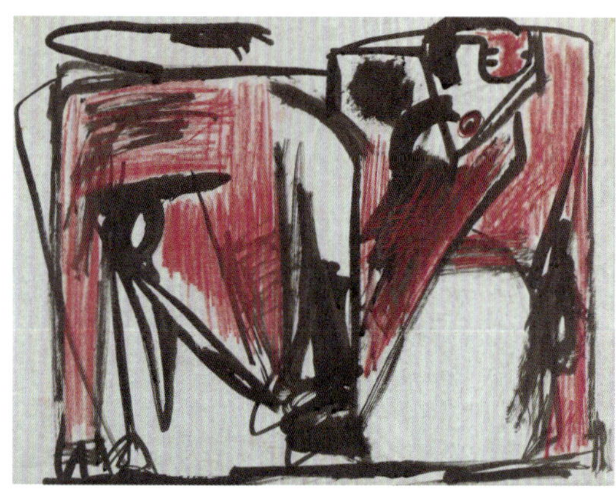

FIG. 3.7 *Bull*, 1954 (cat. 8)

could instead be explored, by looking again at how ideas of expressiveness are interpreted in relation to the work. Indeed, "expressionism," elastically defined, is the term with which Caro's early work has, both at the time and since, been overarchingly characterized. In reviews of Caro's first exhibitions, the rugged physicality of the sculptures was described at turns as "violent," "monstrous," "repellent," but also as deeply moving and evocative of "emotional" states.[20] In more recent accounts, the expressiveness of the figures has been identified with physical conditions rather than psychological ones, going by Caro's much-cited explanation that he wanted to convey a sense of being "inside the body."[21] The almost provocatively banal actions that his figures perform (smoking, waking, taking off a shirt) seem further intended to undermine any too solemn or emotive a reading. But if Caro insisted on his interest in physically oriented rather than emotionally driven ideas, the sculptures are still bound up with "feeling" (Caro's term), expressive of the sentient body.[22] Perhaps it is this ambiguity, the resistance to being defined firmly one way or another, that underlies the romantically inflected readings that his work elicits.

If Caro felt his practice to be limited, it is nonetheless true that his sculpture actively bespeaks his material investment. The work seems so deeply involved in its own materiality that we are constantly referred back to its physical expressiveness. Indeed, clay, the dominant medium in which Caro then worked, has long been seen as inherently gestural and is intimately associated with ideas of sculptural expressionism. This notion was especially germane in the nineteenth century, embodied in the powerful exemplar of Auguste Rodin (1840–1917); but it was carried forth into the early and mid-twentieth century through the very teaching systems from which Caro came. Indeed, Lantéri (Wheeler's influential teacher, and himself of the "Rodin school") articulated this sentiment in not untypical terms: the "original clay sketch," Lantéri wrote in 1904, stood for the sculptor's creative impulse, an object "inspired and worked with feverish haste . . . spontaneous in design and execution."[23] Caro's own lively, energetic modeling suggests a use of

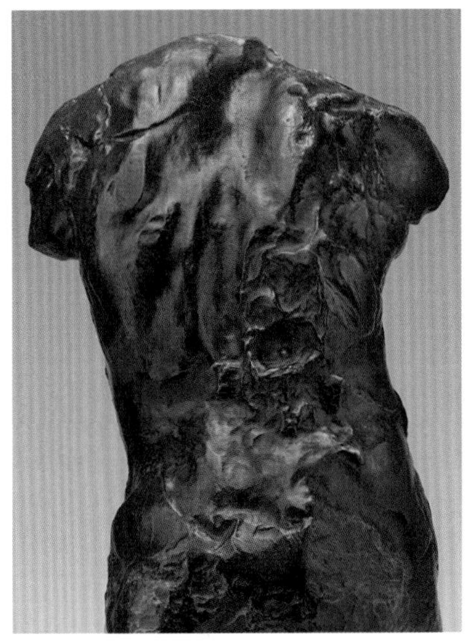

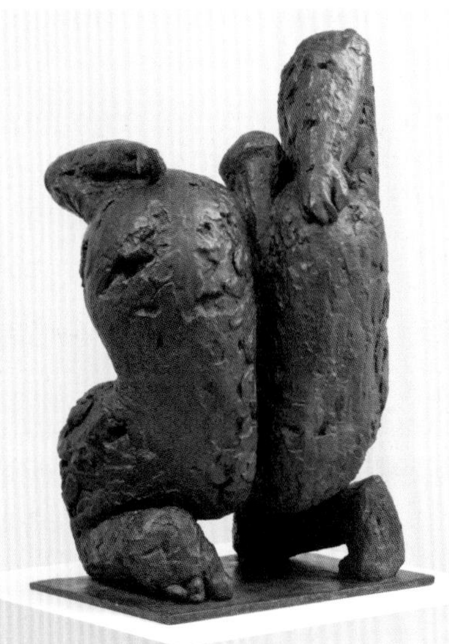

FIG. 3.8 Auguste Rodin, *Walking Man,* detail of back, model 1878–1900, probably cast 1903, bronze, 33¹⁄₁₆ in. (84 cm). National Gallery of Art, Washington, D.C. Gift of Mrs. John W. Simpson

FIG. 3.9 *Man Taking Off His Shirt,* back (cat. 22)

the material that, far from contradicting these associations, closely follows on from them; indeed, the pitted surfaces and gouged forms of his figures are not a world away from Rodin (figs. 3.8 and 3.9).[24] It could be said that Caro's work hardly evinces a struggle with his material constraints but rather manifests his fully engaged exploration, and exploitation, of their inherently expressive potential.

If the introverted posture of *Man Holding His Foot* (cat. 21) had "to do with what it is like to be inside the human body," it might equally well be described as having to do with what it is like to make a sculpture of clay.[25] Its closed, dense form calls to mind the heavy pile of clay from which it barely emerges as a body. *Man Taking off His Shirt* (cat. 22) seems similarly weighed down. The figure is trapped, not in something that suggests a shirt, but in the morass of its clay body. As Caro states, he was interested in conveying the body's daily struggle with gravity, and this idea seems to be mirrored in the heavy weight of the material, not in the sense of a symbolic statement about the sculptor's labor, but rather in that process, form, and image circuitously refer back to each other, suggesting coextensive qualities that convey something of the common condition of gravity.

In light of his subsequent oeuvre, plausible continuities may be found in Caro's intense interest in understanding the nature of materials. In the 1950s there had emerged an absolute imperative to get away from the "tyranny of materials" and the technical conventions involved in their handling that not only limited the possibilities of sculpture but also closed down any newly imagined possibilities for the materials themselves. Materials now no longer bear their connotations as powerfully as they had at the mid-twentieth century and are no longer anchored in the same expectations. Indeed, Caro acknowledges that "sculpture could gain impetus from more feeling for material."[26] Looking back on these years from the vantage of Caro's long and diverse practice, the differences that seemed to divide his work into a "before" and "after" 1960 appear less abrupt. This is not only because of Caro's periodic return to clay and bronze, and to figuration, but also because his approach is now legible as one committed to the exploration of the inherent properties of materials. Already in the early years, Caro's interest in physical qualities was visualized in what he was making, suggesting an intense process of discovery and practical understanding.

Having returned to bronze several times, in most cases Caro now approaches the material with methods that are quite different from those of his training, largely avoiding a return to mode-

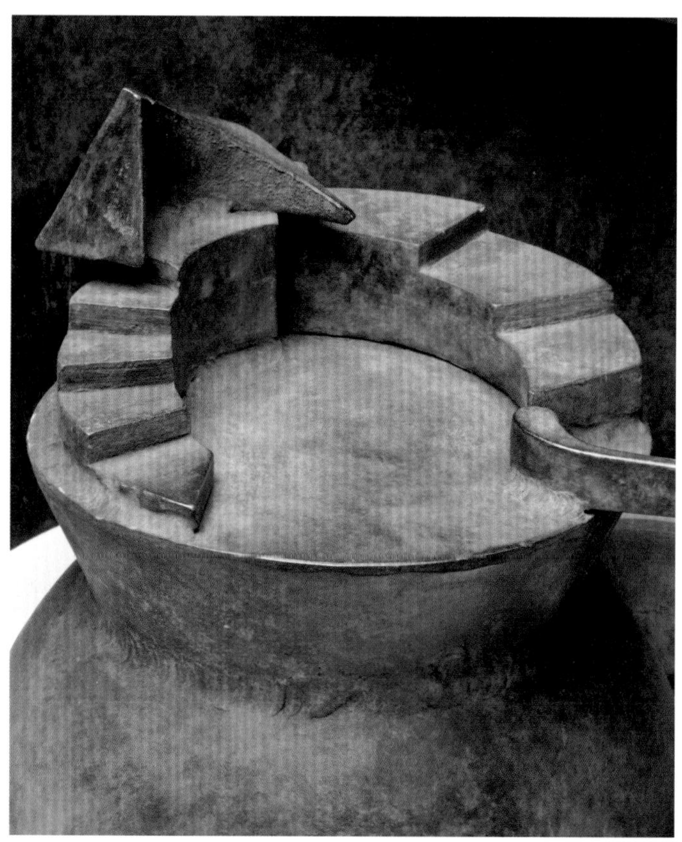

FIG. 3.10 *Cuckoo*, detail (cat. 45)

ling.[27] A recent work such as *Cuckoo* (fig. 3.10) is part cast, part welded. Some of its elements were made by casting leftover pieces in bronze then putting them together with elements from the "piece collection" that Caro accumulates in the studio; in other words, the work is arrived at in a "collage way," "just as has been my custom with pieces of steel."[28] In the case of a yet more recent set of small bronzes made in 2012 (fig. 3.11), the works were cast directly with the "lost wax" process, the most traditional technique conceivable. Yet they were not arrived at through modeling and molding, but by directly folding and bending prefabricated sheets of wax into shapes. Clay has also reappeared in Caro's work, although mostly in the form of potter's—rather than sculptor's—clay, and approached in a manner markedly distinct from the 1950s. Rather than build up a form, let alone use an armature, Caro worked with premade clay slabs—folding, bending, and cutting them into compositions (see cat. 38). As in his work with steel, therefore, Caro has reconfigured his use of more traditional materials in ways that employ the simplest, most direct methods, as given in their ready-formed state, direct from the manufacturer. Thus, much of the character of the work is predetermined—the bendy, flexible curves, the thickness and width of the walls—and is in this sense not unlike Caro's use of the given shapes, widths, and lengths of manufactured steel elements. If these materials seem to stand at opposite ends of sculptural practice, perhaps this has

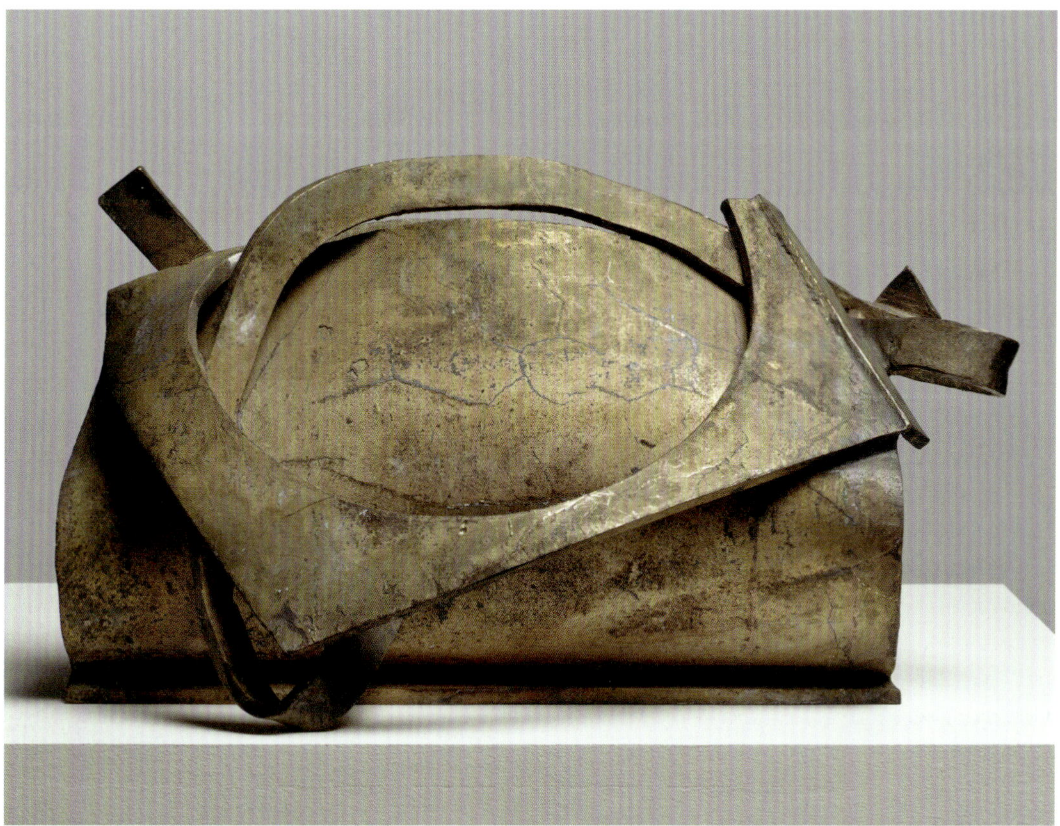

FIG. 3.11 *Sackbut* (cat. 46)

more to do with the ways in which steel has been defined in Caro's oeuvre than with their intrinsic properties.

Smith and the Associations of Steel

Steel—the key to Caro's departure from figuration—represents the polar opposite to clay and bronze, not only because of its inorganic, machinelike, cold, hard qualities, but, more importantly, because it appears free of the burdensome historical references with which the old materials seem laden. Characterized as pure, unencumbered, and "non-referential," steel has been ascribed the purely perfunctory role of supplying a range of shapes and forms from which an unprejudiced vision of sculpture could be crafted, resulting in works that "reminded us of nothing pre-existing."[29]

The notion of the material's neutrality is a central tenet of Caro's abstraction, implying a new kind of internalized, self-referential sculptural idiom free of any externally imposed meanings. This idea aligns closely to the artist's own stated objective "to eliminate references" from his work, so as "to make truly abstract sculpture."[30] And yet the idea that steel—or any material—can be free of references seems fanciful and perhaps should not be taken too literally. Indeed, if we examine the role that steel has played in Caro's oeuvre and consider its historical and practical implications at critical junctures of his career, it emerges as a rather more ambiguous material than standard accounts would allow. Not least in its connection with David Smith, steel had its own resounding historical implications, with which Caro had to grapple from the outset. As he conceded as early as 1966, even "steel's got plenty of art history in it now, unfortunately."[31]

Although the comparison between Smith and Caro may now look rather straightforward and unproblematic, it was deeply competitive at the time and unrelenting. Michael Fried's assertion that "it is above all in comparison with Smith's art that the decisive originality of Caro's fully emerges," was, if meant well, not far from its opposite inflection, as in Hilton Kramer's less kind remark that Caro's were "received ideas—principally the ideas of the late David Smith."[32] Caro countered his alignment with Smith systematically, and the formal differences between the two sculptors are now germane: Caro's "pure abstraction" against Smith's figurelike "totems"; his horizontality against Smith's verticality; the famous elimination of the plinth against Smith's use of bases and wheels; the insistence on an indoor sculpture against Smith's strong identification with the landscape around his studio (fig. 3.12).[33] But perhaps the most striking point of departure between Caro and Smith lies in their conceptions of the material that forms the very basis

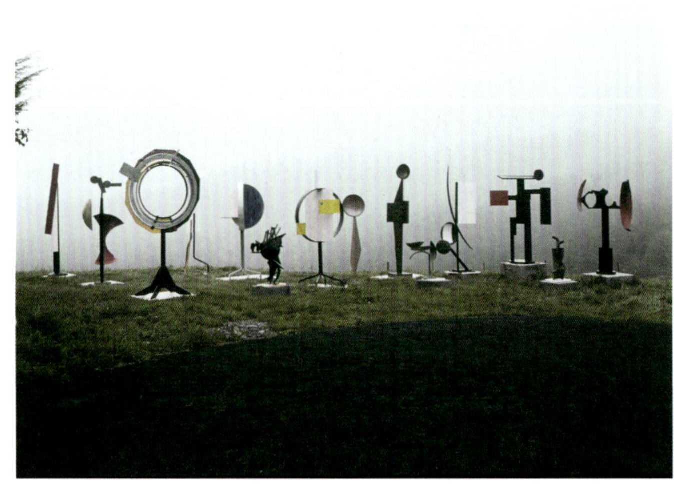

FIG. 3.12 *View of David Smith's sculptures in the upper field, Bolton Landing, New York*, 1961. Photograph by David Smith. © Estate of David Smith/VAGA, New York

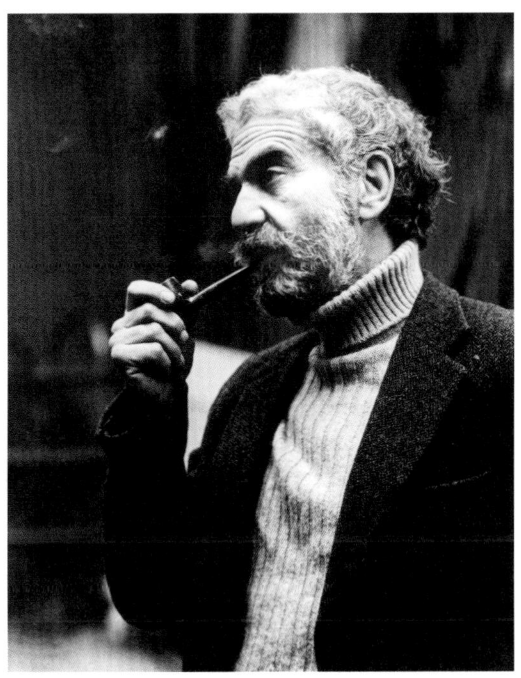

FIG. 3.13 *Anthony Caro,* 1974. Published as the frontispiece to William Rubin, *Anthony Caro,* exh. cat., The Museum of Modern Art, New York, 1975

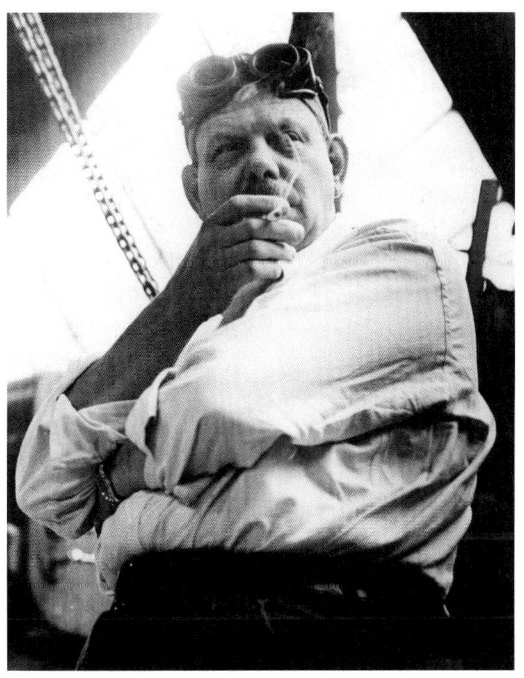

FIG. 3.14 *David Smith,* late 1930s. Photograph by Leo Lances. Copyright, Estate of David Smith/VAGA, New York

of their alignment: in Smith's universe, steel meant something very different than it did in Caro's.

In his self-image as a sculptor, Caro (often photographed in tweed blazer; fig. 3.13) could not be further removed from Smith's gritty personification of the welder-craftsman, heroic steelworker, activist, and union member (fig. 3.14). For Smith, steel offered not only a repertoire of forms, but also a socio-political meaning: his work alluded more or less explicitly to steelworking (as in the self-referential *Home of the Smith*) and the functions of steel, notably war machines.[34] Caro, however, has remained resolutely silent on the industry from which his materials originate and refuses to be drawn on such associations. Almost contrarily, he insists on his dislike of welding ("I loathe anything to do with welding . . . I don't like grinding bits of steel"), his ignorance of engineering (despite his Cambridge degree in the subject), and his dependency on skilled studio assistants.[35] Even in his terminology, Caro sets the material at a distance, referring to "leaf-like" elements,[36] "thin pieces," "metal sticks"[37]—that is, the shape and look of objects rather than their proper technical names. Already early on, when questioned as to whether his "pre-existing elements" presented only "convenient" forms, or if there was "some other intention beyond that," Caro was very clear in his answer: "No. Definitely there isn't any reference to industrial uses and so on. I would really rather make my sculpture out of 'stuff'—out of something that is anonymous."[38]

In light of this and similar comments, Caro's decision, following Smith's untimely death in 1965, to purchase some thirty-seven tons of the sculptor's steel stock, appears quixotic. Absorbing into his own work—in huge quantities and over many years—an unused stock of materials

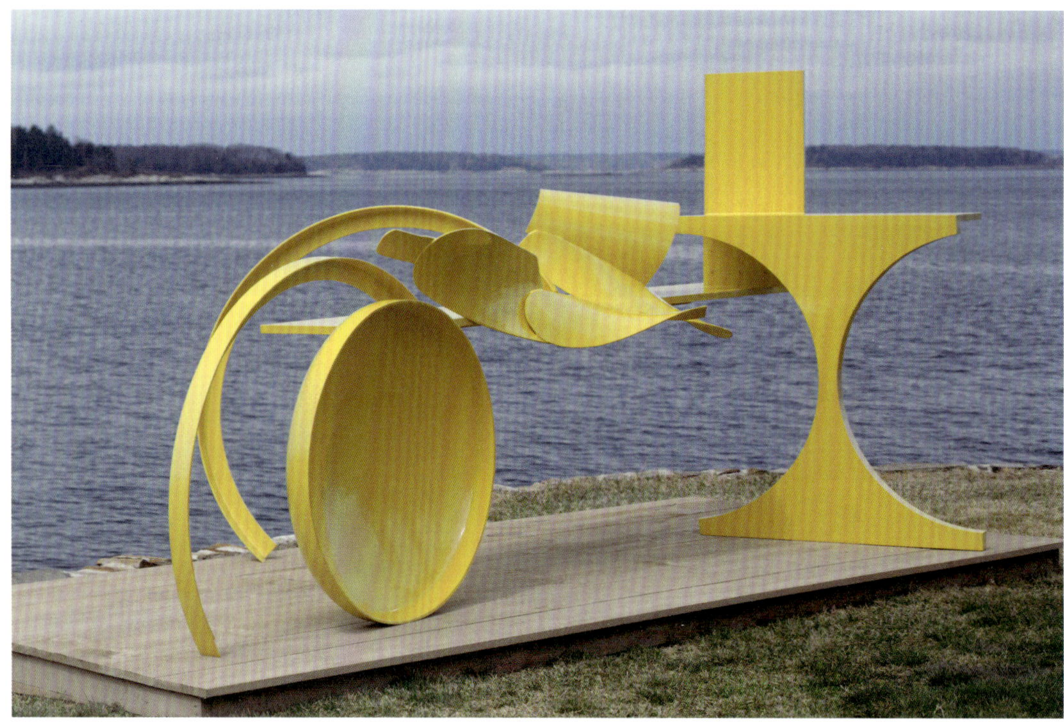

FIG. 3.15 *Sun Feast,* 1969–70, painted steel, 71½ x 164 x 86 in. (181.5 x 416.5 x 218.5 cm)

so strongly identified with another artist, and so deeply evocative of another's vast, unrealized oeuvre, can only suggest an undertaking of a highly charged nature. Steel elements once associated with Smith, such as tank ends, reappear both directly and reconfigured in Caro's work (figs. 3.15 and 3.16). Whether read, as it has been, as a poignant act of homage or as a brave declaration of self-confidence, Caro's purchase of the steel confronted head-on the ever-present taunt of Smith's precedent. But above all, Caro's decision seems provocative and defiant: far from undermining his declared detachment from his material and from steelworking in the Smith manner, it served to amplify his dispassionate stance. Although, privately, Caro found the experience "traumatic,"[39] his public statements have sounded impassive, even cold: Smith's steel was "just stuff"; interestingly "some of the angle-irons were much

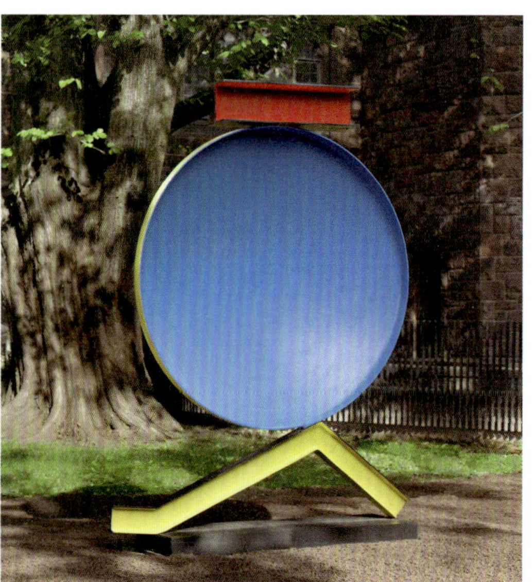

FIG. 3.16 David Smith, *Bec-Dida Day,* 1963, painted steel, 89 x 65 x 18 in. (226.061 x 165.1 x 45.72 cm). Yale University Art Gallery, Charles B. Benenson, B.A. 1933, Collection

thinner than we get in England," but otherwise, "it didn't really mean anything to me."[40]

But if disavowed—and accepted as such—the story behind Caro's inheritance of Smith's steel cannot help but suggest something more emotive. While Caro's sculptures may not evince an explicit response, it is hard not to sense, if fleetingly and obliquely, something of the material's history in the work. Indeed, while this is a specific episode, it also opens the door to a more universal consideration of the particular histories of materials and their ability to carry powerful connotations. In the context of Caro's career, steel is no less overlaid with symbolic allusion than clay and bronze; on the contrary, the hardened image of steel's material impartiality suggests a mythos all of its own, as fully absorbed into Caro's trajectory as the old fine art materials to which it plays antidote.

Caro and the Contexts of Steel

The notion that steel offered Caro a neutral medium goes hand in hand with the prevailing characterization of his work in terms of "pure abstraction" (a phrase used repeatedly and by Caro himself). Yet the sculpture does not entirely bear this out. If a commitment to abstraction is its central precept, it nevertheless remains compellingly suggestive of recognizable things in the world. Indeed, while Caro jettisoned the kind of literal figurative images that appeared almost germane to modeling, his abstract work, as is often noted, is still reminiscent of familiar, human qualities.[41] These lingering allusions have been most consistently related to the horizontality of works such as *Midday,* said to recall the reclining figures of Henry Moore (fig. 3.17).[42] Seldom taken as a contradiction to Caro's "pure abstraction," such figural echoes nevertheless unsettle the certainty that this phrase suggests. As Paul Moorhouse has put it, the "sculptures are defiantly abstract, yet the sensations they evoke are familiar."[43] A set of less determinable qualities remains in play, suggesting that the work is not as straightforwardly quantifiable as has been allowed. An ambiguity remains, and I would suggest that this has to do not only with figurative resemblances but with the material's own associative content;

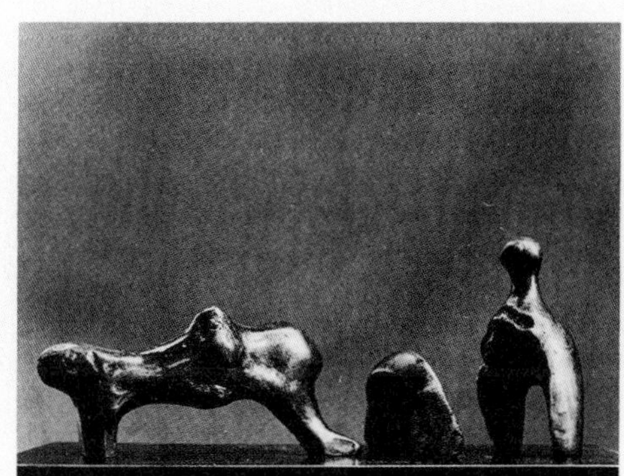

Henry Moore, *Three Piece Reclining Figure: Maquette No. 4*, 1975, 18 cm long. Reproduced by kind permission of the Henry Moore Foundation.

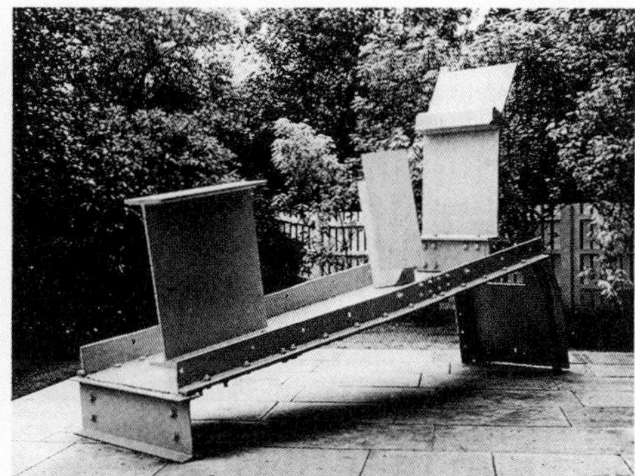

Anthony Caro, *Midday*, 1960, steel painted yellow, 238·7 × 96·5 × 365·7 cm.

FIG. 3.17 Plate from Peter Fuller, "Anthony Caro Talks about Henry Moore," *Modern Painters* 1: 3 (Autumn 1988), p. 10

indeed, Caro's work overtly and continually refers us back to the real-world origins of its physical constituents.

If Caro's steel and scrap metal seems cold and mechanical, it nevertheless embodies its own kind of humanity, not of a representational kind, but in the sense that it comes out of human endeavor and production. Several different kinds of object types appear in Caro's work. There are sculptures that incorporate discarded parts from objects no longer serviceable, which are either clearly identifiable or retain at least a semblance of their former purpose: the scissor handles of *Table Piece VIII* (cat. 25); the various kinds of instruments of the *Writing* series (fig. 3.18); the tools of the *Catalan* series (cats. 37 and 38); and a range of more ambiguous parts from defunct machinery, equipment, and engines, such as the ploughshares of *Table Piece XCVII* (cat. 30). In other sculptures, the elements were either bought off the shelf, such as the famous I-beams, or taken out of their normal chain of production, such as the frayed ends of rolled steel, which would normally disappear back into the melting pot.[44] These elements can be less readily pinned down to a specific function, but if less routine to our lived experience than scissors and tools, they are far from alien. Despite their hugely varied forms and sources, Caro's sculptures largely consist of materials that are patently utilitarian in origin and call to mind the breadth of human industry from agriculture to shipping, road and bridge building, and other kinds of large-scale construction and manufacturing enterprises.

Caro tends to reconfigure his raw materials through cutting, assemblage, and joining rather than fundamentally alter their properties; even when painted, the original product remains largely undisguised. The abstraction of Caro's work thus resides in a visual culture that is very familiar. Far from appearing "anonymous," its physical elements are directly representative of themselves, and can hardly help but bring to mind something of their past life. Coursing through Caro's work, especially from the 1970s onward, when scrap metal, rather than stock steel, becomes the predominant material, one could pick out any number of works bearing the resounding marks of a former life. *Drummer's Book* (fig. 3.19), is one such example. A slab of clay, representing the book of the title, is bracketed (or bound) by pieces of metal that read as handles. Detached from their original context and repurposed for a new sculptural one, the history of these metal parts is barely suppressed: their wrought, manmade solidity points to a particular kind of use and clearly speaks of a former industrial environment. If only vaguely and for a brief moment, a residual sense of the object's past reality remains, reaching back to an image of formerly thriving large-scale operations such as shipbuilding, once the mainstays of the British manufacturing industry.

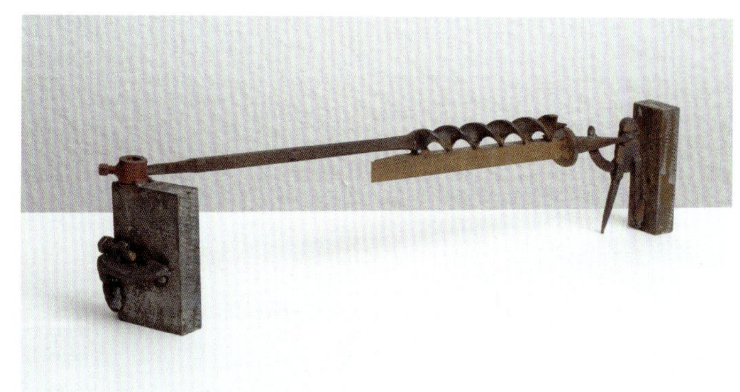

FIG. 3.18 ***Writing Piece "By,"* 1978, painted steel, 6 x 25½ x 3½ in. (15.2 x 64.8 x 9 cm). Private collection**

It may be "sheer coincidence," as Caro insists, that steel and scrap metal became important sculptural mediums at a time when heavy industry and large-scale manufacturing were undergoing tremendous change (to Smith, of course, it was no coincidence).[45] In the late 1960s British Steel became nationalized; in the 1980s it was again privatized. While Caro's work does not read in terms of socio-political meaning, let alone suggest a content motivated by labor issues, it physically and visually resides in the history of its materials, which may be imprecisely recognizable but is in many ways rather emotive. Scrapyard metal, if not exactly time-specific, is nevertheless reflective of the changing conditions that give rise to its materials. Over five decades Caro's work has incorporated remnants from defunct equipment and outdated machines, and the resulting sculptures are not entirely free of the pathos evoked by the historical course of its parts. The worn, used handles of *Drummer's Book* suggest a lifetime of handling, touch, and work; they also appear industrially old-fashioned, their newly non-operational role as sculpture intrinsically tied to their status as obsolescent, redundant.

Implications of decay, disuse, and deterioration are never far away from Caro's sculpture, partly because it often consists of elements that imply abandonment, but also because decay is part of the physical fabric of the material. Steel is prone to rust and corrosion, qualities that Caro's sculptures both manifest and resist. In the polished, thinly painted steel table sculptures made around 1966 and 1967 (see cats. 29 and 30), shininess gives the appearance of a flawlessly sealed surface; the glossy finish acts as skin and protective patina. But close-up, that seal appears fragile; uneven passages, bubbles, scratches, and imperfections become visible, interrupting the alluring gloss of the surface and bringing into focus the strangely vulnerable quality of this hard, recalcitrant material. Even in the case of large works such as *Midday,* painted with repeated heavy layers of gloss applied without prior stripping back, a sense of necessary preservation prevails.

Caro stopped applying color to his sculptures in the mid-1970s and began instead to emphasize the physical roughness of the material through its natural coloration. In the large-scale *York* or *Flats* series, as well as the table sculptures made from the same type of rolled steel, the material has been varnished to arrest the natural process of rusting. But the emphatic visuality of the rust nevertheless keeps in play a sense of the inevitability of corrosion. The larger *Flats* (such as *Cliff Song,* or *Fathom,* both 1976) have a wall-like, obstructive frontality, which reminds of abandoned barricades, prone to collapse at any moment. A similar sense of precariousness is suggested in the smaller-scale works, such as *Table Piece CLXVIII* (fig. 3.20). Made up of heavy slabs of steel that are joined together like torn strips, the work just balances at the edge of its support. The pieces that form its lower parts appear perilously suspended, as though their own weight has already begun to tear the flimsy welding seams that join them to the upper parts. The edges of the steel are soft and ragged, not unlike the edges of torn

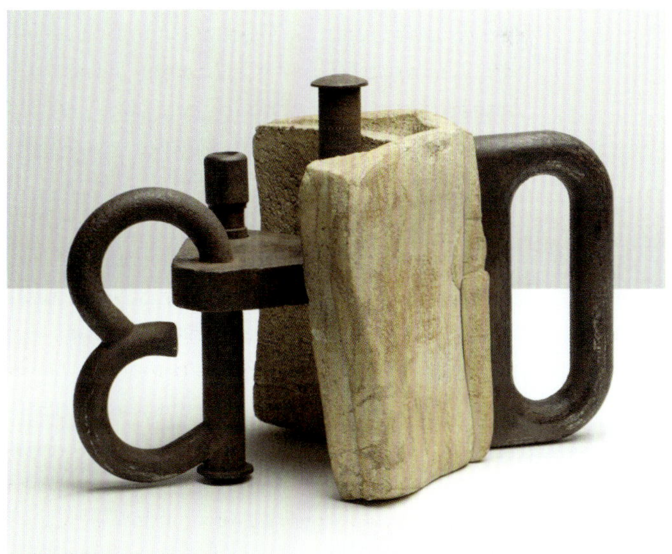

FIG. 3.19 *Drummer's Book* (cat. 39)

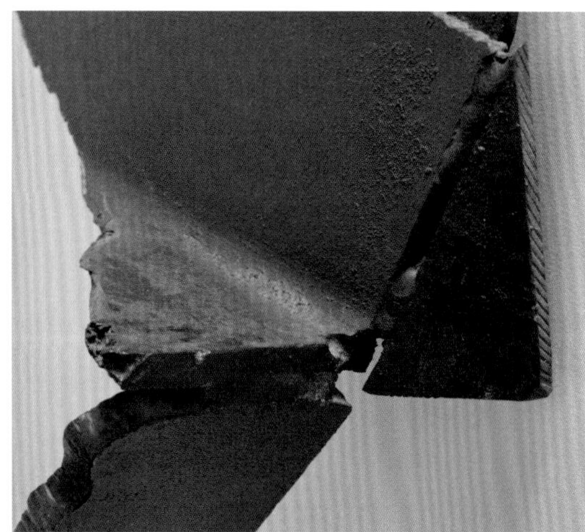

FIG. 3.20 *Table Piece CLXVIII*, detail (cat. 31)

paper. There is something unsettling about the idea that these heavy slabs might be torn—by a machine—as easily as we might tear a sheet of paper. The poised elegance of the piece reinforces its strangeness—it has something warm, familiar, and domestic about it, and even coheres into a semi-human form, sitting on a ledge, beckoning to us. Yet its material, and the idea of how this material was formed, also conjures up an image of an engulfing, hot, dangerous environment, where outsized sheets of rolled metal are forged by human ingenuity.

Not all of Caro's works are as warmly elegant. In a late 1970s series of complex pieces, which includes *Table Piece CCCXLVI—Tim's Grader* (fig. 3.21), there is a different kind of disjunction. Rather than evoke the factory, *Tim's Grader* suggests a handmade device. Its composition is exaggerated and elaborate, and its components hint at some kind of crudely crafted contraption, like a bear trap or snare. The widths of steel look sharp and knifelike, and imply the potential to injure, while the lengths of wire suggest a cage or entrapment device. Far from conjuring up a light, detached, purely self-referential world of sculptural abstraction, Caro's work is deeply serious in tone and disturbingly evocative of the darker aspects of our material world.

A photograph showing Caro's North London studio in 1978 captures a sense of the abundance of "stuff" that marks the starting point of the sculptor's working process (fig. 3.22). An array of bits and pieces clutters the floor, at first glance appearing disparate and chaotic, but soon cohering visually into a sequence of potential objects: we can almost see the parts beginning to resolve into sculptural assemblages. What is brought across so vividly by the moment caught here is how close Caro's sculptures stay to the raw material. As he has often emphasized, he works in consciousness of the material's own voice ("you've got to let the steel talk to you, and you must not give it orders too much," he said recently).[46] But although materials are the acknowledged agents of Caro's sculptures, the potential force of their own expressive implications has on the whole been overwhelmed by the large claims that abstraction needed to make very early on in Caro's

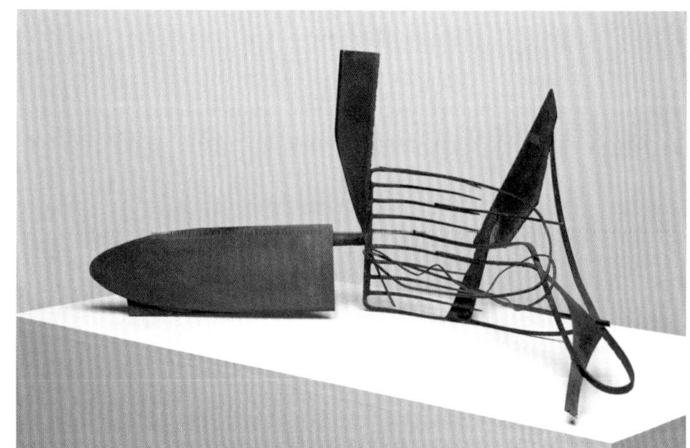

FIG. 3.21 *Table Piece CCCXLVI—Tim's Grader*, 1976/1977, steel, 23½ x 58 x 34 in. (59.7 x 147.3 x 86.4 cm). Private collection, London

career. Those claims—to a watershed, to a newly found objectivity that could neutralize the baggage of a recognized fine art language—have long ceased to be the urgent imperatives of Caro's sculpture and can no longer hold the work hostage. Caro was and remains resolutely an object maker. Across the decades, regardless of the challenges thrown at his kind of sculpture, he has remained deeply invested in material, composition, and the endlessly nuanced possibilities of structuring parts. Those are the large claims of his work; and the changing materials that he has deployed to keep that practice alive and interesting over six decades are its imperatives.

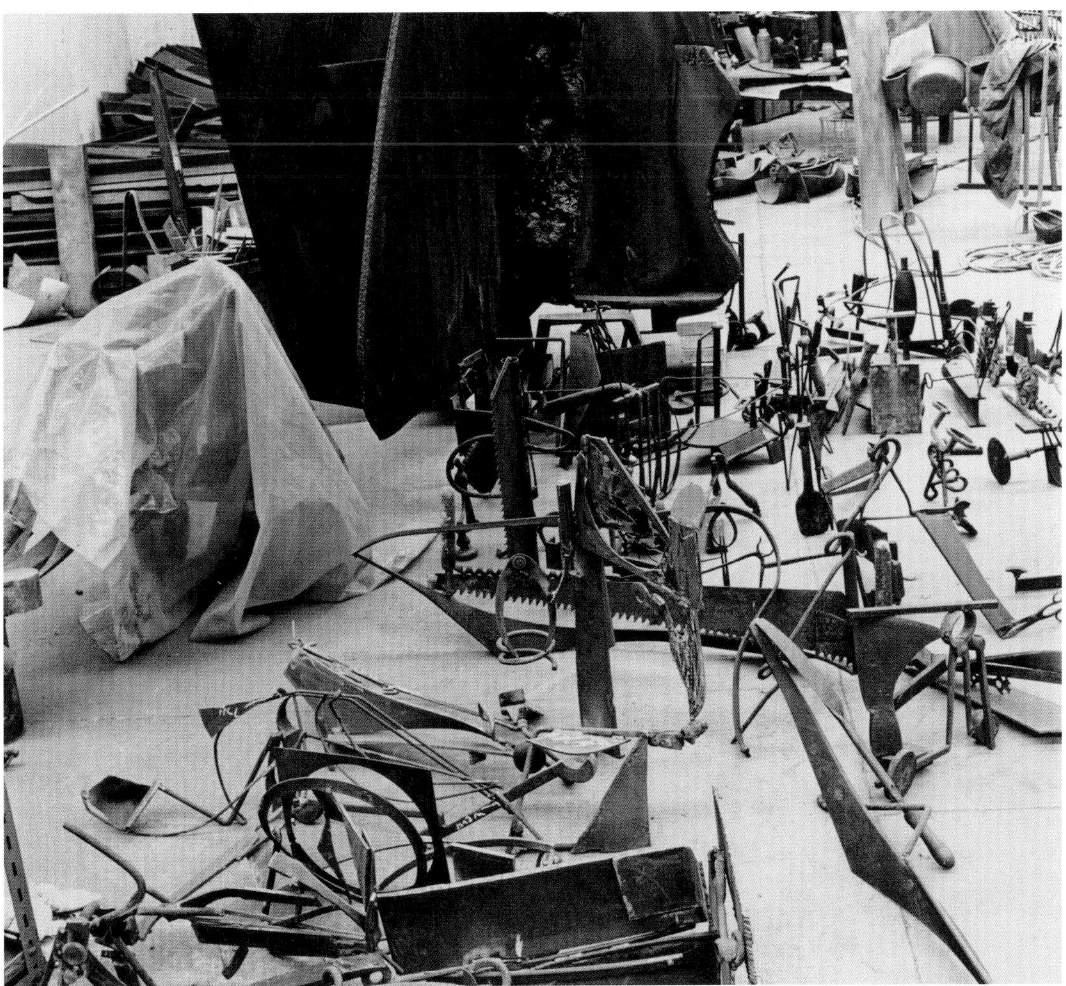

FIG. 3.22 Caro's studio, June 1979. Photo: Carlos Granger

Acknowledgments: My thanks to Sir Anthony Caro, Pat Cunningham, and Jackie Honsig-Erlenburg for providing helpful information. I am also grateful to Penelope Curtis and Nick Mead for their comments on drafts of the essay.

NOTES

1. A selection of the extensive literature is provided in the bibliography.
2. Key texts, all reprinted in Richard Whelan, *Anthony Caro* (London and New York: Penguin, 1974), include: Clement Greenberg, "Anthony Caro" (1965); Michael Fried, "Two Sculptures by Anthony Caro" (1968), and "Caro's Abstractness" (1970). See also Michael Fried, "Introduction," in *Anthony Caro: Sculpture 1960–1963* (London: Whitechapel Art Gallery, 1963) and "Introduction," in *Anthony Caro's Table Sculptures* (London: British Council, 1977).
3. Alex Potts, "Anthony Caro: Early One Morning," in *Modern British Sculpture,* Penelope Curtis and Keith Wilson, eds. (London: Royal Academy of Arts, 2011).
4. For example, Paul Moorhouse: "Caro's achievement, in his late thirties, is to have created . . . a body of work so radical in its implications, and so yet so [*sic*] completely authoritative in its means of expression, as to have changed the course of sculpture." See Moorhouse, ed., *Anthony Caro* (London: Tate Publishing, 2005), 8.
5. Peter Fuller, "Anthony Caro Talks about Henry Moore," *Modern Painters* 1, no. 3 (1988): 10. A similar idea of Caro as "an Englishman" with "different attitudes" to his American peers, appears in Phyllis Tuchman, "Anthony Caro: Sculpting Space," *Sculpture* 16, no. 8 (Oct. 1997): 15.
6. To Fuller, Caro retorted that his categories were too "simplistic"; not only does the idea of Moore's "naturalism" and "pastoral" references make "a romantic trap which obscures our view," America wasn't all "urban"; "in 1963 I was making . . . steel sculpture in the heart of the Vermont countryside." See Fuller, "Anthony Caro," 10.
7. This underpins, for example, the organization of the recent five-volume set of books on Anthony Caro, edited by Karen Wilkin (Aldershot: Lund Humphries, 2010): Mary Reid, *Drawing in Space*; Wilkin, *Interior and Exterior*; Bryant, *Figurative and Narrative Sculpture*; H. F. Westley Smith, *Small Sculptures*; and Moorhouse, *Presence*.
8. A comprehensive and well-illustrated account of Caro's student years and early career is in Barker, *Quest for the New Sculpture,* 15–53.
9. Andrew Forge, "Andrew Forge Interviews Anthony Caro," *Studio International* 171, no. 873 (Jan. 1966): 7.
10. For an account see Penelope Curtis, "How Direct Carving Stole the Idea of Modern British Sculpture," in David Getsy, ed., *Sculpture and the Pursuit of a Modern Ideal in Britain, c. 1880–1930*, (London: Ashgate, 2004), 291–316.
11. Anthony Caro in an unpublished interview by Noel Chanan, 1974, as cited in Barker, *Quest for the New Sculpture,* 47.
12. Charles Wheeler citing from *The Times* in 1966, in *High Relief: The Autobiography of Sir Charles Wheeler, Sculptor* (Feltham: Country Life Books, 1968), 64.
13. Edouard Lantéri published a three-volume book, *Modelling: A Guide for Teachers and Students* (London: Chapman & Hall, 1902), which takes its place in a long line of books on modeling as the foundation of sculptural practice, often written by sculptors and teachers linked with the South Kensington schools. For a recent account, see Ann Compton, "Plastic Pleasures: Reconsidering the Practice of Modeling through Manuals of Sculpture Technique, c. 1880–1933," *Journal of Modern Craft* 3, no. 3 (Nov. 2010): 309–24.
14. See Barker, *Quest for a New Sculpture,* 16.
15. Fuller, "Anthony Caro," 7. For an illuminating account of Moore's evolving production methods, and their similarity to, as well as departure from, traditional studio practices, see Anne Wagner, "Scale in Sculpture: The Sixties and Henry Moore," *Tate Papers* 15 (Spring 2011).
16. See Barker, *Quest for the New Sculpture,* 32.
17. Phyllis Tuchman, "An Interview with Anthony Caro," *Artforum* 10 (June 1972): 56–58. See Barker, *Quest for a New Sculpture,* 47–49.
18. Anthony Caro to the author, Jan. 3, 2012.

19. Terry Fenton, *Anthony Caro* (London: Academy Editions, 1986), 7.
20. Examples include Simon Bone, *Guardian,* Jan. 9, 1957, cited in Barker, *Quest for the New Sculpture,* 73; and Nevile Wallis, "At the Galleries: Different Worlds," *Observer,* Jan. 13, 1958.
21. Tuchman, "An Interview with Anthony Caro," 55.
22. As in the famous statement: "I want to make sculpture about feelings, not ideas," recording of an interview of Anthony Caro by Lisa Lyons, April 26, 1975, The Museum of Modern Art, New York.
23. Lantéri, *Modelling: A Guide for Teachers and Students,* 2:152.
24. For Caro's response to Rodin see the chapter "Anthony Caro on Rodin," in *What Makes a Masterpiece? Encounters with Great Works of Art,* Christopher Dell, ed. (London: Thames and Hudson, 2010), 24.
25. Tuchman, "An Interview with Anthony Caro," 55.
26. Tuchman, "An Interview with Anthony Caro," 55.
27. An exception is the group of figurative works made in between 1983 and 1988. See Julius Bryant, *Anthony Caro: The Figure* (London: Royal British Society of Sculptors, 2010).
28. Anthony Caro to the author, Jan. 19, 2012.
29. Moorhouse, *Anthony Caro: Presence,* 16. Wilkin, *Interior and Exterior,* 11.
30. Forge, "Interviews," 7.
31. Forge, "Interviews," 9.
32. Michael Fried, "Introduction," in *Anthony Caro* (London: Hayward Gallery, 1969), 11. Hilton Kramer review of Anthony Caro's exhibition at the Whitechapel, 1968, cited in Barker, *Quest for the New Sculpture,* 178. The comparison is invoked again and again. See for example Kay Larson's review of Caro at Storm King, a sculpture park in New York State that also owns a significant David Smith collection, "The Steel-plated Theories of Anthony Caro," *New York Magazine* 14, no. 35 (Sept. 7, 1981): 58–59.
33. For Caro's attitude to siting his sculptures outdoors, see my "Anthony Caro at Chatsworth," in *Caro at Chatsworth* (Salisbury, UK, and Bakewell, UK: New Art Centre and the Chatsworth House Trust, 2012).
34. See Rosalind Krauss, "Smith's Imagery: The Cannon, the Totem, the Sacrifice", in *Terminal Iron Works: The Sculpture of David Smith* (Cambridge, Mass.: MIT Press, 1971), 51–116.
35. Interview of Anthony Caro by Lisa Lyons.
36. Anthony Caro to Noel Chanon, as cited in Barker, *Quest for the New Sculpture,* 186.
37. Lutz Haufschild, "Conversations with Anthony Caro," *Arts Magazine* 9, no. 38–39 (Jun. 1978): 35.
38. Forge, "Interviews," 9.
39. Letter from Anthony Caro to Michael Fried, 1968, cited in Barker, *Quest for the New Sculpture,* 174.
40. Recording of an interview of Anthony Caro by Tim Marlow, Nov. 2005.
41. Alex Potts has discussed this ambiguity persuasively in "Early One Morning."
42. See for instance Charles W. Millard, "The Reclining Figure and the Development of Modern Sculpture," *Hudson Review* 27, no. 2 (Summer 1974): 234–44; and Norbert Lynton, "Anthony Caro," in *Five Sculptures by Anthony Caro* (London: Arts Council of Great Britain, 1982), 13.
43. Paul Moorhouse, *Anthony Caro,* 22.
44. See Jeremy Hunt *Anthony Caro: Flats* (Salisbury: New Art Center, Roche Court, 2007).
45. To the author in a private conversation, Dec. 16, 2011.
46. To the author in a private conversation, Dec. 16, 2011.

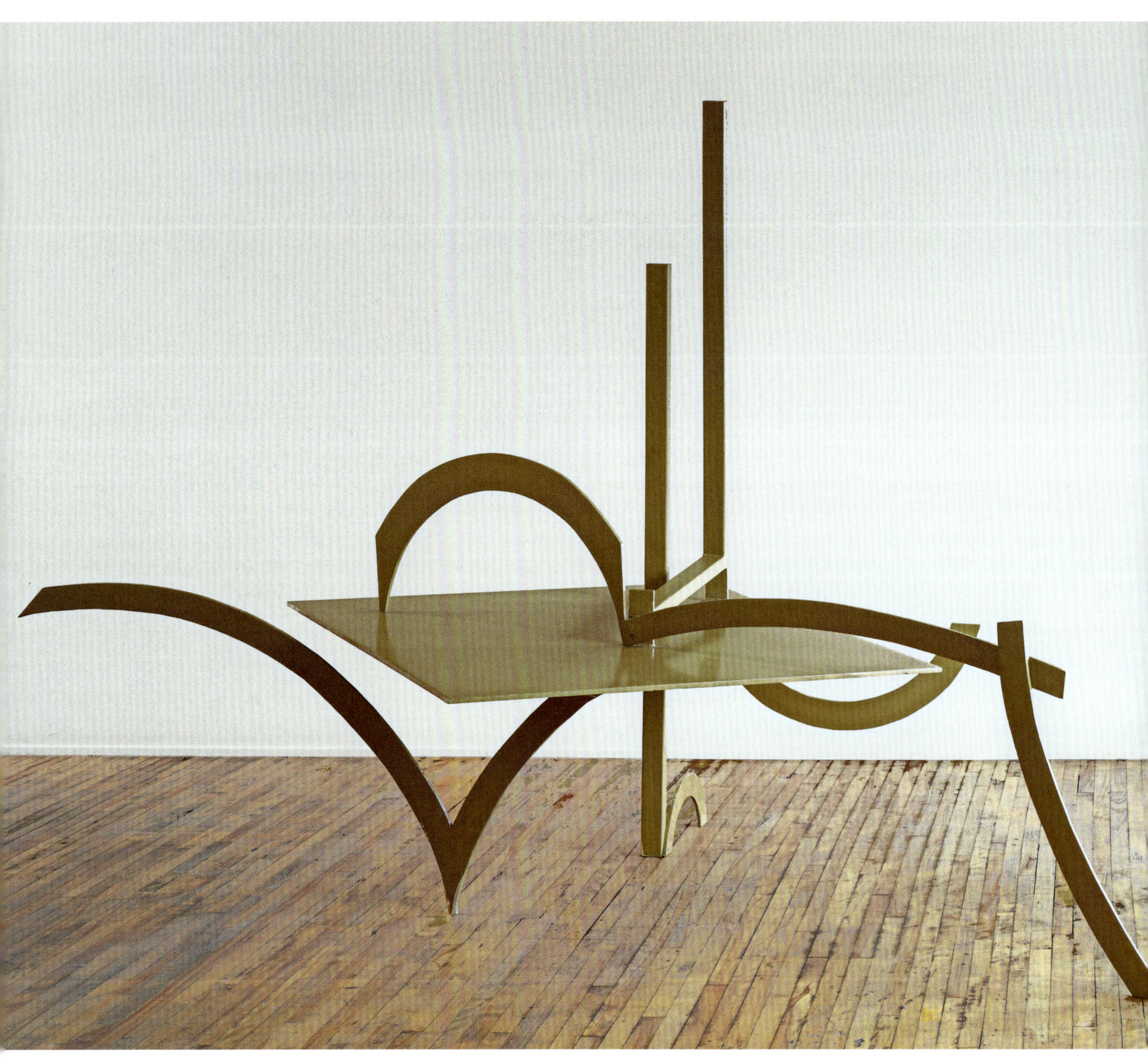

Of Acorns and Oaks, “Sons” and “Fathers”

Robert Storr

Let’s back up and slip sideways before jumping forward. After all, art history is an intricately matrixed, hopscotchlike game of leapfrog, a game that should be played on heavily trafficked sidewalks and roadways and never on a one-way street.

In 1967 Bruce Nauman cast a bas-relief torso of a man with his arms tied behind his back and titled it *Henry Moore Bound to Fail* (fig. 4.2). Many commentators, including this one, have mistakenly thought that the work was a Duchampian joke at the expense of the old modernist master of British art. It was not. Eager to clarify his intent, Nauman talked about the piece in two interviews. In the first, an exchange with *Avalanche* founding editor Willoughby Sharpe in 1970, the artist responded to a query about the importance of titling his art:

> I don’t know. There’s a certain amount of perverseness involved, because the piece could probably just have been left the way it was. I mean, it could just as well have stood without any kind of descriptive title. It could have just been ‘bound to fail.’ When I made the piece a lot of young English sculptors who were getting publicity were putting down Henry Moore, and I thought they shouldn’t be so hard on him. Because they’re going to need him.[1]

FIG. 4.1 *Trefoil* (cat. 33)

In a second interview, in 1972, with an art history student at Pomona College, Lorraine Sciarra, Nauman was even more explicit:

> There were several pieces that dealt with Henry Moore about that time, and they had to do with the emergence of the New English sculptors Anthony Caro and [William] Tucker and several other people. There was a lot written about them. Some of them sort of bad-mouthed Henry Moore—the way Moore made work was old fashioned and oppressive and all the people were really held down by his importance. He kept other people from being able to work that anyone

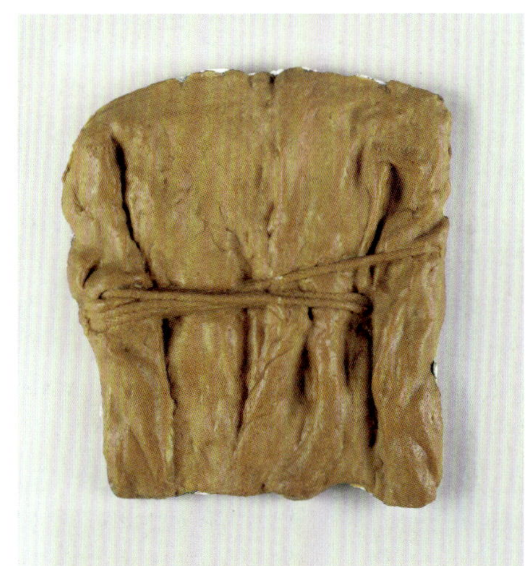

FIG. 4.2 Bruce Nauman, *Henry Moore Bound to Fail,* 1967, wax over plaster, 26 x 24 x 3 in. (66 x 61 x 8.9 cm). Private collection © ARS, NY and DACS, London 2012

would pay attention to. So he was being put down, shoved aside and the idea I had at the time was that while it was probably true to a certain extent, they should hang on to Henry Moore, because he did some really good work and they might need him again.[2]

Vault forward three decades. On the cover of the catalogue for his 1998 mid-career survey show at the Museum of Contemporary Art in Los Angeles, the California conceptual artist Charles Ray appears in a full bleed photograph standing behind the work of another artist (fig. 4.3). The piece is *Early One Morning* (1962) in the collection of the Tate Gallery, London. Its author is Anthony Caro.

Conversing in 2005 with art historian Michael Fried, among the leading formalist critics to have emerged in the 1960s from the generation following that of Clement Greenberg, Charles Ray explained the affinity for Caro that produced this unusually prominent, oddly self-effacing homage:

In 1971 at the University of Iowa I enrolled in a sculpture class that was taught by Roland Brenner, who had been a student of Caro at St Martins in the early 1960s. Brenner was very strict in his approach to teaching the sculpture studio class. We learned to weld and were taken to the scrap yard to buy metal. We drew or sketched our ideas directly with the material at hand. He walked around and encouraged our configurations to move in certain directions. We looked at a lot of slides of Caro's work, as well as other contemporary sculptors. The crit phase of

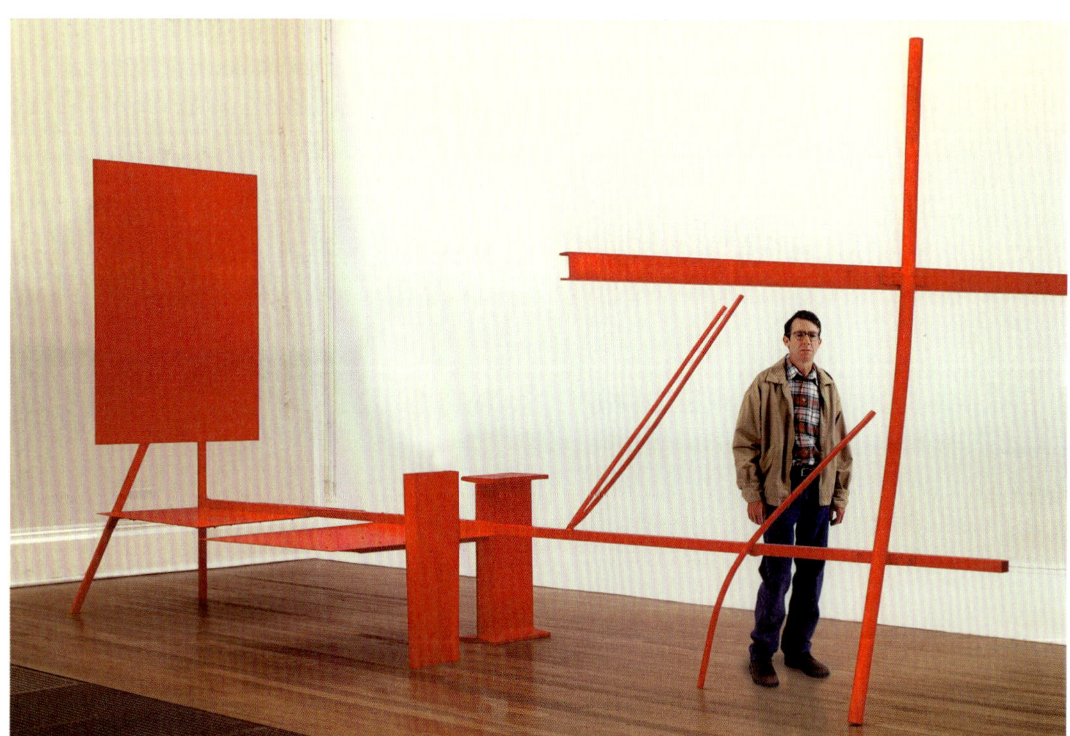

FIG. 4.3 Charles Ray, Self-portrait with *Early One Morning*. Montage created for the cover of *Charles Ray*, Museum of Contemporary Art, Los Angeles, exhibition catalogue, 1998. Digital adaptation by Martin Shoesmith, 2012

> the studio was constant. A lot of the students felt the class was too dictatorial. For me, it was liberating. As a young student I was unaware of the historical context, but I found this phase of Constructivism a wonderful time and place to enter sculpture. I really didn't need to understand what I was doing. Caro's work was like a template; I saw it as almost platonic. The formal rules as taught by Brenner were a kind of nourishment for me. The actual working in the studio was, in a sense, the expression. I was taught that the finished sculpture was maybe the end of a paragraph. Once a sculpture was completed it was critiqued and put back on to the scrap pile. This way of working taught me to think sculpturally rather than to think about sculpture. At this time in my life the historical context of high Modernism was really beyond my grasp. I saw Caro as super-contemporary. His work was, and is, so alive. It bridges a gap between the inside and outside of my mind.[3]

"What about Caro's *Early One Morning* from 1962?" Fried then inquired. "It seems to have been a work you were particularly interested in?" To which Ray replied at length:

> I'm still amazed by the experience of viewing *Early One Morning*. It is sculptural disjunction compressing and expanding space in such a hallucinogenic way. The sculpture seems to be an armature that space clings to like clay. In 1962 The Beatles were singing, 'I want to hold your hand.' The hallucinogenic scene didn't explode onto pop culture until five or six years later. Not that this sculpture was prophetic of the coming youth culture involvement with drug experiences, but it was so born in its time. It is so alive in its making that it seems unlikely ever to die.
>
> *Early One Morning* is a work that I gauge myself by. I never re-created it, but at one time I wanted to use it as an image on an announcement poster for a show I was having at the ICA in London. There's a wonderful painting by Edward Hopper with a young woman sitting nude on an unmade bed in a hotel room. I wanted to have a young woman sitting nude on the I-beam of *Early One Morning*. Caro agreed in principle. The sculpture is very fragile. The aluminium tubes and plate are so extended structurally that it's almost magic that the sculpture stands at all. Caro did not want a public image of it that would suggest it might be strong enough to be sat on. He very generously gave me permission to photograph a model standing near it, but I declined, as that would not work for what I was attempting to do. I was trying to make a picture. I was thinking about time and its necessity for contemplation. Around the same time I was attempting to return to abstract sculpture. I was struggling. Every move I made bumped into genre problems. I had a photo of *Early One Morning* on my bookcase. A gallon apple cider jug somehow was turned on its side directly in front of the photograph. It instantly hit me that here was a possible solution to my sculpture problem. I could take the genre of a ship in a bottle and use its space to create a sculpture within—a short cut out of my problem? I began trying to assemble abstract sculptures in bottles. They never did what I wanted them to do. I learned that a ship in a bottle is not sculptural. You never need to walk around the back, or see it from the side. The bottle is a

frame and you view the ship and the feat of its construction in a pictorial way. I did remain very interested in the space inside a bottle and eventually made *Puzzle Bottle* in 1995 [fig. 4.4]. There is abstractness to the space of *Puzzle Bottle*. The figure is really the armature to build both the space and the bottle that contains it. After making *Puzzle Bottle* I started working on a sculpture for Documenta and the sculpture show in Münster in Germany. I spent a year learning how to make my own clothes and shoes. My contribution was going to be a short 35mm film entitled *Self-portrait with Home-made Clothes*. It was to play as a trailer in the local movie theatres. There was a similarity to *Puzzle Bottle* with the utilization of space associated with media and genre. I didn't finish the clothes in time to make the film. A few years later I had to come up with an image for the catalogue of another show. So that's me in my home-made clothes digitally placed in front of [*sic*] *Early One Morning*![4]

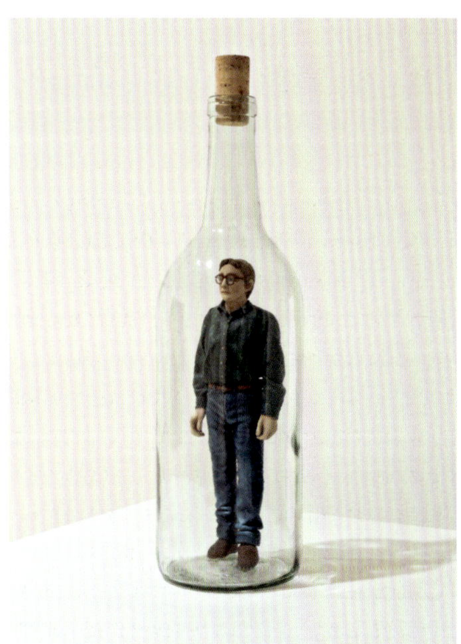

FIG. 4.4 Charles Ray, *Puzzle Bottle,* 1995, glass, painted wood, cork, 13⅜ x 3¾ x 3¾ in. (33.97 x 9.53 x 9.53 cm). Whitney Museum of American Art, New York; purchased with funds from the Contemporary Painting and Sculpture Committee and Barbara and Eugene Schwartz. Photo: Sheldan C. Collins. © Charles Ray, Courtesy Matthew Marks Gallery

And there you have it: tradition. And a formalist tradition, at that! All without aid of the Eliotic Trotskyism—T. J. Clark's memorably mordant phrase—of Greenbergian ideology. But a tradition fortified by the very impurities that Greenberg, Fried, and their cohort vainly struggled to banish from art during the decades when modernist art, as they understood it, was constantly ceding ground to the new concepts and new practices that were mistakenly lumped together as postmodernist.[5] Practices that had demonstrably developed out of the strains of modern art that Greenberg and his disciples had been at such pains to write off or at very least to obscure.

If it sounds like I am beating a dead horse, consider not only that such obsolete orthodoxies have never been fully or frankly recanted by those who so ardently, if not arrogantly, propagated them as revealed truth; neither does the statute of limitations ever run out on art historical fraud committed when the past is redacted to expunge inconvenient precedents for views or practices a given critic or scholar opposes. Nor is there ever a moratorium on pointing out that predictions of the future used to buttress weak positions in the present have failed to materialize in the forms anticipated, and have instead taken other, supposedly theoretically impossible or aberrant forms, or simply "dematerialized" altogether, as was the fate of "modernist" sculpture in the 1970s. Meanwhile the radical irony of the situation is that Nauman's prediction *has* come true even though

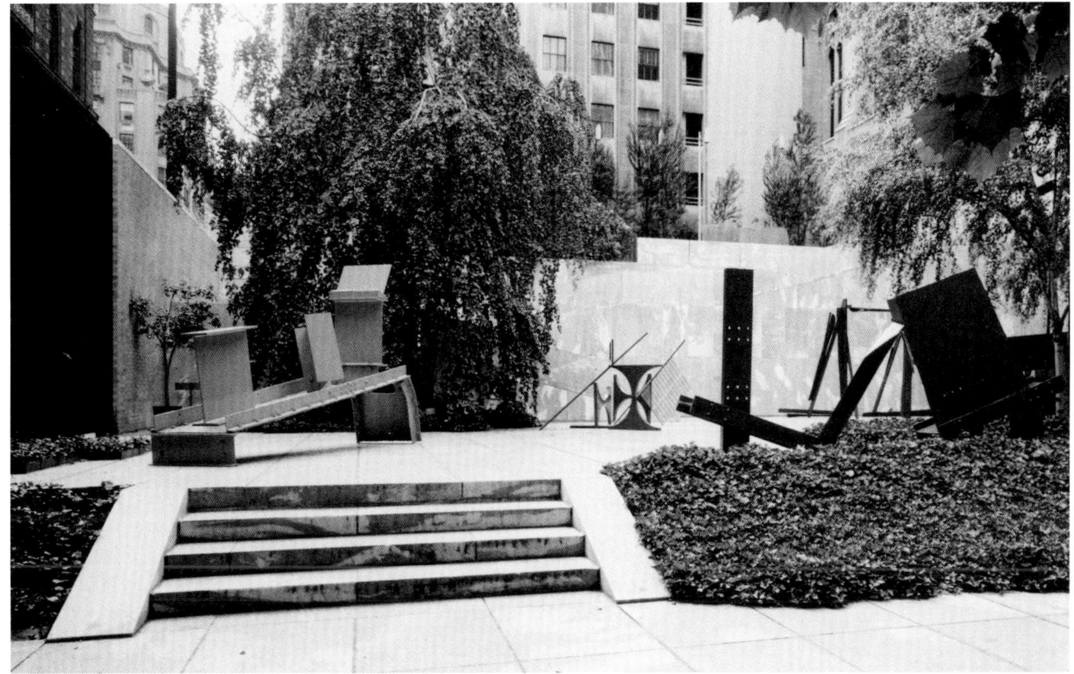

FIG. 4.5 Installation view of Caro's retrospective at the Museum of Modern Art, New York, 1975

Fried, in his influential 1966 polemic against minimal and postminimal sculpture, "Art and Objecthood," declared Nauman's type of multimedia, spectator-engaging work an anathema.[6] For just as Nauman had foreseen, younger artists ready to slough off the burden of the fathers would find that they needed those patriarchs—and as Louise Bourgeois, among others, was to prove, a handful of matriarchs—after all. Moreover, Caro, who worked for Henry Moore as a studio assistant, never categorically renounced him no matter how his critical advocates sometimes framed the Oedipal dynamic involved, and despite the severe assessment of Moore that appeared in some of his own published comments.[7] For Caro clearly needed his example as much as Ray needed Caro's, along with that of Nauman and the post-Duchampian heritage Nauman epitomized.

The principle being advanced might conceivably have been established with briefer quotations from Ray and Nauman. However, the aim here is not only to argue against conventional shorthand interpretation of the anxiety of influence, but instead to advocate for the candid recognition by emerging artists of the debts that are demonstrably owed their seniors, and recognition by senior artists of the debts they sometimes owe their juniors in return. Because, if anyone outside the old-line modernist museological and academic hierarchies can be credited for championing Caro as a pivotal figure and restoring him to a place of honor in contemporary sculptural discourse, it is Ray. Furthermore, it is Ray's manner of reading his own work—with its characteristic admixture of literalness and uncanniness, its replication or re-presentation of banal things and images (department store mannequins, house-

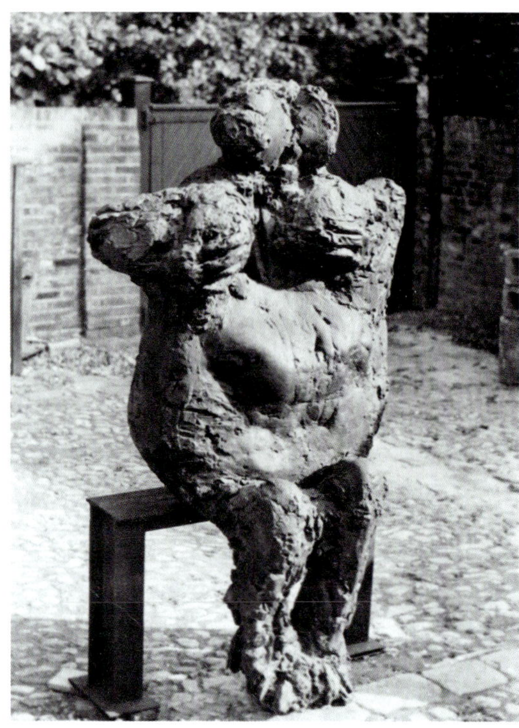

FIG. 4.6 *Woman's Body,* 1959 (destroyed), clay, 74 x 40 x 34 in (188 x 101.6 x 86.4 cm)

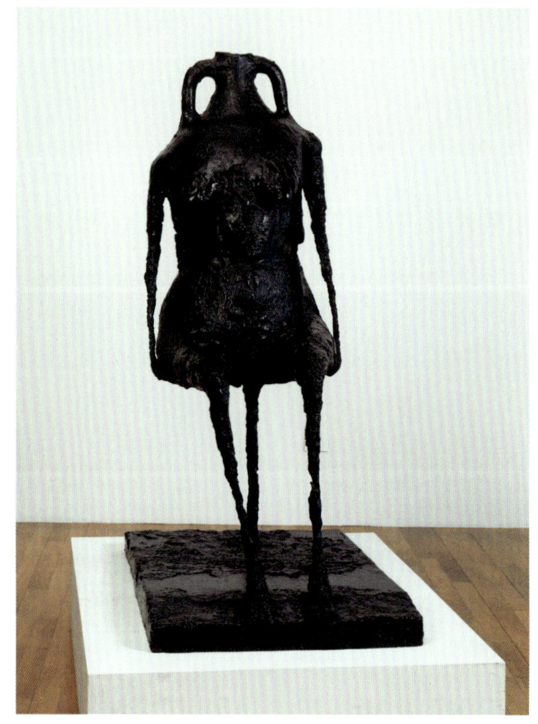

FIG. 4.7 Germaine Richier, *L'Eau (Water),* 1953–54, 56¹¹⁄₁₆ x 25³⁄₁₆ x 38¹¹⁄₁₆ in. (144 x 64 x 98.3 cm). Tate, London, purchased out of funds provided by Lord Sainsbury and Sir Robert Sainsbury, 1956. © Tate, London, ADAGP, Paris, and DACS, London, 2012

hold objects, and large machines), and its extreme as well as subtle discrepancies of proportion or barely perceptible kinesis—through the intersecting vectors of influence represented by a glimpse of an Edward Hopper interior and multiple, sustained glimpses from different angles of Caro's *Early One Morning*—grasping glimpses one might call them, *pace* Willem de Kooning[8]—that inspires the following brief art critical glances at Caro's work that follow, since as coevals, Ray and I came to our revisionist respect for canonical modernism along comparably oblique paths.

My first exposure to Caro came with walking into the garden of the Museum of Modern Art in 1975 when William Rubin—then chief curator of painting and sculpture and the premier though far from undisputed institutional exemplar of formalist aesthetics in America—was installing Caro's retrospective, just five years after Rubin's similarly intentioned apotheosis of the younger Frank Stella.[9] I say similarly intentioned because all of Rubin's shows were aimed at making history by confirming the status of a contemporary artist in the presence of the modernist old masters already enshrined on 53rd Street: although in keeping with the strategies described above for enforcing consensus by tidying up art history, Rubin had consigned to MoMA storage much of the evidence that art history had ever diverged from the Greenbergian mainstream, evidence that his predecessors, Alfred Barr first and foremost among them, had assiduously amassed and

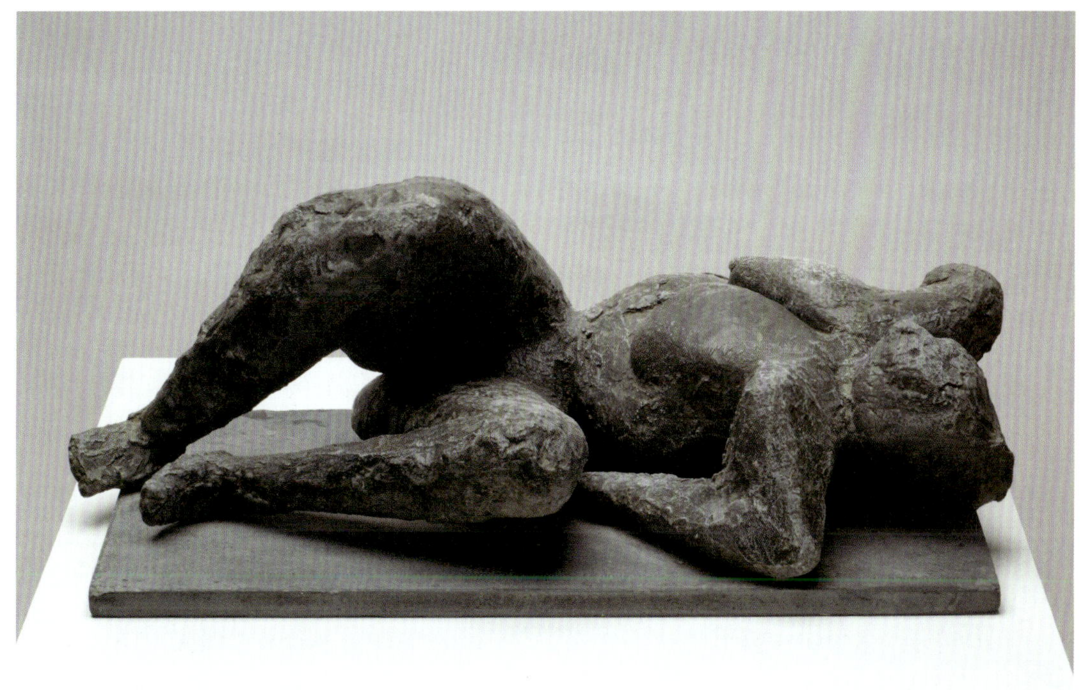

FIG. 4.8 *Woman Waking Up* (cat. 24)

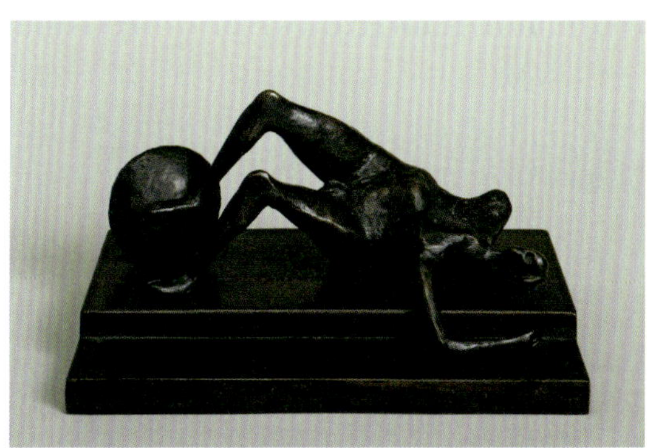

FIG. 4.9 Henry Moore, Maquette for *Fallen Warrior,* bronze, 5½ x 6⅛ x 10 7/16 in. (14 x 15.5 x 26.5 cm). Tate, London, Presented by Gustav and Elly Kahnweiler 1974. © Tate, London, 2012

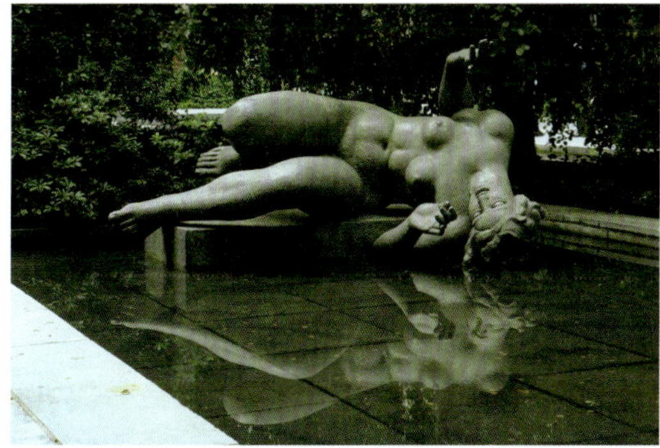

FIG. 4.10 Aristide Maillol, *The River,* 1943, lead, 53 x 90 x 66 in. (136.5 x 228.6 x 167.7 cm). The Museum of Modern Art, New York, Mrs. Simon Guggenheim Fund. © 2012 Artists Rights Society (ARS), New York / ADAGP, Paris and DACS, London

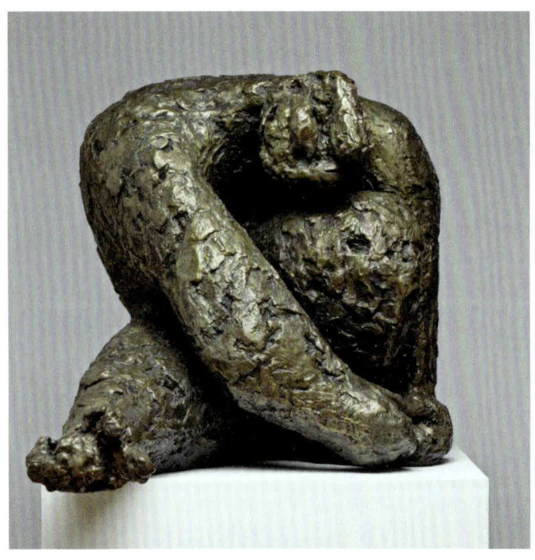

FIG. 4.11 *Man Holding His Foot* (cat. 21)

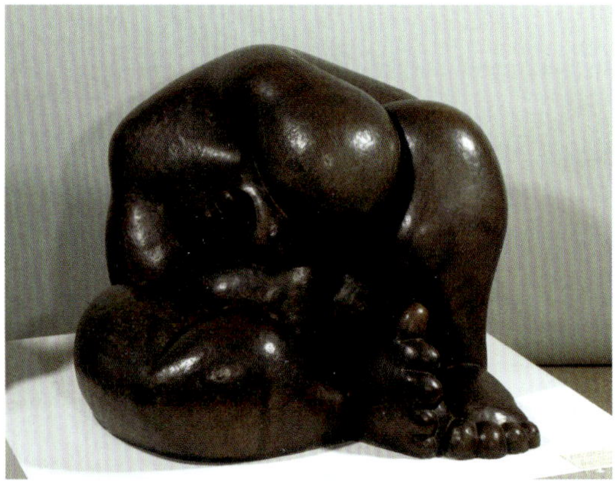

FIG. 4.12 Henri Laurens, *L'Adieu (The Farewell)*, 1941, gilded bronze, 28 x 33 7/16 x 33 1/16 in. (73 x 85 x 84 cm). Centre Pompidou, Paris. © Centre Pompidou, MNAM-CCI, Dist. RMN / Droits réservé, ADAGP, Paris, and DACS, London, 2012

preserved. But that spring day in 1975 I was blissfully unaware of the backstory and bedazzled by the visual splendor that my behind-the-scenes tour of an exhibition in the making had to offer (fig. 4.5). The garden was fresh and green and the colors of Caro's painted steel assemblages were fresh as well, like industrial steel blossoms amid the pale, variegated marble setts that pave Phillip Johnson's geometric layout of flower beds and marble platforms, which, I later learned from MoMA art handlers, was nicknamed "Dead Bunnies in the Snow."[10] And, I was amazed to discover how much I felt at home among these polychromed, postcubist structures, how much I instinctively felt the "rightness" of the artist's compositional methods and decisions—"rightness," I confess, being the ineffable *sine qua non* of formalist art—having already developed a powerful resistance to the logic according to which such abstraction was to be admired or at least deferred to as the "only" valid extension of the grand lineage of Julio González, Picasso, Henri Matisse, and David Smith. (Parenthetically, unwillingness to embrace abstraction was not the sticking point; I had already experienced the revelation of Robert Ryman's mid-career survey at the Guggenheim in 1972.[11] His multifarious, materialistic, intuitively innovative paintings, along with his eschewal of art historical determinism, were my touchstones for rejecting the Greenberg-Rubin model for extrapolating the future from the past, and Sol LeWitt's 1968 *Sentences on Conceptual Art* provided a correspondingly clear verbal refutation of formalist thinking.[12]) In short, I was won over despite my deep-seated disinclination to like things that I had been force-fed in school, and despite the ranks of authorities, living and dead, marshaled in front of and behind the work in display; I was won over by the sculptures themselves as I encountered them one-by-one.

That show did not include examples of the work with which the present exhibition begins, specifically Caro's Mooresque figures of the 1950s. Before the appearance of Diane Waldman's 1982 monograph, most fans of Caro in this country were barely conscious of how deeply immersed he had been in the raw-boned aesthetics of Moore's monumental men and women; still fewer knew how long that apprenticeship to the neo-archaic had lasted.[13] The first of these pieces, reproduced in Waldman's book, *Half-Life-Sized Figure* (a studio exercise the artist destroyed), dates to 1948, and is as much Aristide Maillol or Georg Kolbe as Moore, while the last, *Woman's Body*, from 1959 (fig. 4.6) is more than halfway to early Eduardo Paolozzi by way of Germaine Richier (fig. 4.7). The three bronzes in this show come from the middle of that formal and temporal trajectory, and two belong to Caro's private collection, indicating their abiding importance to him, and the third belongs to Phillip King.

Of the trio, *Woman Waking Up* (fig. 4.8) is the most Moore-ish of all. It recalls a number of reclining figures Moore himself carved or modeled, figures that seem in the process of levering themselves up from or collapsing onto the ground (fig. 4.9). The contrapposto twist at the hips and flex in the shoulders embedded in this pose exploit

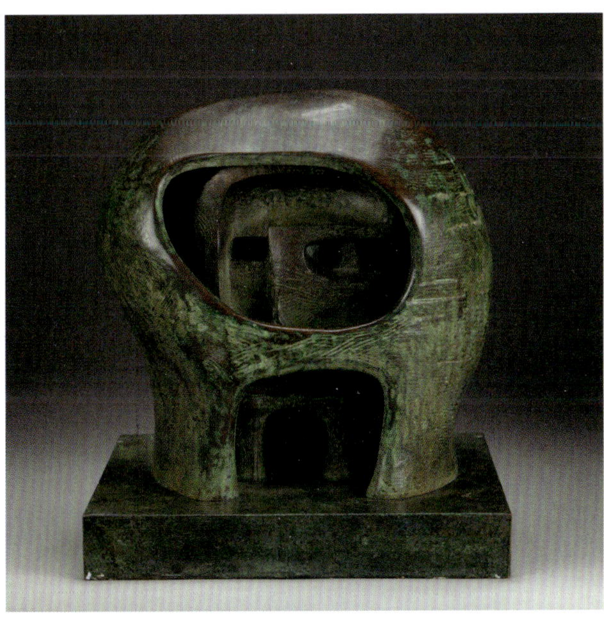

FIG. 4.13 Henry Moore, *Helmet Head No. 3,* 1960, bronze, 13⅞ x 12 x 12 in. (35.2 x 30.5 x 30.5 cm). Yale Center for British Art, New Haven, Paul Mellon Collection. © Estate of the Artist

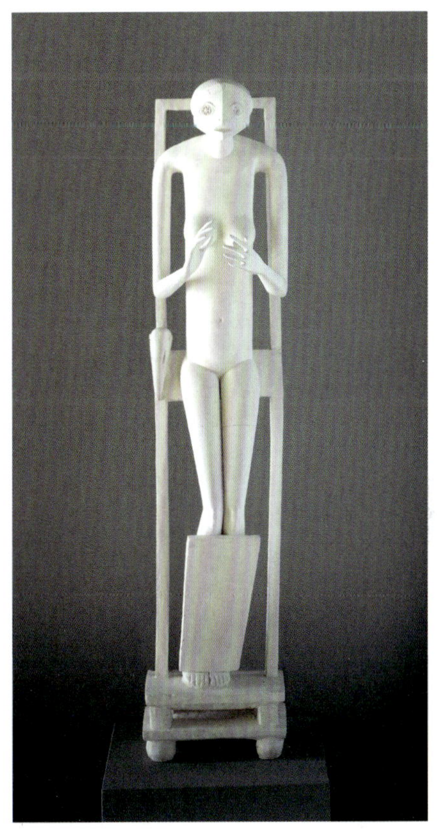

FIG. 4.14 Alberto Giacometti, *Hands Holding the Void,* 1934, brush and ink, oil paint, pastel, charcoal, and wash on wove paper mounted on marbled brown-gray paper, 61½ x 13½ x 11½ in. (156.2 x 34.3 x 29.2 cm). Yale University Art Gallery, New Haven, anonymous gift. © 2004 Artists Rights Society (ARS), New York / Succession Alberto Giacometti (Fondation Alberto et Annette Giacometti, Paris/ADAGP, Paris and DACS, London), 2012

horizontality rather than verticality as their foil, thereby lending active vigor to a composition that might otherwise suggest the classic passivity of odalisques stretched out under the admiring gaze of presumably masculine viewers, much as Aristide Maillol's rendition of Dina Vierny does in *The River* (fig. 4.10), a work that was little more than a decade old when Caro made his. By contrast *Man Holding His Foot* (fig. 4.11) and *Baby with a Ball* (cat. 23) are compact and obdurate, with the former evoking Henri Laurens's *The Farewell* (fig. 4.12) in its massive convolutions, while substituting a kind of caveman bestiality for the pathos of Laurens's wartime icon of mourning. Centered on a snoutlike nose, bulging eyes, and a broad mouth/muzzle, the man's head surmounts a knotted body of hunched shoulders and haunches, articulated in pitted lumps of clay that resemble startling enlargements of Moore's rough surfaces, just as in their graininess extreme photographic blow-ups resemble once evenly toned parts of the larger prints from which they were extracted. *Man Holding His Foot* is a further regression from Moore's own regressive transformations of the classical human form, the id of postwar expressionism tracked to its lair. *Baby with a Ball* reprises Moore's *Helmet Heads* and positions one atop an outsized torso with stunted or as yet underdeveloped limbs, that torso being perforated by round holes of different diameters, holes that harken back to Barbara Hepworth's and Moore's repeated opening of sculptural monoliths in the 1930s. The iconography leaves one guessing as to Caro's exact symbolic intent, but the pudgy hands clutching the ball held out to the viewer summon the specter of Alberto Giacometti's *The Invisible Object (Hands Holding the Void)* (fig. 4.14), and morph it into its opposite, replacing a beautiful, mysterious woman groping for the intangible with an unlovely and implacable child clinging to the real as it discovers the physical world one palpable object at a time.

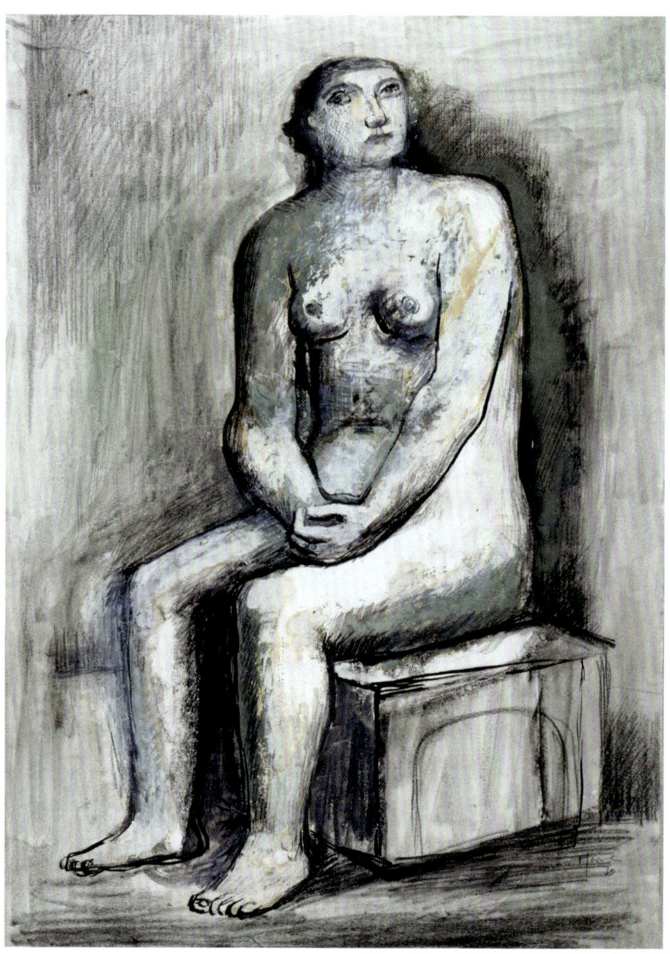

FIG. 4.15 Henry Moore, *Seated Figure,* 1930, brush and ink, oil paint, pastel, charcoal, and wash on wove paper mounted on marbled brown-gray paper, 20³⁄₁₆ x 14⁷⁄₁₆ in. (51.3 x 36.7 cm). Henry Moore Foundation, Hertfordshire. Photo: Michel Muller. Reproduced by permission of The Henry Moore Foundation

By comparison, the drawings Caro made in the period 1951–52 display Moore's influence at its fullest, including the older artist's direct tutorial intervention in the form of correction in his hand. Although larger than sketchbook studies, virtually all could have come from one of Moore's notepads but for their residual signs of awkward apprenticeship (fig. 4.15). Together they attest to the degree to which the practices of traditional academic training by a master still applied despite the aesthetic shift from neoclassical paradigms to nominally modern ones. In this there is nothing very unusual. Max Beckmann, for one, also had the habit of drawing on the work of his students to show them how it should be done — while a student at the School of the Museum of Fine Arts in Boston the young Ellsworth Kelly watched the German master do this—and the idiom Caro learned in Moore's studio was by the time he came into his circle as codified as that of a German Bauhaus, Dutch de Stijl, or Soviet Vkhutemas pedagogue imparting the systems of their respective schools to eager acolytes.[14]

The notion that "modernism" in and of itself "freed" students to express themselves in their own fashion is a myth that persists ideologically, despite the ample evidence that what modernism accomplished was to supplant one paradigm with another. When Moore tutored Caro, he did very much what other first-rate or at least committed teachers have done, ranging from Josef Albers (mentor to countless artists of consequence, from Robert Rauschenberg to Eva Hesse) through Thomas Hart Benton (mentor to Pollock and counterweight to his other chosen role models, such as David Alfaro Siqueiros and José Clemente Orozco), and that was, in Pollock's grateful assessment of Benton, to give him "something against which to react very strongly later on; it was better to have worked with him than with a less resistant personality."[15]

It was equally crucial that Caro started out by contending with the unyielding personality of Moore, and, later on, reacting to him (the younger man certainly did). As with Pollock, Picasso was a catalyst for this process but for Caro was ultimately not the solution to the challenge posed by Moore; in some measure, one assumes, Picasso's manner of manipulating fragmented volumes,

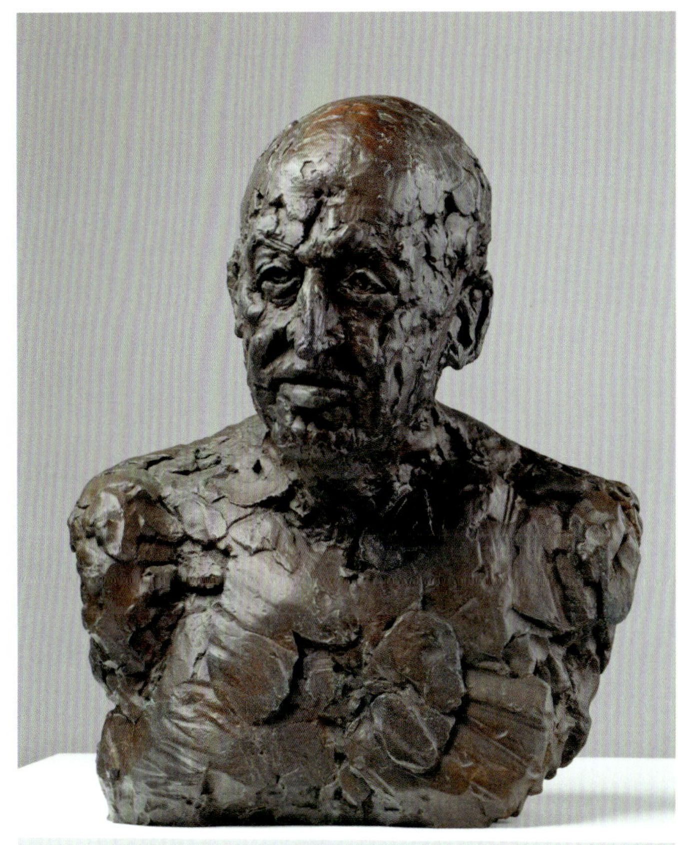

FIG. 4.16 *Bust of Clement Greenberg,* 1987/88, bronze, 22 x 18 x 14 in. (54.5 x 44.5 x 35.5 cm). Private collection, London

while retaining a semblance of their original heft and solidity, was already incorporated into Moore's way of thinking and working. Shedding Moore was shedding Picasso too, at least the mid-1930s to mid-1940s quasi-surrealist, quasi-neoclassical Picasso, in whose work Moore's art was steeped. However, in the thick linear armatures and flat color of Caro's Picassoid bulls—a 1954 bronze in the Art Gallery of Ontario collection renders these bovine studies as forceful masses—and human bodies the protean Spanish master takes one last bow on the stage where Caro's development played itself out. Meanwhile, there are hints of

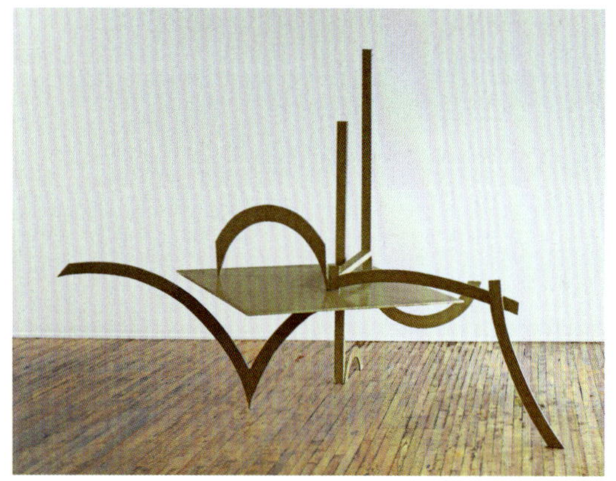

FIG. 4.17 *Trefoil* (cat. 33)

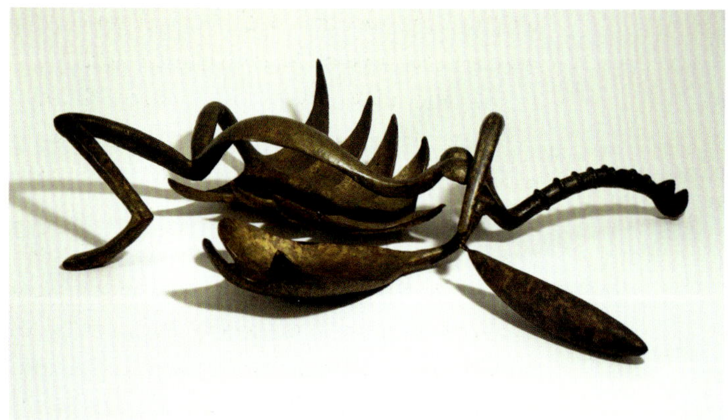

FIG. 4.18 Alberto Giacometti, *Woman with Her Throat Cut,* 1932 (cast 1949), bronze, 8 x 34 x 25 in. (20.3 x 87.6 x 63.5 cm). The Museum of Modern Art, New York. © The Museum of Modern Art, New York/ Scala, Florence and Succession Alberto Giacometti (Fondation Alberto et Annette Giacometti, Paris/ ADAGP, Paris and DACS, London), 2012

an alternative approach, one based on floating planes, firm tracery, and a vibrant full-spectrum palette. Caro's 1959 encounter, at the home of his friend and contemporary William Turnbull, with American critic, studio coach, and power player Clement Greenberg, marks the turning point in his career. And as problematic, if not destructive, as Greenberg's tutelage proved for numerous partially or entirely formed talents, Pollock chief among them, as well as for many less fully developed aspirants who came into his orbit, it had an undeniably positive effect on the thirty-four-year-old Englishman. After Moore, Greenberg was, in essence, the second resistant personality who gave shape to Caro's artistic identity. Two years later, that effect was readily apparent in Caro's work. The pictorialism of Matisse and the constructivism of David Smith replaced the "conservative" monumentality of Moore and Picasso, giving free rein to the gift for the bold, airy, spatial inventions upon which Caro's reputation ultimately rests. Doubling back from that breakthrough, years later Caro ironically paid tribute to his American mentor with a return to the rough plasticity of his Moore-ish clay and bronze pieces. Modeled from life between 1987 and 1988—Greenberg died in 1994—Caro's portrait bust is a fair and respectful likeness of its unprepossessing subject that follows the example of similar tributes to greatness thumbed and knifed by countless academic sculptors, while indirectly referencing classical Roman realism—which is fitting to the extent that Greenberg saw himself as the proconsul of art at the dawn of America's mid-twentieth-century imperium (fig. 4.16).

By contrast, *Orangerie* (cat. 34) and *Sun Feast* (see fig. 3.15) show Caro at the height of *his* powers, as does the earlier *Trefoil* (fig. 4.17). These are the sculptures that blew fresh breezes through the over-cultivated, rapidly calcifying groves of formalist art at the end of the 1960s. And these were the works that established Caro as the only heir of David Smith capable of matching his gift for gestural improvisation and compositional surprise and equipoise. However, gone for the most part were the aggressively industrial tropes of

Smith's constructions, with I-beam and rivet-based works such as *Midday* (1960), *Sculpture 7* (1961), and *Lock* (1962) on through *Tantrum* (1970), and *Halfway* (1970–71) being the qualified exceptions, the I-beam cross-section in *Early One Morning* having been reduced to its primary function as ready-made fulcrum for other elements that have been custom cut and are linear or planar in ways that are patently pictorial.

With works such *Orangerie*, Caro picked monolithic sculpture up off the ground, stretched its wings and legs and ruffled its feathers, and then released it to move wherever it wished, which often appeared to be in multiple directions simultaneously—though usually along a readily discernible, if seemingly disarticulated, axis, like so many double-jointed flamingos trying to regain their feet in order to take flight. The avian analogy has been chosen to avoid the darker associations that attend Alberto Giacometti's *Woman with Her Throat Cut* (1932), a work that in any case differs from Caro's steel assemblages as much in its cast-bronze qualities and relatively small scale as it indirectly resembles them in its combination of splayed limbs and compound convexities and concavities.

That said, bringing sculpture low, and allowing it to lever itself from the floor or off a plinth, were among Caro's signature formal gambits. In the many 'table pieces' from the 1960s until the present day, that gambit paid off handsomely. Some, such as *Table Piece VIII* (1966), *Table Piece XLII* (1967), *Table Piece LXXX* (1969), *Table Piece XCVII* (1970), and *Table Piece CLXVIII* (1973–74) (see cats. 25–31) play artfully with gravity by

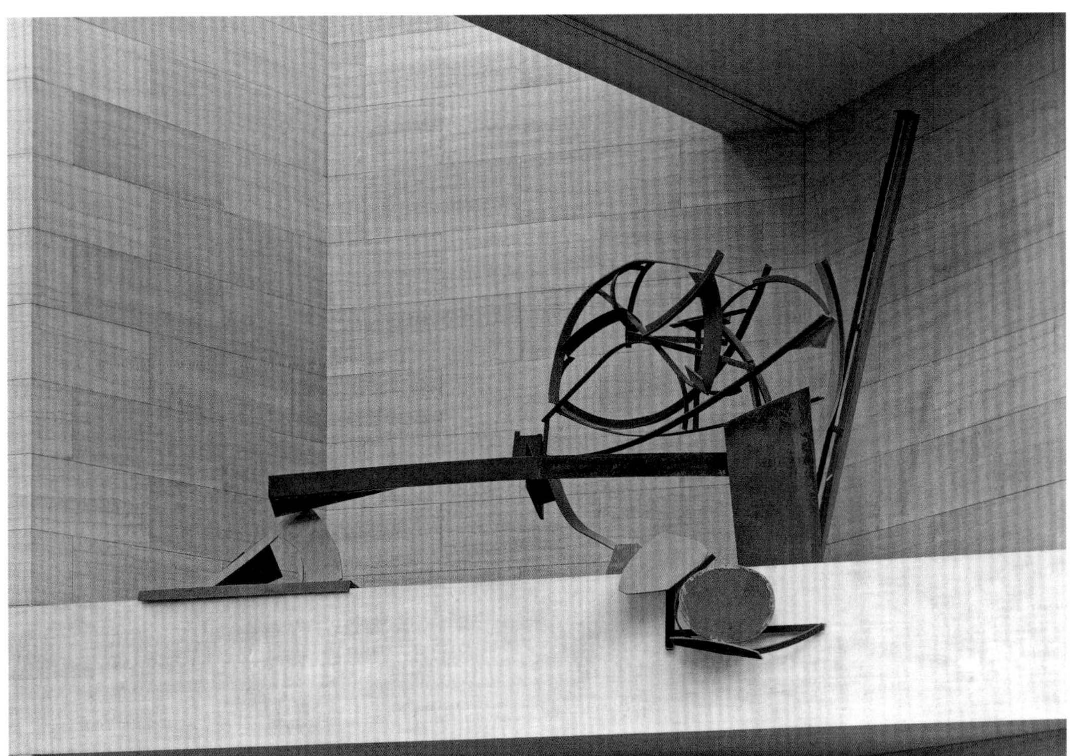

FIG. 4.19 *Ledge Piece*, 1978, welded steel, 171 1/16 x 243 1/8 x 106 in. (434.5 x 617.6 x 269.2 cm). National Gallery of Art, Washington, D.C., Gift of the Collectors Committee

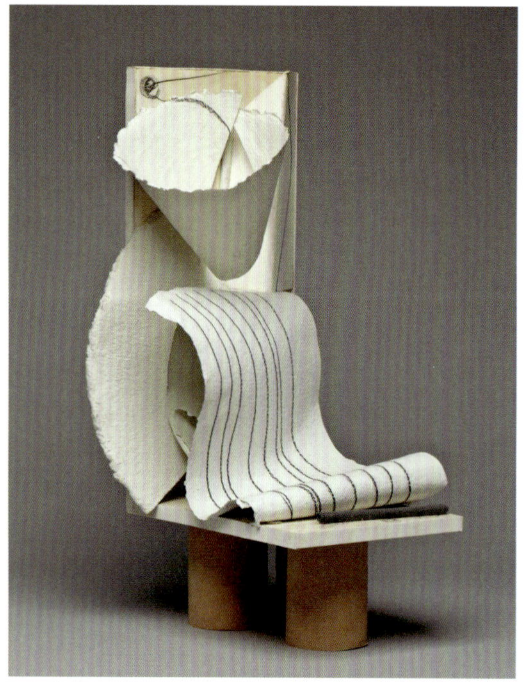

FIG. 4.21 *Paper Sculpture No. 98* (cat. 50)

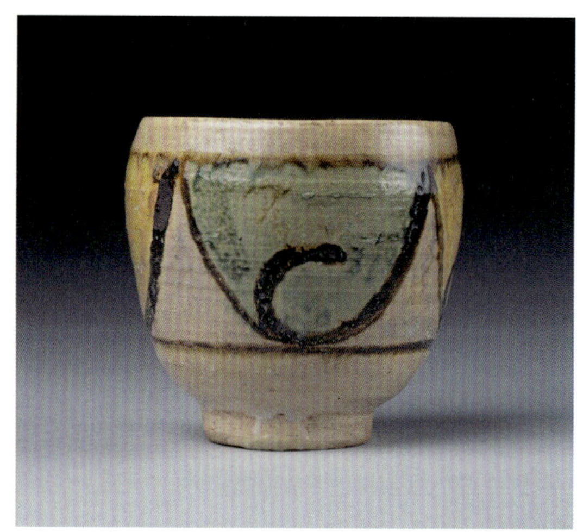

FIG. 4.22 Bernard Leach, *Tea Bowl,* 1921–29, thrown earthenware, fired, glazed, and painted raku, 3⁷⁄₁₆ x 3 in. (8.7 x 8.9 cm). Victoria and Albert Museum. © The Leach Pottery, St Ives / Victoria and Albert Museum, London

suggesting that they might simply fall apart and over the edge of their support; *Ledge Piece* (1978) in the I. M. Pei wing of the National Gallery of Art, Washington, D.C., enlarges this illusion to nearly heroic scale, and elevates it in an architectural setting such that it threatens to cascade down on spectators below (fig. 4.19). Other table pieces from the 1980s through the 1990s, and on into the second decade of the new millennium—*Cuckoo* (cat. 45) rates as a table piece—incorporate what appear to be architectural motifs or allusions, but seem at times as if they have collapsed into themselves like sodden suitcases crammed with shoes and other volume-retaining contents that incompletely hold their shape, or like the insides of fossilized crustaceans whose sub-carapace walls have grown thick as if they had been transformed from organic into mineral substances. Naturally, such a description does not claim the artist's intent as its source, but merely seeks to provide vivid terms of comparison for opening up the field of associations implicit in Caro's protean forming, much as the French phenomenologist Gaston Bachelard did in his suite of books devoted to the poetics of space and of the classical elements, earth, water, and fire. And as Bachelard argued—and by example proved—one doesn't have to be a surrealist to dream worlds within worlds.[16]

The balance of the works in this small anthology of studio pieces show Caro experimenting with materials quite unlike the traditional ones with which he began—clay and bronze—or the by now traditionally modern one with which he made his name—raw and painted steel. Specifically, they reveal his encounter with Japanese craft traditions in paper (fig. 4.21), porcelain, and stoneware, and with traditional Japanese brush painting. This late life shift in orientation away from European antiquity (Caro's Moore period), and European and American modernism (the 1960s through the 1980s), is not so anomalous as it might at first appear, and does not signify the sudden effects of a "globalized," Pacific Rim obsessed art world on a heretofore essentially Transatlantic artist. After all, from the 1920s onward when Bernard Leach set up his first pottery in the coastal town of St. Ives (fig. 4.22)—the home of such native talents as the naïve painter Alfred Wallis, later the center of activity for a whole community of modernists including Ben Nicholson and Barbara Hepworth, and in honor of that history, the site of a branch of the Tate Gallery, London—and fostered a dialogue between East and West that aligned the British Arts and Crafts movement as conceived by the polymath William Morris with Chinese and Japanese tendencies he had studied, tendencies that during this period developed their own complex dialectic between the supposedly "timeless" aesthetics of the past and the insistent "presentness" of modern art.

The tensions between East and West, then and now, are palpably implicit and—in the case of a stoneware piece like *Minoan* (cat. 38)—verbally explicit in much of Caro's recent production. So too is the combination of process and art historical precedent, for as much as *Paper Sculpture No. 60* and *No. 98*, and *Floor Paper Sculpture No. 51* (cats. 48–50) seem to presage aspects of Caro's turn to ceramics and *washi* paper, they even more obviously evoke the hybrids of neoclassicism and cubism that preoccupied Picasso from 1914 onward, and took on surrealist attributes in the 1930s in works such as *Composition with a Glove* (fig. 4.23) as well as a strange convergence of the metaphysical still lifes of Giorgio de Chirico (an unmistakable influence on the Picasso work just cited), and the form-folding and furling cubo-futurist *Bottle in Space* (1919, Museum of Modern Art, New York) of Umberto Boccioni, with an aside in *Paper Sculpture No. 98* to Frank Stella's recent constructed sculpture and reliefs. Morphological similarities with *Drummer's Book*, *Little Book of Opera*, and *Small Wedge Book* (cats. 39–41) also suggest a probable awareness on Caro's part of Marcel Broodthaers's poetry career-ending, art career-launching exercise in sculptural self-censorship, *Pense-Bête* (fig. 4.25). This was featured in the Tate Gallery retrospective of the Belgian neo-dadaist's work in 1980, although no artist occupies a position further from Brood-

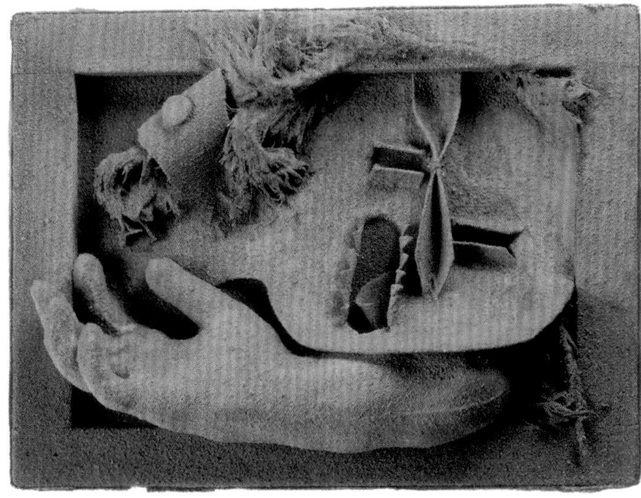

FIG. 4.23 Pablo Picasso, ***Composition au gant (Composition with glove),*** 1930, cardboard, plants, and glove, sown and glued to back of canvas stretcher and coated with sand, partially painted, 10 13/16 x 14 x 3 1/8 in. (27.5 x 35.5 x 8 cm). Musée Picasso, Paris. Réunion des Musées Nationaux/Art Resource, New York. © RMN / Béatrice Hatala and Succession Picasso/DACS, London 2012

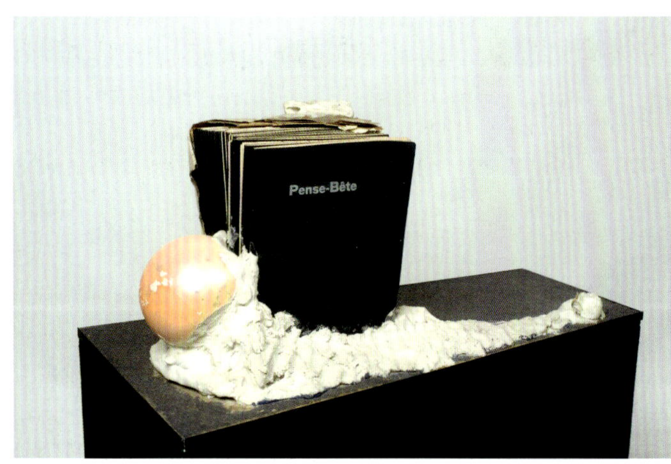

FIG. 4.25 **Marcel Broodthaers, *Le Pense-Bête,* 1964, books, paper, plaster, plastic sphere, and wood. Collection S.M.A.K./Flemish Community, photography: Dirk Pauwels © DACS 2012**

thaers's postmodernist conceptual approach and formal sensibility and procedures than the inveterate modernist shape maker Caro.[17]

Still, the self-consciously art history-minded dimension of Caro's oeuvre over its long trajectory remains, perhaps, its most salient characteristic. Beginning with his assimilation of Moore's work—especially that elder's assimilation of Mesopotamian, Greek, Roman, meso-American, African, and medieval European monolithic sculpture, along with cubism and surrealism as epitomized in the objects made by Picasso—it continued with his absorption of David Smith's anti-monolithic handling of many if not all of the same paradigms, and has displayed itself in asides to Asian art, as just noted, as well as in three-dimensional palavers with some of the younger artists who have regarded him as a role model to be embraced rather than as an elder to be shunned or attacked. In particular, I am thinking of Richard Deacon's eccentric variations on constructivism while recalling works seen in Caro's studio in the 1990s that seemed in their curves and volumes to respond to the example of Deacon, even as Caro took an unanticipated detour into post-impressionism with the sculptural variations on Vincent van Gogh's *Chair* (1888, National Gallery, London), and Édouard Manet's *Déjeuner sur l'herbe* (1862–63, Musée d'Orsay, Paris) (fig. 26).

All of which reminds us of the basic pictorialism of the art history-making—as distinct from art history-elaborating or -pastiching—works Caro created after his separation from Moore, works that could not have been without that apprenticeship, works such as *Early One Morning.* In the 1960s Bruce Nauman defended Moore when critical consensus among a rising generation of "late modernists" had judged him and his most devoted and deferential acolytes as bound to fail. In the 1990s Charles Ray spoke up for Caro at a moment when the majority of postmodernists had long since convinced themselves that Caro

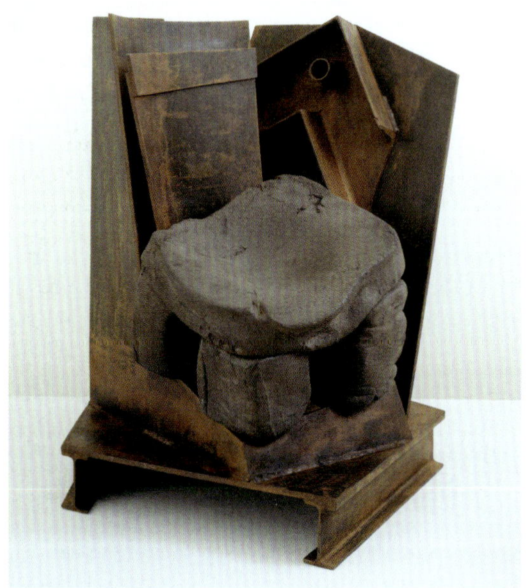

FIG. 4.26 ***Van Gogh Chair IV,* 1997, stoneware and steel, 35 x 26½ x 24 in. (89 x 67.5 x 61 cm). Private collection**

was "irrelevant" to "the discourse," or worse, a nagging, Lear-like father figure who denies that his time is up and refuses to go away.

Yet, as we should by now have learned from the myriad ways in which modernism keeps making its presence felt in ostensibly postmodern art, "relevance" is always a matter of to whom something or someone is relevant and when—and why. Moore's significance to Nauman, a significance sufficient to inspire a handful of related works in several media during the crucial early years of Nauman's formation in the 1960s, including one of his greatest and most influential sculptures, is a case in point. As previously noted, Caro's relevance to Ray was so great that he photoshopped himself looking like a geeky student into a picture of *Early One Morning*, and used that picture, rather than one of his own works, as the lead image of the catalogue of his first retrospective. At this juncture it is anybody's guess—or may yet be an archivist's trophy discovery—how Moore greeted Nauman's advocacy, but it is certain that archaizing figurative sculptors today are looking at him and his work anew. How Caro feels about Ray as his champion would be interesting to know but it is nevertheless plain that the vigor of his protean production, like the abiding freshness of his signature achievements, makes him impossible to ignore and that his most radical sculptures constitute the branches of clustered oaks that persistently expand the periphery of the thicket, which they anchor by dropping acorns while other trees and bushes loose seeds to the wind. Adapting to epistemic ruptures and political and cultural revolutions the way cells absorb and adapt to abrupt mutations or changes in their environment, that organic process is how modernist tradition came into being, and how it has continued to evolve despite ideological efforts to contain that process or cut it off. A survivor's survivor and currently as much of an artist's artist as he is a British cultural icon, Caro is the proof.

NOTES

1. Willoughby Sharpe, "Interview with Bruce Nauman," *Arts Magazine* 44, 1970, reprinted in *Please Pay Attention Please: Bruce Nauman's Words. Writings and Interviews*, ed. Janet Kraynak (Cambridge, Mass., and London: MIT, 2003), 44.
2. Lorraine Sciarra, "Bruce Nauman, January, 1972," reprinted in *Please Pay Attention Please*, 155-171, quotation on 159.
3. Interview between Charles Ray and Michael Fried "Early One Morning . . . Charles Ray and Michael Fried on Anthony Caro," *Tate Etc.* 3 (Spring 2005), 50-53.
4. Ray is in fact depicted standing behind *Early One Morning*, rather than in front of it.
5. T. J. Clark, "Clement Greenberg's Theory of Art," in *Pollock and After: the Critical Debate,* ed. Francis Frascina (Harper & Row: New York, 1985), 50.
6. Michael Fried, "Art and Objecthood," *Artforum* 5, no. 10 (June 1967): 12–23.
7. Anthony Caro, "The Master Sculptor," *Observer*, London, November 27, 1960, 21.
8. Willem de Kooning, "Content is a Glimpse: Interview with David Sylvester" (1963), reprinted in Kristine Stiles and Peter Selz, eds., *Theories and Documents of Contemporary Art: A Sourcebook of Artists' Writings* (Berkeley: University of California Press, 1996), 197–99.
9. William Rubin, *Anthony Caro*, exh. cat. (New York: Museum of Modern Art, 1975); William Rubin, *Frank Stella*, exh. cat. (New York: Museum of Modern Art, 1970).
10. The phrase "dead bunnies in the snow" was frequently heard in use by MoMA staff during the author's tenure there as Senior Curator of Painting & Sculpture.
11. Diane Waldman, *Robert Ryman*, exh. cat. (New York: Solomon R. Guggenheim Foundation, 1972).
12. Sol LeWitt, "Sentences on Conceptual Art," *Art-Language* 1, no. 1 (May 1969).
13. See Diane Waldman, *Anthony Caro* (New York: Abbeville, 1982).
14. Beckmann style of studio critique as described to the author by Ellsworth Kelly ca. 2001.
15. Pollock on Benton, *Art and Architecture* 61, no. 2 (Feb. 1944); as quoted in Clifford Ross, ed., *Abstract Expressionism: Creators and Critics, an Anthology* (New York: Abrams, 1990), 137
16. Gaston Bachelard, *The Poetics of Space*, trans. Maria Jolas (New York: Orion, 1964).
17. Marcel Broodthaers and Michael Compton, *Marcel Broodthaers: the Tate Gallery*, exh. cat. (London: Tate Gallery, 1980).

Changing Settings

Anthony Caro in Conversation with Julius Bryant

(October 27, 2011)

JB: The idea for this exhibition came during my fellowship at the Yale Center for British Art (fig. 5.1). Revisiting the Center, one's relationship to art is less like that of a visitor at a temporary exhibition and more like that of an owner at home. This seemed the ideal place to experiment with showing your smaller, more intimate, sculptures. You once said, "all my sculpture is intimate," yet you make large sculptures for exhibitions. From having worked with you on three exhibitions, be-

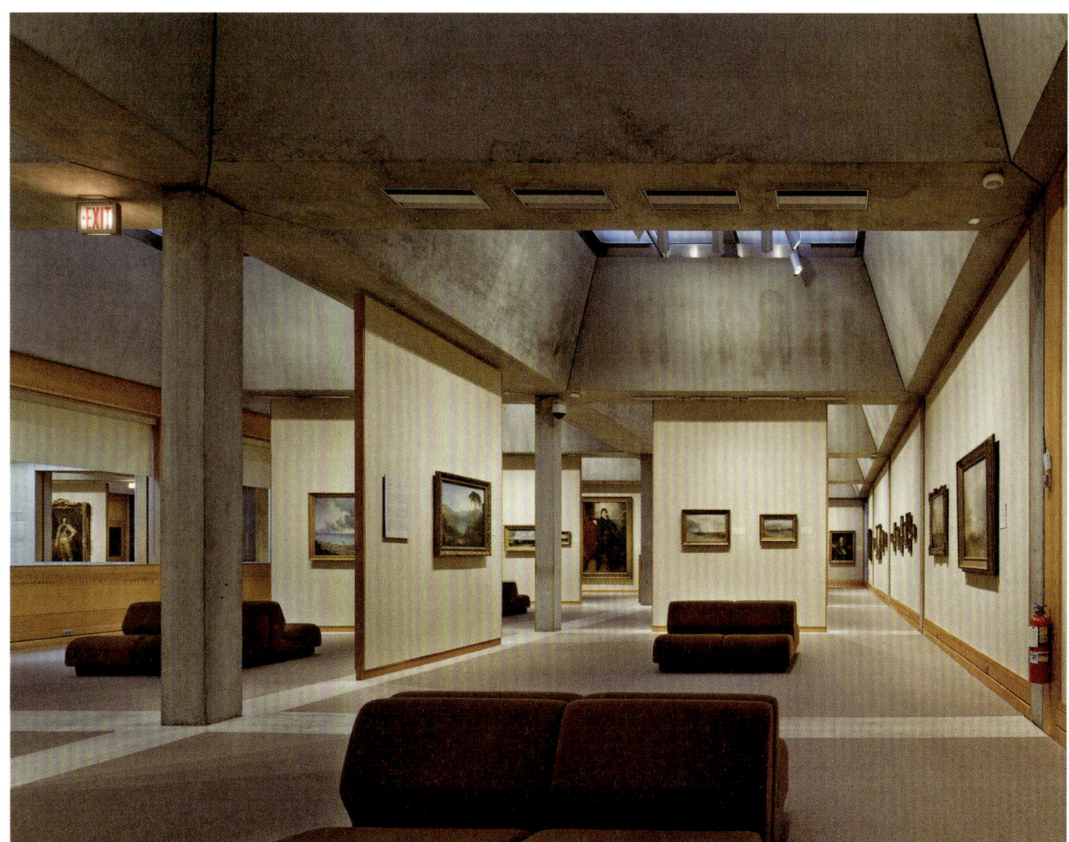

FIG. 5.1 View across the top floor of the Yale Center for British Art. © Francis Dzikowski/Esto

tween 1994 and 2010, I know how much effort you put into perfecting the viewing conditions and the placement of each sculpture. You make precise architectural models of galleries and scale models of your own sculptures. It seems to be a key aspect of your work that you have not talked about, and no one has written about, so I would like to explore it here. Is your painstaking attention to exhibition installation a way to keep the intimacy of the studio when a work goes public?

AC: I'm not a curator. There have been shows done without my being there—shows that have been installed by other people who are familiar with my sculptures—and I've sometimes been surprised and delighted by the results. In a retrospective of my work in the Museum of Contemporary Art, Tokyo, in 1995, the architect Tadao Ando had the walls of a room angled from the vertical, which played off against the tilted steel slabs in the sculptures. It was an inspired move—one I would never have expected to work—but it made a spectacular room. How a sculpture gets seen is of the utmost importance: when I speak of my sculpture being intimate I mean that I strive for a one-to-one relationship with the viewer. My works are not monuments to be looked up at or seen from a distance. There are practical reasons for the scale models I use. They are made after the sculpture is finished. My sculpture is often heavy and has to be moved in parts so it's best to get it more or less right in the scale model rather than try to move things about in the gallery.

JB: Let's talk about the very different places where you've shown sculpture, which have ranged from the Museum of Modern Art in New York (see figs. 4.5 and 5.3) to the Trajan Markets in Rome (see fig. 2.1).

AC: Making the work is what matters. One then tries to make sure they are displayed to their best advantage.

JB: In that case let's begin with your choice of studio space. You once said how you learned from Ken Noland, when you first met him in 1959, the benefits of working in a small studio, close-up.

AC: After I came back from my first trip to New York in 1959 I was working in my small studio at home—a one-car garage where you cannot stand back. It prevented me from relying on an older aesthetic, on ideas of balance or composing. After I found my present studio, which used to be a piano factory, I still liked sometimes to work at home, and at weekends at my Dorset cottage. But I now feel I can treat this big studio as my private space even with assistants to help me.

JB: For Battersea Park in 1966 Alan Bowness curated the exhibition of three generations of British sculpture, from Henry Moore to Phillip King. How did you feel about showing your sculpture in the open air?

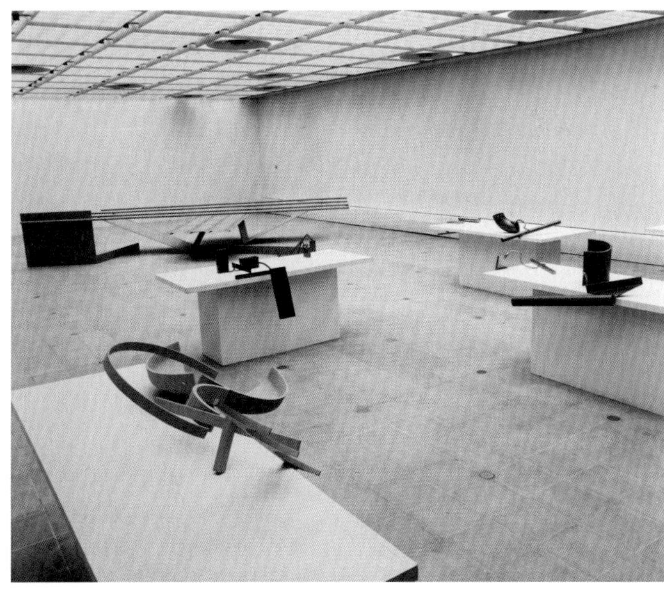

FIG. 5.2 **Installation view of Caro's solo exhibition at the Hayward Gallery, London, 1969**

AC: I don't like grass and bushes and trees much. Sculptures among trees and grasses can look like garden gnomes or eighteenth-century statues in formal flower beds. By and large, landscape damages sculpture and sculpture damages the landscape, I've seen few open-air sites that are suitable for sculpture, and these are often formal, contained places. Sculpture needs containment, unless it is a sculpture specifically made for the open air. *Goodwood Steps* holds its own out-of-doors. That one you can see from afar or close-up. I made it first for an inside setting, in 1996, at Dean Clough in Halifax. It began as a site-specific sculpture, but when we put it outside at Goodwood it became a work that you not only look at but also look through. It does not reflect the landscape, rather it acts as a kind of counterpoint to it. And it frames the landscape.

JB: Like *Promenade* (see fig. 7.6)—when it was installed in the Tuileries Gardens in Paris in 1996; then in Holland Park in London (1998), the viewer discovered it sequentially, as many sculptures in one; as you walked alongside, you had to approach it from an oblique angle, like reading a great pediment from left to right.

AC: This exactly makes my point.

JB: So what are the ideal places to show sculpture?

AC: I prefer to show my sculpture in an anonymous white room because then what you look at is just the sculpture itself. In the 1960s and '70s the Kasmin Gallery (see fig. 7.4) was the best

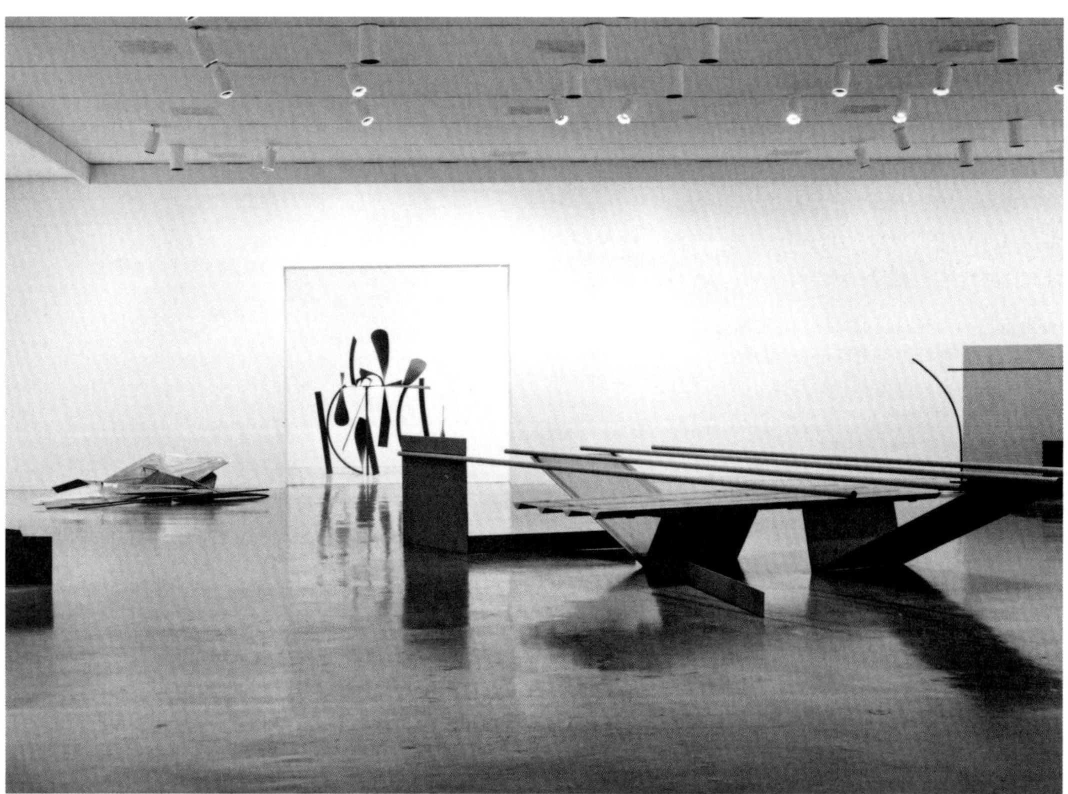

FIG. 5.3 Installation view of Caro's retrospective at the Museum of Modern Art, New York, 1975

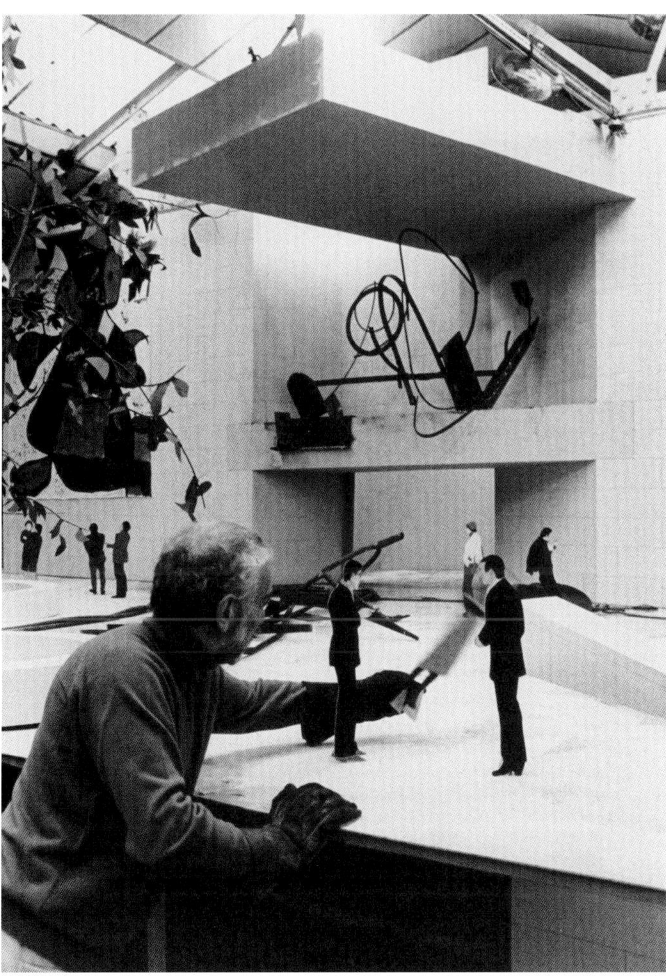

FIG. 5.4 Caro working on his installation model for the East Building, National Gallery of Art, Washington D.C., showing an early version of *Table Piece CCCXCI* (see fig. 4.19) above the entrance to the study center, 1977

setting I have come across. You came off Bond Street into a dark passage, walked along, turned, and there, after the second turning, was this wonderful light room—it was like a box for treasures—a perfect showing space. In the Emmerich Gallery in New York, which André Emmerich designed himself, spaces to right and left allowed you to see the works individually, without interruption.

JB: For your mid-career retrospective in 1969, curated by Michael Fried, did the Hayward Gallery (fig. 5.2) provide these kinds of ideal spaces?

AC: When it first opened many people hated the gallery, but I didn't. I liked the downstairs spaces, even though the floors were different. I showed *Early One Morning* on the left, a large space, and then on the right in the long gallery with a wooden floor I showed *Titan*. You came upon each work separately. You could look down on *Early One Morning* from slightly above.

JB: For your retrospective at the Museum of Modern Art in New York, in 1975, curated by Bill Rubin, was the experience much the same?

AC: Yes but outside, the upper part above what was then the restaurant, was a problem. You could see the buildings on 53rd Street, and I was afraid that the scale would be wrong, that they could not stand in such a setting. I had seen works there, by Barnett Newman and others, which were much bigger, and I thought my work would shrink, but it didn't (see figs. 4.5 and 5.3).

JB: In 1978 you made a sculpture for a specific setting, for the new East Building of the National Gallery of Art in Washington, DC, a vast diagonal space designed by I. M. Pei.

AC: I. M. Pei asked me if I would make a sculpture there. It is in a difficult place at the back of the atrium—a corner ledge over an interior doorway leading to the Library and Study Center. This building was telling the sculpture to fit in with it. The atrium is massive, with many viewing points at different distances and different levels. In the end I had to give instructions to the fabricators by walkie-talkie from various viewing points at different levels. I had started by making a model of the ledge in my studio in Camden Town, and then making a table piece on it. But when I worked in the building itself I found myself changing it again and again. Finally I welded a great mass of scrapped steel parts together and

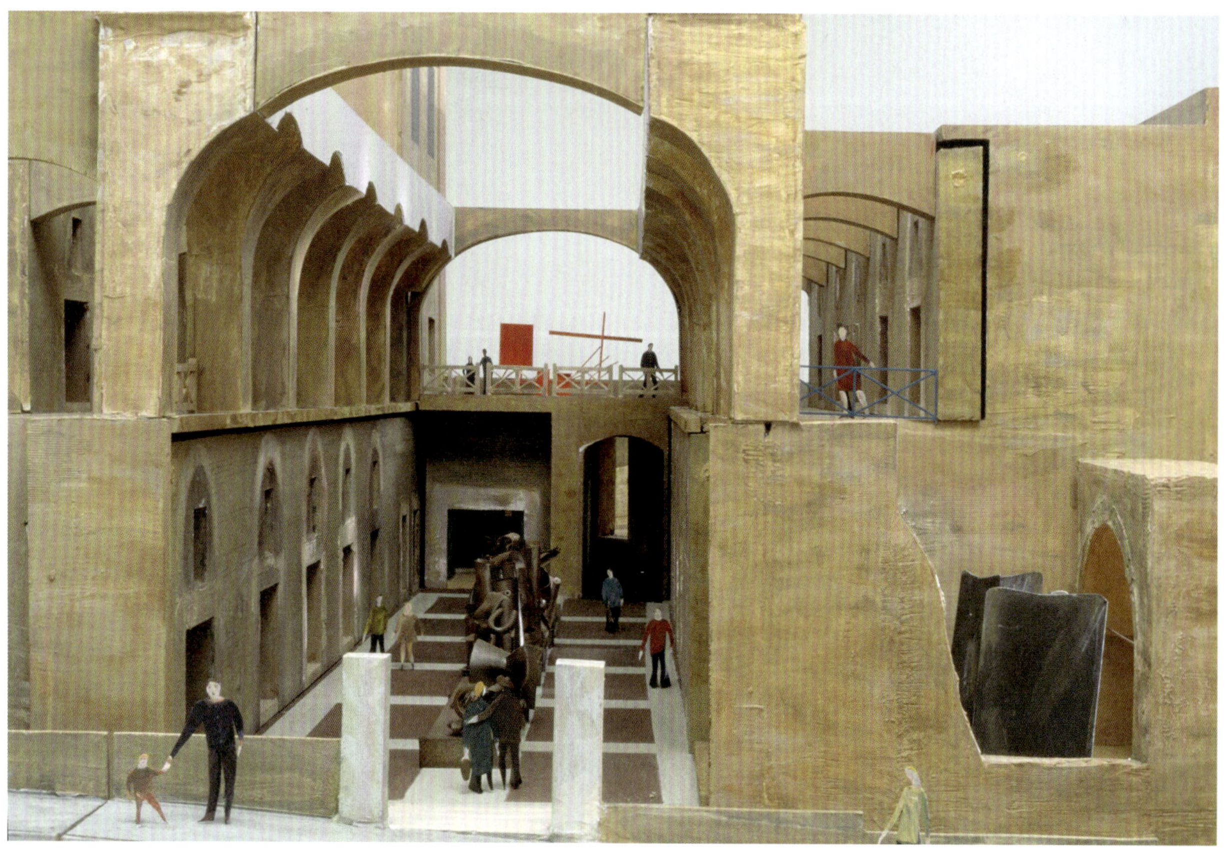

FIG. 5.5 Scale model for *After Olympia* and *Early One Morning* at the Trajan Markets, Rome, 1992

lifted it up on the ledge and this became my starting point. I was then able to work in a spontaneous way, just as I do at home (fig. 5.4).

JB: The Serpentine Gallery in Kensington Gardens is a pavilion, where you had a show in 1984. Were the flowing space and ample daylight an advantage?

AC: The indoor spaces at the Serpentine are fine. Outdoors, it is too open for my liking. An open-air place where I enjoyed installing my work was the Trajan Markets in Rome (figs. 5.5 and 5.6).

JB: That was in 1992, with Giovanni Carandente, who had organized the David Smith show in the Roman amphitheater in Spoleto, Italy, in 1962, and the Henry Moore show in Forte Belvedere, Florence, in 1973. How did the Trajan Markets help the open-air setting?

AC: In Rome the ancient remains of shops on the street became compartments that contained and isolated each work, each within its own frame.

JB: Was there an intimacy, from the small size of each ruined house limiting the number of people who could enter?

AC: It's not a question of seeing the sculpture with other people or being alone. At a concert you can have a sense of intimacy with music while being part of a big audience or listening to a big orchestra. Within exhibitions I think we artists try

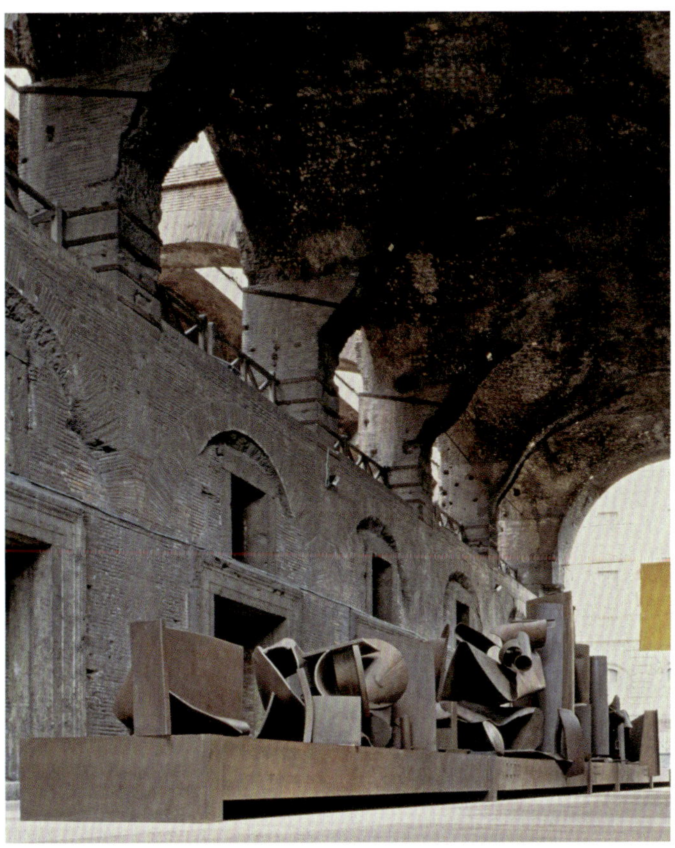

FIG. 5.6 *After Olympia,* installed at the Trajan Markets, Rome, 1992

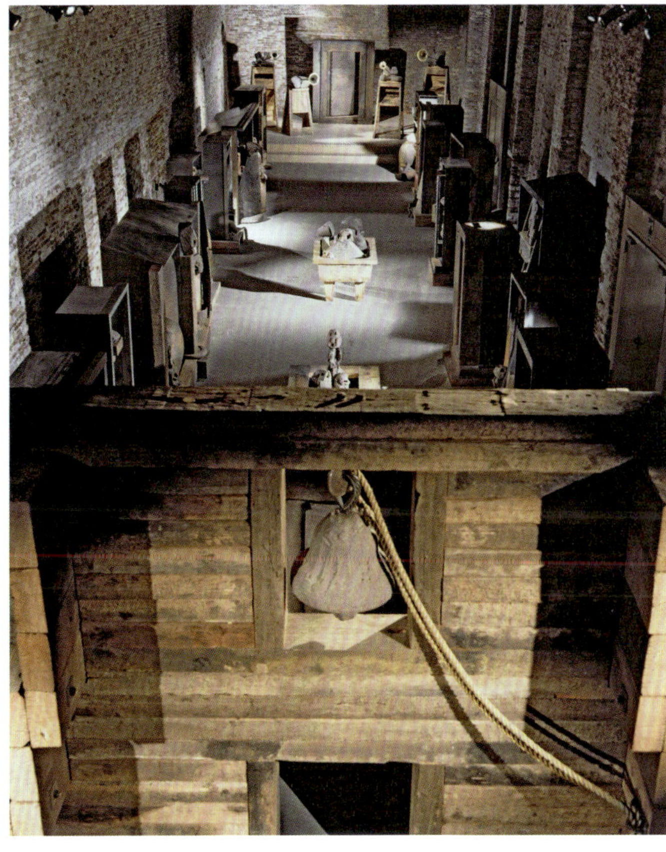

FIG. 5.7 *The Last Judgement,* 1996–99, installed at the Antichi Granai, XLVIII Venice Biennale (1999). Museum Würth

to replicate, in some way, what we are feeling in our own studios. That's the kind of intimacy I'm after.

JB: For the Venice Biennale in 1999 you presented *Last Judgment* (fig. 5.7) in the Antichi Granai delle Zitelli, in the Giudecca. How did that setting influence the way people looked at the sculpture?

AC: These old buildings have a resonance.

JB: When *Last Judgment* was shown at Tate Britain, in the Duveen Galleries, for your retrospective in 2005, did it look very different?

AC: Very, the space was cavernous. It was difficult to come to terms with it.

JB: You have exhibited twice on the roof terrace of the Metropolitan Museum of Art in New York: in 1988, *After Olympia,* and this year, a group of individual works. How did the setting inform your choice of sculptures?

AC: Well, you can't go far wrong with that setting. It is a space that carries so much—all those skyscrapers in the distance. A wonderful place for sculpture—you've got a tremendous plus from the start.

JB: The *Chapel of Light* you created in 2008, for the Church of St. John the Baptist in Bourbourg, in the Nord-Pas region of France, near Calais, was

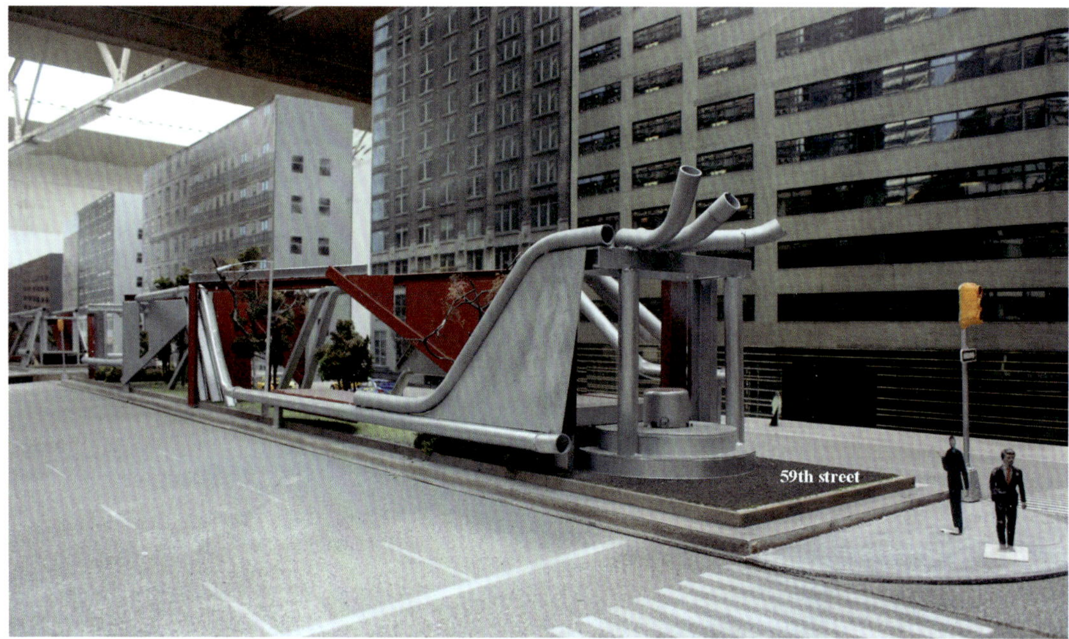

FIG. 5.8 Studio model, 2011, for Caro's planned temporary installation in Park Avenue, New York

your first multipartite site-specific sculpture, a permanent installation. What lessons had you learned about conceiving sculpture for a specific place, since working in the East Building in Washington thirty years before? Why did you feel things could go better there? (see fig. 4.19)

AC: I had a big model made, one-tenth scale, which was useful in placing and designing the font and the towers. When it came to the apse, the setting was so strong that I decided to make a full-scale replica in my London studio, and I made each of the niche sculptures there and later fitted and fixed them in the church itself. When I first saw the ruined choir it was separated from the nave, because the three arches had been walled up. But one day when I arrived I found that the wall had been opened up, and from the west end of the nave you could see this gorgeous light streaming in. I had to fit in glass walls to separate the choir from the main body of the church. This was for both aesthetic and religious reasons. As well as making the choir into a Catholic baptistery, I wanted to make a place of private contemplation for people of all religions or none. This is why I insisted on the door from the town direct into the *Chapel of Light*.

JB: Park Avenue, New York, is your current project, a temporary sculpture down the central island for three blocks. This is a totally public space, but is it actually contained, by the skyscrapers, like a vast outdoor room? (fig. 5.8)

AC: It is an urban canyon and it controls the way the sculpture is to be seen. It needs to be experienced from a pedestrian standpoint—from the sidewalks, from the passenger seat of a car travelling at perhaps 30–40 miles an hour passing alongside, or from the windows of buildings fronting the Avenue. The sculpture is also a kind of container for the trees and shrubs already on the median. Working with the model is not easy. It is pretense: I have to pretend I am only three inches high.

JB: Can we end with your thoughts about showing at the Yale Center for British Art? Louis Kahn's galleries are on the human scale of rooms, so they have that sense of containment, of enclosure and intimacy, and then surprise you with great vistas that tempt you with art from afar. There is also the wealth of changing daylight and Kahn's respect for the sculptural qualities of his construction materials.

AC: It's a lovely building. I also like Kahn's earlier building, the Yale University Art Gallery [1953] across Chapel Street. But the Center offers much more than a white gallery space. The rich use of different materials gives gravity. I'm sure my sculpture will look at its best.

Overleaf: *Table Piece LXXX* (cat. 28)

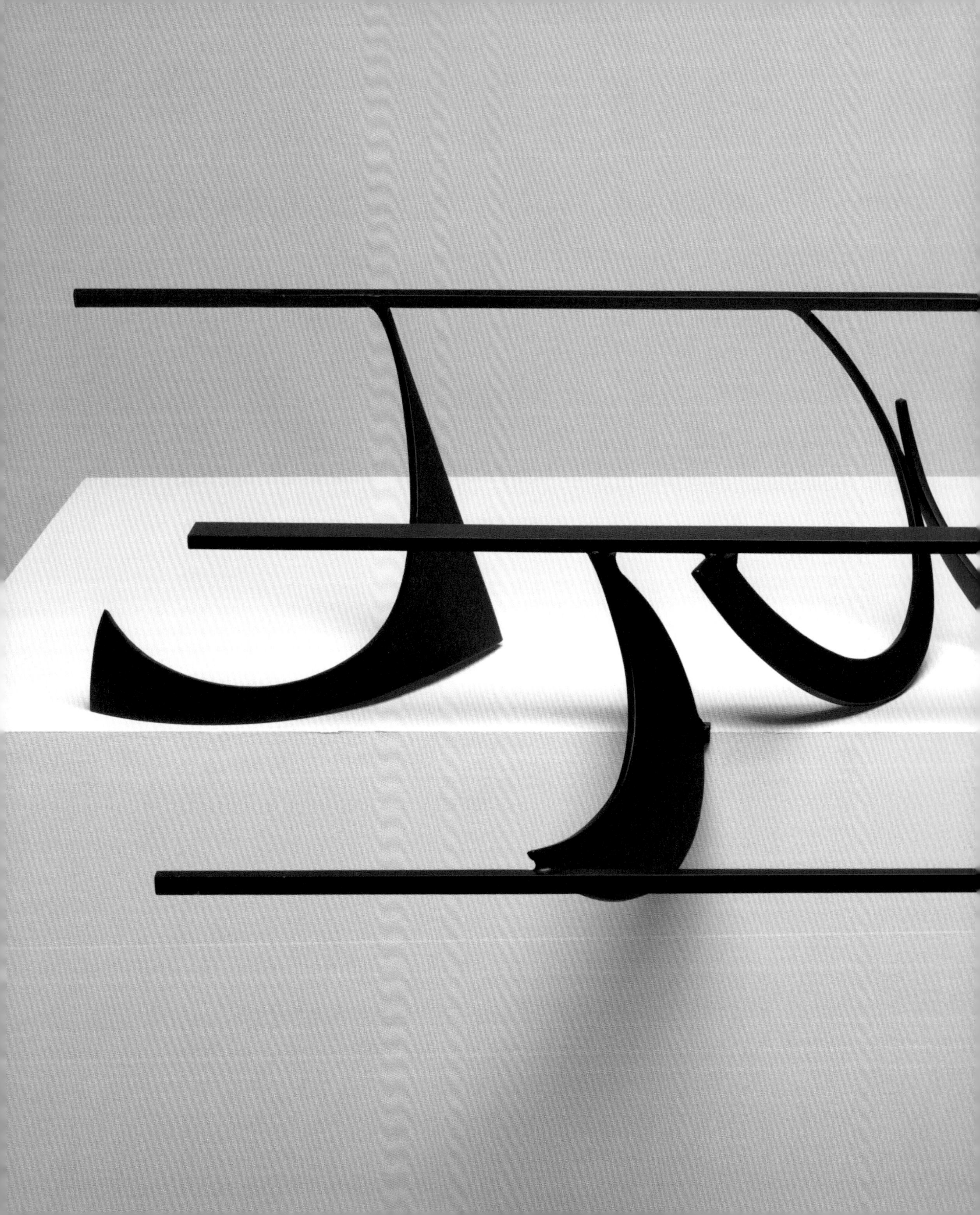

Catalogue

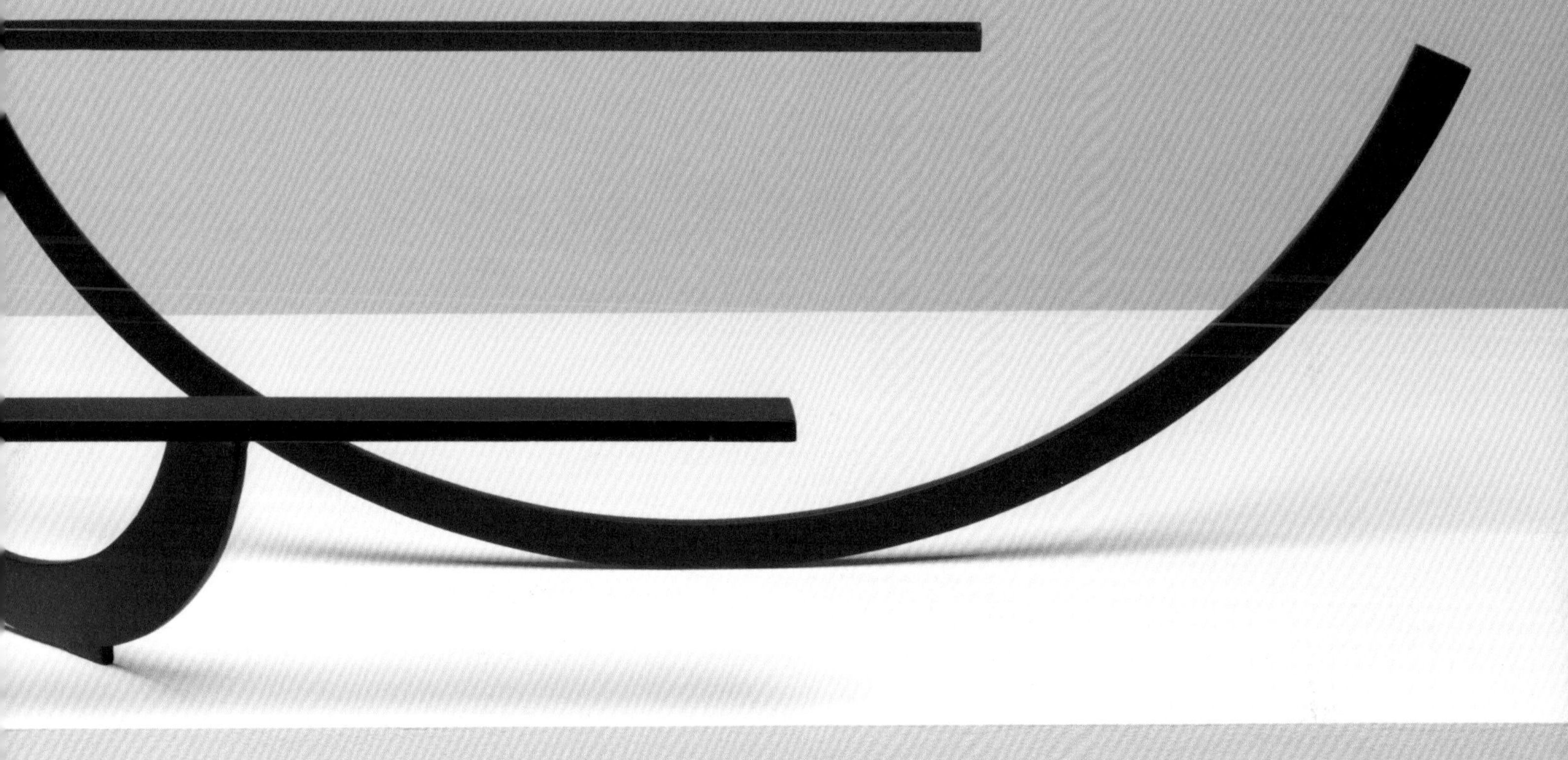

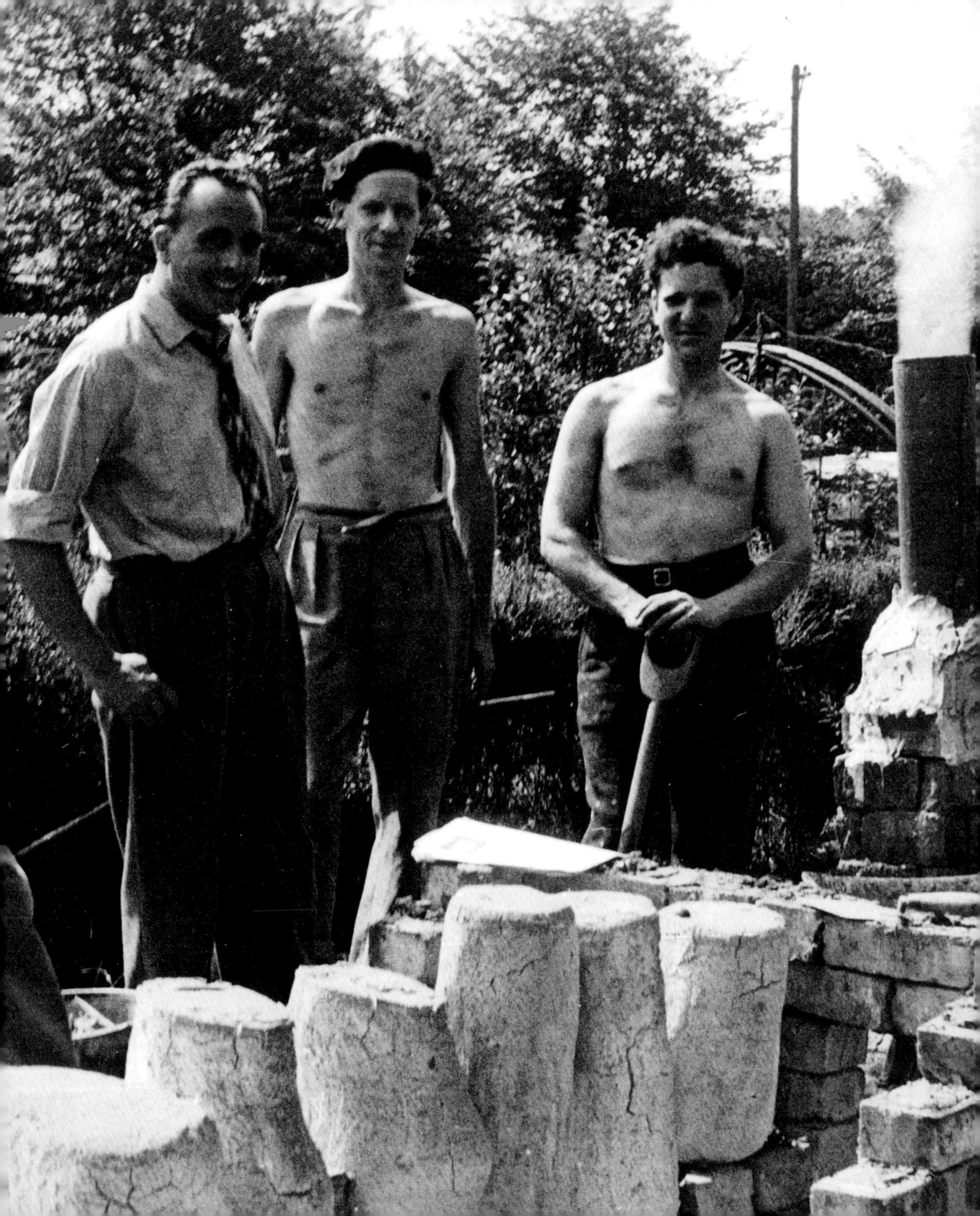

Early Life-drawings and Henry Moore

The human figure is a central theme in Anthony Caro's art. As a student of sculpture at the Royal Academy in London (1947–52) Caro benefited from a traditional if conservative training, grounded in patient, analytical observation of the human figure. During the two years he worked as Henry Moore's assistant (July 1951–August 1953), Caro continued at the Academy part-time, and as a regular in the life-class. At Moore's home and studio, Hoglands, at Much Hadham in Hertfordshire, Caro helped to build and operate Moore's new bronze foundry. He learned to cast waxes into bronze and to color bronzes through patination. Caro also enlarged Moore's model of *Draped Reclining Figure* (1952–53) tenfold, before it was cast into bronze for the Time-Life building in London.

Moore was fifty-three, Caro twenty-seven. Moore encouraged Caro to borrow books from his extensive library, and discussed with him the art of Africa, the surrealists, Picasso, and others; indeed, Caro felt "the doors of a whole world of art which I had not known as a student he opened for me."[1] Moore introduced Caro to visiting curators and critics such as Kenneth Clark, Herbert Read, David Sylvester, and Alan Bowness. Moore also took a strong interest in the drawings Caro made in the Royal Academy Schools. Caro recalls:

> I was so much into volume that it seemed to me false to have to put it down on a flat sheet of paper. Moore's attitude was 'Well, let's try and break down the flatness of the paper, we'll try and make it work in a way like reality works.' For this reason he explained to me a logical system of the laws of light, inventing a light source; the more a surface was turned away from that light source the darker it became; also that perspective and intensity could work equally well on a figure drawing as on the drawing of a landscape. . . . Moore recommended the practice of drawing because if you draw a lot you can do a lot far quicker than making sculpture and this is a real plus when you are changing fast.[2]

Working as Moore's assistant provided more than a technical training and an understanding of how a workshop could be run. It was also inspiring, as Caro recalls:

Caro with Alan Ingham (center) and an unidentified Italian sculptor (left) building the foundry at Henry Moore's studio, Much Hadham, 1951

"There was something compelling in Henry's conviction . . . that made me look all the harder. I felt more challenged around Moore than I ever had before."[3]

In the sixteen drawings by Caro that survive with Moore's annotations, mostly in the margins, the older artist is present also in the central figures, which recall Moore's own drawing style. They reveal his concern for expressing volume by first setting the depth of the model's chair in perspective, for identifying key curves and swells, for defining depth through extreme shadow, and Moore's signature technique of applying contour lines to define three-dimensional form. As the drawings are by an artist who still saw himself as a student they do not seek to express a personal style or an individual response to the human figure. Nevertheless, they clearly respect principles for composing volume and space through tense and relaxed forms that can be found in some of Caro's most abstract sculptures.

CAT. 1
Seated Man (with corrections by Henry Moore), 1951/1952
Charcoal and pencil on vellum paper, 22 x 15⅛ in. (55.7 x 38.7 cm)
D0058
Private collection, London

CAT. 2
Seated Figure (with corrections by Henry Moore), 1951/1952
Charcoal, ink, wash, and white color on vellum paper, 22 x 15 in. (55.8 x 38.1 cm)
D0032
Private collection, London

CAT. 3
Seated Woman (with corrections by Henry Moore), 1951/1952
Charcoal, pencil, and wash on vellum paper, 22⅛ x 15 in. (56.2 x 38.2 cm)
D0060
Private collection, London

CAT. 4
Seated Woman (with corrections by Henry Moore), 1951/1952
Pencil and charcoal on vellum paper, 21¾ x 14½ in. (55.3 x 36.9 cm)
D0074
Private collection, London

CAT. 5
Seated Figure (with corrections by Henry Moore), 1951/1952
Charcoal, ink, and wash on vellum paper, 22 x 15 in. (55.8 x 38.1 cm)
D0034
Private collection, London

CAT. 6
Woman with Pot, 1951/1952
Charcoal and wash on vellum paper, 22⅛ x 14¾ in. (56.1 x 37.4 cm)
D0045
Private collection, London

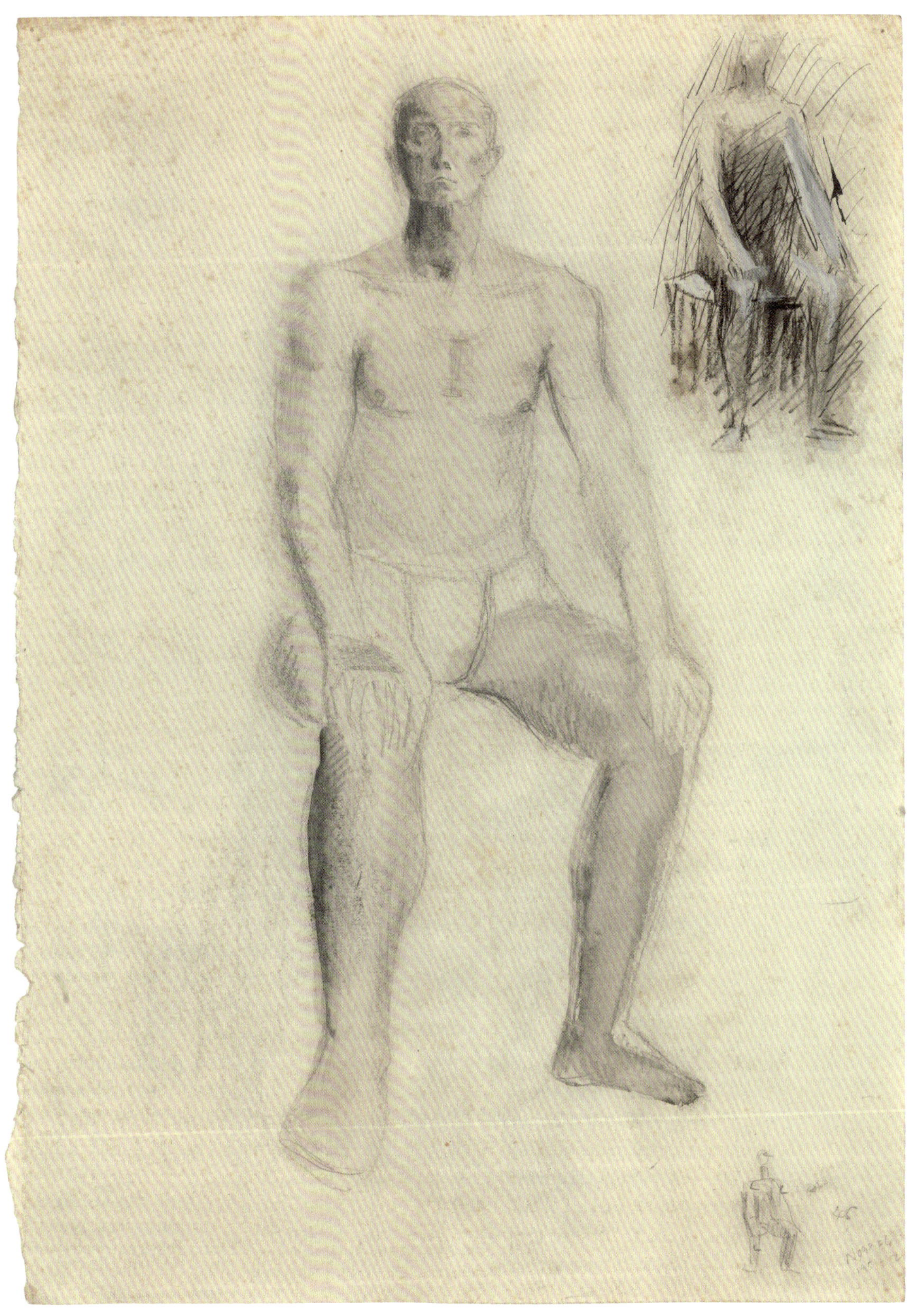

CAT. 1

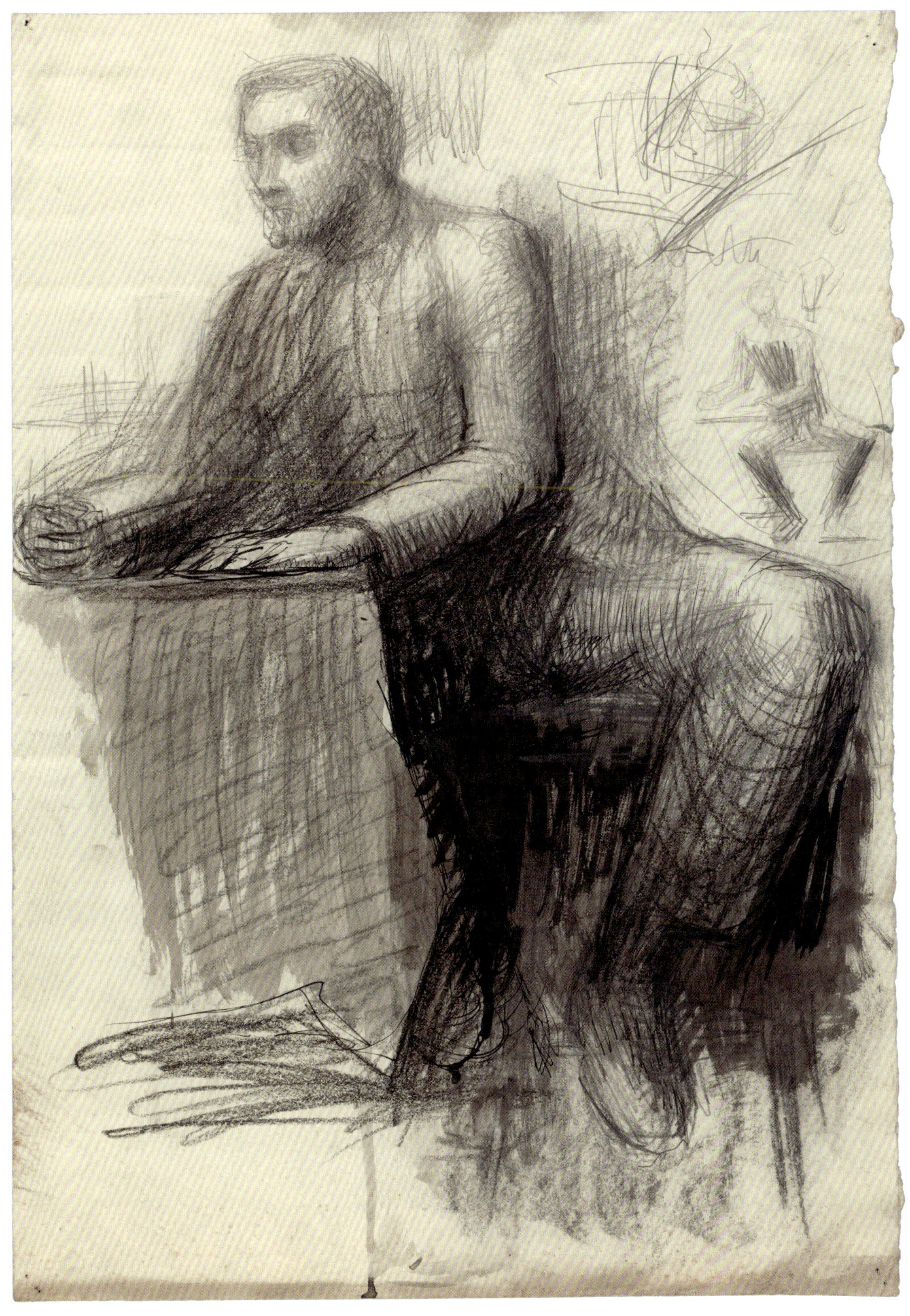

CAT. 2

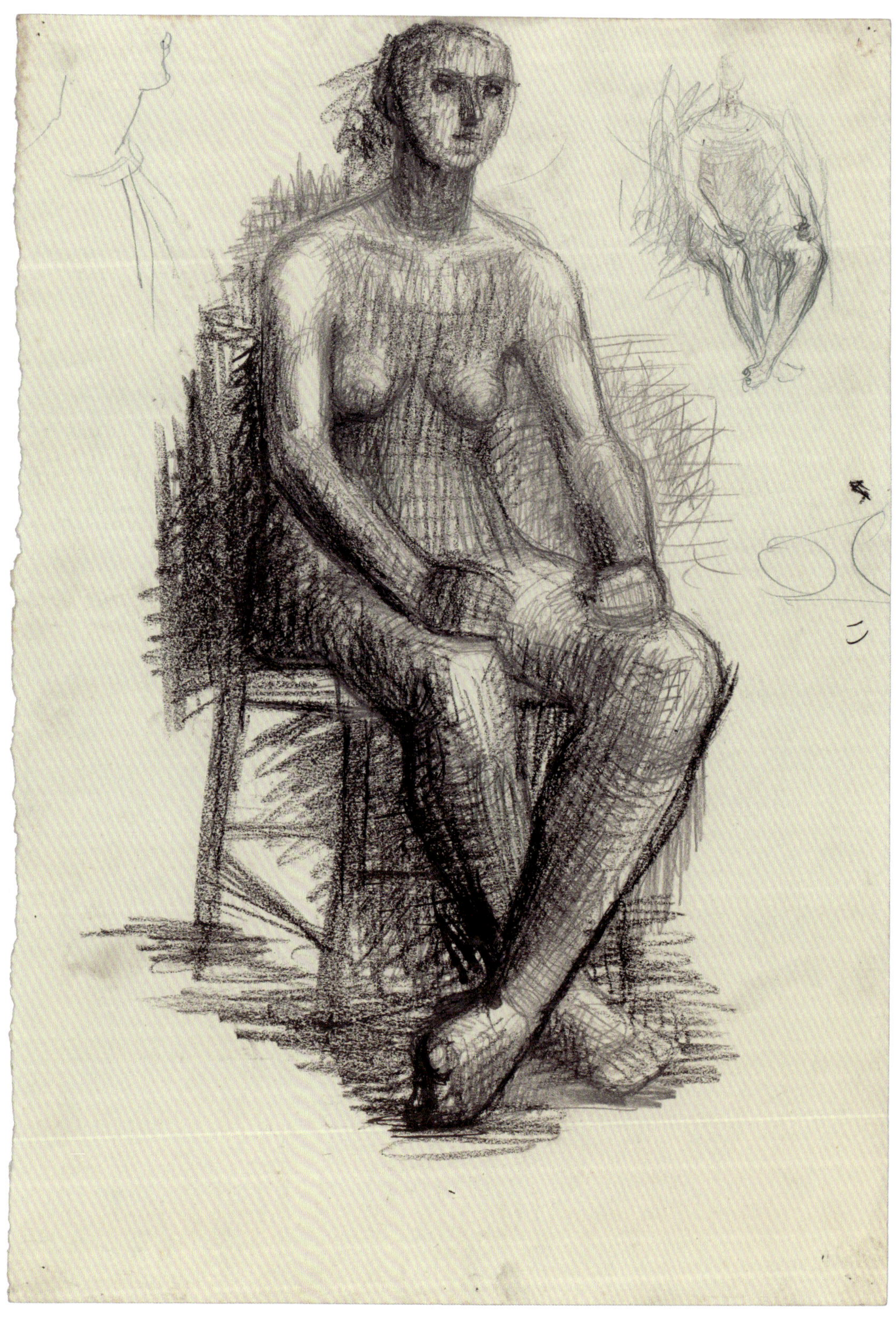

CAT. 3

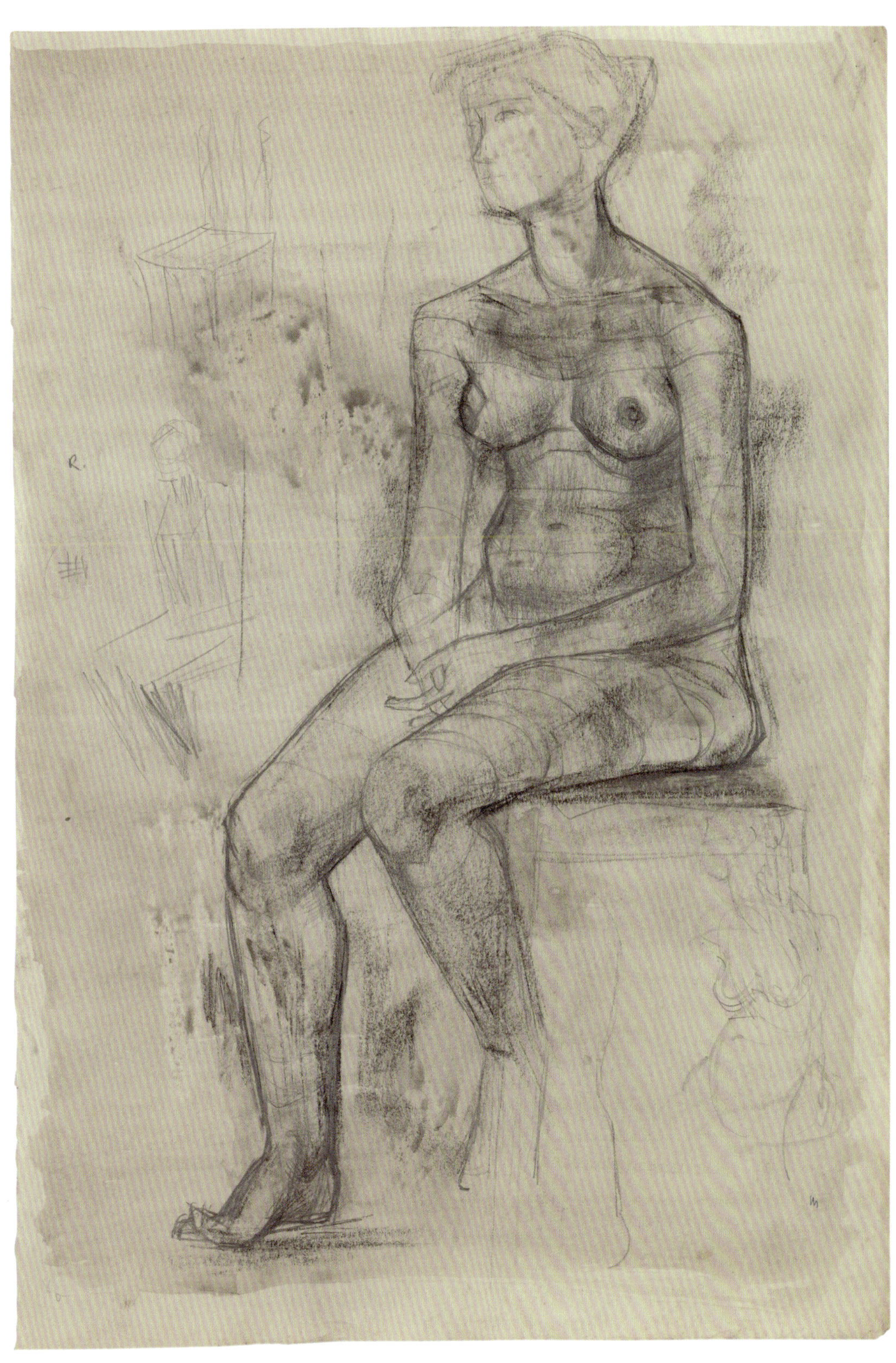

CAT. 4

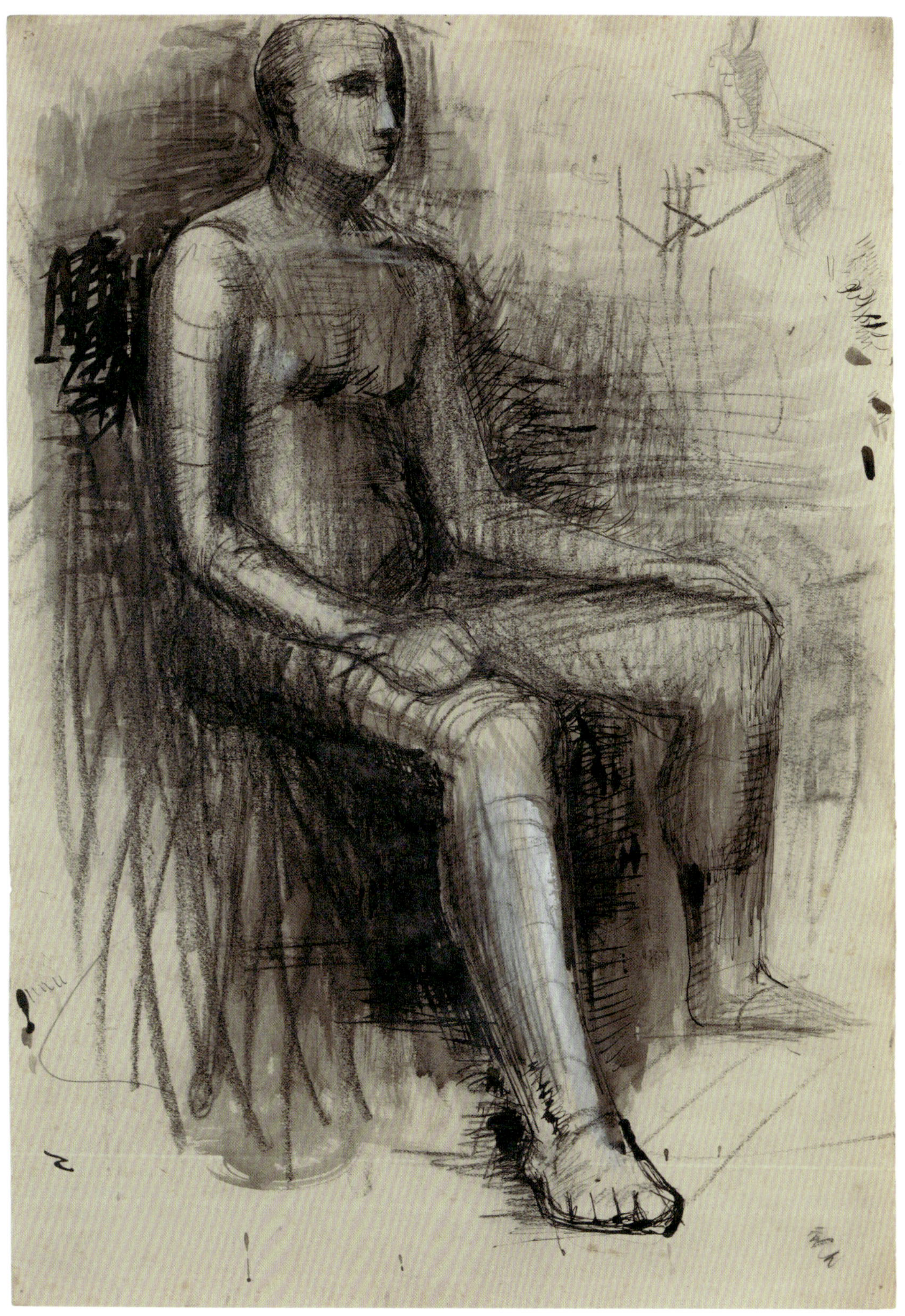

CAT. 5

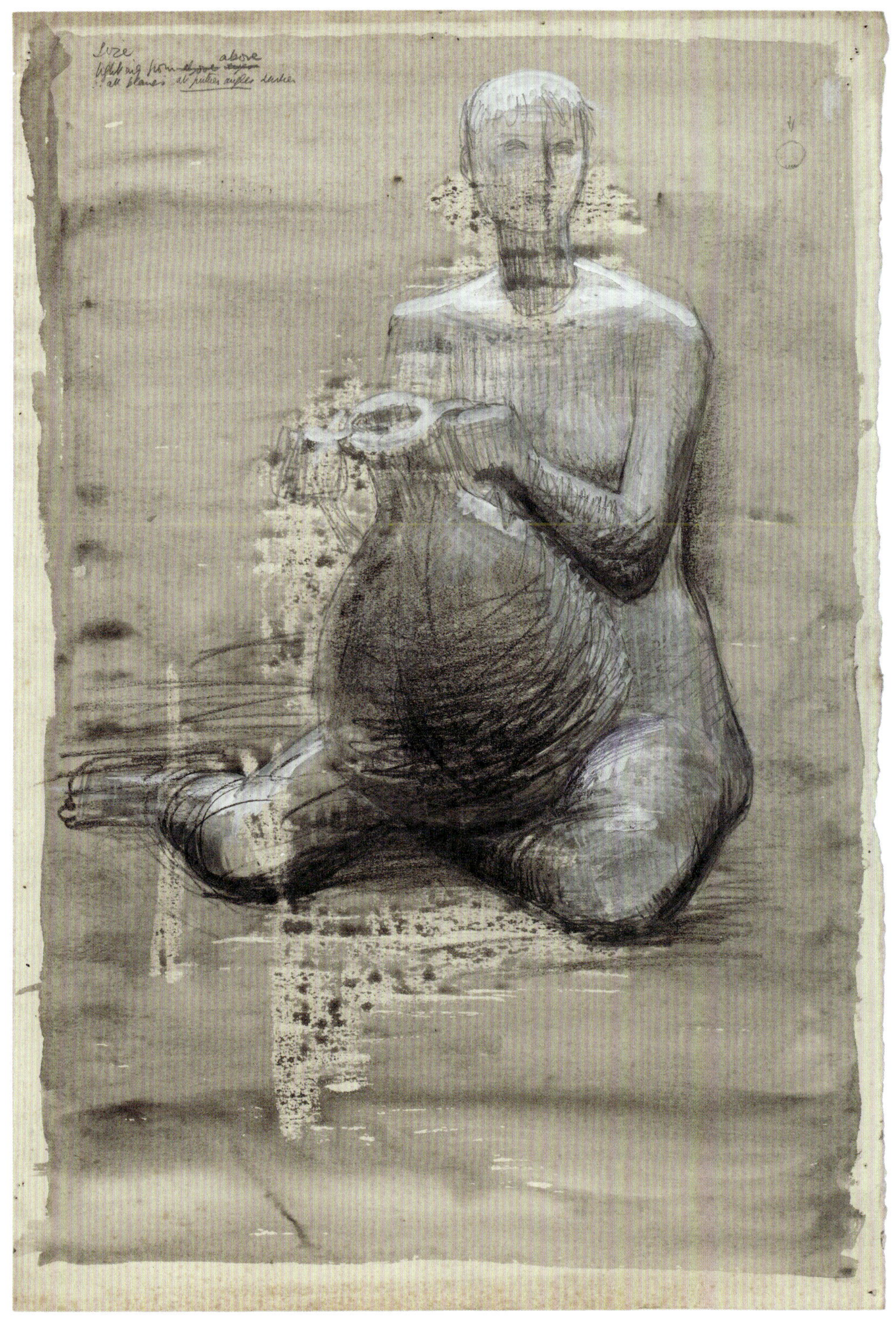

CAT. 6

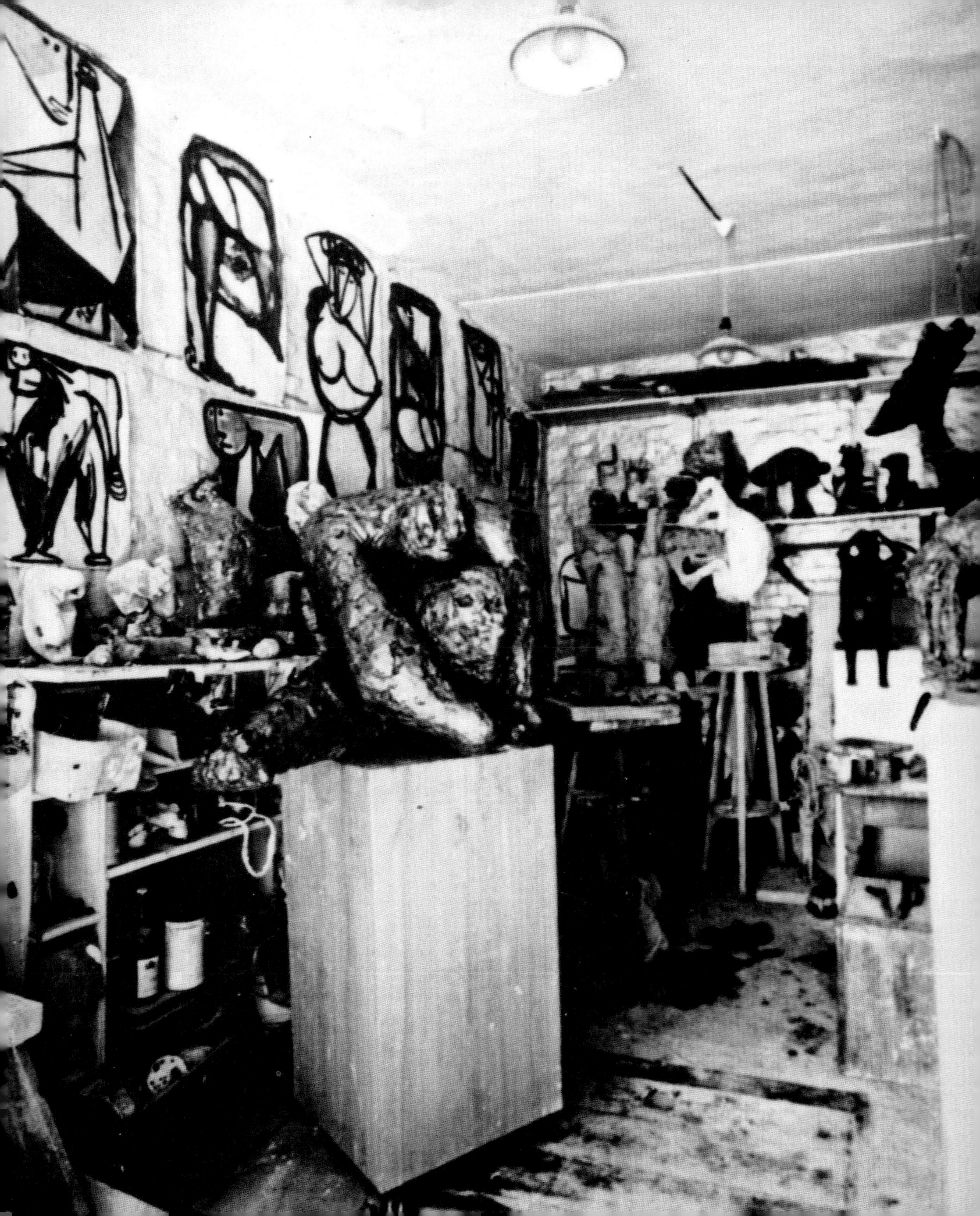

Early Drawings and Bronzes

After the student drawings from the Royal Academy's life-class, the first sign of Caro's ambition to find his own artistic language is a series of drawings of bulls, made in an expressionist idiom during his final months with Moore. Real bulls tethered nearby, and images of bulls and cats by Picasso, of a bird by Elizabeth Frink, and similar works by Reg Butler, Lynn Chadwick, and Eduardo Paolozzi, inspired him. The last sculptures he made while working for Moore in 1953 included small bronzes of aggressive bulls, their heads bowed in anger. Caro recalls the echoes of the advent of the Cold War in the "angst" conveyed by British sculptures shown at the Venice Biennale in 1952, identified ever since as the "Geometry of Fear" group from Herbert Read's catalogue essay.[4] Caro was not part of this group of artists, but with hindsight he can see how he may have been responding to the mood of the times.

More disturbing than the drawings of angry bulls are the ones of men, to which they relate directly. Seen together, they present a creeping metamorphosis—a bull transforming into the Minotaur and then into a screaming man. Caro had been impressed by Francis Bacon's paintings of crouching naked men in barren rooms; a similar sense of frustrated aggression unites the series. The figures share a sense of anxiety, as the men seem to press against the edges of their sheets of paper like caged beings. Like other drawings from this period, of a baby holding a ball, the studies of bulls and confined figures have their counterparts in Caro's sculpture, and represent rare moments when his works on paper and sculptures address the same theme.[5] His practice of making sculptures and drawings in series is traditionally credited to the examples of David Smith and Kenneth Noland (whom he first encountered some years later), but here we see Caro already making sequences of works, perhaps recalling Moore's advice that drawing could be a faster way to work through his ideas.

Caro moved back to London in 1953 when he started teaching at St. Martin's School of Art. In a carefully composed photograph from around 1955 he presents his work to date in his garage studio in Hampstead, arranged almost like a personal exhibition. The walls are lined with works on paper, painted in ink with a brush, some in-filled with color like stained glass windows. Most of these rare examples of Caro's work as a graphic artist or painter survive in his personal collection. While not

Caro's studio at his home in Hampstead, ca. 1955

related to his sculptures in the traditional sense, as "preparatory" works, they nevertheless can be seen as exploring the same themes. They are painted on cheap paper with speed and intensity, in the same passionate and provocative way that he is known to have taught life-drawing to sculpture students at St. Martin's. Not only a sense of Cold War angst, but also perhaps of the ambition to break free from the dominant influences of his long training, pervade this "caged figure" series.

The photograph of Caro's small garage studio also depicts two sculptures exhibited in 1955, in *New Sculptors and Painter-Sculptors* at the Institute of Contemporary Arts, the first group show in which Caro took part. The sculptures attracted interest from the critics, including Basil Taylor and David Sylvester. *Man Holding His Foot* (cat. 21), the first sculpture that Caro made in London, was singled out for praise. Sylvester wrote that it revealed, "besides the influence of Picasso and Henry Moore, a sheer sculptural power indicative of rare promise."[6] It clearly relates to his drawings of the same subject. From the same year, *Woman Waking Up* (cat. 24) explores a similar expressionist use of exaggeration to convey "what it is like to be inside the body," when gravity seems to press you down.[7] Like the bronze *Baby with a Ball* (cat. 23), it is a cast collage of found objects and follows the example of Moore and Picasso. But in technique, form, subject, and surface it is clearly the work of an artist struggling to find his own expressive language for sculpture.

CAT. 7 (overleaf)
***Bull*, 1953/1954**
Brush, ink, and pastel on newsprint paper, 18⅛ x 23⅛ in. (46 x 58.7 cm)
D0173
Private collection, London

CAT. 8 (second spread)
***Bull*, 1954**
Brush, ink, and chalk on newsprint paper, 18⅛ x 23⅛ in. (45.9 x 58.6 cm)
D0189
Private collection, London

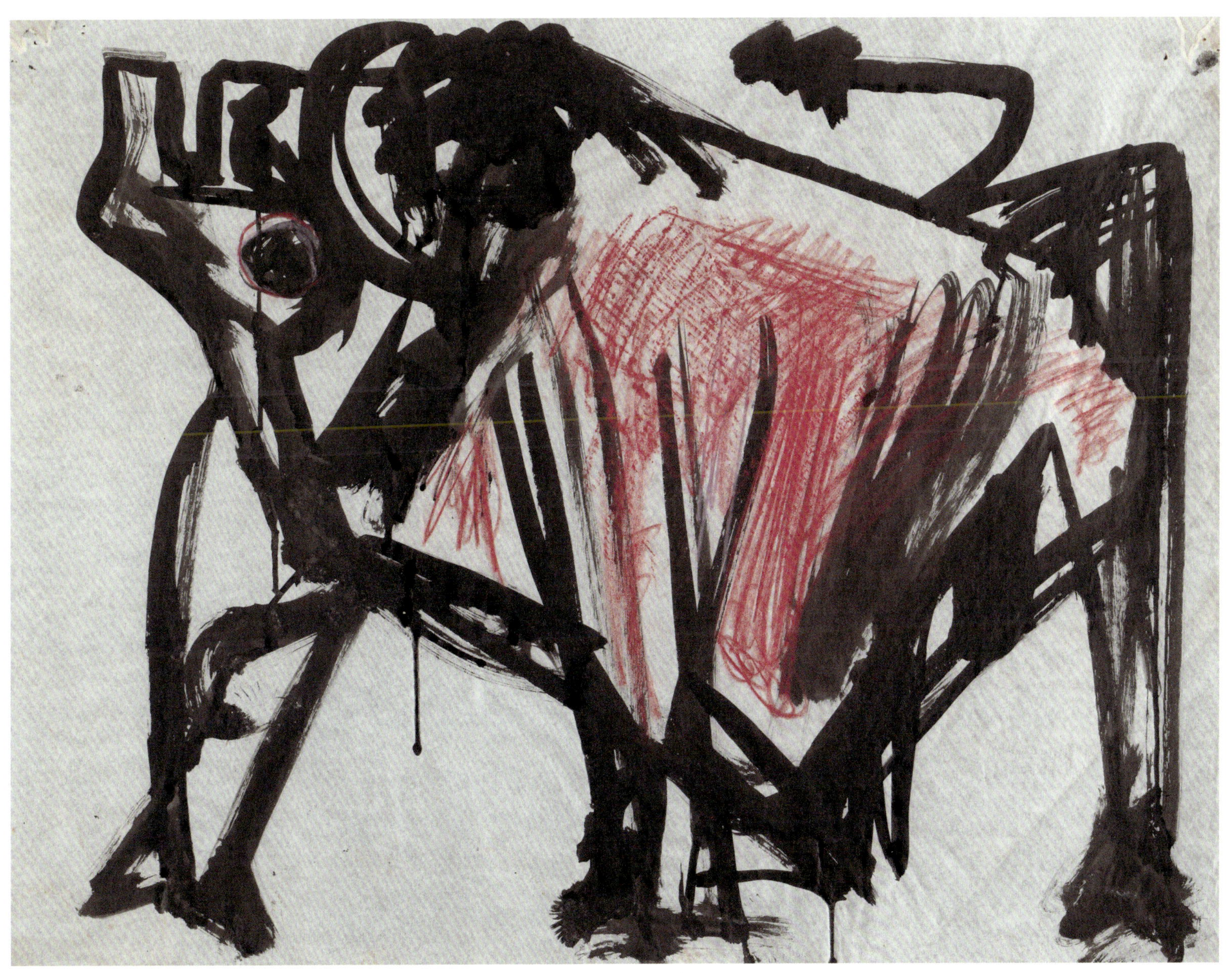

CAT. 7

CAT. 8

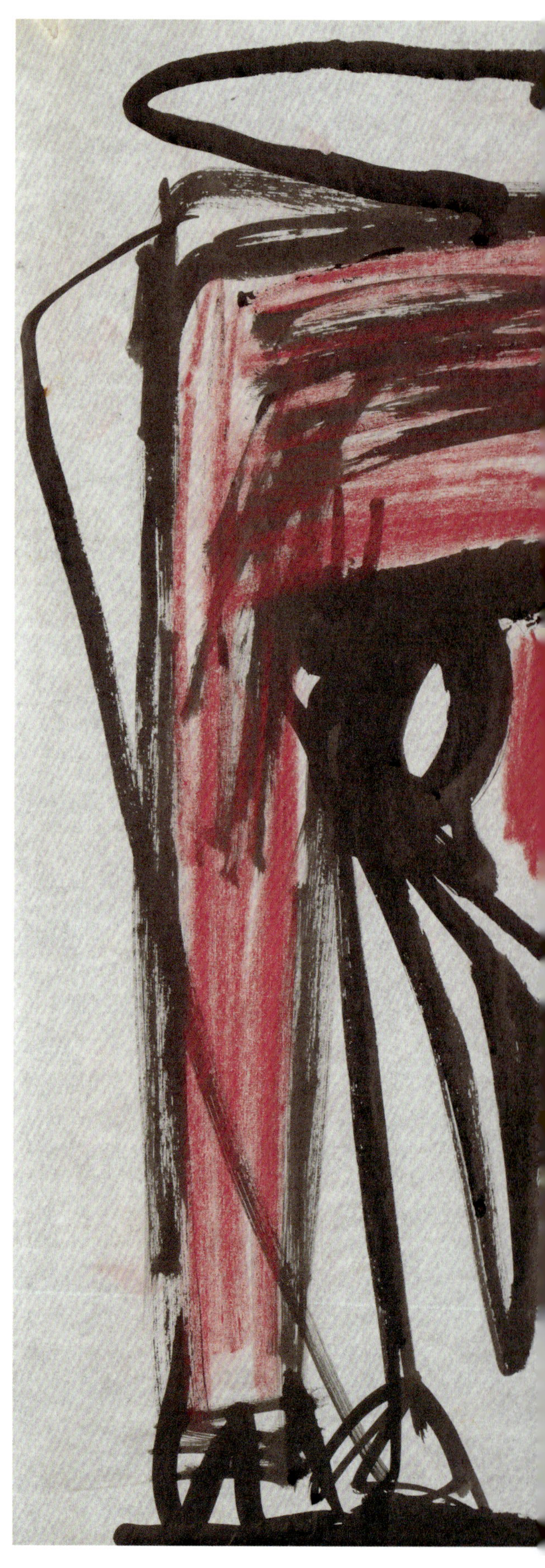

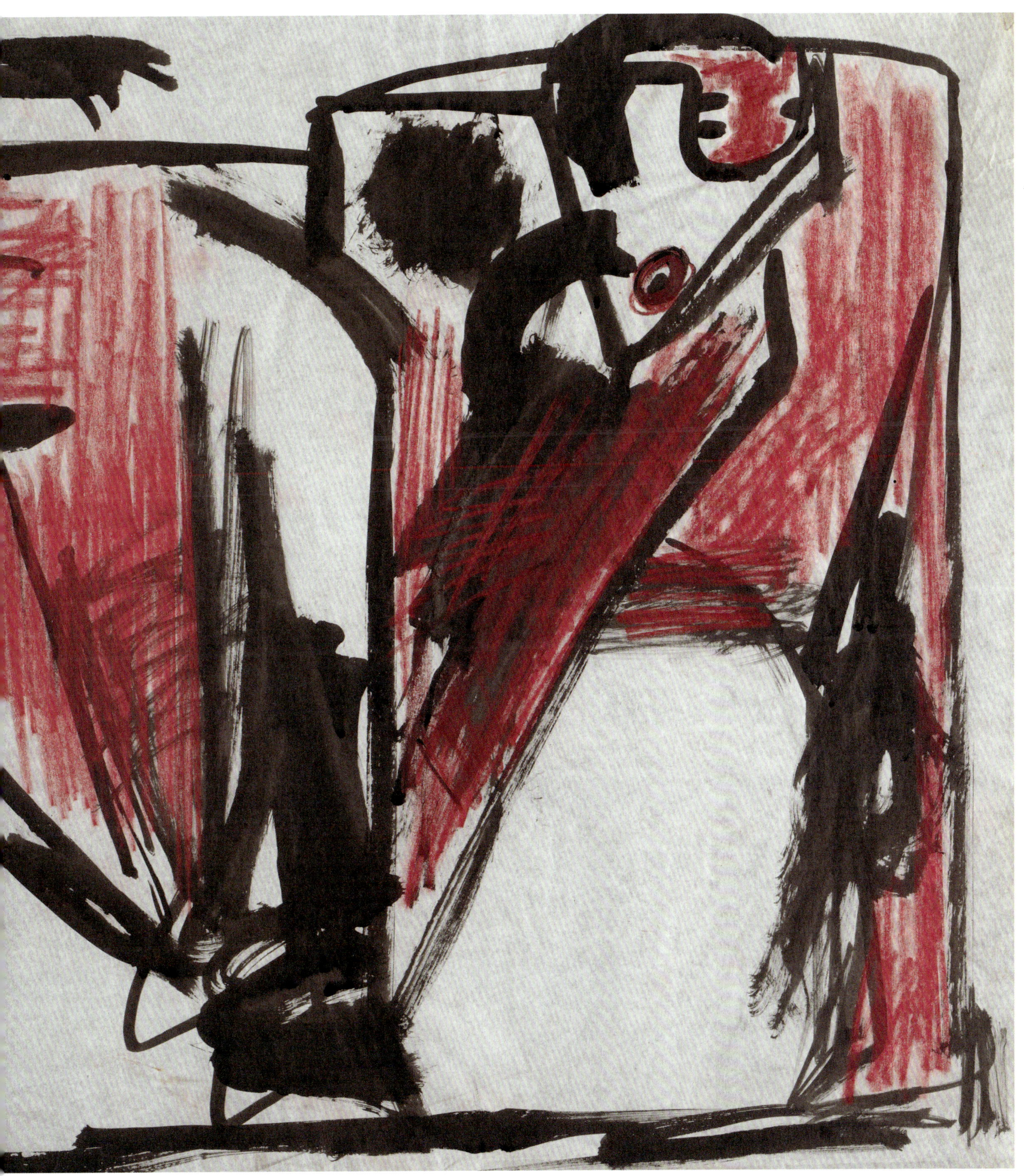

CAT. 9 (facing page)
***Bull*, 1954**
Brush and ink on newsprint paper, 18⅛ x 23⅛ in. (46 x 58.7 cm)
D0190
Private collection, London

CAT. 10 (overleaf, left)
***Bull*, 1954**
Brush and ink on newsprint paper, 18 x 23⅛ in. (45.5 x 58.6 cm)
D0194
Private collection, London

CAT. 11 (overleaf, right)
***Figure*, 1954**
Brush and ink on newsprint paper, 18 x 23⅛ in. (45.6 x 58.6 cm)
D0205
Private collection, London

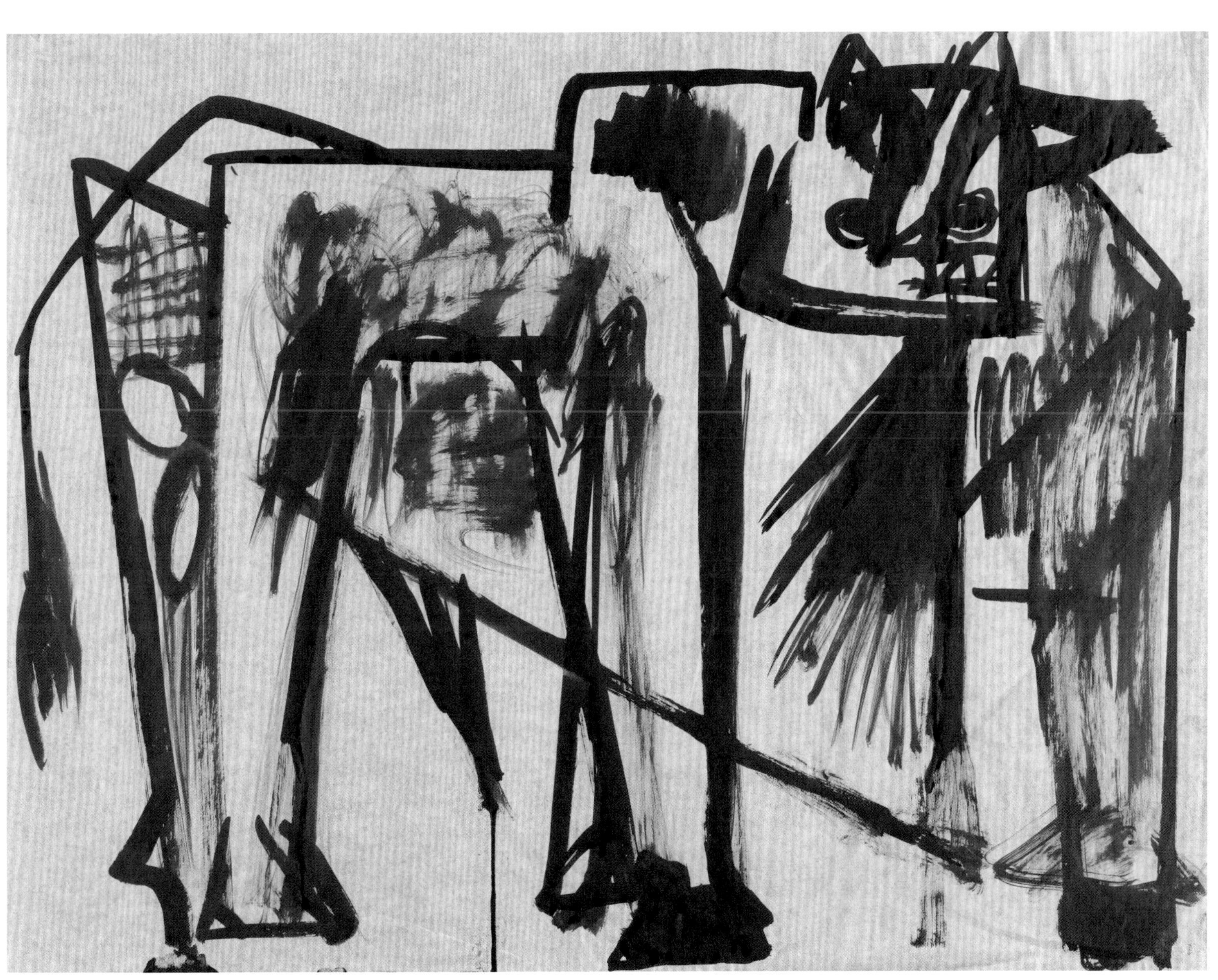

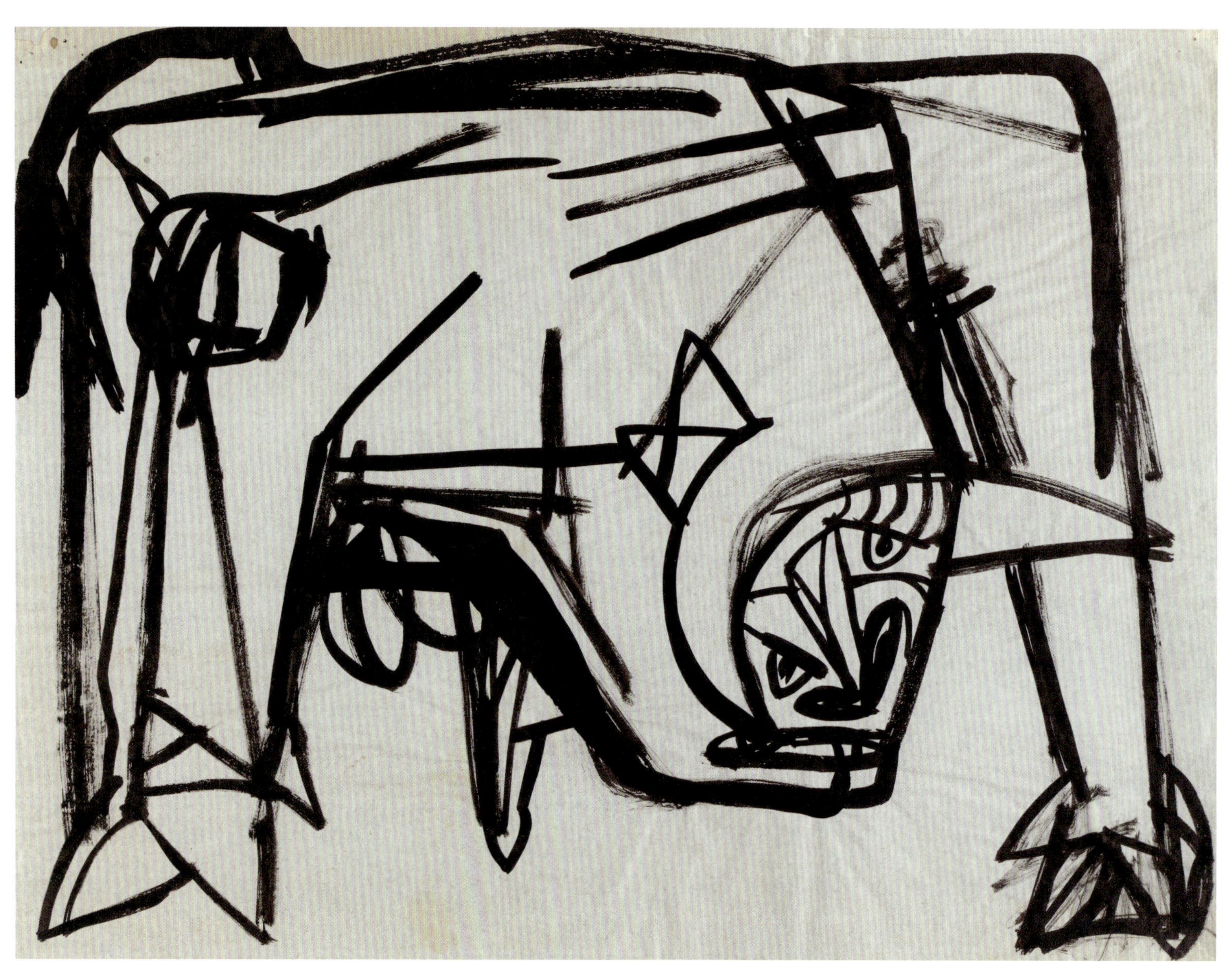

CAT. 10

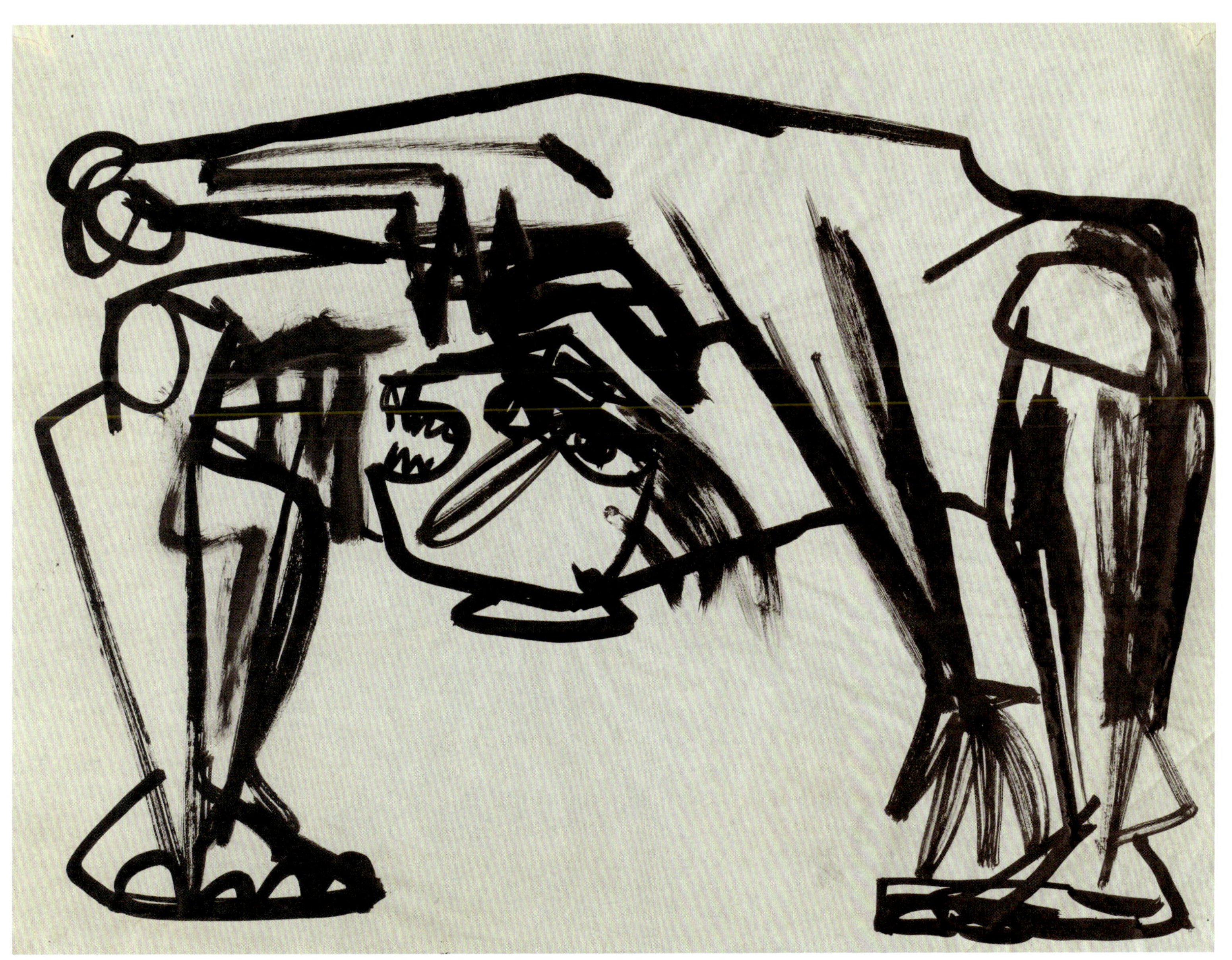

CAT. 11

CAT. 12 (facing page)
Figure Kneeling, 1954
Brush and ink on newsprint paper, 18 x 23 in. (45.6 x 58.5 cm)
D0201
Private collection, London

CAT. 13 (overleaf, left)
Seated Figure, 1954
Brush and ink on newsprint paper, 21⅛ x 16½ in. (53.6 x 41.7 cm)
D0214
Private collection, London

CAT. 14 (overleaf, right)
Figure, 1954
Brush and ink on newsprint paper, 21 x 16½ in. (53.4 x 41.6 cm)
D0216
Private collection, London

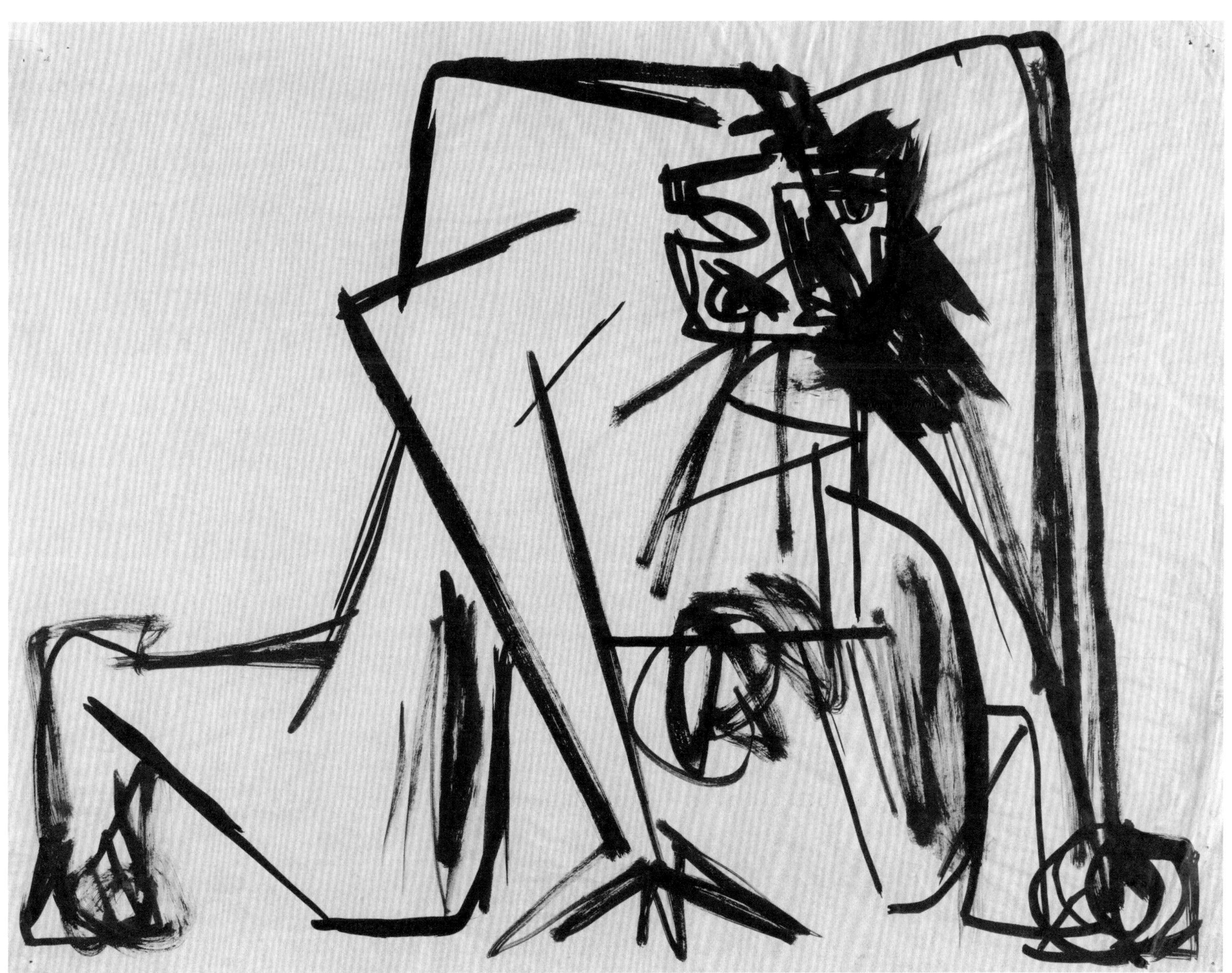

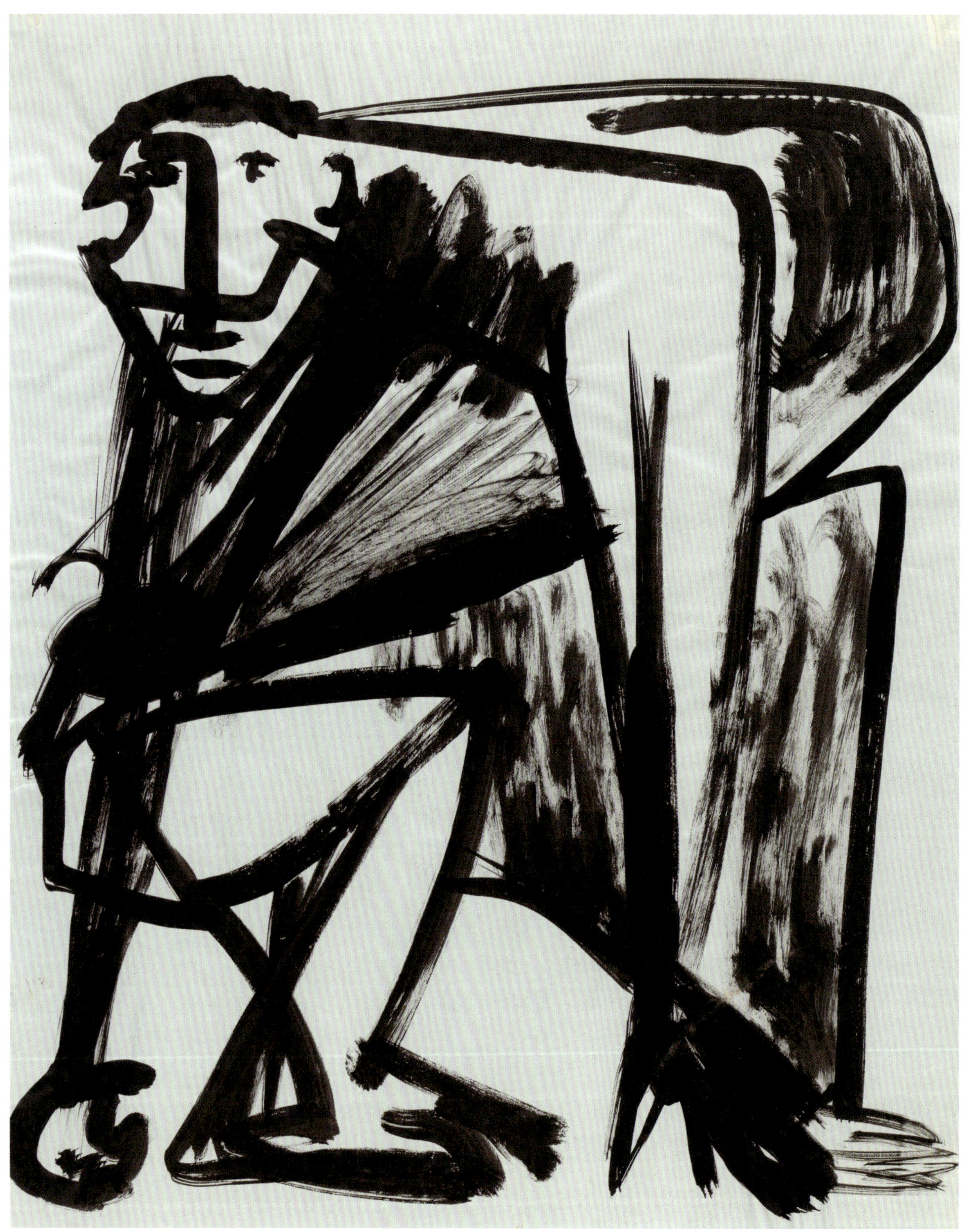

CAT. 13

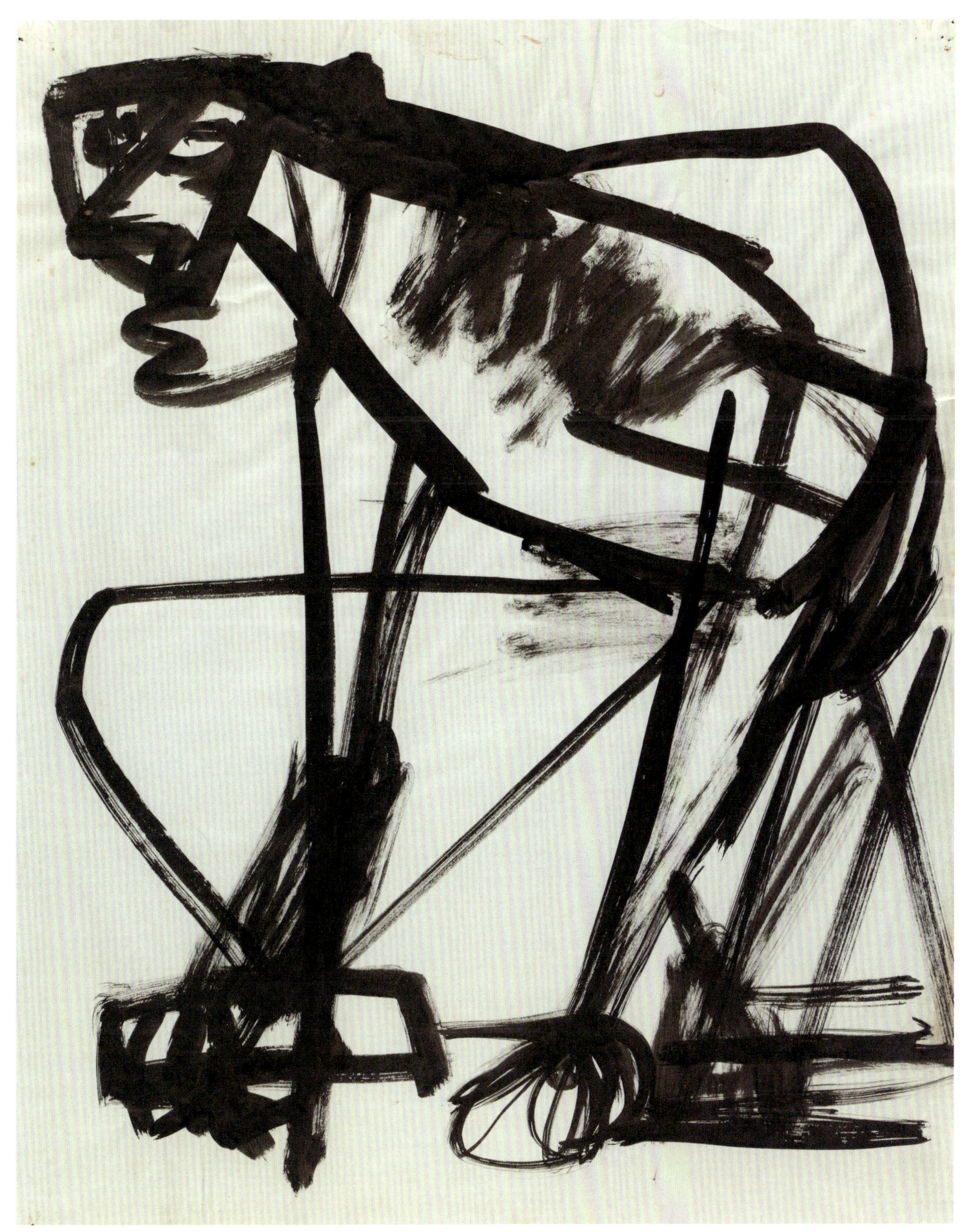

CAT. 14

CAT. 15 (facing page)
Figure, 1955/1956
Brush and ink on newsprint paper, 23 x 18 in. (58.5 x 45.5 cm)
D0248
Private collection, London

CAT. 16 (overleaf, left)
Baby with a Ball, 1954
Brush and ink on newsprint paper, 23½ x 18 in. (58.6 x 45.8 cm)
D0222
Private collection, London

CAT. 17 (overleaf, right)
Baby with a Ball, 1954
Brush and ink on newsprint paper, 23 x 18 in. (58.5 x 45.7 cm)
D0225
Private collection, London

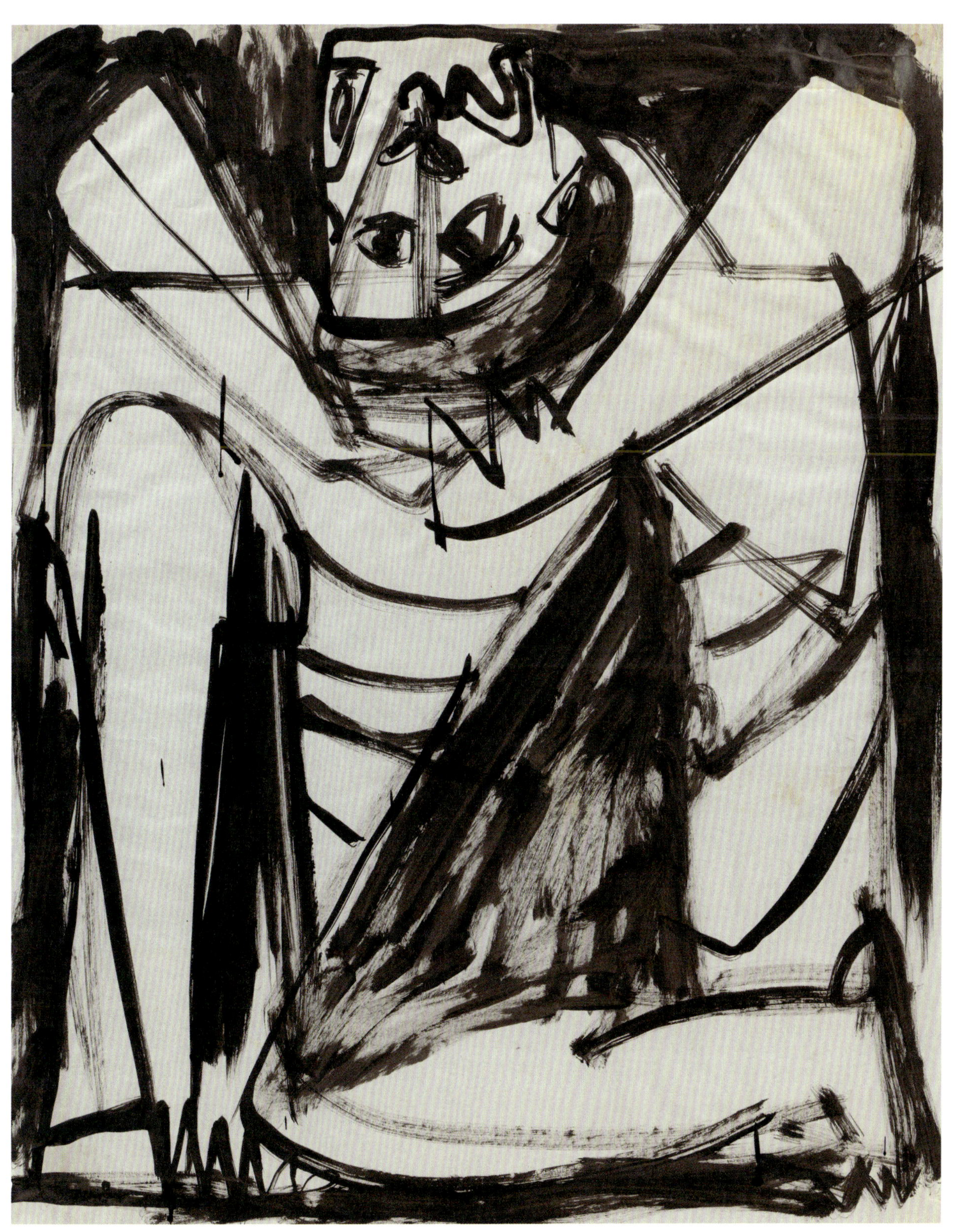

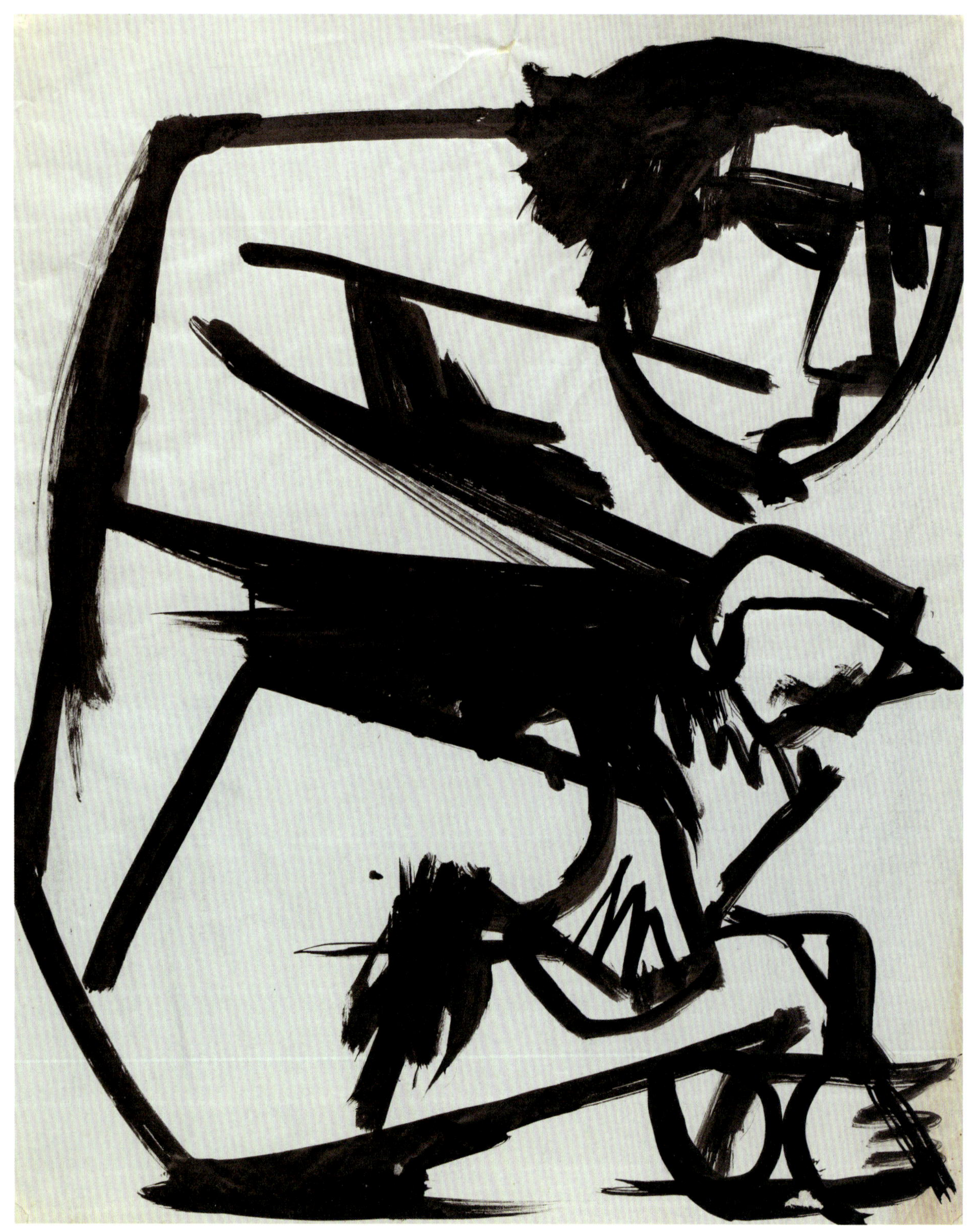

CAT. 16

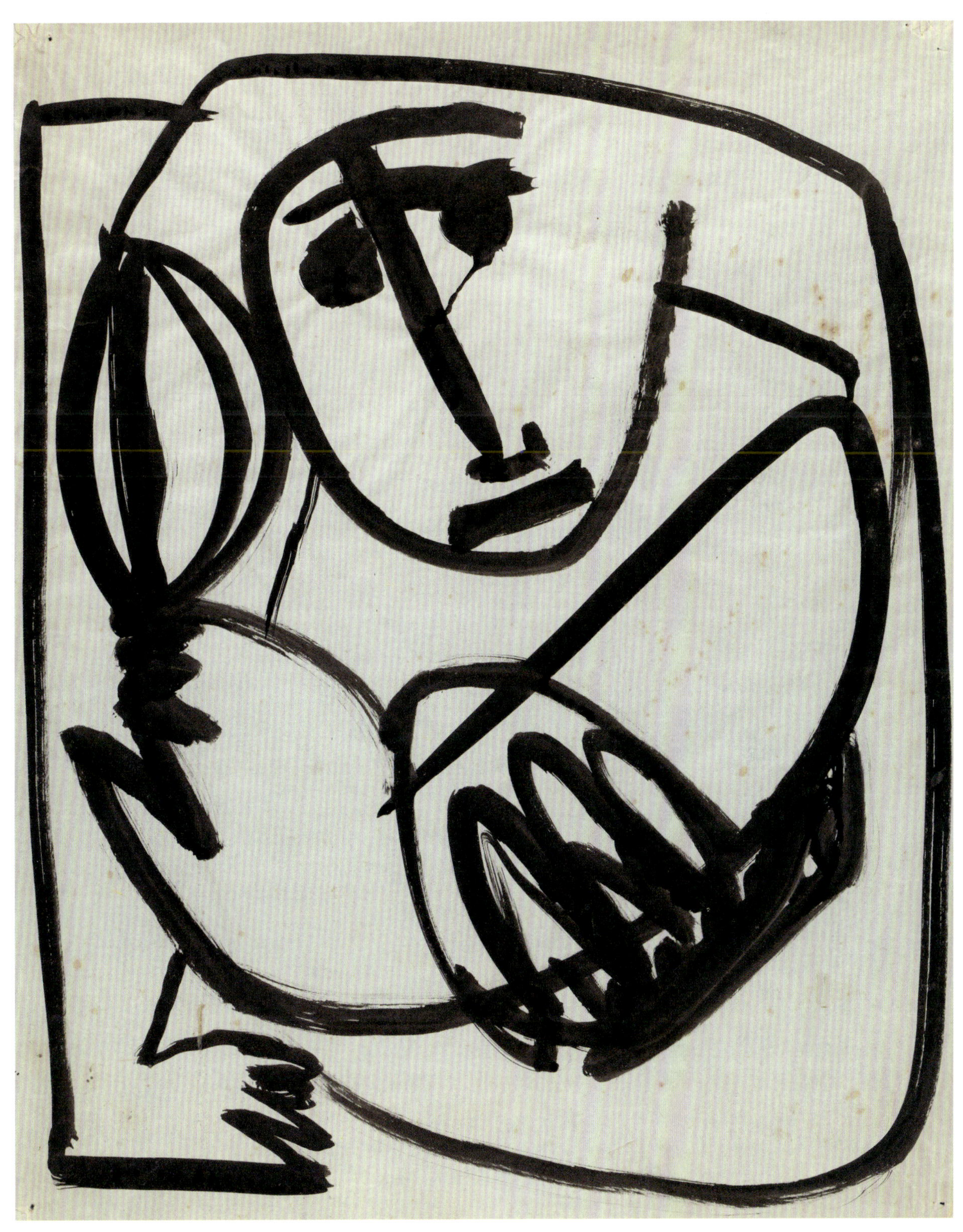

CAT. 17

CAT. 18 (facing page)
Figure, 1955/1956
Brush, ink, and paint on newsprint paper, 32¾ x 20¾ in. (83.4 x 52.9 cm)
D0247
Private collection, London

CAT. 19 (overleaf, left)
Warrior, 1955/1956
Brush, ink, and paint on newsprint paper, 32¾ x 20¾ in. (83.3 x 52.9 cm)
D0251
Private collection, London

CAT. 20 (overleaf, right)
Figure, 1955/1956
Brush, ink, and paint on newsprint paper, 33 x 21 in. (83.8 x 53.3 cm)
D0246
Private collection, London

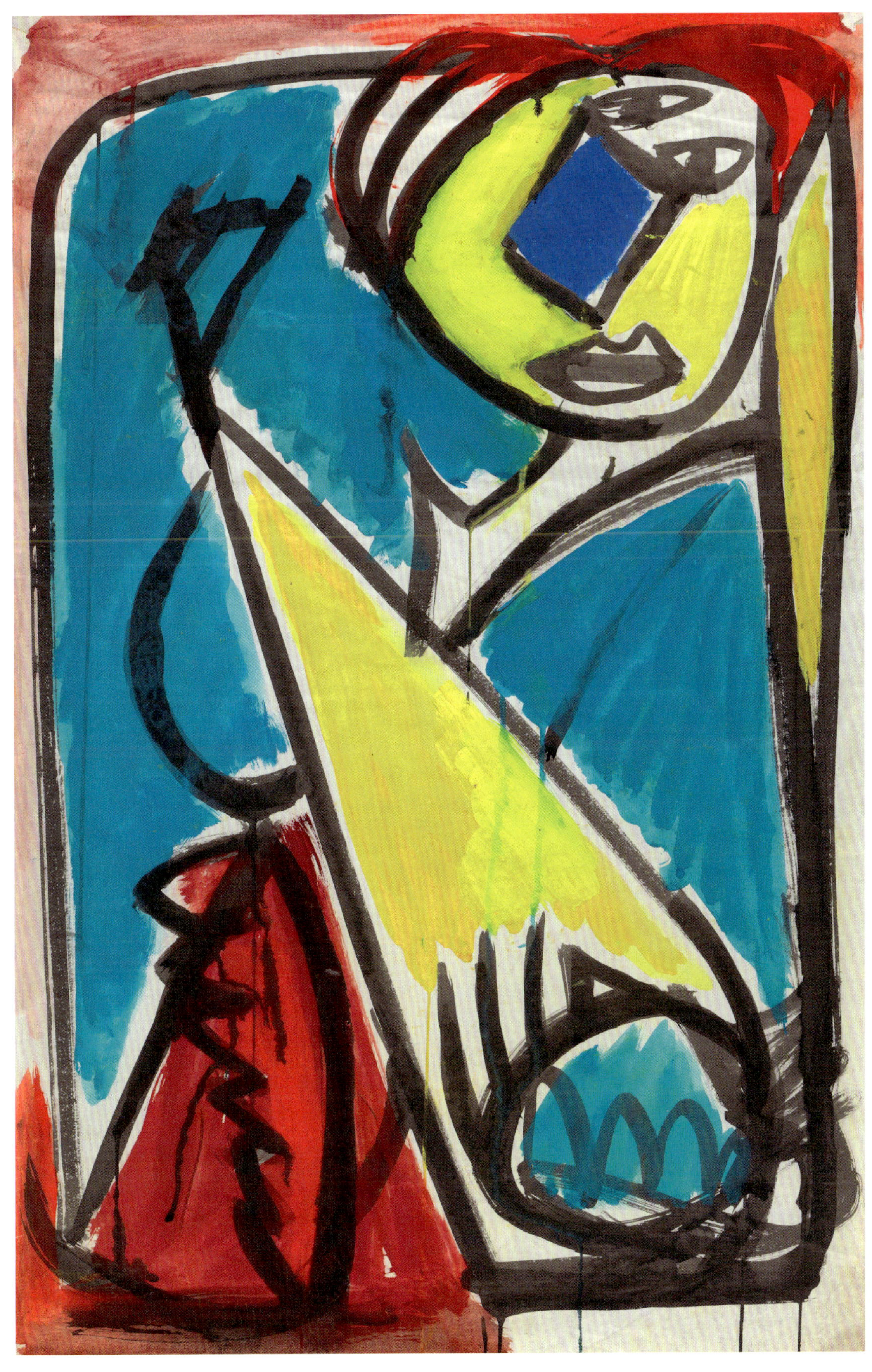

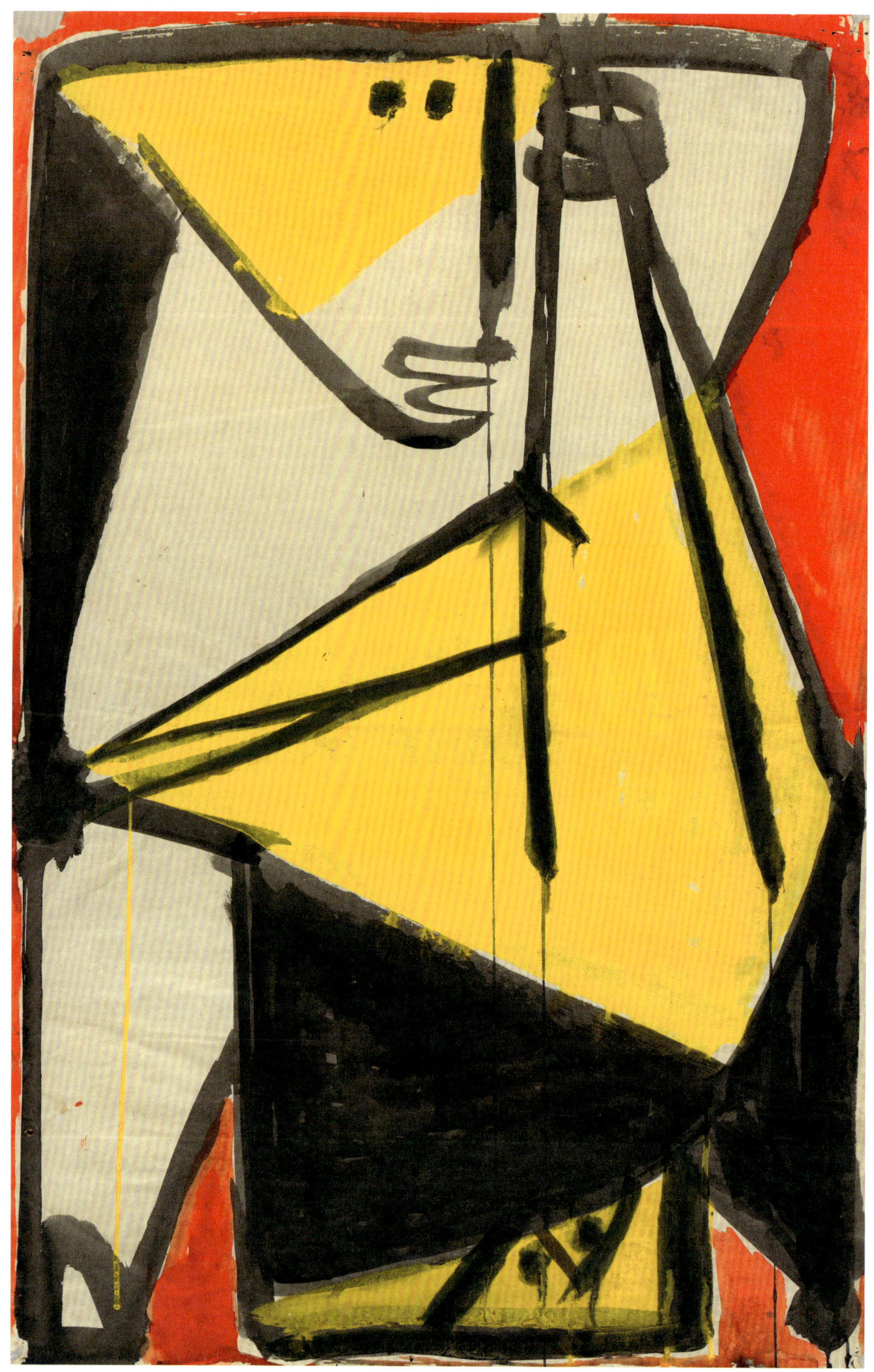

CAT. 19

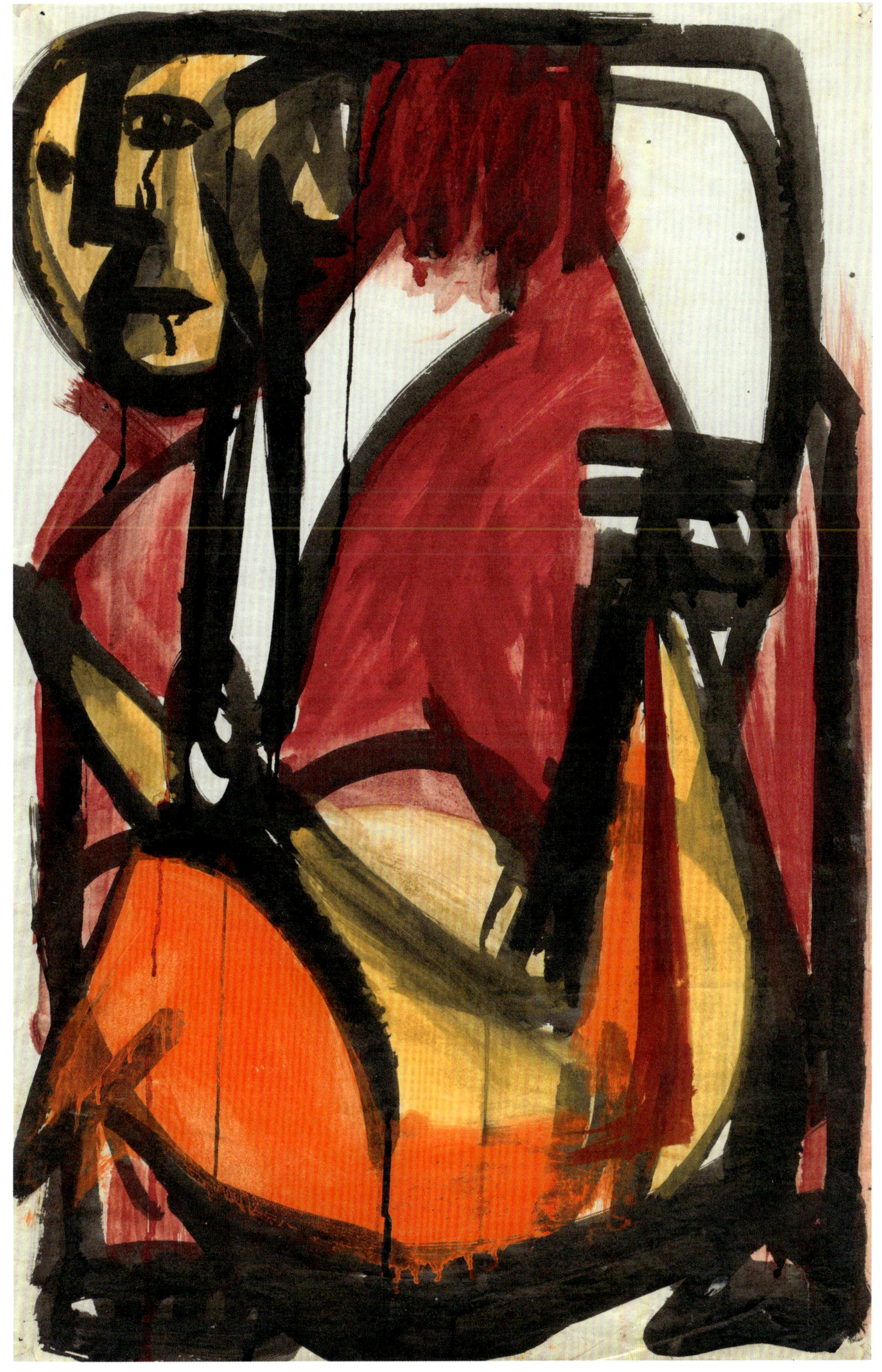

CAT. 20

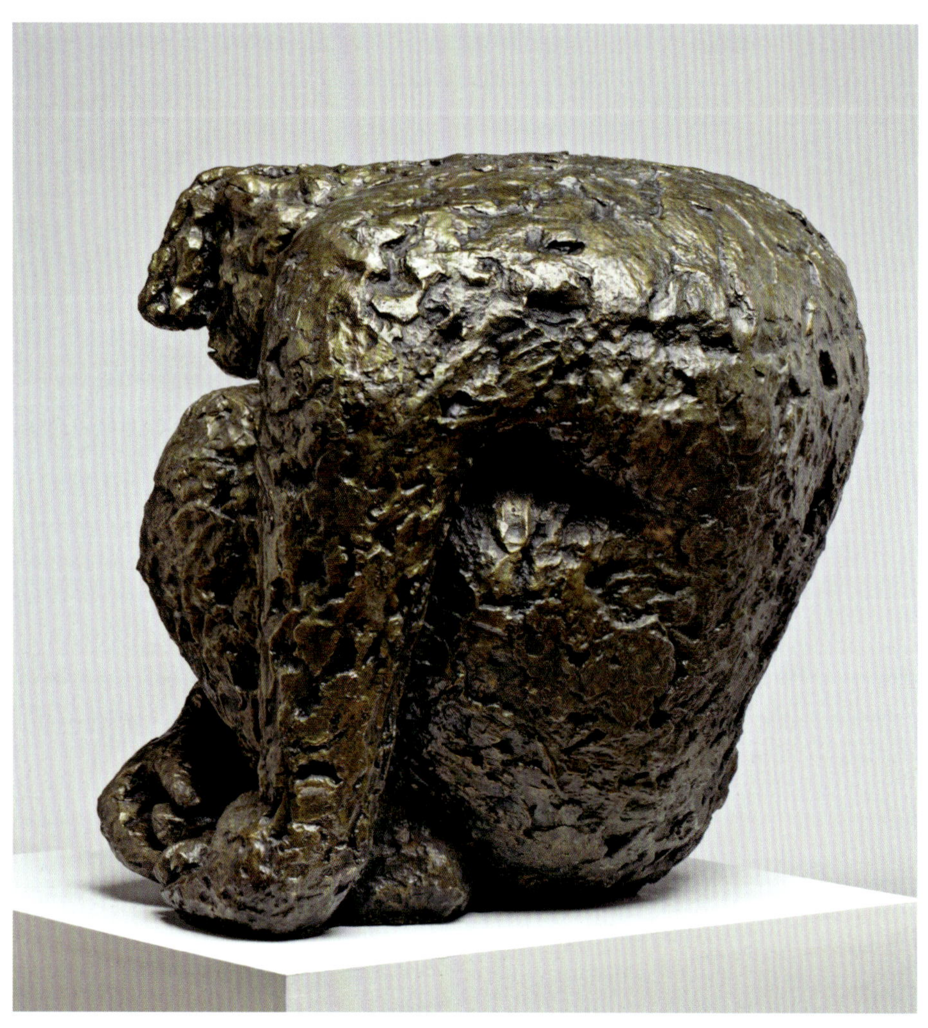

CAT. 21

***Man Holding His Foot*, 1954**

Bronze, height: 26½ in. (67.3 cm)

A0053

Private collection, London

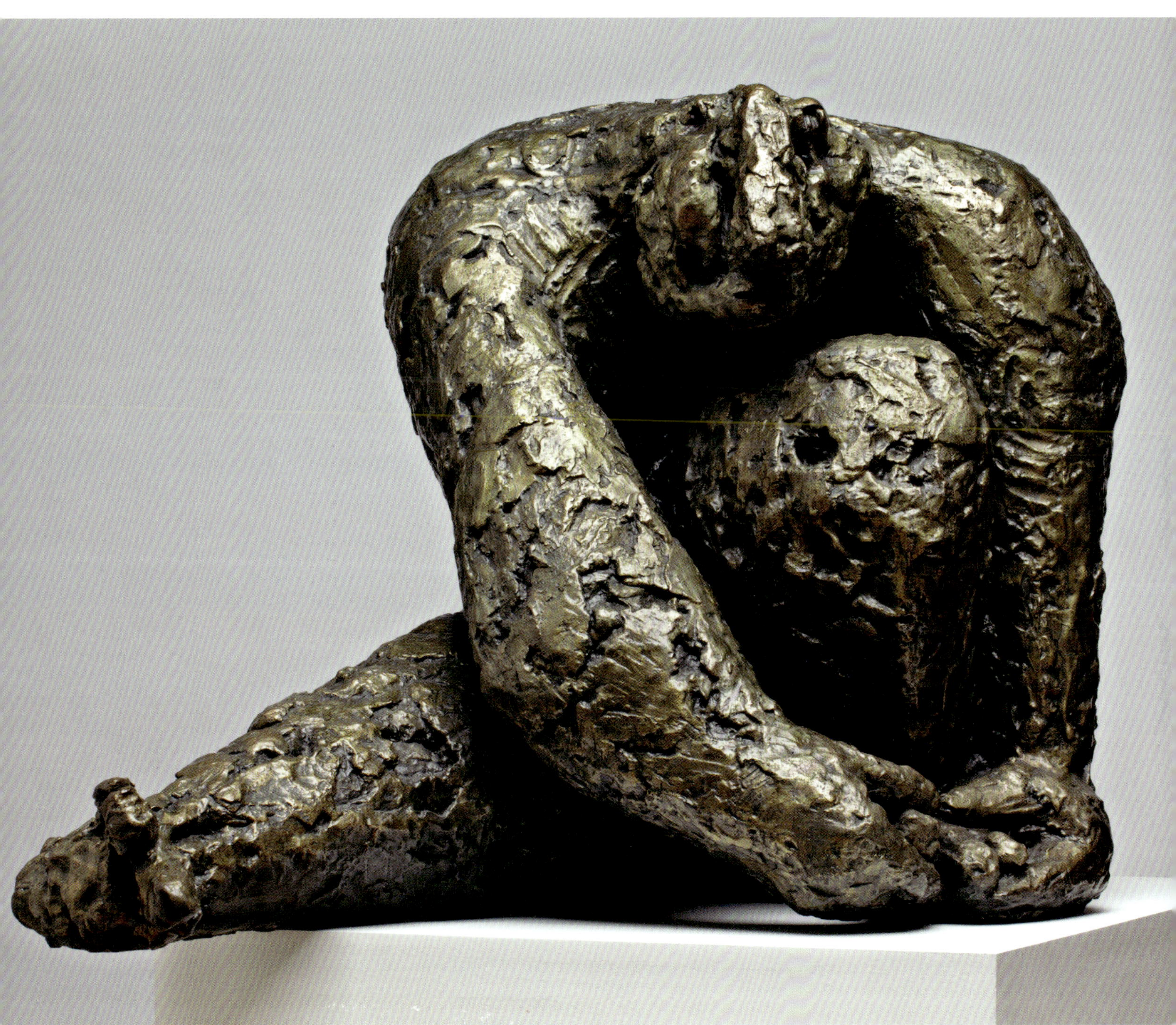

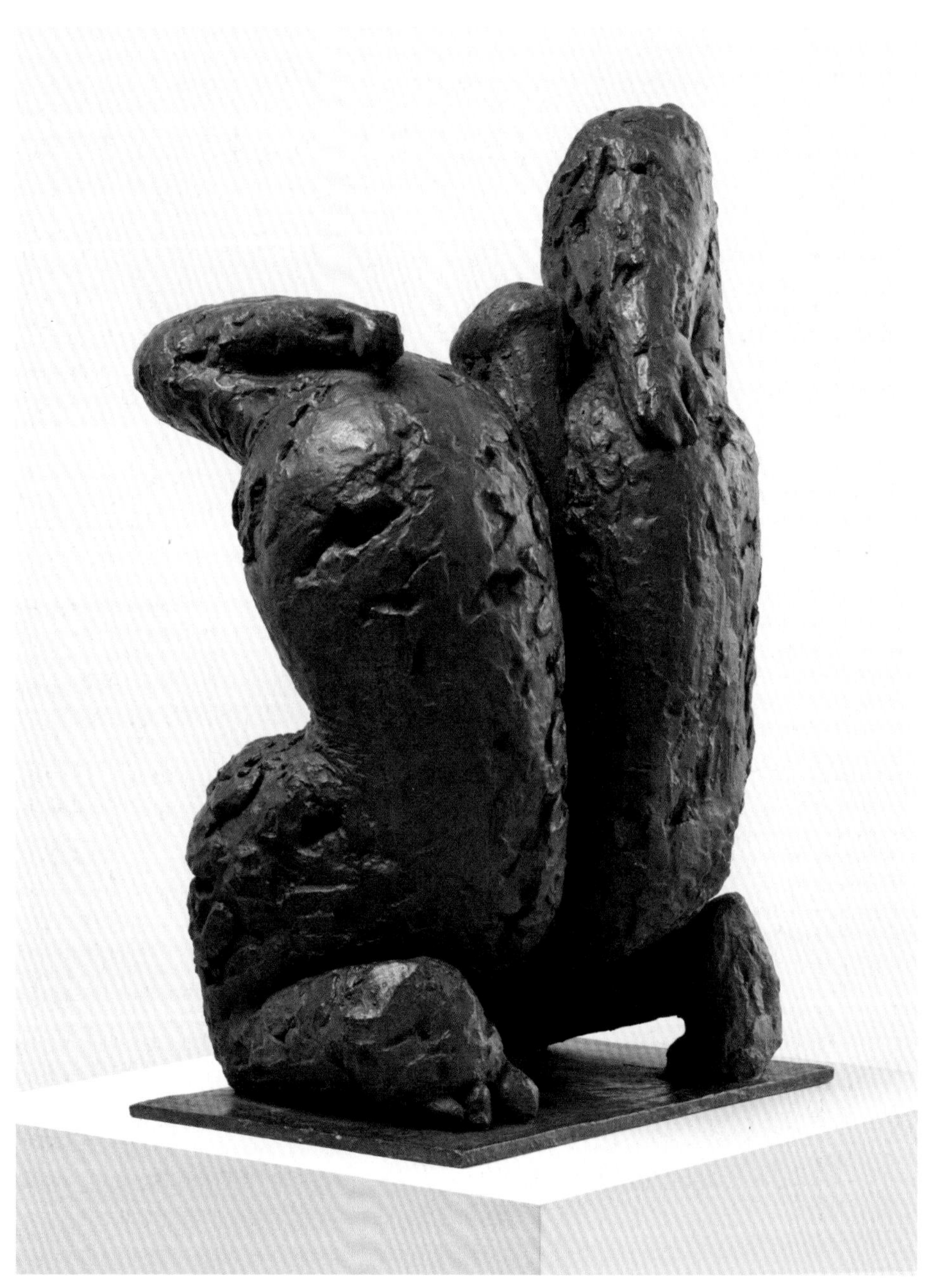

CAT. 22
Man Taking Off His Shirt, 1955/1956
Bronze, 31 x 18¼ x 18½ in. (78.7 x 46 x 47 cm)
A0069
Mr. and Mrs. Phillip King

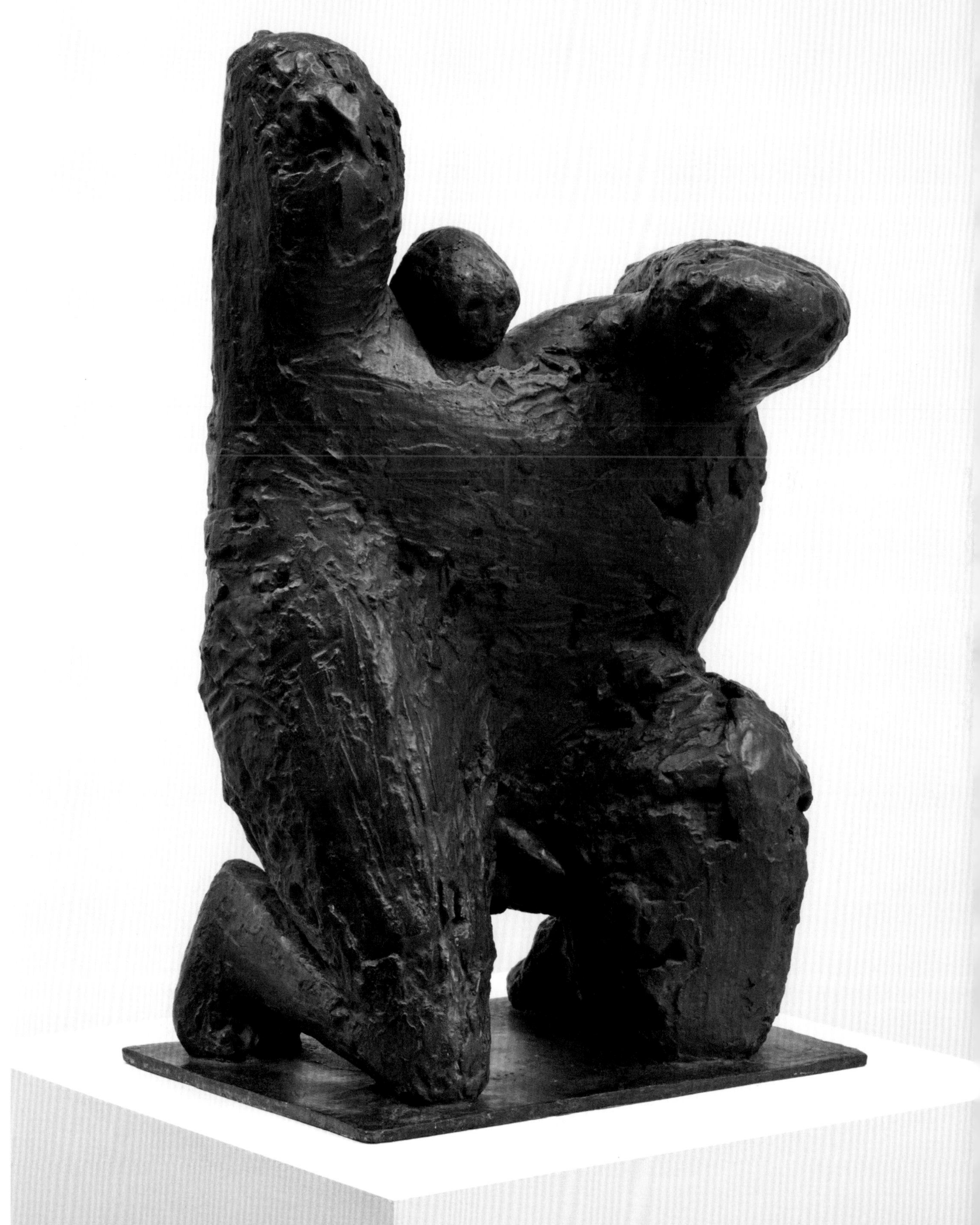

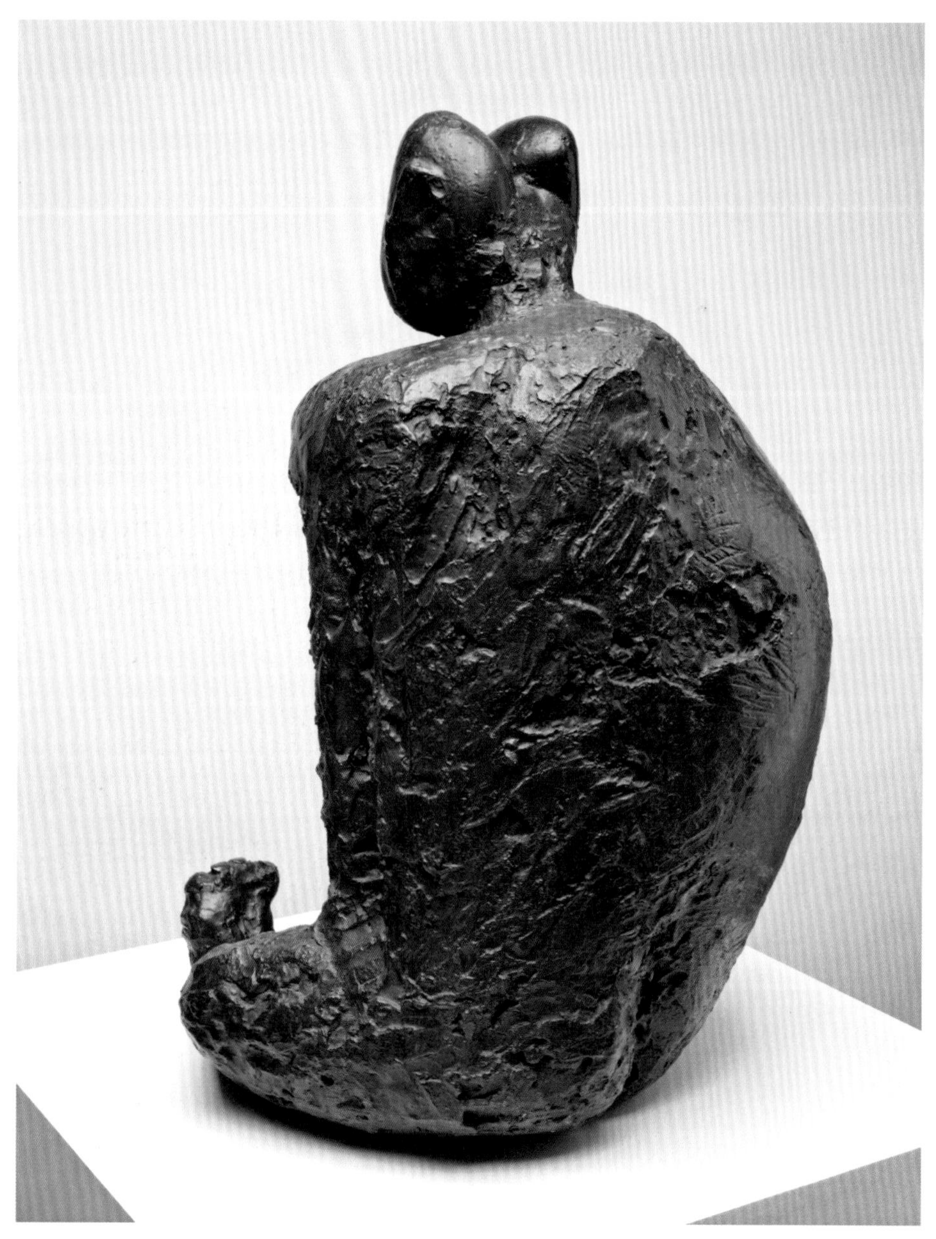

CAT. 23

Baby with a Ball, 1955

Bronze, 30 x 18⅞ x 20½ in. (76 x 48 x 52 cm)

A0060

Private collection, London

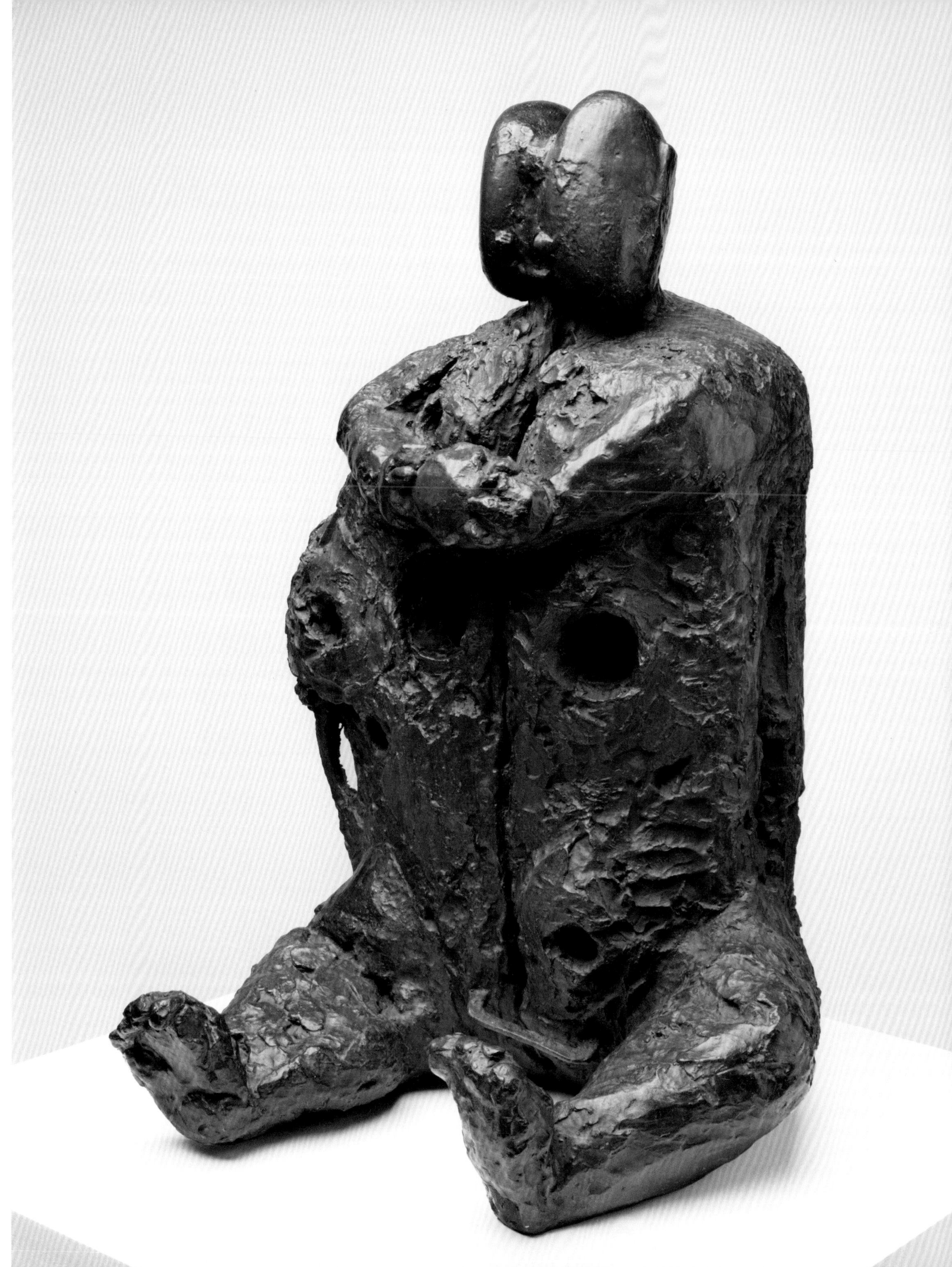

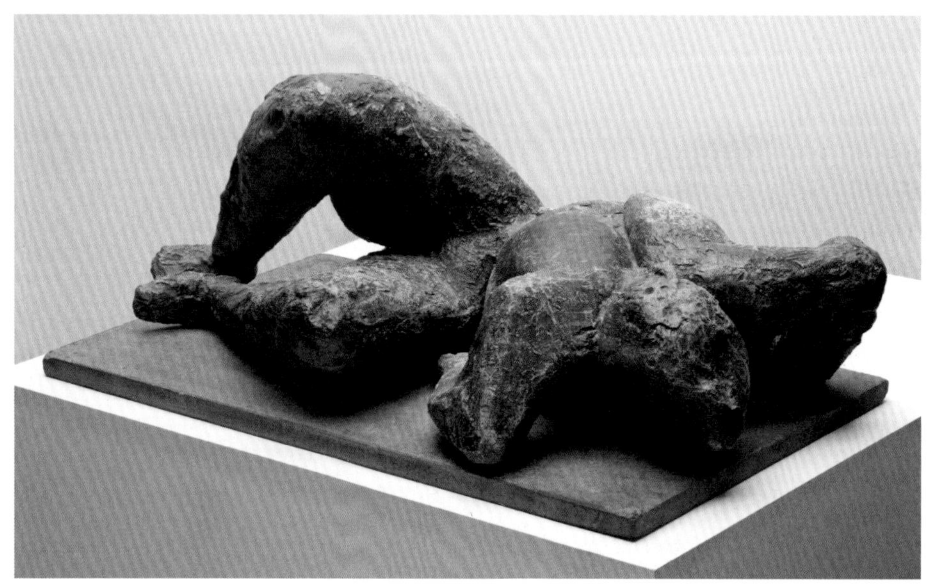

CAT. 24
Woman Waking Up, 1955
Lead, 12 x 26 x 15 in. (26.7 x 67.9 x 34.9 cm)
A0067
Private collection, London

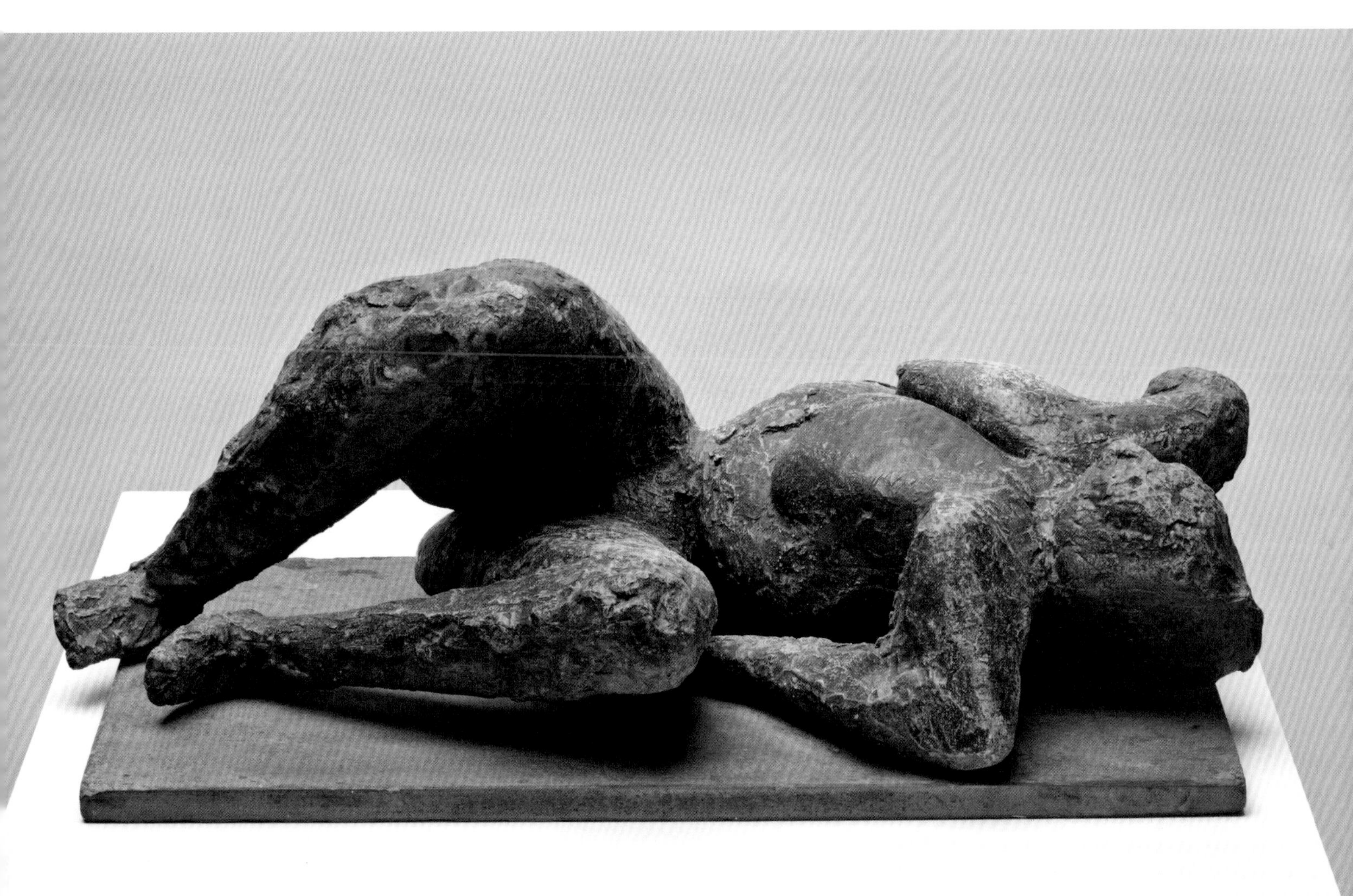

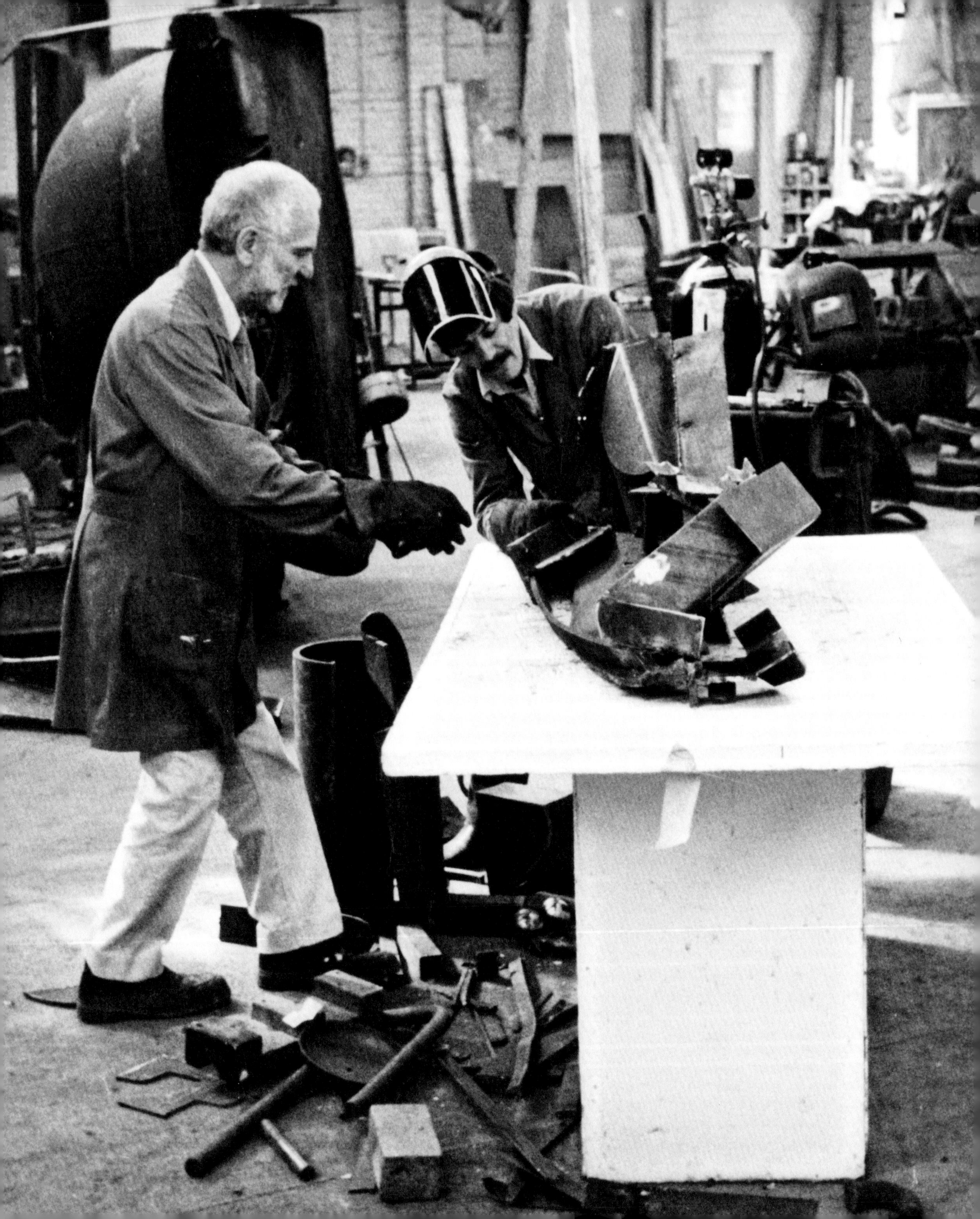

Table Sculptures

In 1959 Caro visited the United States where he admired the work of color field painters such as Kenneth Noland and Jules Olitski, as well as the sculpture of David Smith. Upon his return to London, he committed himself to two key changes: to make freestanding sculptures without plinths, and to work in recycled steel, cut and combined through a collage process. He launched his new sculptural vocabulary in a solo exhibition (Whitechapel Art Gallery, London, 1963) to a mixed critical reaction. Partly through the impact of his teaching at St. Martin's School of Art, he encouraged a generation to explore the potential of freestanding steel collage. Alongside the sculpture of his leading contemporaries Eduardo Paolozzi and William Tucker, Caro's example was seen as an Anglo-American alternative to Henry Moore, Barbara Hepworth, and Reg Butler.

Freestanding sculpture soon revealed its own limitations, for without plinths each sculpture had to be large enough not to be overlooked. Typically, Caro also soon felt the need for change, particularly when he saw that the themes he was exploring were becoming formulae for other sculptors. Caro had made small sculptures while with Henry Moore but never followed Moore's practice of enlarging from sketch models to full-scale works. The risk of making small works is that they can look like maquettes or scale reductions and so lose the direct relationship with the viewer's own body that Caro had achieved by dispensing with the plinth. The solution emerged in a conversation with Michael Fried in 1966 when the art historian encouraged him to make a series of "table pieces" that reclaim and use their supports in a new way.[8]

Rather than sitting isolated on plinths, Caro's table pieces reach into the viewer's own space. By springing over or reaching down the vertical sides they also use balance and counterweight as a key compositional theme, so much so that a sense of suspense can almost seem to tease the viewer. This space below offered an opportunity that the larger sculptures on the floor did not allow. Composing over the table's edge also makes it clear that these are complete, self-sufficient works and not scale models of freestanding sculptures. Caro conveys this sense of smaller sculptures being of a scale that still relates to the viewer's body in another way, by including elements familiar from everyday life: hand-sized objects such as

Caro with his assistant, Pat Cunningham, making a table sculpture in the Camden Town Studio, ca. 1981, with *Ocean* (Yale University Art Gallery) in the background

the three scissor handles in *Table Piece VIII* (cat. 25). Caro enhanced their surfaces with a variety of finishes, polishing and lacquering the steel and spraying it with automobile paints. In *Table Piece XLII* (cat. 26) the glowing green finish gives the piece a seductive sense of jadelike translucency. These qualities enhance the intimate appeal of the sculptures.

Precedents for using the table surface as part of the sculpture can be found in the art of Alberto Giacometti and David Smith; in Caro's games of balance there also are echoes of Degas' bronzes, which he much admires. As compositions of discrete elements these sculptures also recall still-life paintings.

Caro composed many of the small *Table Pieces* in the evening: he temporarily spot-welded them together in his garage studio in Hampstead, then handed them over to his assistants in the morning in his Camden Town studio to consolidate, after which he would make further refinements. He recalls: "I used to work on larger things there, then in the evenings come back and it would be rather like drawing. . . . Making table sculptures is fun, very open and loose."[9] As with drawings, these *Table Pieces* provided Caro with the opportunity to work alone and experiment, as if sketching fast, and he took ideas back into his larger works.

CAT. 25 (overleaf)
Table Piece VIII, 1966
Steel, polished, 27 x 13 x 20 in. (68.5 x 33 x 50.8 cm)
B0008
Private collection, London

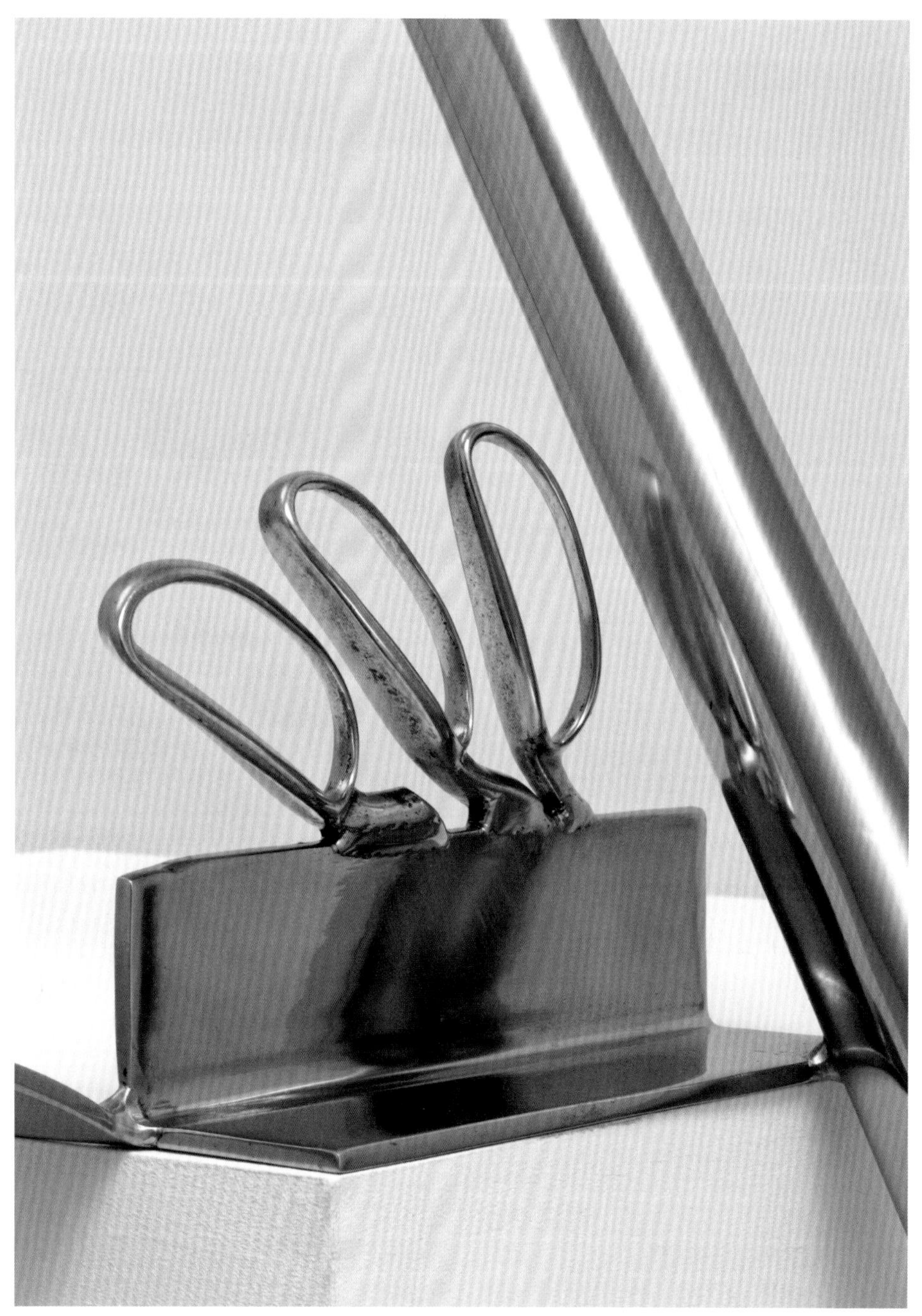

CAT. 25

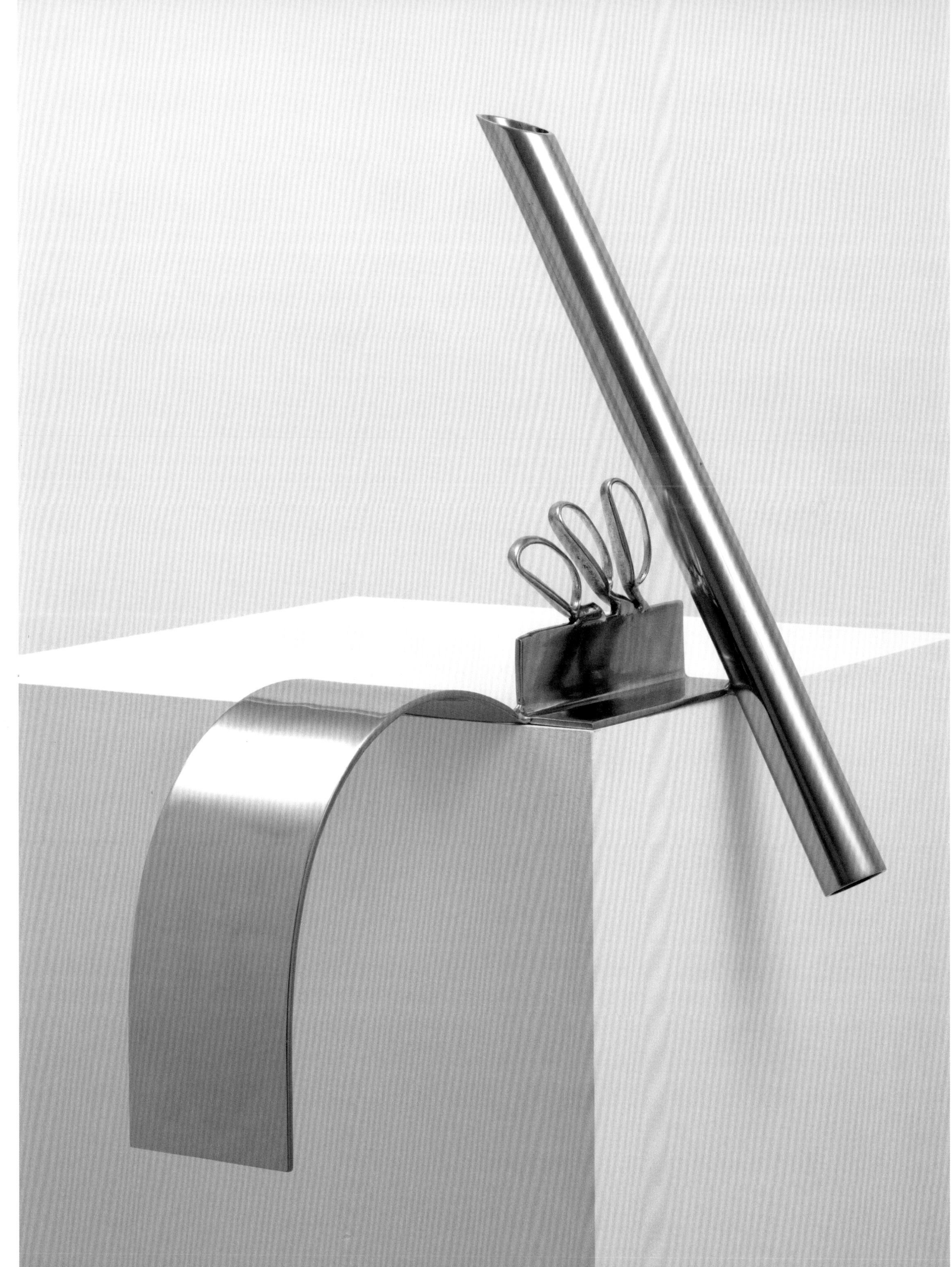

CAT. 26

Table Piece XLII, 1967

Steel, polished and sprayed, 23½ x 15½ x 29 in. (59.7 x 39.4 x 73.7 cm)

B0042

Private collection, London

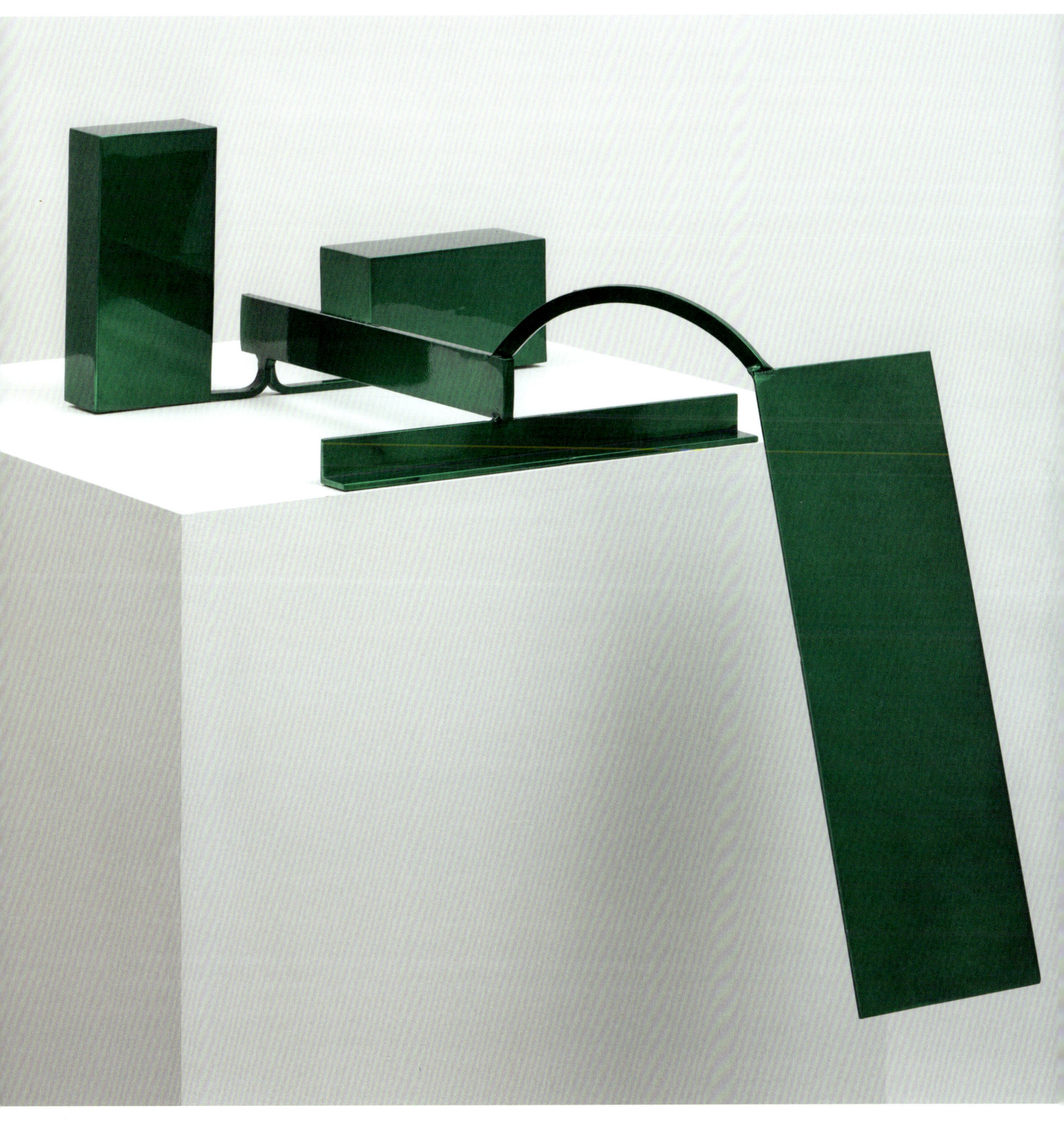

CAT. 27

Table Piece LIX, 1968

Steel, sprayed, 11½ x 17 x 19 in. (29.2 x 43.2 x 48.3 cm)

B0059

Private collection, London

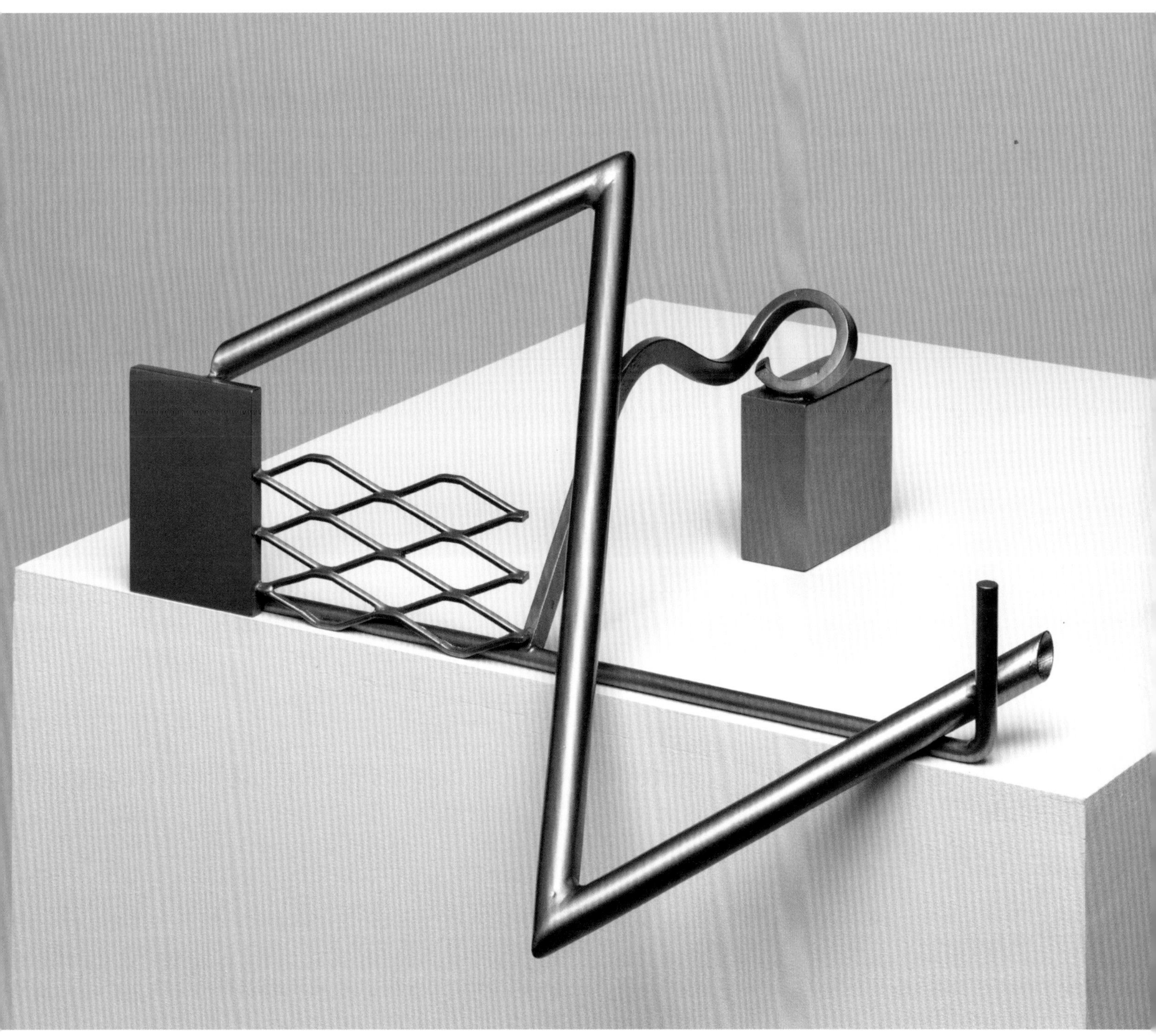

CAT. 28
Table Piece LXXX, 1969
Steel, painted, 13½ x 53 x 20 in. (34.3 x 134.6 x 50.8 cm)
B0079
Private collection, London

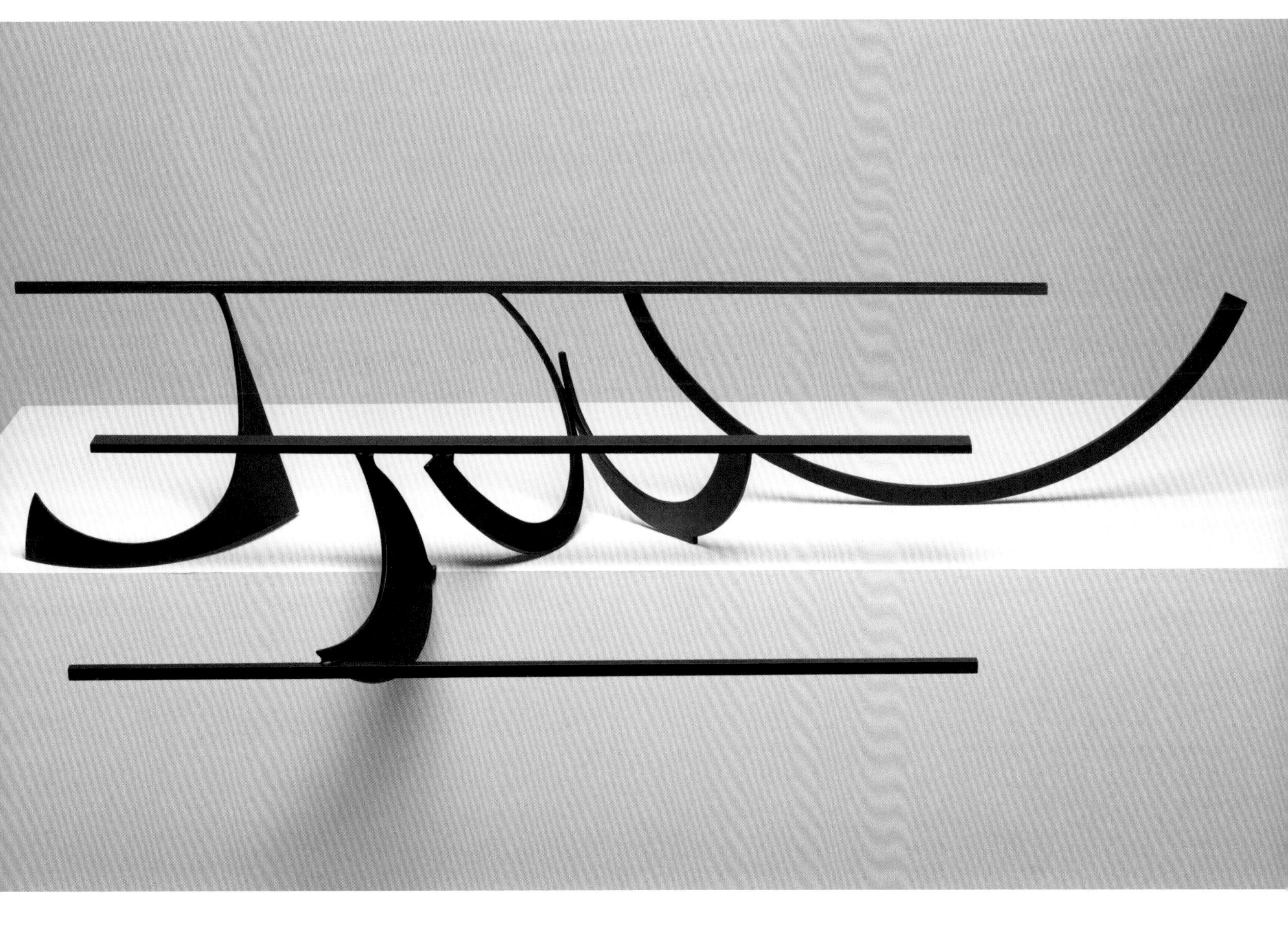

CAT. 29 (facing page and overleaf)
Table Piece CII, 1970
Steel, painted, 29½ x 80 x 34 in. (74.9 x 203.2 x 86.4 cm)
B0106
Yale University Art Gallery, Katharine Ordway Fund

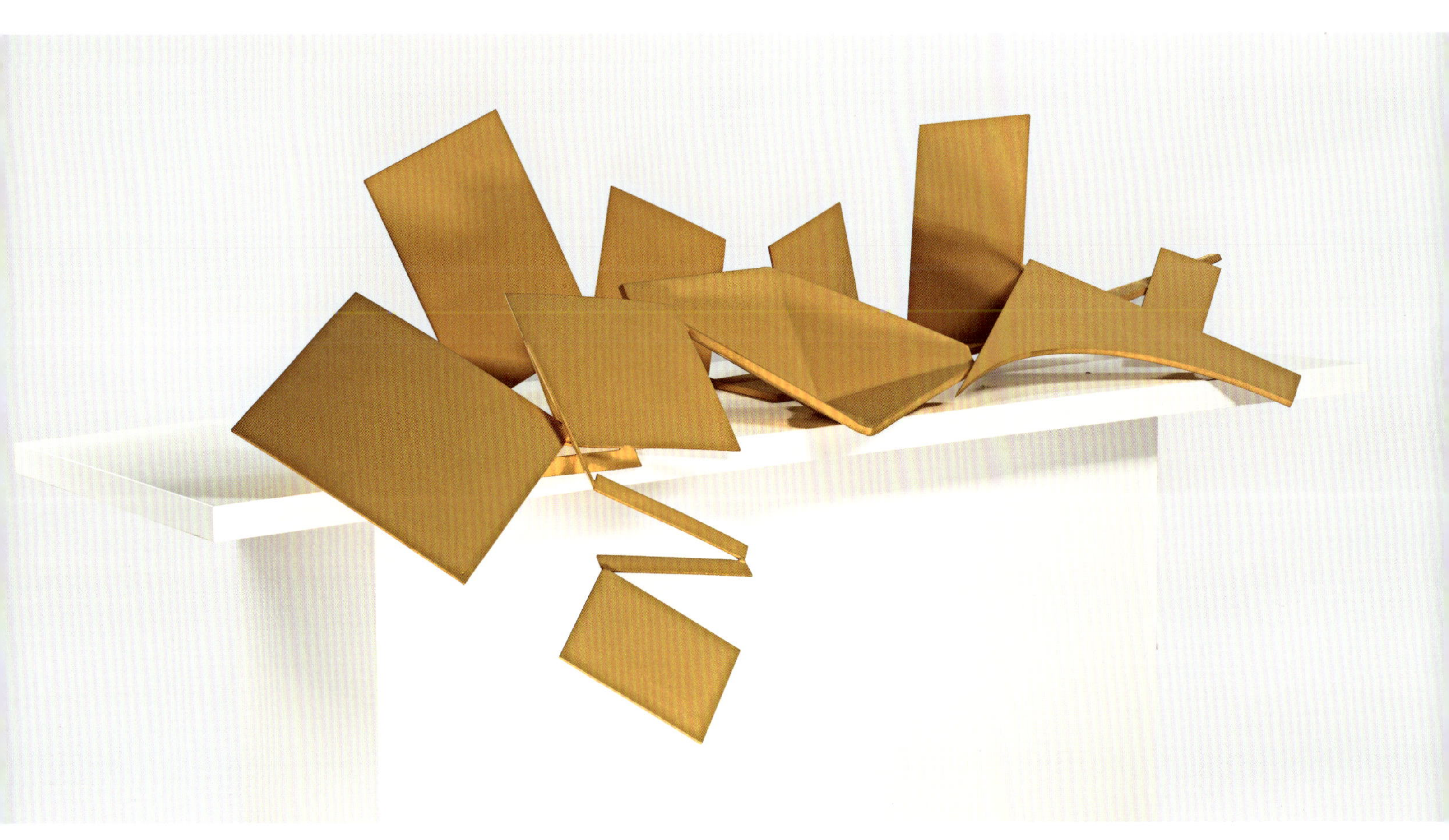

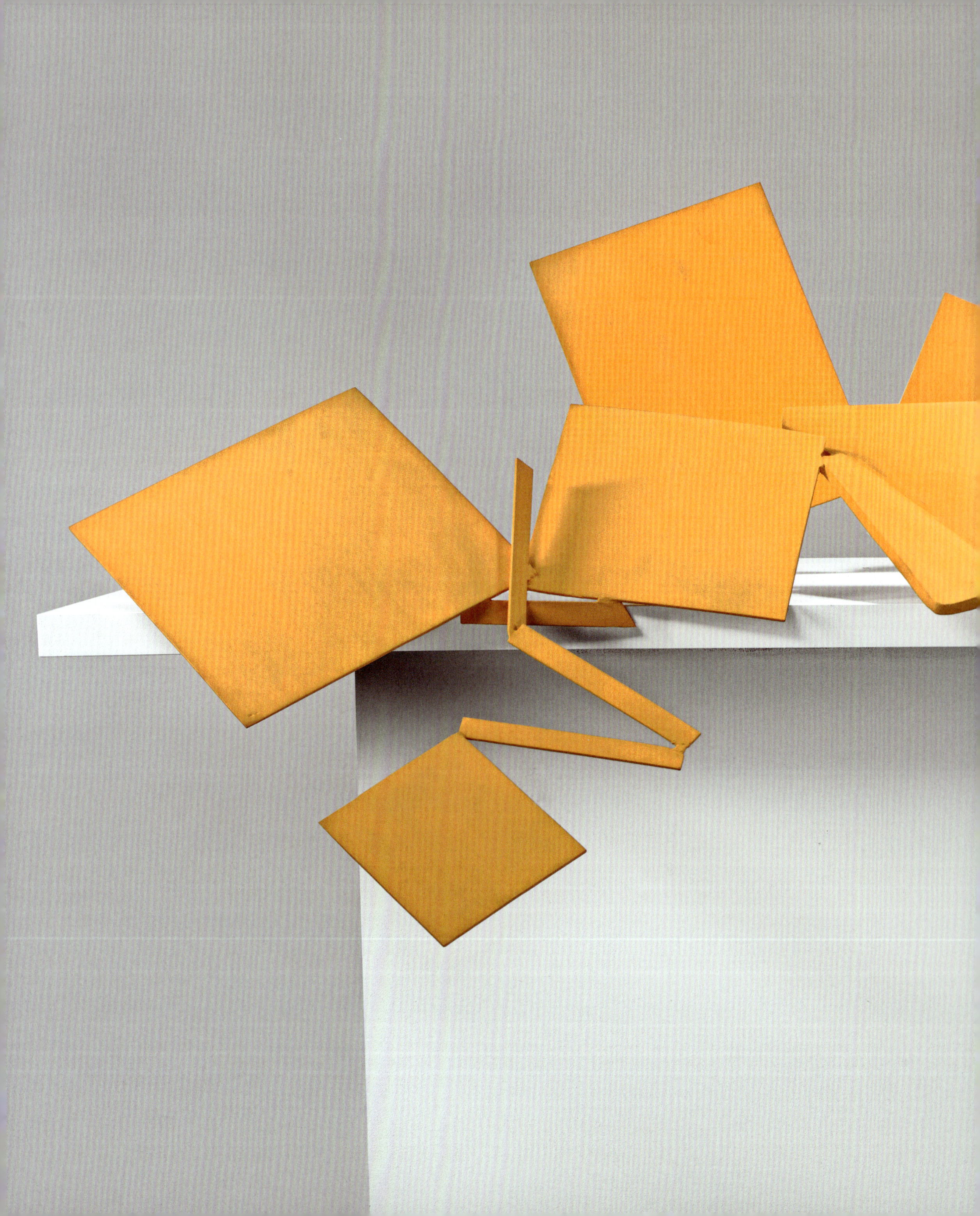

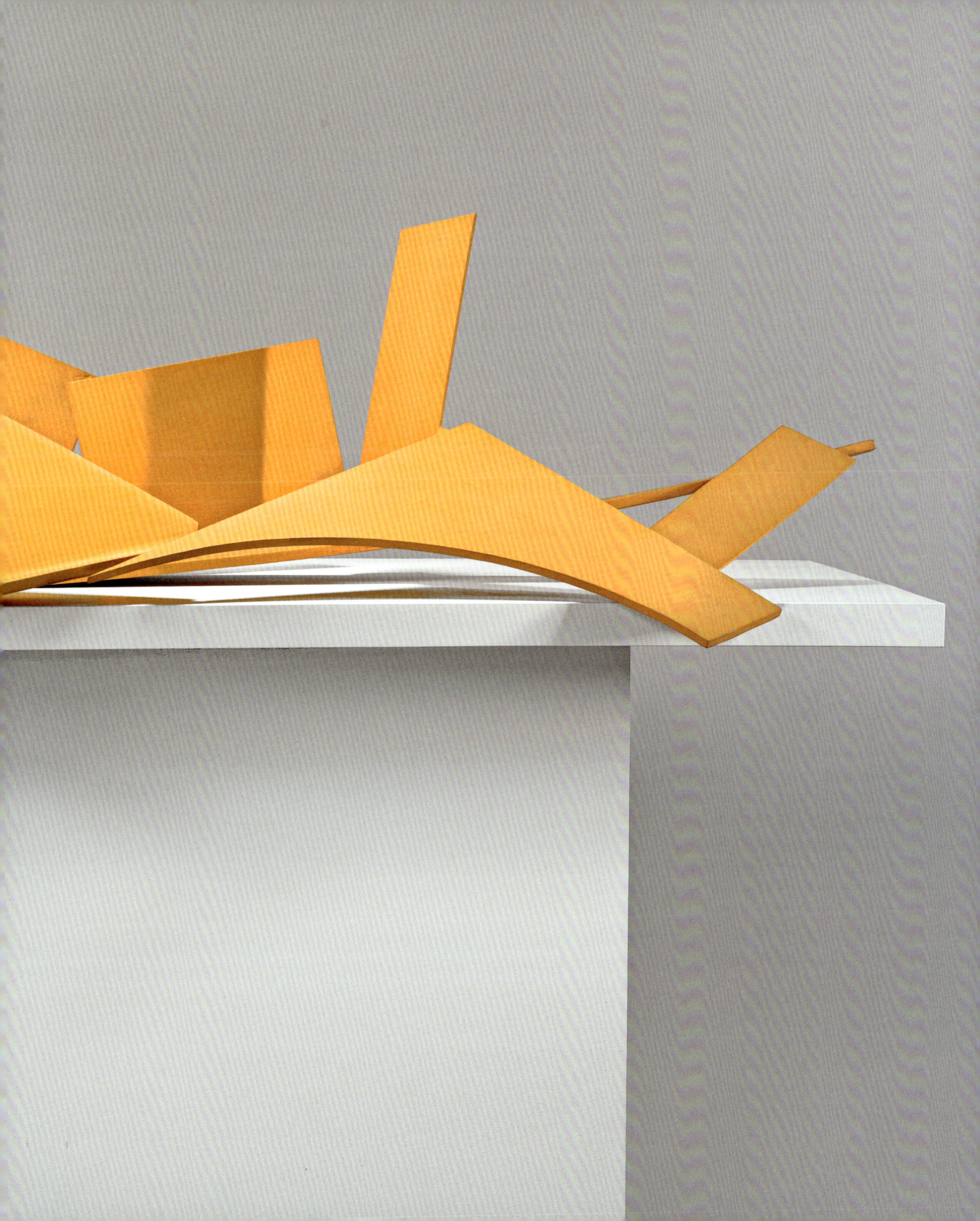

CAT. 30

Table Piece XCVII, 1970

Steel, painted, 25 x 53 x 44 in. (63.5 x 134.6 x 111.8 cm)

B0095

Private collection, London

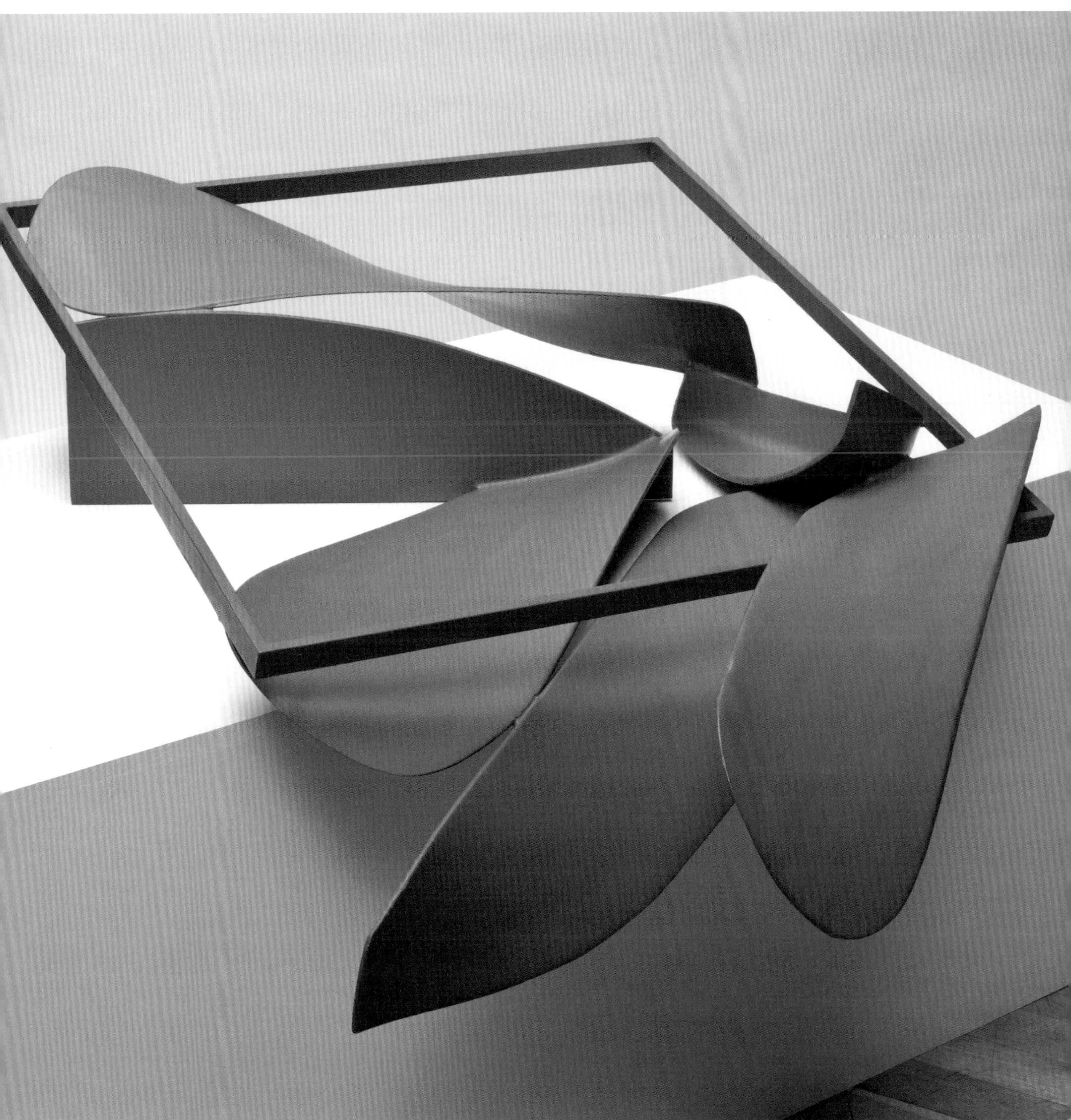

CAT. 31

Table Piece CLXVIII, 1973–4

Steel, varnished, 49 x 30 x 18 in. (124.5 x 76.2 x 45.7 cm)

B0173

Collection of Clifford Ross

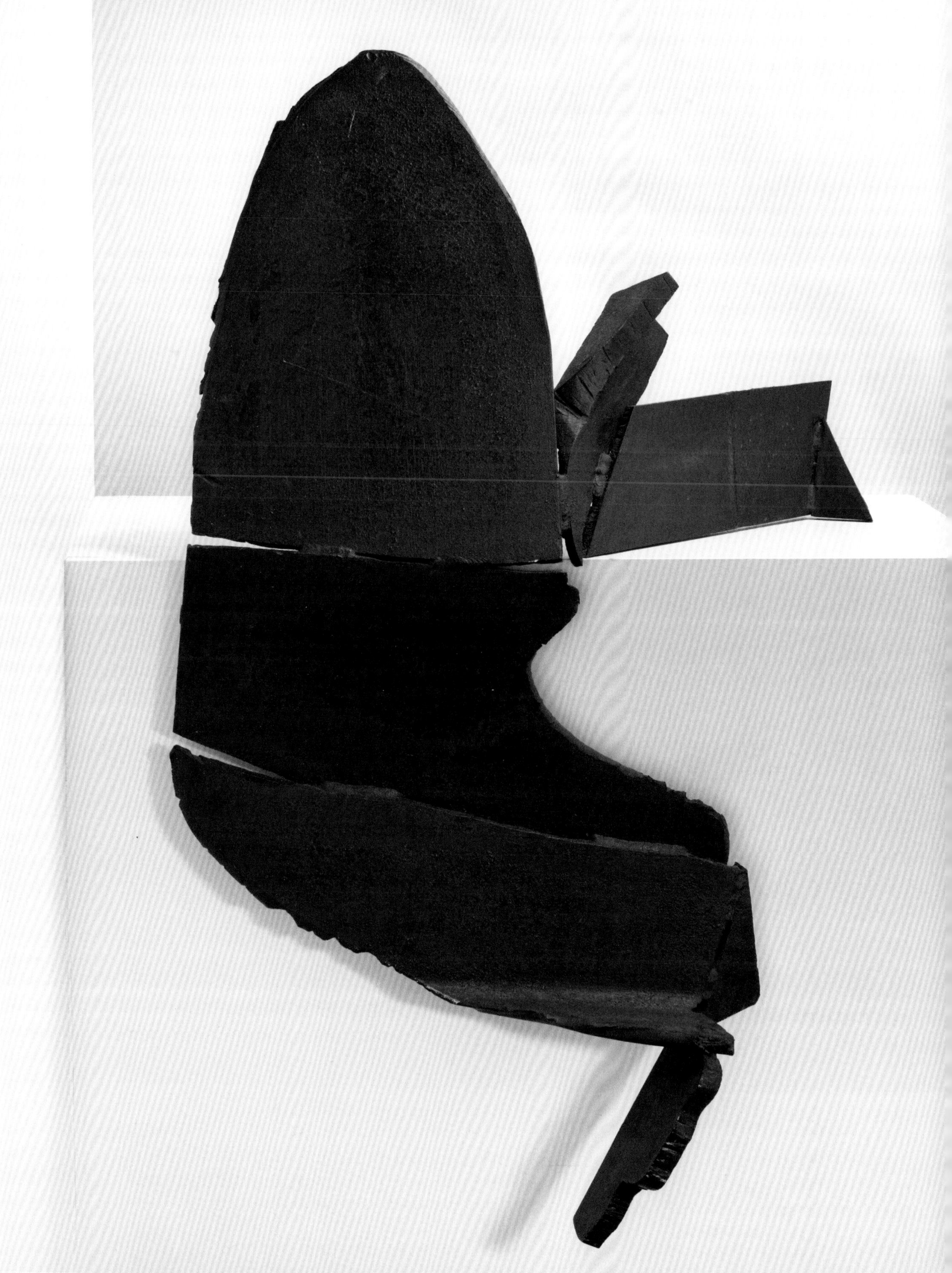

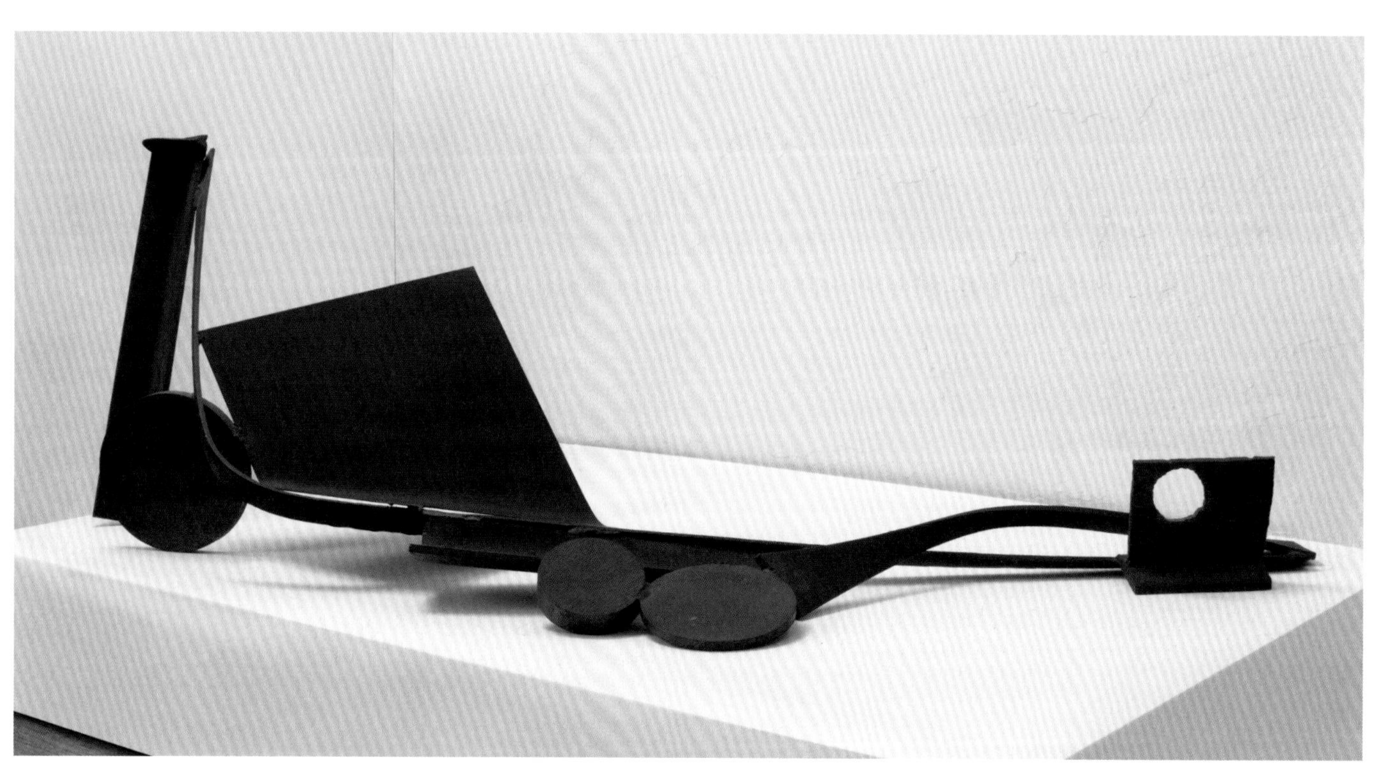

CAT. 32

***Table Piece Z-69*, 1981/1982**

Steel and sheet steel, rusted and varnished, 20 x 60½ x 13 in. (51 x 153.5 x 58.5 cm)

B1243

Collection of Karen Wilkin

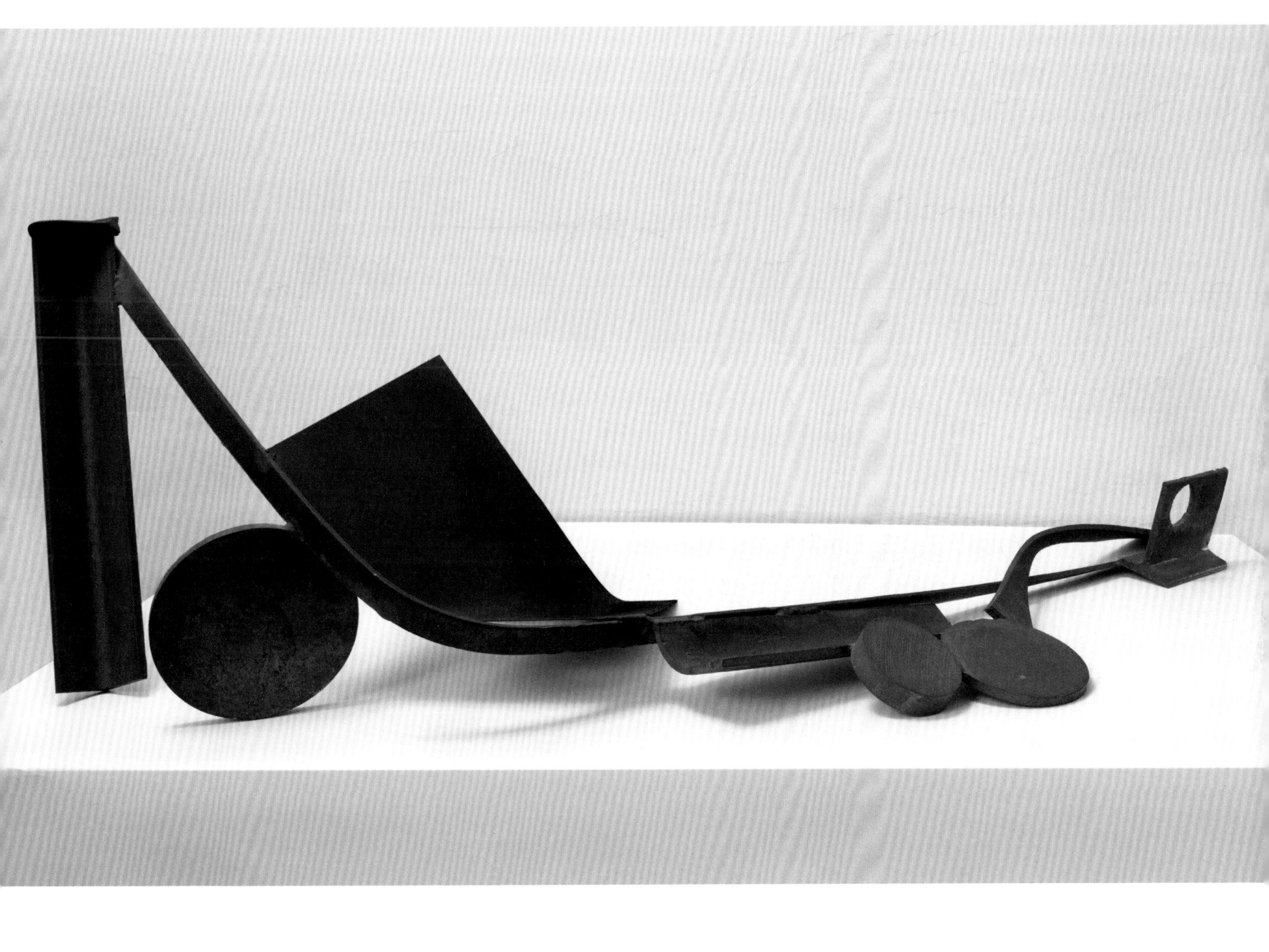

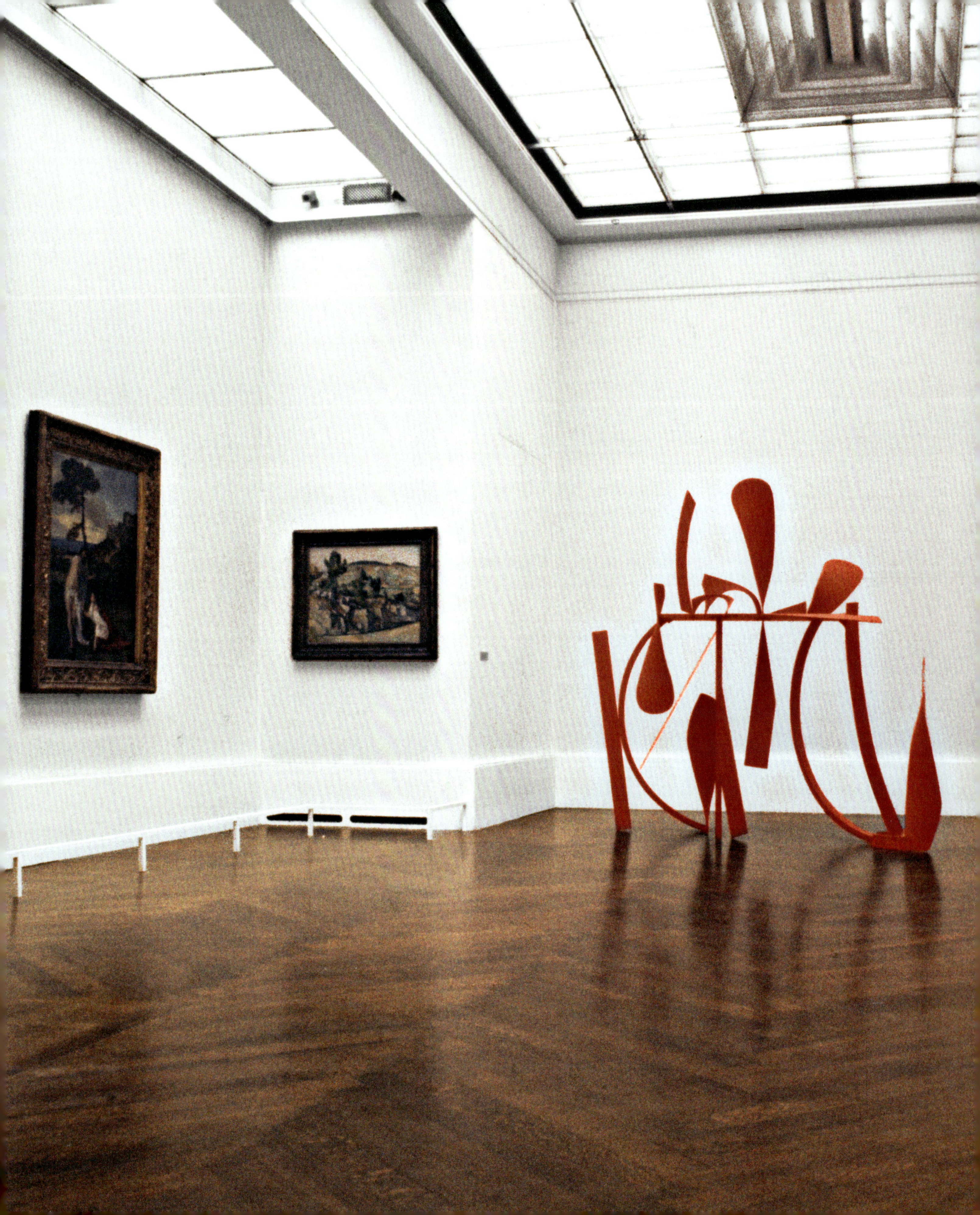

Floating Color

During the Table Pieces series, Caro discovered the potential presented by the horizontal plane at the top of the pedestal. By incorporating this element into freestanding sculptures Caro was able to return to the direct sense of encounter that he achieved by dispensing with pedestals while continuing to explore the space 'below' each work. The "table" plane provides a stable element around which compositions can seem to spring and dance; it also draws the floor into the experience of a sculpture, as a parallel plane.

Trefoil (cat. 33), for example, has as its central element a square tablelike plane, parallel to the ground, which seems to hover above the floor between springing arcs that appear to slice through the plane. It has a sense of perfect poise, like a prima ballerina about to spin.

New sources of raw materials inspired change. In 1967, two years after David Smith's death, Caro bought his unused stock of steel from the estate, which included the shell-like ends sliced off container tanks. One of these can be seen in *Sun Feast* (see fig. 3.15). This actually began as a table sculpture, until Caro decided that the long steel workbench on which he composed could be part of the whole object . Following the chance discovery in 1968 of a sale of small plowshares, Caro approached an aircraft manufacturer (De Havilland) for old propeller blades. The result, *Orangerie* (cat. 34), clearly works as an expansion on the table theme: a central horizontal plane forms the axis around which the composition almost seems to rotate. Like giant brushstrokes or musical notes drawn as a baroque score, twisting lines and planes dance; lacking any actual or implied volume, the work is both sculptural and pictorial.

The use of orange paint to enhance the sense of blocks of colour was inspired by an exhibition on Matisse that Caro saw at the time, which featured his late compositions of large color paper cutout collages from the end of his career. *Table Piece XCVII* (cat. 30) uses similar materials to splash across a plinth like an adventurous tropical plant, restrained indoors only by the tilted frame. The effect of a single strong but soft colour is to lighten the sculpture and suggest it is floating.

Orangerie in the exhibition *Artist's Eye*, National Gallery, London, 1977

Seemingly both heavy and weightless, it conveys an uplifting sense of joy in the viewer that is also achieved with spectacular effect in *Table Piece CII* (cat. 29). The perfect match between color and form (whether the soft matt salmon pink of *Orangerie* or the brilliant gloss yellow of *Trefoil*) enhances the flow through the composition and sense of weightlessness. The choice of color is a key contribution of the artist Sheila Girling (Caro's wife). Its importance is most apparent if one imagines these sculptures painted in different colors.

CAT. 33 (overleaf)
***Trefoil*, 1968**
Steel, painted, 83 x 100 x 65 in. (211 x 254 x 165 cm)
B0920
David and Audrey Mirvish, Toronto, Canada

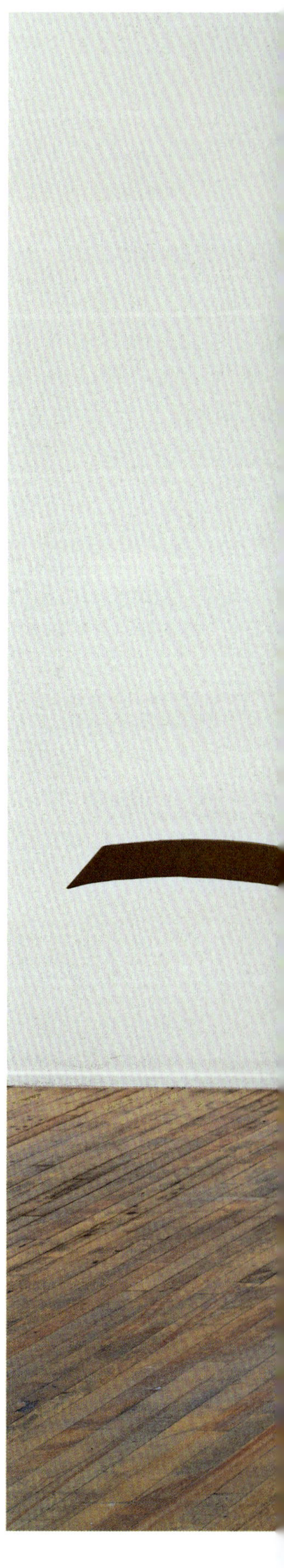

CAT. 33

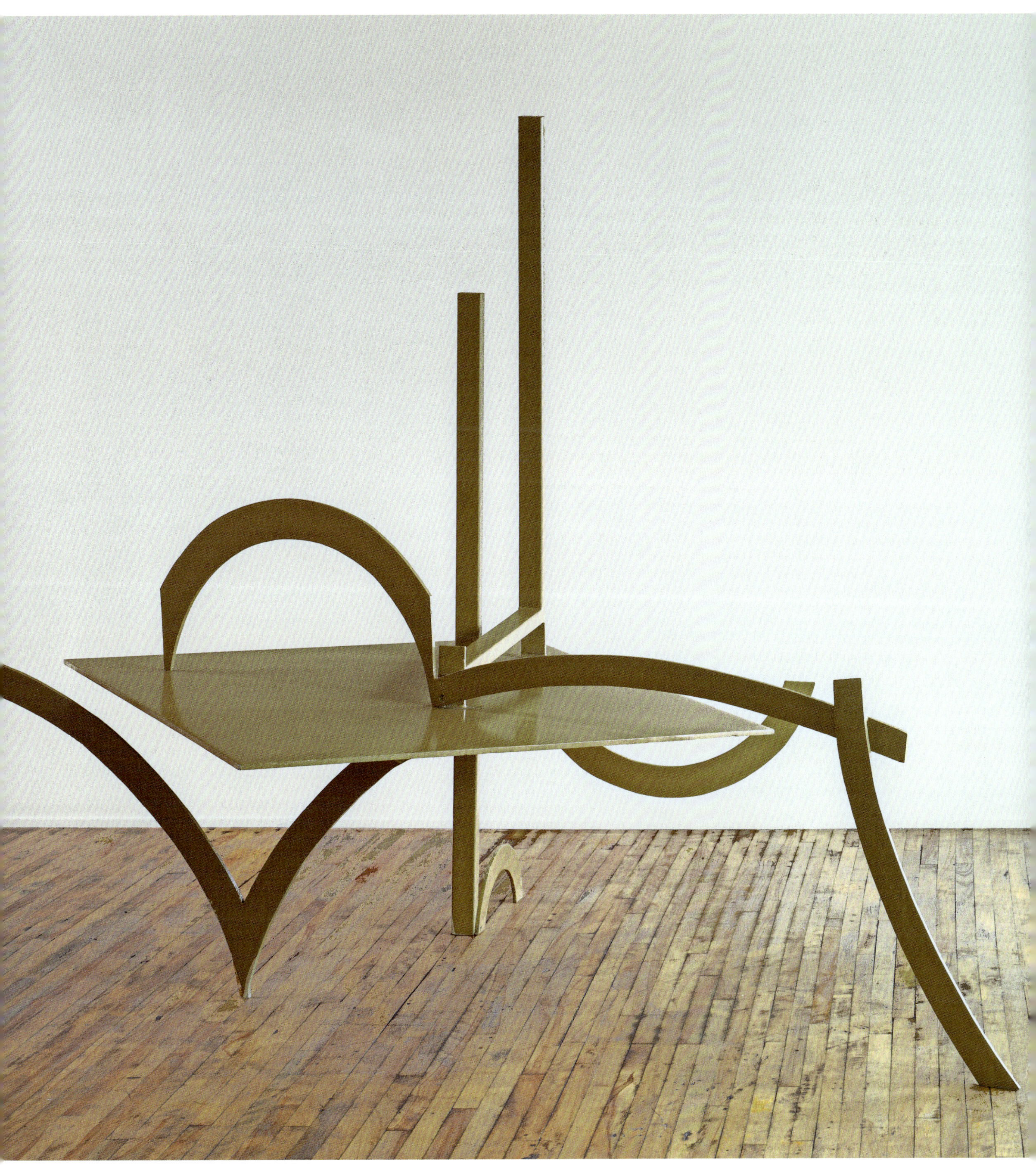

CAT. 34
Orangerie, 1969
Steel, painted, 88½ x 64 x 91 in. (225 x 162.5 x 231 cm)
B0929
Museum of Fine Arts, Houston

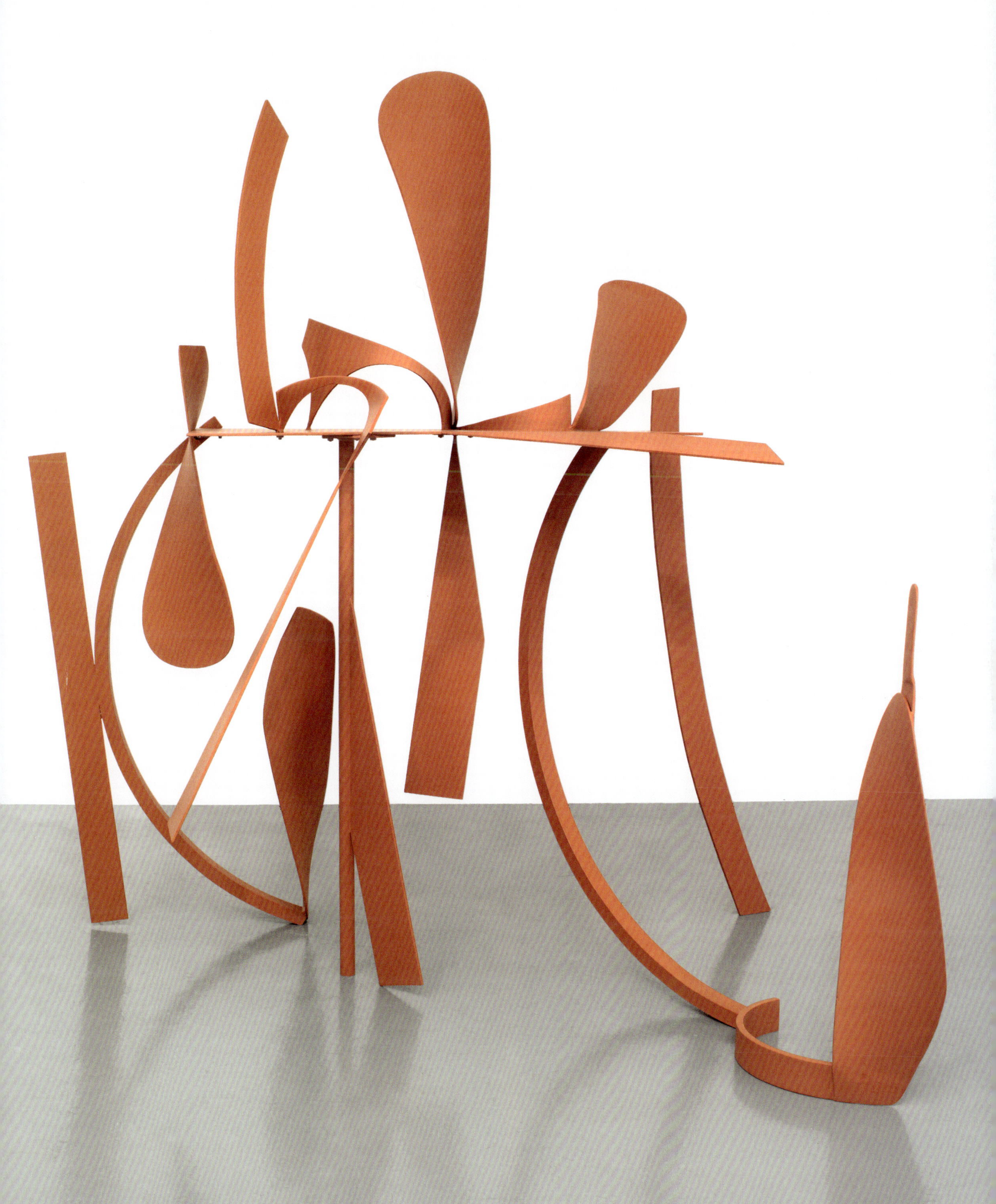

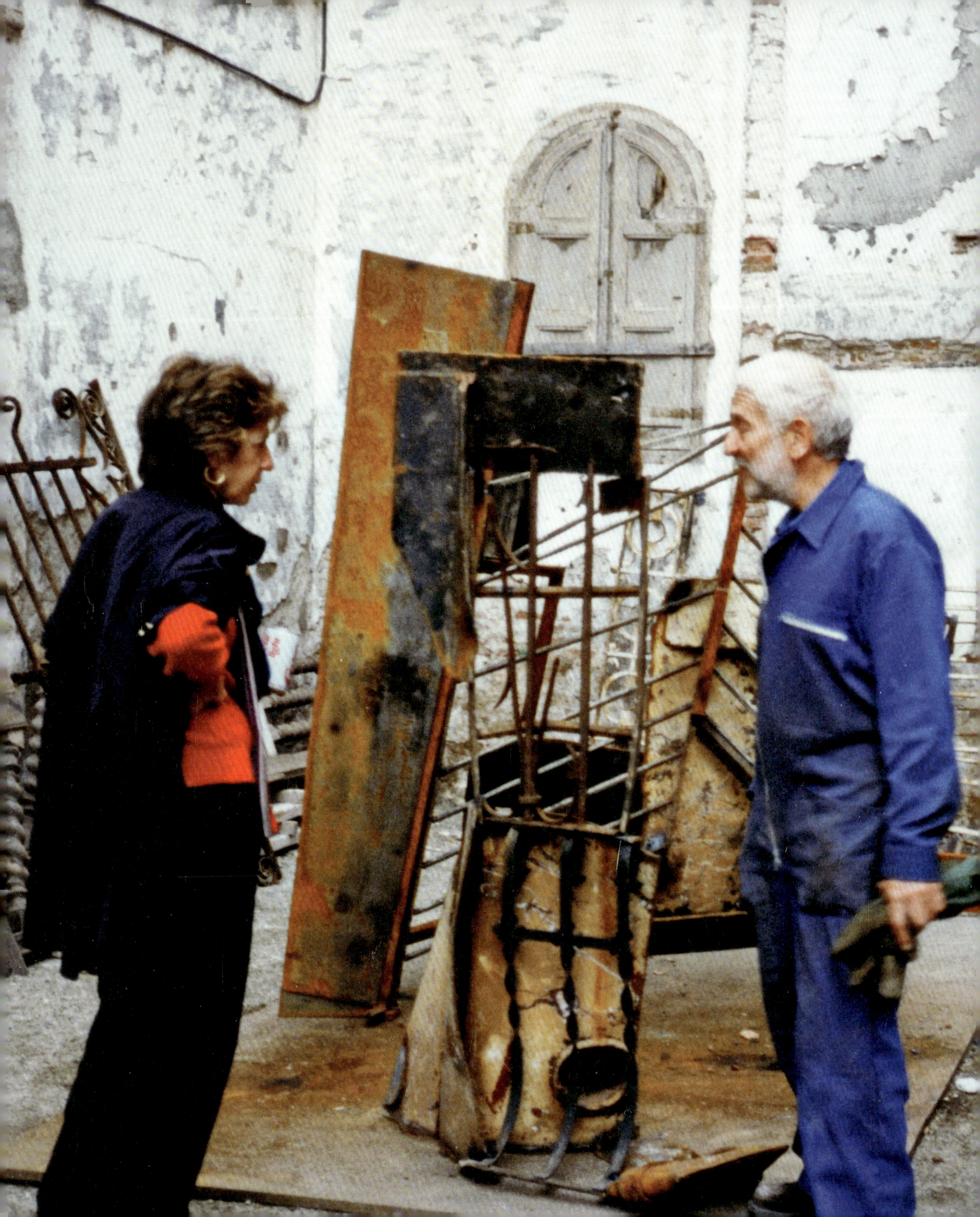

Drawing in Space

Working on a smaller scale with table supports led Caro to make lighter, more calligraphic sculptures. The most celebrated of these is *Table Piece LXXXVIII* (cat. 35) known as *Deluge* after William Rubin compared it to Leonardo's drawing of tumbling waves in the Royal Collection, London.[10] The similarity is entirely coincidental, yet Caro and Leonardo clearly share a delight in tracing the flow of interlocking arcs of energy, twisting in their descent through tight curls to coil and eddy. In the sensuality of its curves, which cascade over the table edge as if ready to embrace the passing viewer, *Deluge* possesses an intimacy of appeal quite unlike *Orangerie* or *Sun Feast*, for all their seductive arabesques.

Caro is a trained draftsman but he only returned to life-drawing in 1983, after an absence of nearly twenty years. In his almost life-size studies of the female nude he clearly enjoys drawing with exuberant sweeping gestures of the charcoal. This love of line partly explains the series of linear sculptures that Caro began in Barcelona in 1987. Inspired by the traditional Catalonian art of wrought iron, as seen in the city's characteristic curling balconies and balustrades that cast sharp shadows from strong silhouettes, he chose to work with local steel from architectural salvage. After shipping new sculptures and materials back to London, he produced a series of tall, flat table pieces that work like windows or screens, such as *Catalan Maid* (cat. 36), suggesting in its title the curved outline of a local girl seen at a window. In his *Catalan Scrawl* (cat. 37) Caro draws linear dances that catch and beguile the eye. From different angles the interplay of lines and planes suggest voids and invisible volumes floating in and out of focus. David Smith made similar intricate, upright collages on this intimate scale, which seem all the more remarkable for being almost two-dimensional when viewed from the side.[11] Caro said at the time: "Picasso, Gaudí, González and Míro were all alive in my mind; the resulting sculptures introduce something of the drawing of this part of Spain, which I felt I subconsciously assimilated."[12]

Caro with Helen Frankenthaler at the Triangle workshop, Barcelona, Spain, May 1987

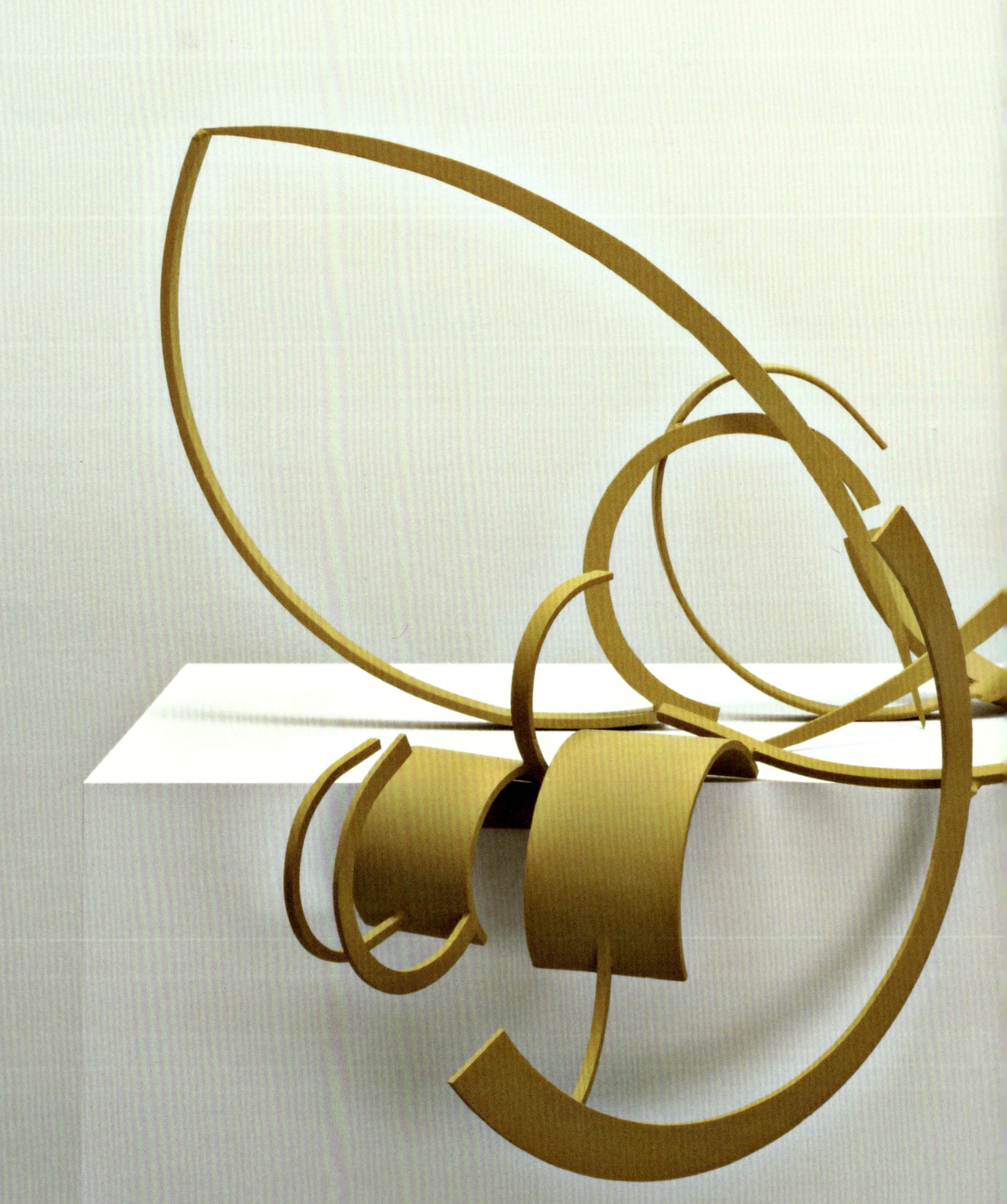

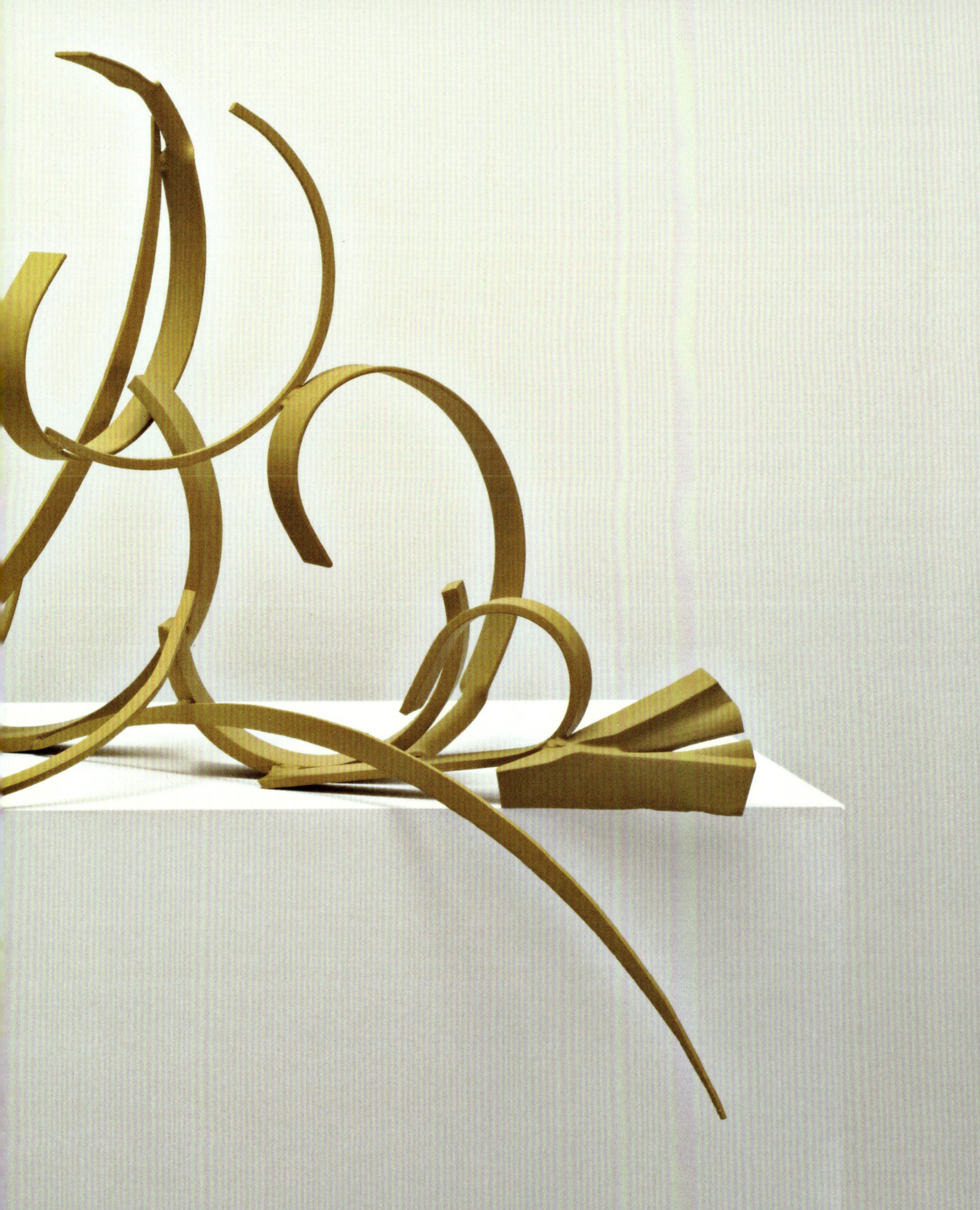

CAT. 35 (previous spread)
Table Piece LXXXVIII – Deluge, 1969
Steel, painted, 40 x 63 x 38 in. (101.6 x 60 x 96.5 cm)
B0086
Museum of Modern Art, New York
Gift of Guido Goldman in memory of Minda de Gunzberg

CAT. 36 (facing page)
Table Piece "Catalan Maid," 1987/88
Steel, rusted and fixed, 53 x 27 x 15½ in. (134.5 x 68.5 x 39.5 cm)
B1825
Private collection, London

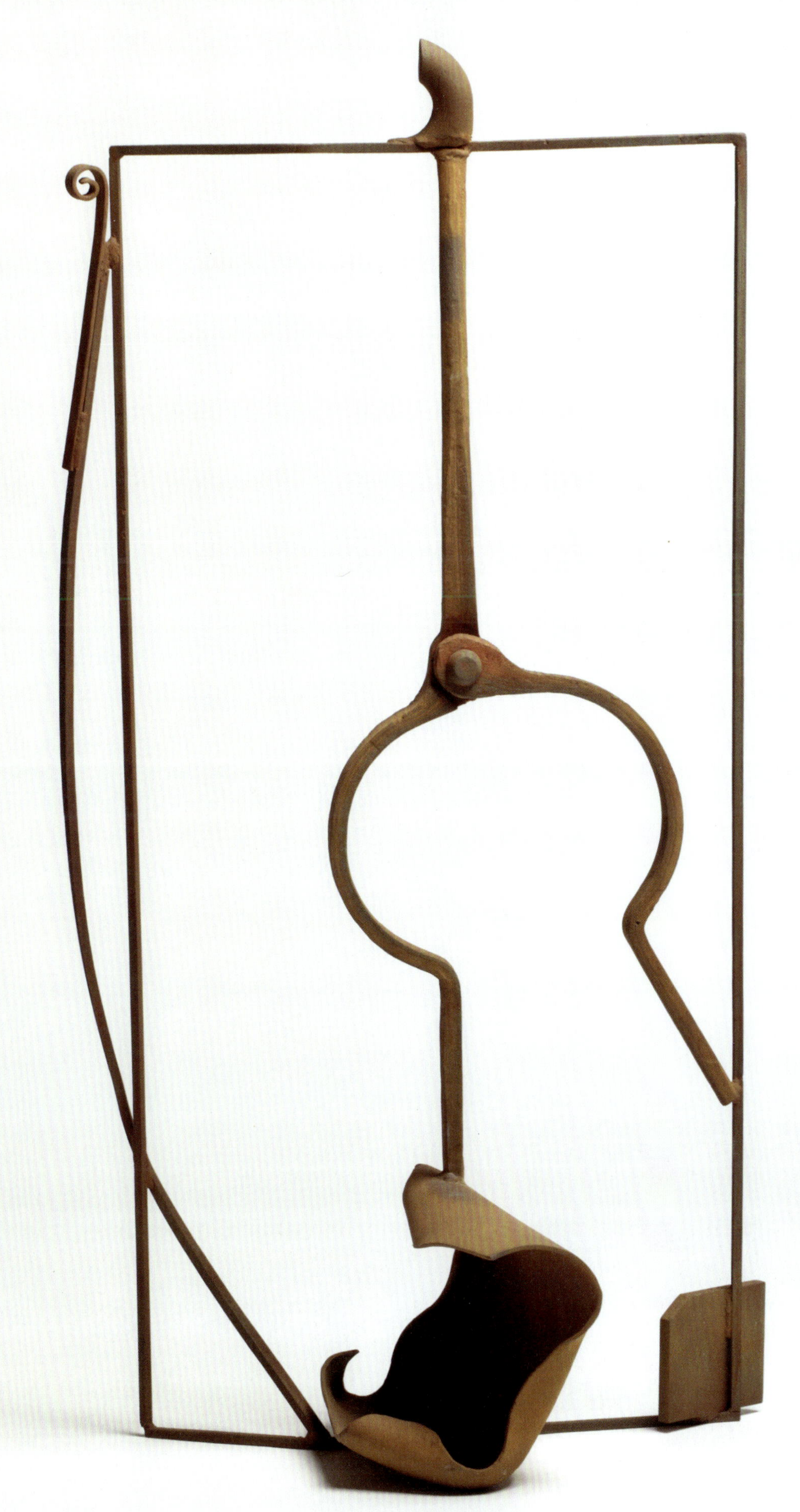

CAT. 37

Table Piece "Catalan Scrawl," 1987/88

Steel, rusted and fixed, 41 x 40 x 13 in. (104 x 103 x 33 cm)

B1848

Private collection, London

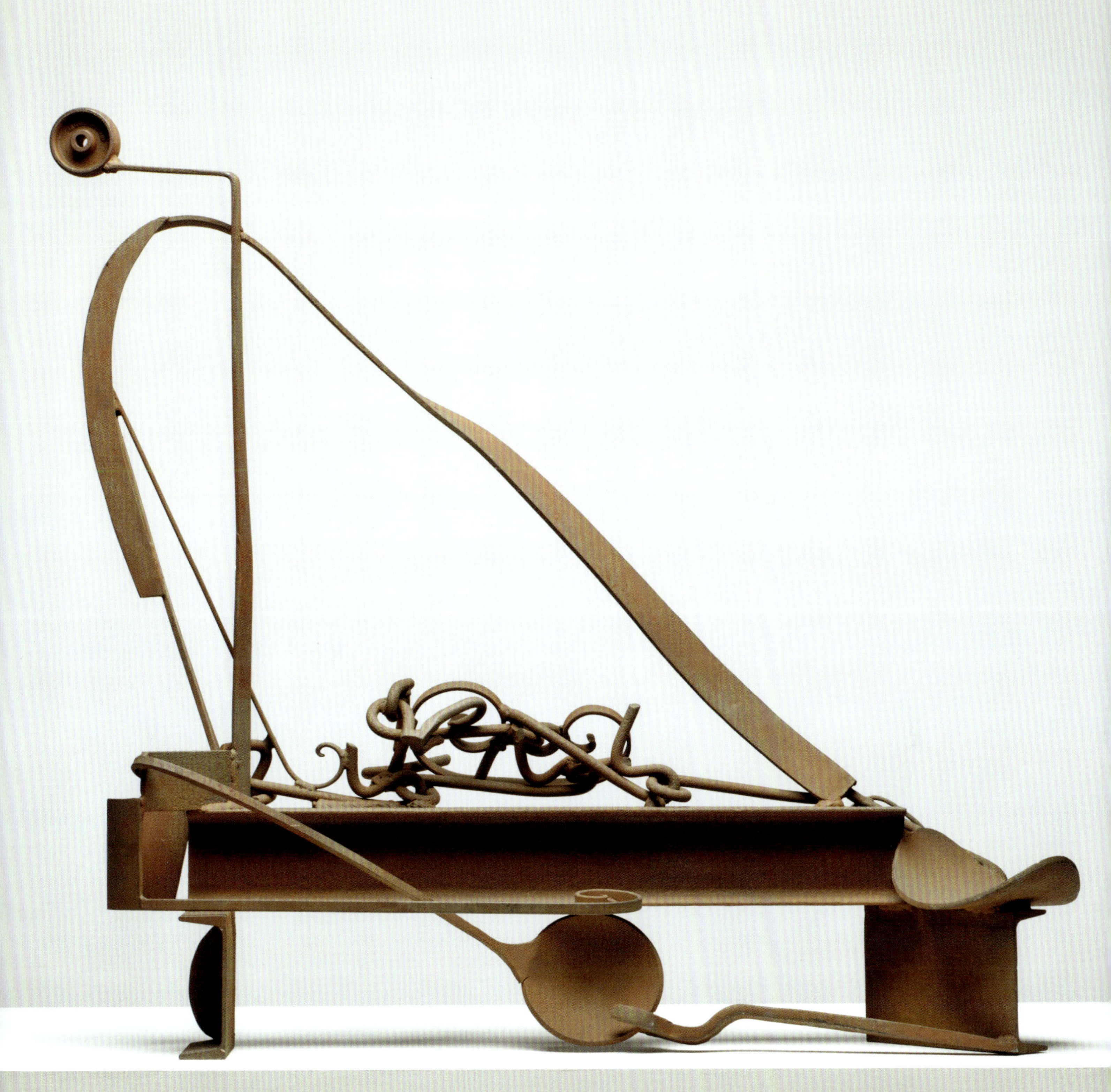

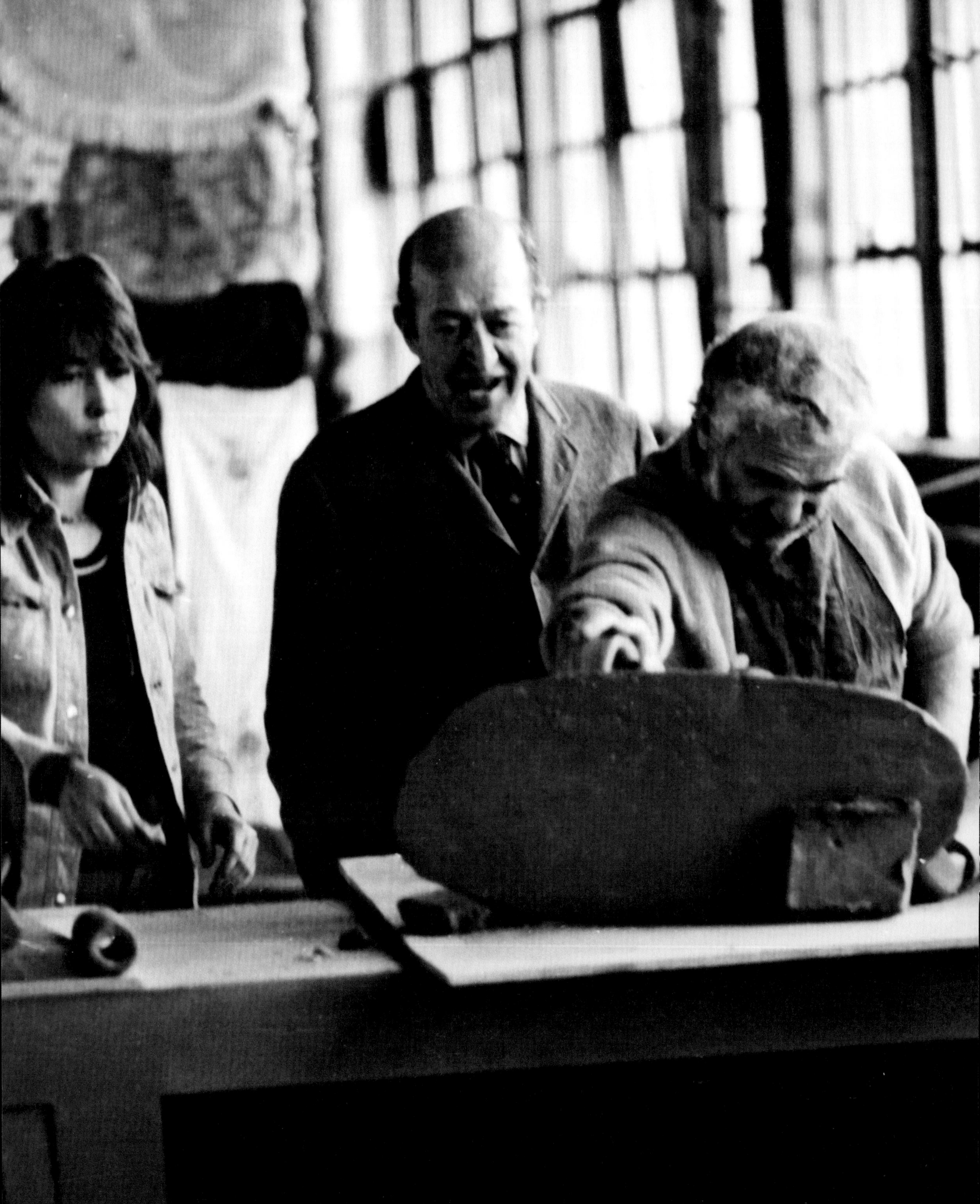

Ceramic Sculpture

Caro has always enjoyed working with other artists, right from the time when, as a schoolboy, he helped out in the studio of the sculptor Charles Wheeler. Although Caro is now strongly associated with steel, clay has also been a lifelong interest, ever since he started modeling sculptures at the age of fifteen. This was the oily modeling clay he rejected in the 1960s in favor of steel. In 1975 Clement Greenberg told Caro that clay was "the open road to free form," when he invited him to join an experimental workshop run by the ceramist Margie Hughto at Syracuse University.[13] Other invited artists included the painters Jules Olitski, Helen Frankenthaler, and Larry Poons. Hughto was using slabs of stoneware clay that could be folded like lead sheets or heavy rugs and had to be worked more swiftly than modeling clay, before it dried. Rather than return to modeling, Caro let the material dictate the form and used the stoneware clay as a medium for collage. Together with clay pots and tubes, the soft, malleable medium provided a more volumetric range of options than that offered by steel. In 1988–89 he worked with Paul Chaleff on the first of three occasions, which led to the "Hudson" series of abstract architectural sculptures in stoneware, such as *Minoan* (cat. 38). In scale, it is a tabletop sculpture, yet its boxlike structure, toasting scars from the kiln, and evocative title suggest some austere archaeological find, now half-revealing its precious contents, mummified by the dry air of an ancient tomb.

In contrast, the series of "Book" sculptures made from stoneware and porcelain come from another world—born in the south of France, where Caro worked with the ceramist Hans Spinner in his studio near Grasse on the Côte d'Azur. To the ceramic "books" he added steel and brass elements, such as handles and wedges, that read like quotations, bursting out of the pages and coming to life. In *Little Book of Opera* (cat. 41) the polished brass seems to spring from the pure white porcelain, like single notes from a score or precious coins from a purse. He first exhibited the *Book* series at Annely Juda Fine Art in London in 1998, installed in rows on freestanding shelves like a library. These are among Caro's smallest and most intimate works.

Caro making sculpture with Margie Hughto while Clement Greenberg offers advice, Syracuse University, 1975

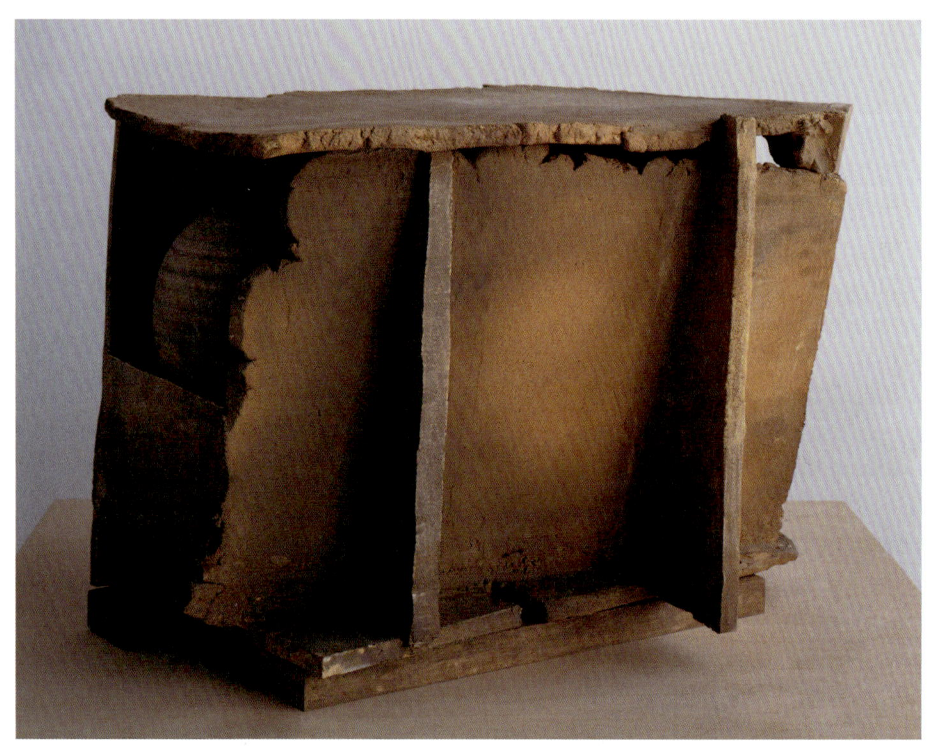

CAT. 38
***Minoan*, 1990–91**
Stoneware, 23 x 31½ x 24 in. (58.4 x 80 x 61 cm)
B2088
Metropolitan Museum of Art, NYC
Gift of Dawn F. Bennett and Martin S. Davidson, 2002

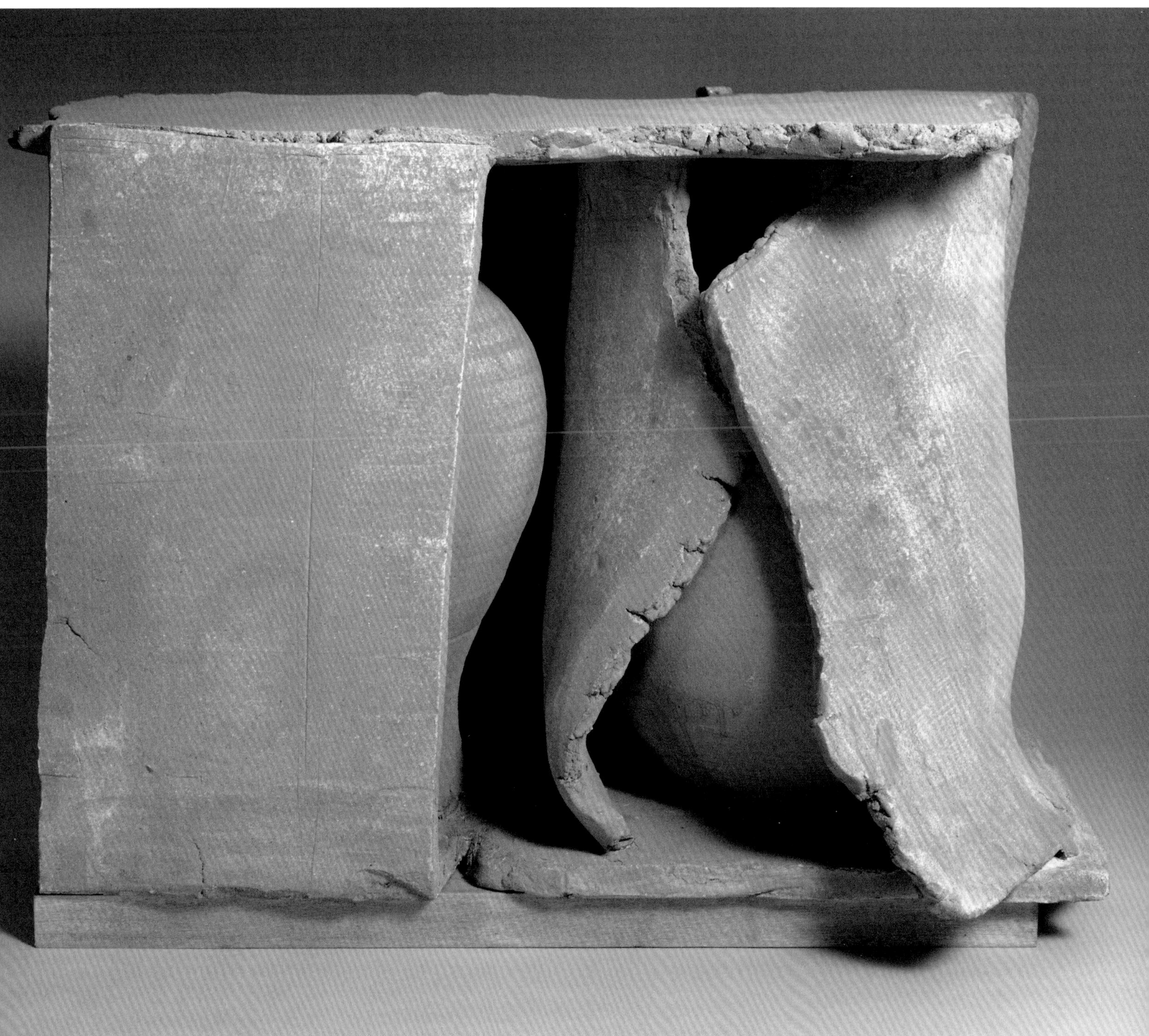

CAT. 39
Drummer's Book, 1995/1996
Ceramic stoneware and steel, rusted, 13½ x 12 x 20 in. (34 x 30.5 x 51 cm)
B2414
Private collection, London

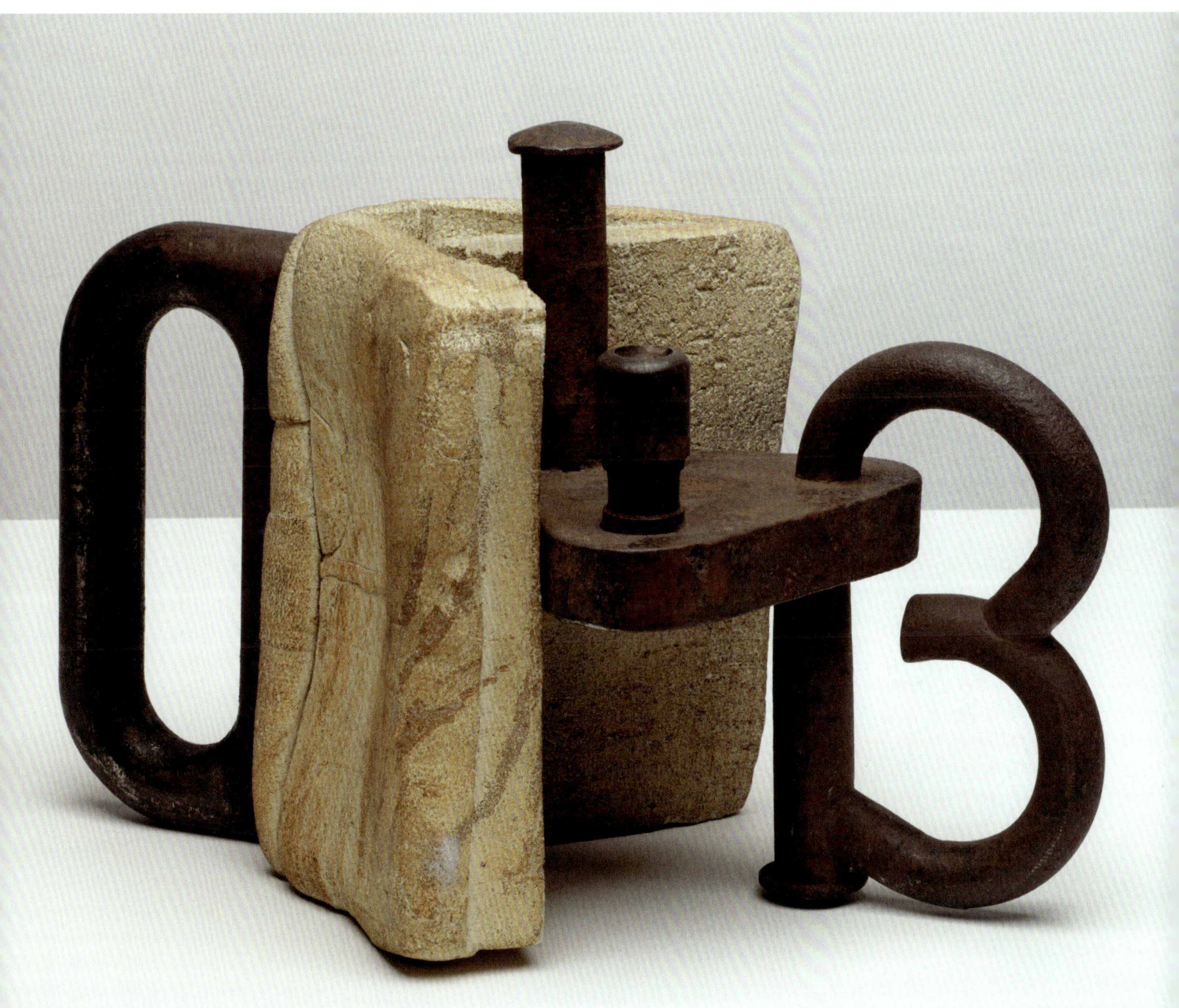

CAT. 40

Small Wedge Book, 1996/1997

Porcelain and steel, 6 x 10 x 3 in. (15 x 25.5 x 7.5 cm)

B2423

Private collection

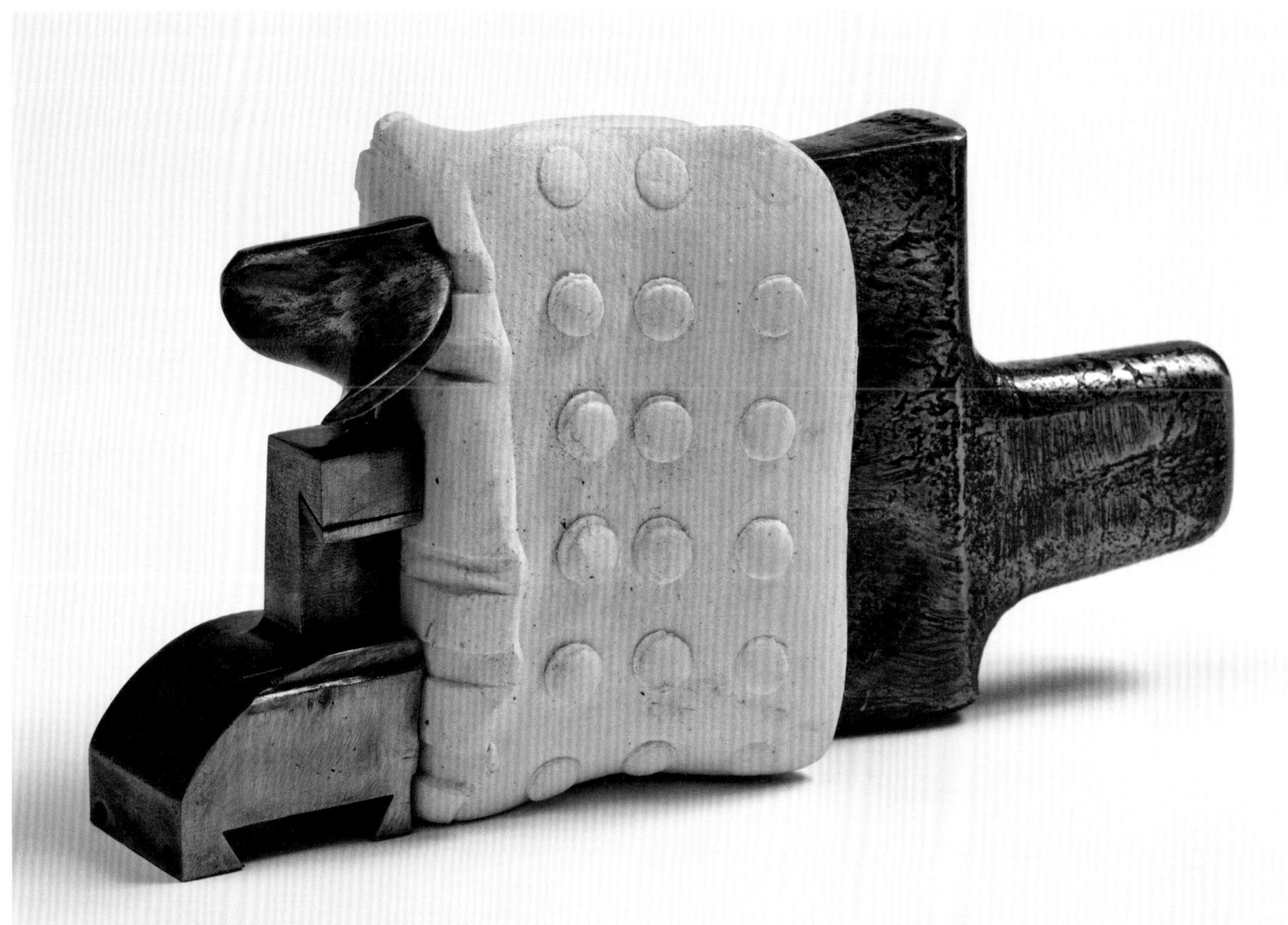

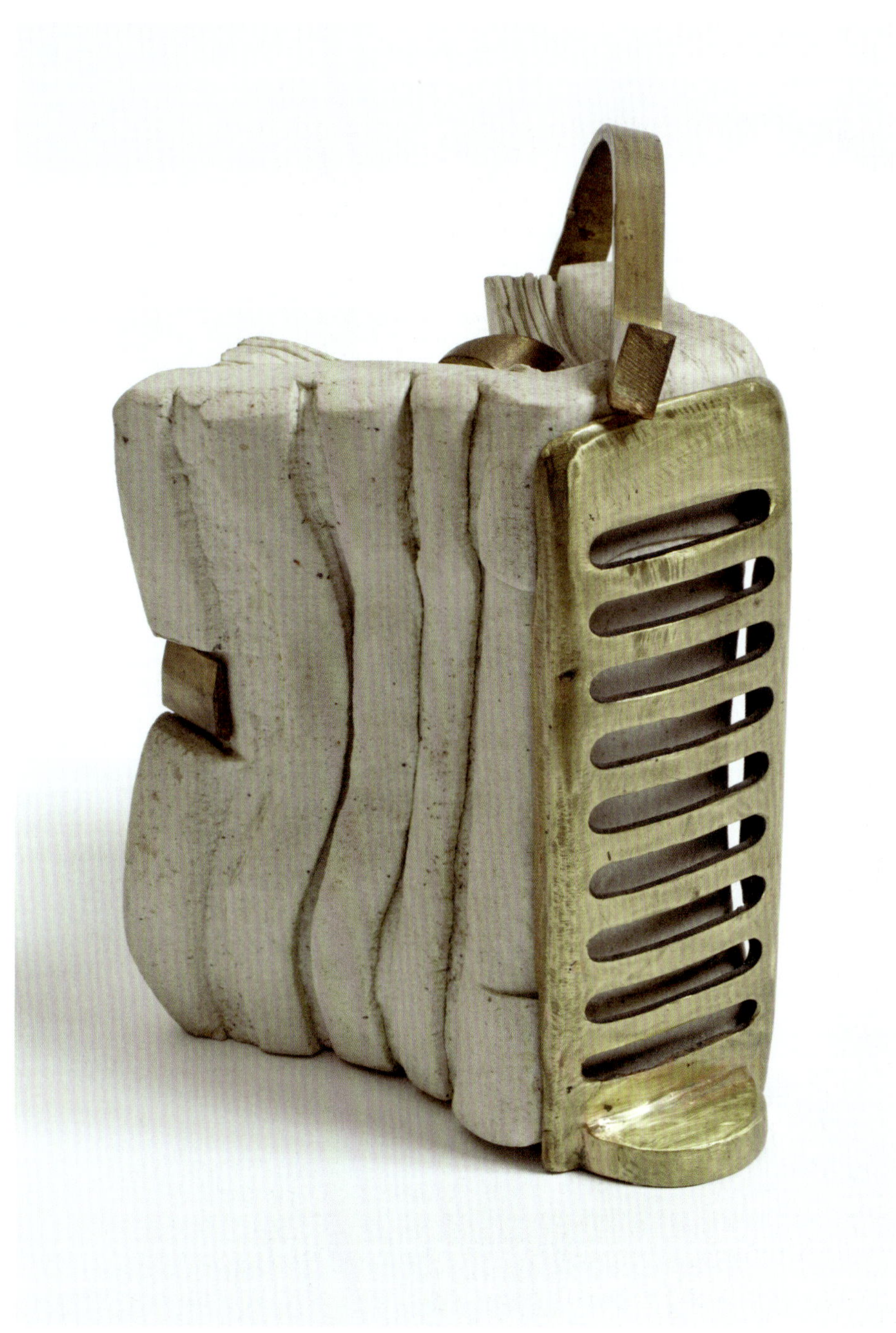

CAT. 41
Little Book of Opera, 1996/1997
Porcelain and brass, 6 x 8 x 4 in. (15.5 x 20 x 10.5 cm)
B2432
Private collection

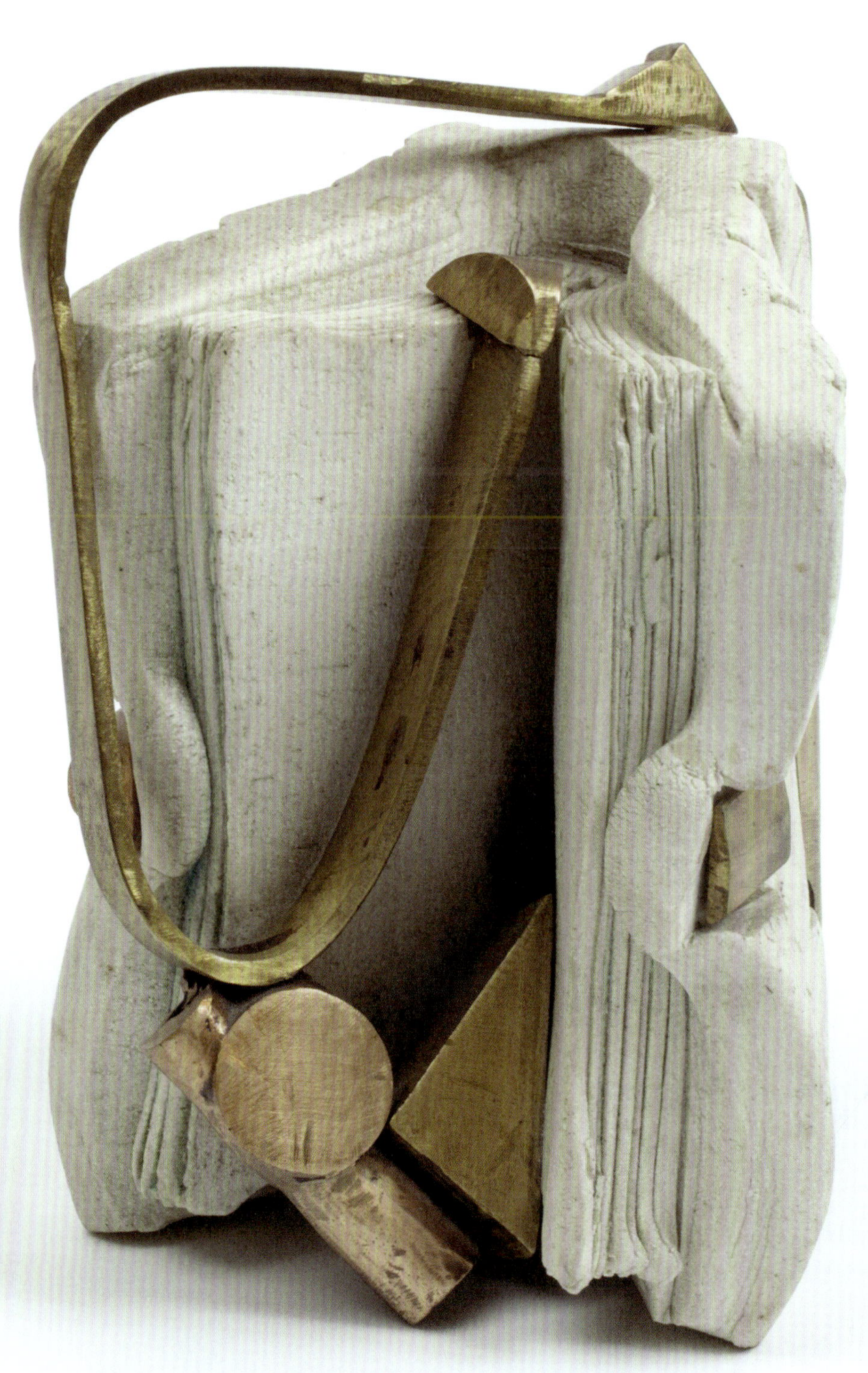

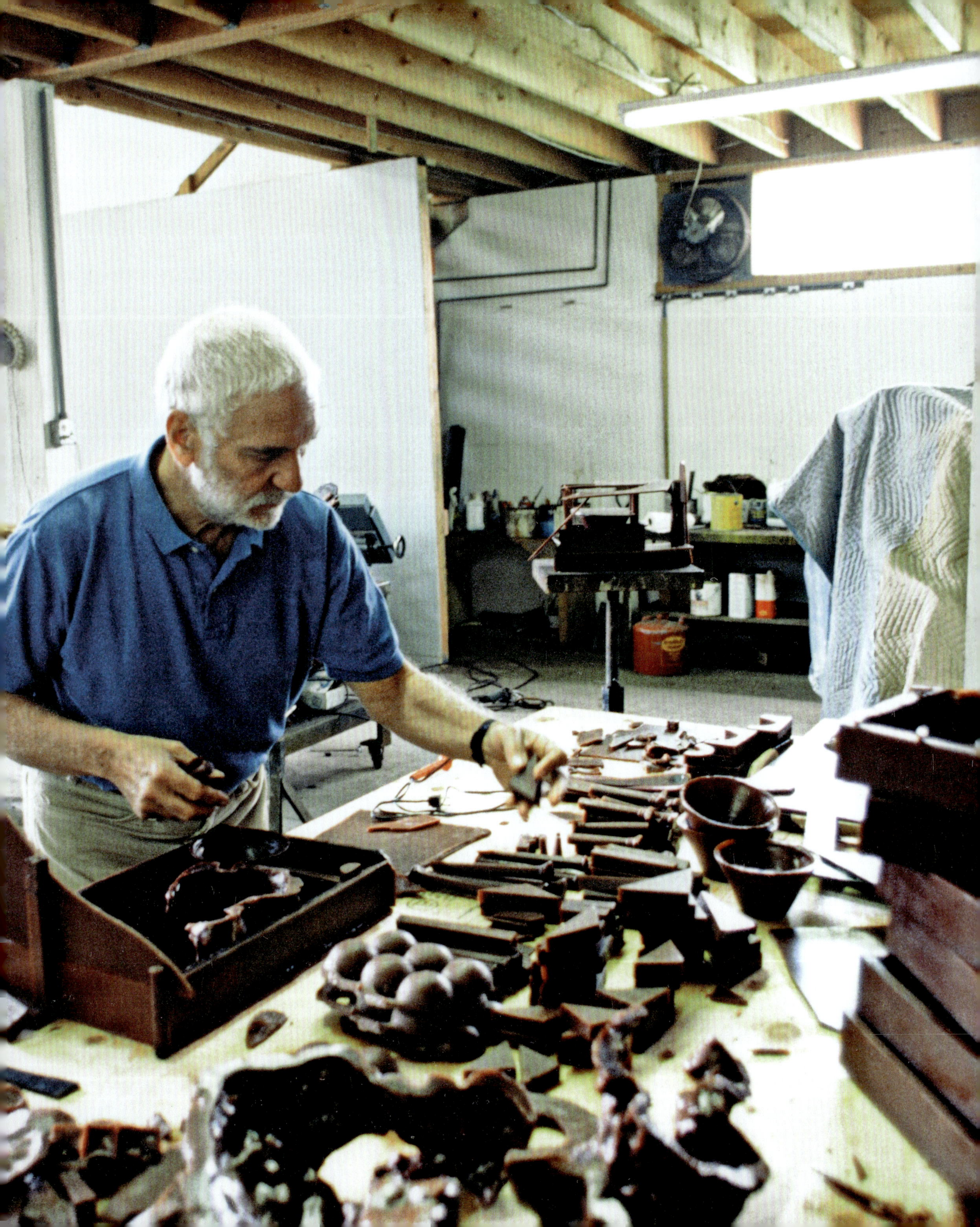

Table Bronzes and Silver

After clay, stone, and marble, bronze is the most ancient and traditional of materials for sculpture. Having established a new career as a sculptor working directly in steel collage, twenty years passed before Caro turned to bronze again. He had avoided the medium, not only as it required the intermediary services of a commercial foundry to translate wax models into permanent sculpture, but also because of its loaded art historical associations.

The first group of abstract bronzes he exhibited (at Kenwood, in 1981) revealed his new process of bronze collage, through which he retained direct control of the finished work. He first cast the components, then combined them by hand in a process he had developed while working in stoneware clay at Syracuse University in 1975. The greater weight of bronze, however, makes it much more difficult to improvise quickly, as Caro had been able to do in steel, spot-welding, alone, in his garage studio in the evenings. One also needs four hands to hold the bronze part, the welding rod, and the welder. A solution was to compose first in models made of cardboard and wood, which he made at his Dorset cottage at weekends. Once cast, he would work further on them with his assistants in the Camden Town studio—through his customary collage process but at a necessarily slower speed. Some of Caro's most intense, inwardly focused tabletop compositions resulted from this process.

One series began with the many traylike, shallow wooden boxes he received as gifts when visiting Korea for his retrospective exhibition in Seoul (1989). When combined in a table bronze like *Scrawl Zone* (cat. 43), such rectilinearity creates a structure that resembles an architectural model, evoking an Eastern palace temple. In *Box of Tricks* (cat. 44) one may recognize the enriched remains of a machine's box casing: there are tubes pinched into a pair of cushionlike forms and a bronze of a human limb, as used in another series of bronzes inspired by Indian figure sculptures.[14] It invites the viewer to look down from above, on an internal, walled composition, like a miniature courtyard, its title suggesting a conjuror's tray of magic toys.

Some of the bronzes from the 1980s have a quality of color patination so painterly that on close scrutiny it almost dissolves surface form. Silver provides an even more reflective effect. While closer to steel than bronze in responding to Caro's

Caro composing table bronzes in his Camden Town studio, 1989

improvisatory approach to composition, this precious metal also carries associations with gifts and celebrations. Caro first experimented with silver alone at his Dorset cottage, while making a gift for his wife to mark their twenty-fifth wedding anniversary. The inherent value of the material (Caro has also made sculpture in gold) calls for painstaking precision, like that exercised by a painter of portrait miniatures, or a jeweler.[15]

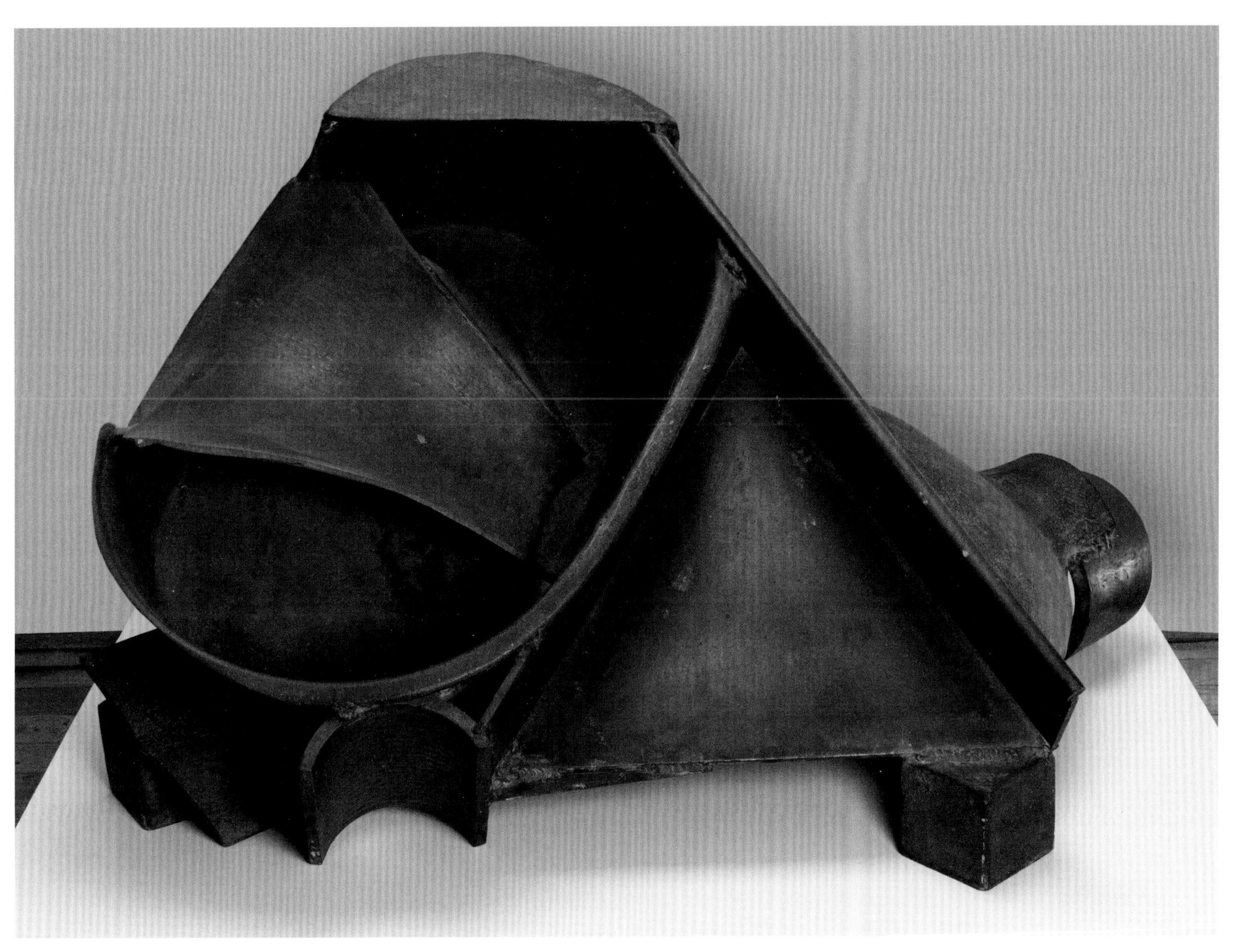

CAT. 42
***Barcarolle (Table Bronze)*, 1981**
Bronze and brass, cast and welded, 20 x 33½ x 24½ in. (51 x 85 x 62 cm)
B1546
Private Collection

CAT. 43
Scrawl Zone (Table Bronze), 1989/1990
Bronze, cast, 10 x 17 x 13 in. (25.5 x 43 x 33 cm)
B2034
Private Collection

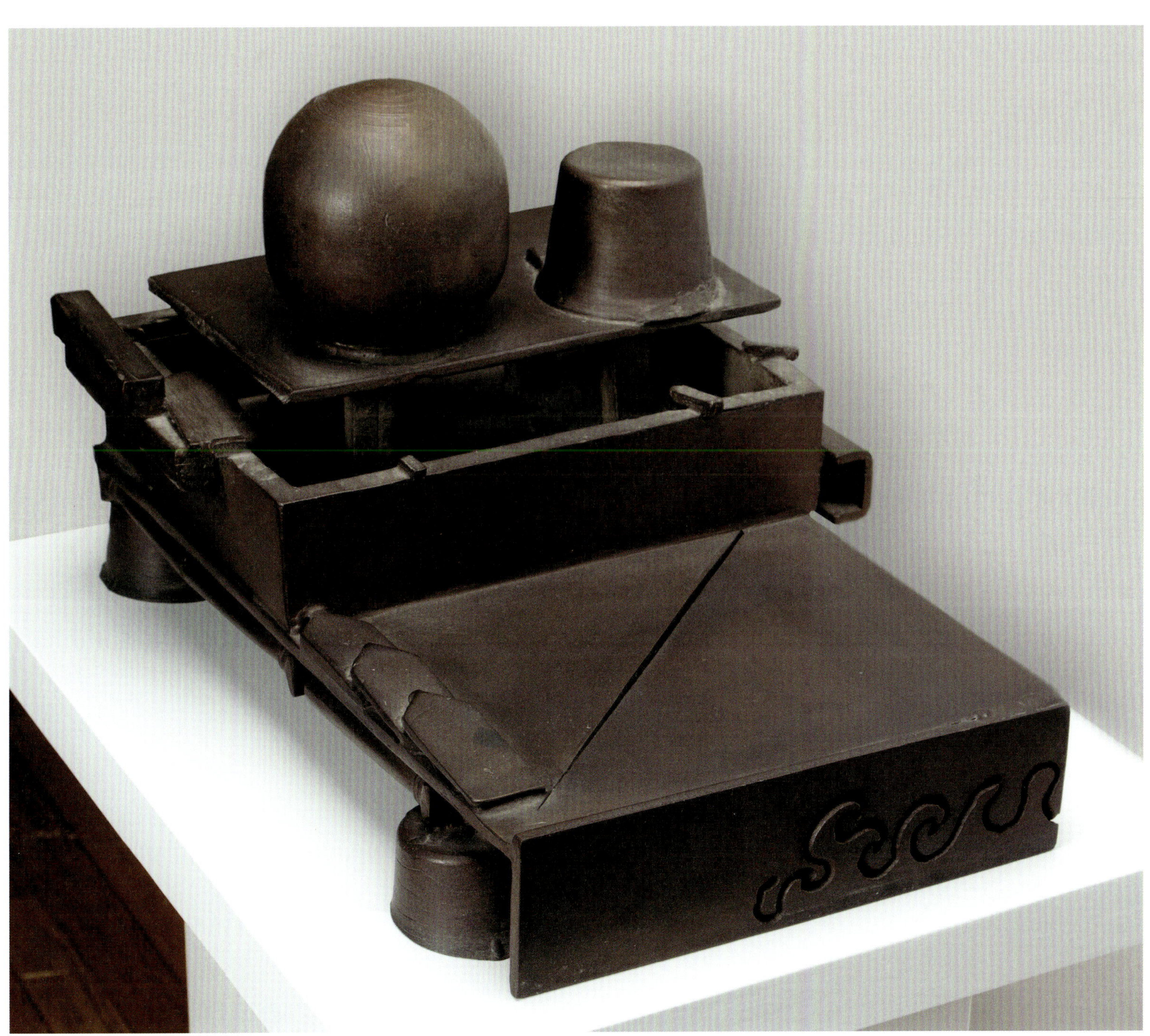

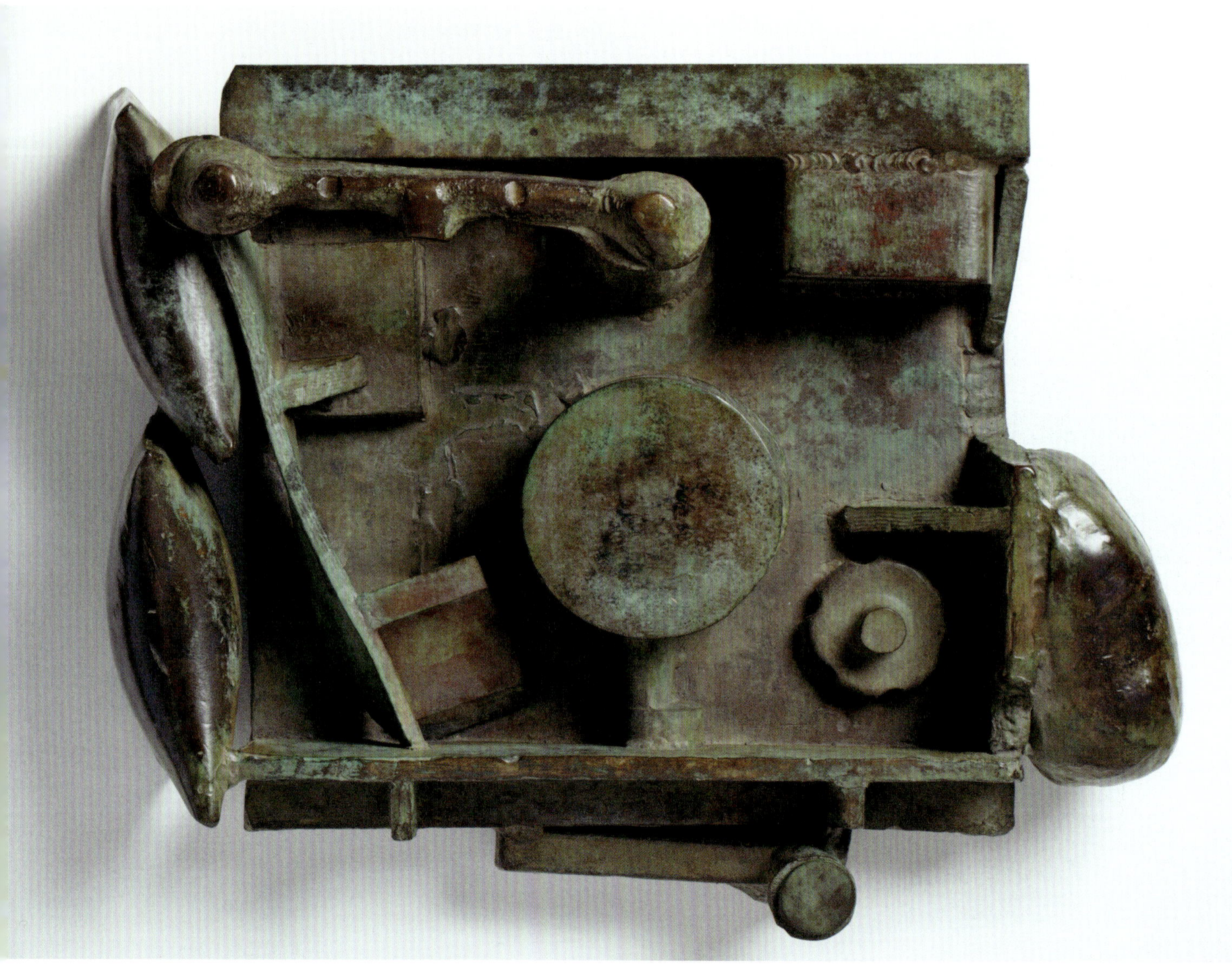

CAT. 44
***Box of Tricks (Table Bronze)*, 1992**
Bronze, cast and welded, 6 x 18 x 14½ in. (15 x 46 x 37 cm)
B2150
Private Collection, London

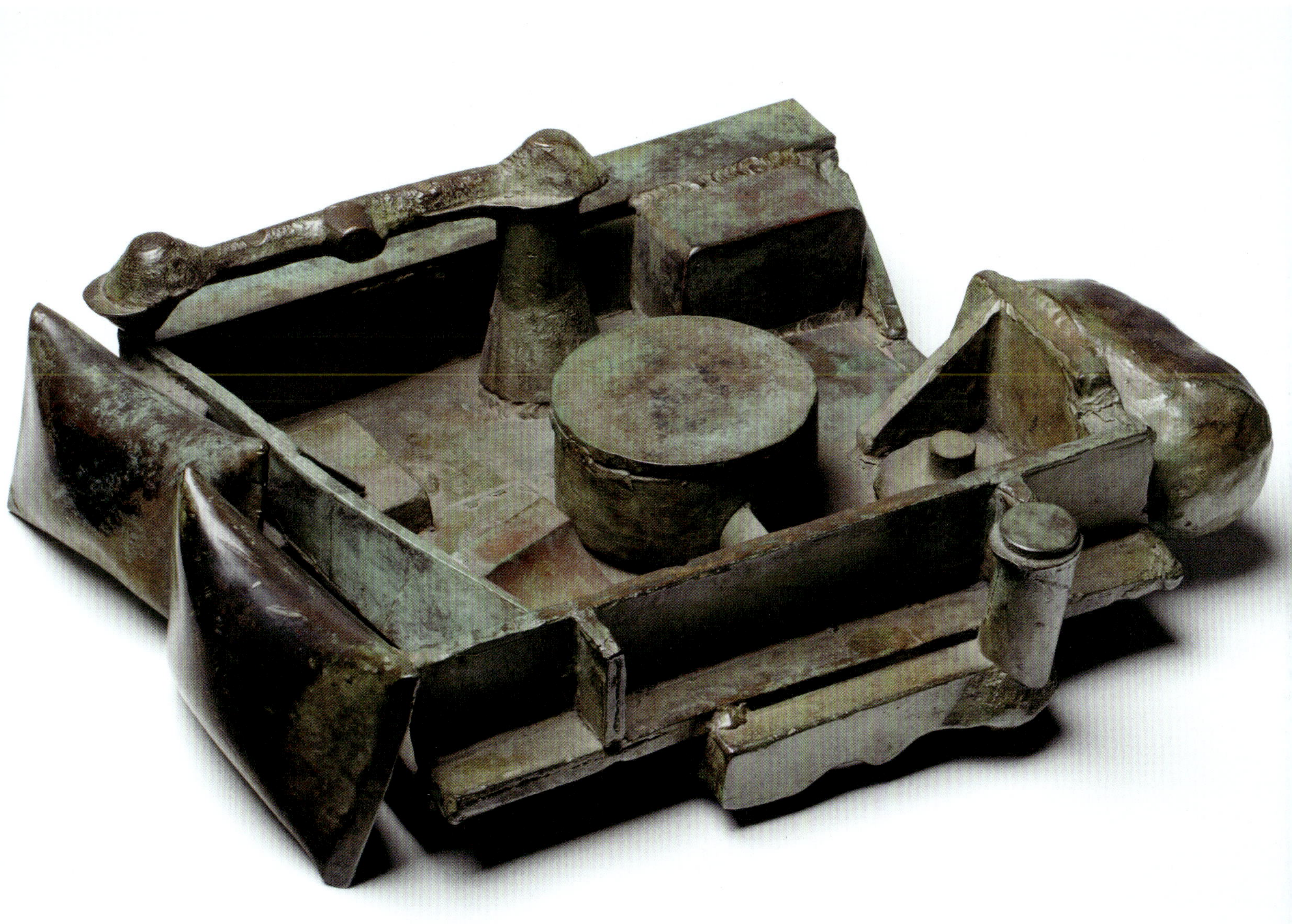

CAT. 45

Cuckoo, 2011

Bronze, cast and welded, 7½ x 12 x 9½ in. (19 x 31 x 24 cm)

T0207

Private collection, London

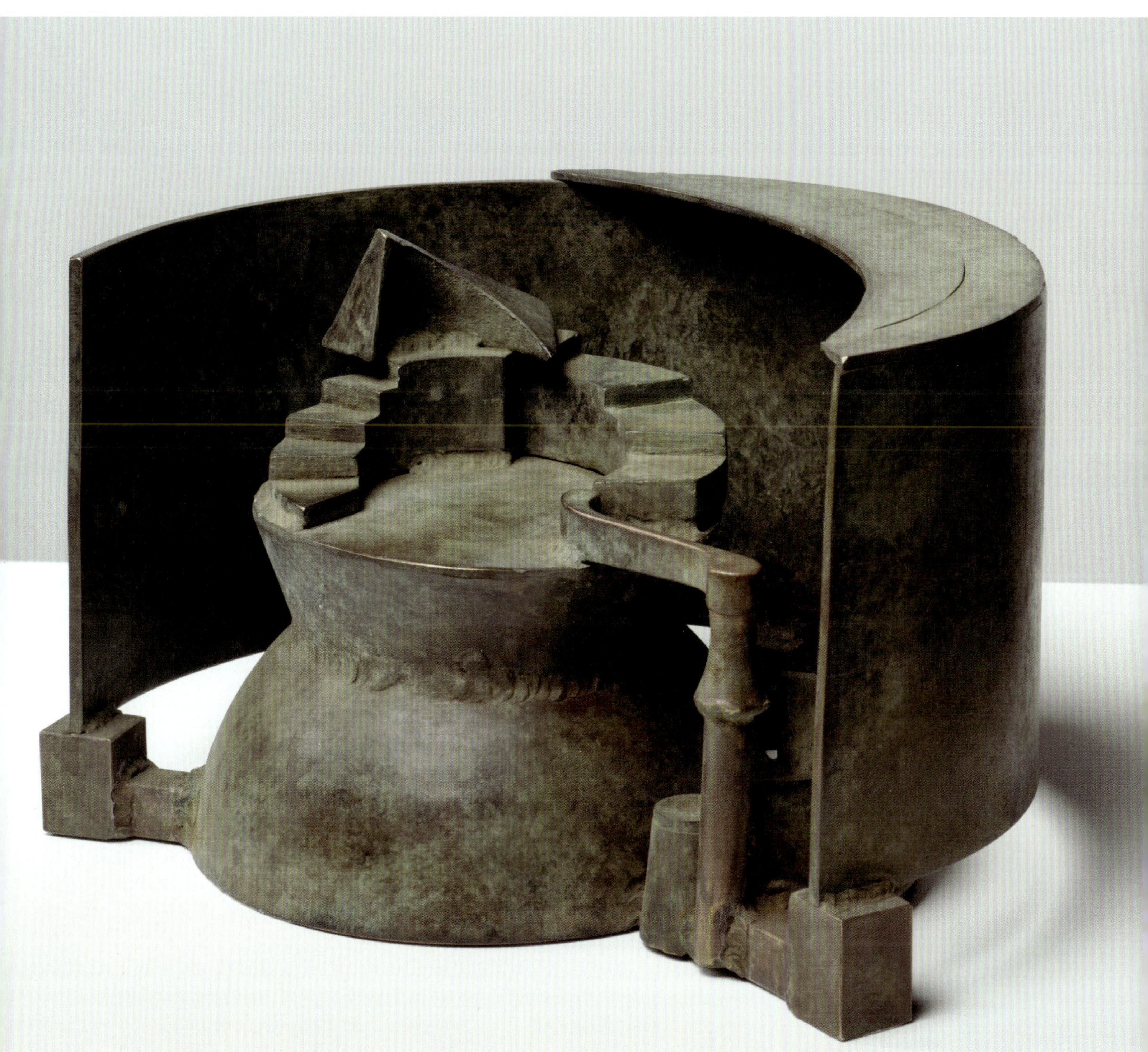

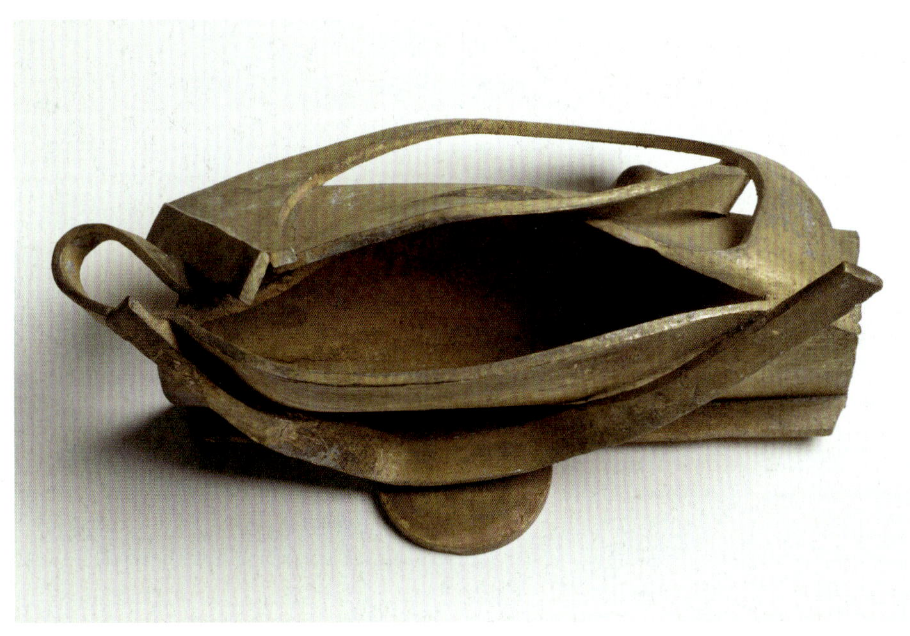

CAT. 46
***Sackbut*, 2011/2012**
Bronze, cast, 10 x 18 x 11½ in. (26 x 45 x 29 cm)
T0224
Private collection, London

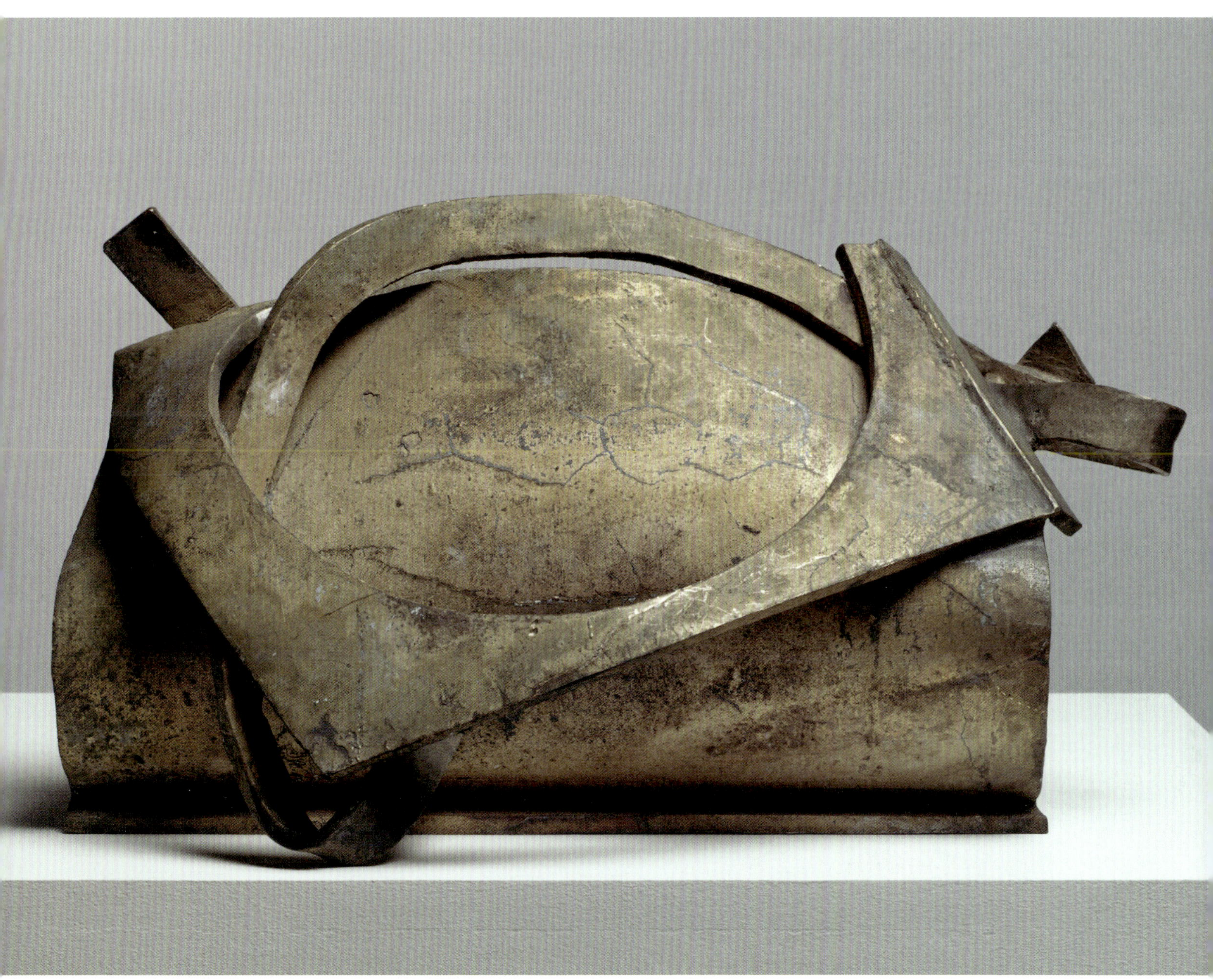

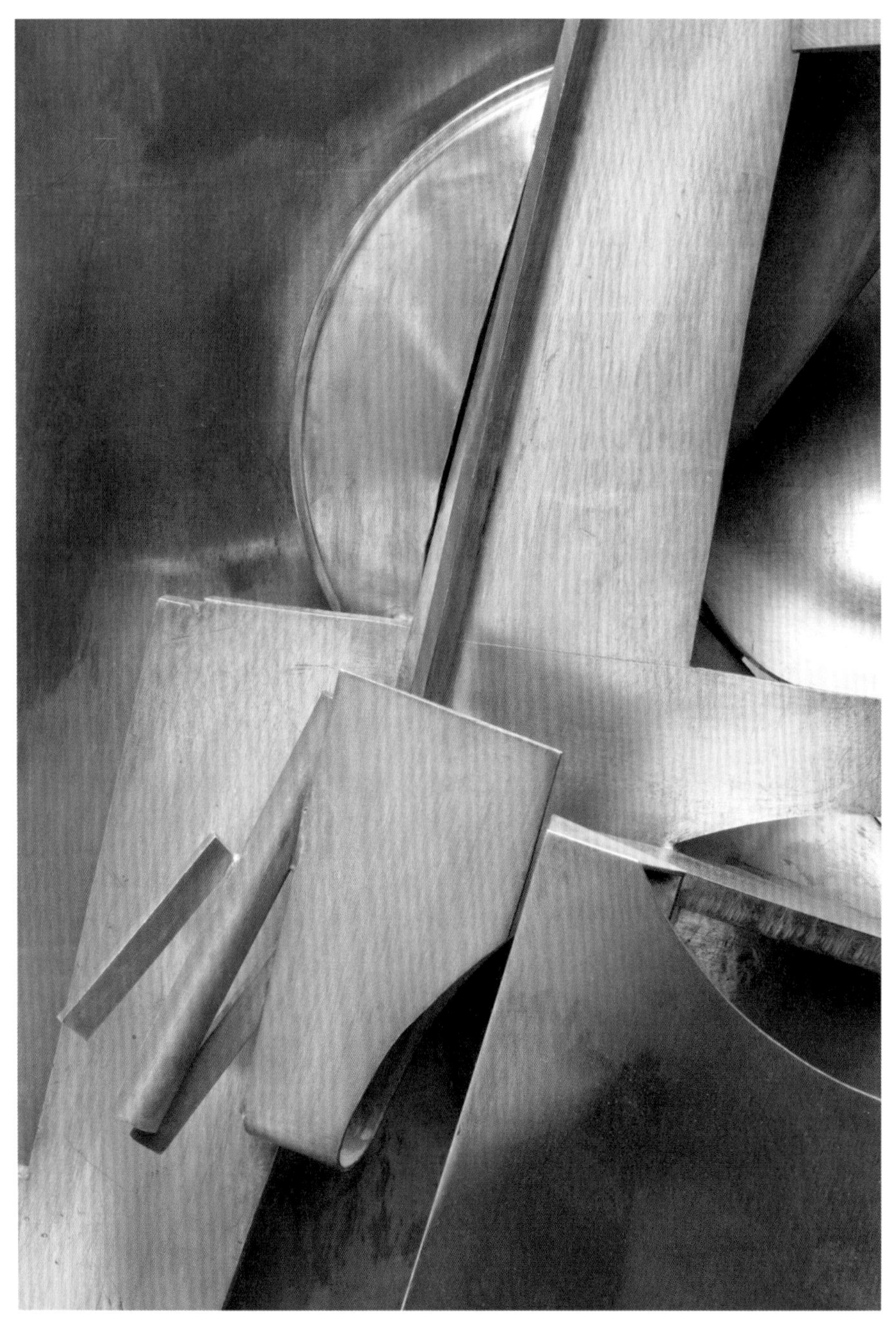

CAT. 47
***Silver Piece 30*, 1984/1985**
Silver, 19 x 11½ x 13½ in. (47 x 29 x 34 cm)
B1737
Private collection, London

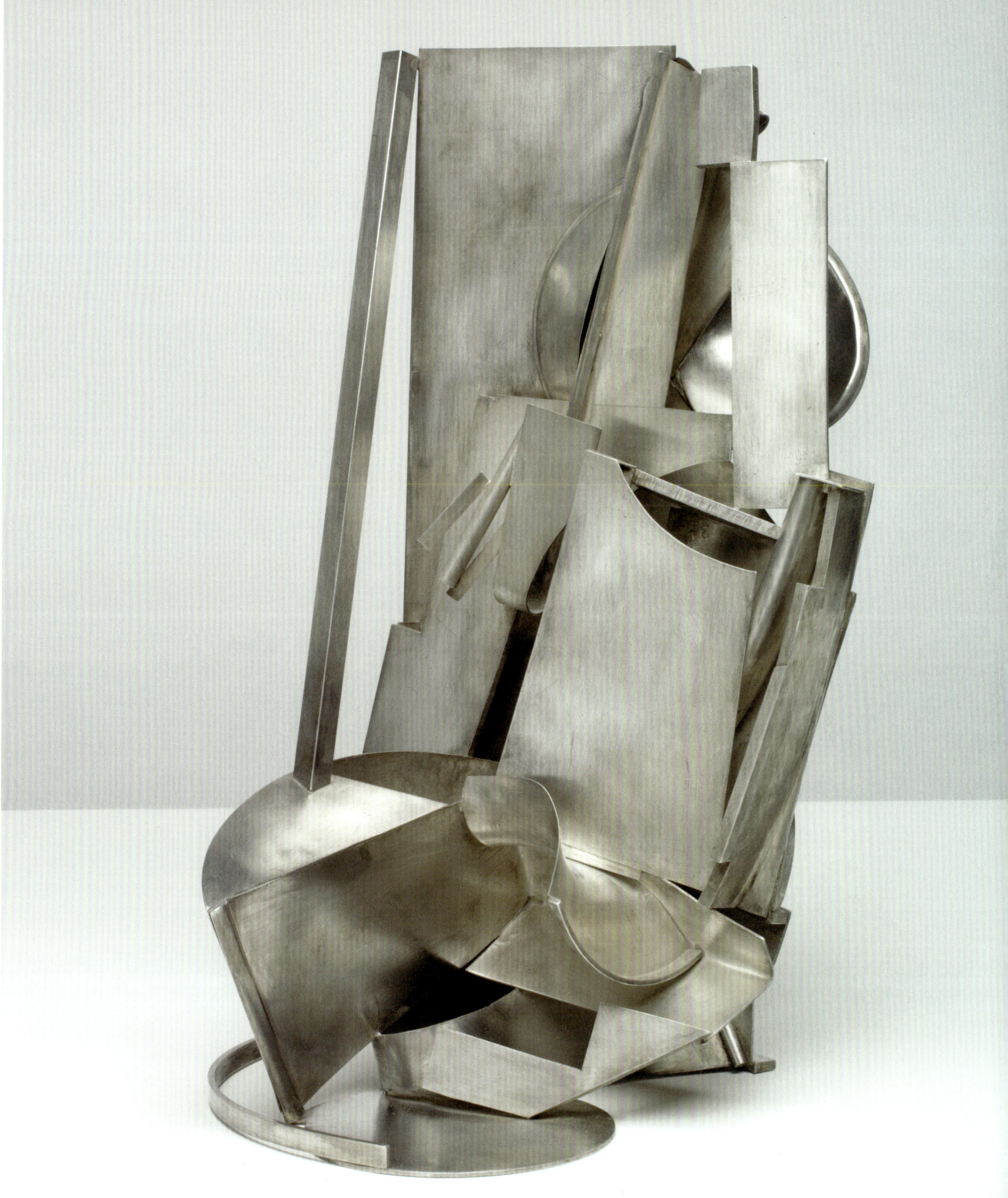

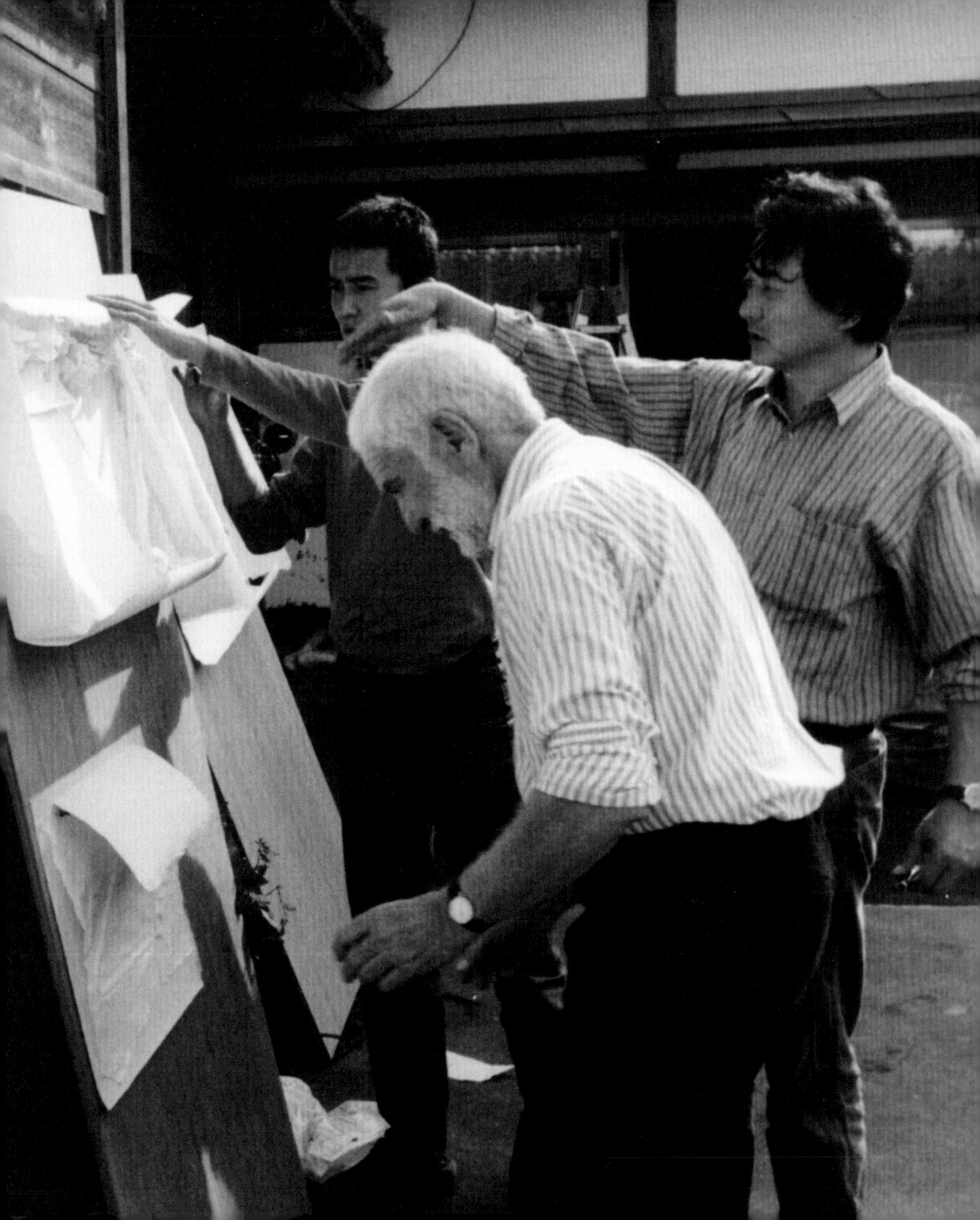

Paper Sculpture

Paper can be the most pliable and fragile of materials for a sculptor to use, demanding a lighter touch; yet despite its relative lack of resistance, it has its own distinctive qualities. In Caro's hands it became the means to merge the sculptural and graphic arts. Beyond the pictorial effects of sculptures in bas-relief, with their foregrounds and backgrounds, Caro incorporated drawn lines, shading, color, and molding. These are the works in which he comes closest to painting, by using color as part of the process rather than at the end, to complete a sculpture.[16]

Caro first worked with the master printmaker Kenneth Tyler in 1981. At his studio and paper mill in Bedford, New York, Tyler made paper for bespoke printing and also facilitated projects in paper pulp with leading artists including Robert Rauschenberg (1974), Robert Motherwell (1975, 1979), Ellsworth Kelly (1976), Helen Frankenthaler (1978), Kenneth Noland (1978), Frank Stella (1984), and David Hockney (1978, 1985).[17] With Tyler, Caro worked with wet paper containing a hardening agent, neither making images nor cutting or tearing paper, but rather folding, molding, and impressing it, before draping it (over furniture and other supports) and then leaving it to set firm overnight. Next morning he would pin the sheets to the wall and add color, line, and more sculpted paper. Despite the practicalities of their backboard supports and protective Perspex cases, these wall-mounted works almost literally achieve the state of "weightlessness" that has been a theme throughout Caro's career. The rich, thick handmade paper also gives them a sense of softness like ruffled bedclothes.

When Caro was invited to visit Japan for the first time in 1990, for the opening of three exhibitions of his sculpture in Tokyo, he asked if he could work with a traditional papermaker. His hosts located Mr. Ohé and his family in the village of Obama, which gave its name to a series of paper sculptures that was begun in Japan and completed in Dorset and London. The *washi* paper that the Ohé family had made for generations was much stronger than Tyler's (in medieval times the same paper was used to make armor for Japanese archers). Caro used it for molding forms and imprinting objects that were readily to hand, like scissors, coat hangers, carpet beaters, and even roof tiles. Sent from Japan to Dorset, the white papers were enhanced in Caro's coastal cottage with color tissue paper, pastel, gouache,

Caro making paper sculpture with Mr. Ohé at Obama, Japan, 1990

watercolor, and crayon, to bring out their sculptural qualities. They were then further worked on in the London studio, some with the addition of picture frames.[18]

The third group of paper sculptures dates from Caro's return visit to Tyler's studio in 1993. Following on from his series of boxes and traylike sculptures made the year before in bronze, he used paper to construct tiny, rectilinear containers recalling origami, and added visual strength to these nestlike forms with bold, solid colors. In 1999 he made a final visit to Bedford to work with Tyler on a series that became the "Paper Book Sculptures." As with the stoneware "books" Caro had made with Hans Spinner in 1995, the creative process involved two stages. In Bedford, Caro and Tyler made V-shaped wedges from heavy rag paper, to which Caro added lengths of rope, aluminum rods, cardboard tubes, and lead discs. These robust little collages have a visual strength far beyond their scale. It is as if Caro has condensed lessons learned from welding sheets of rusty steel into something one could fit in a pocket. Or in sporting terms, they "punch above their weight."

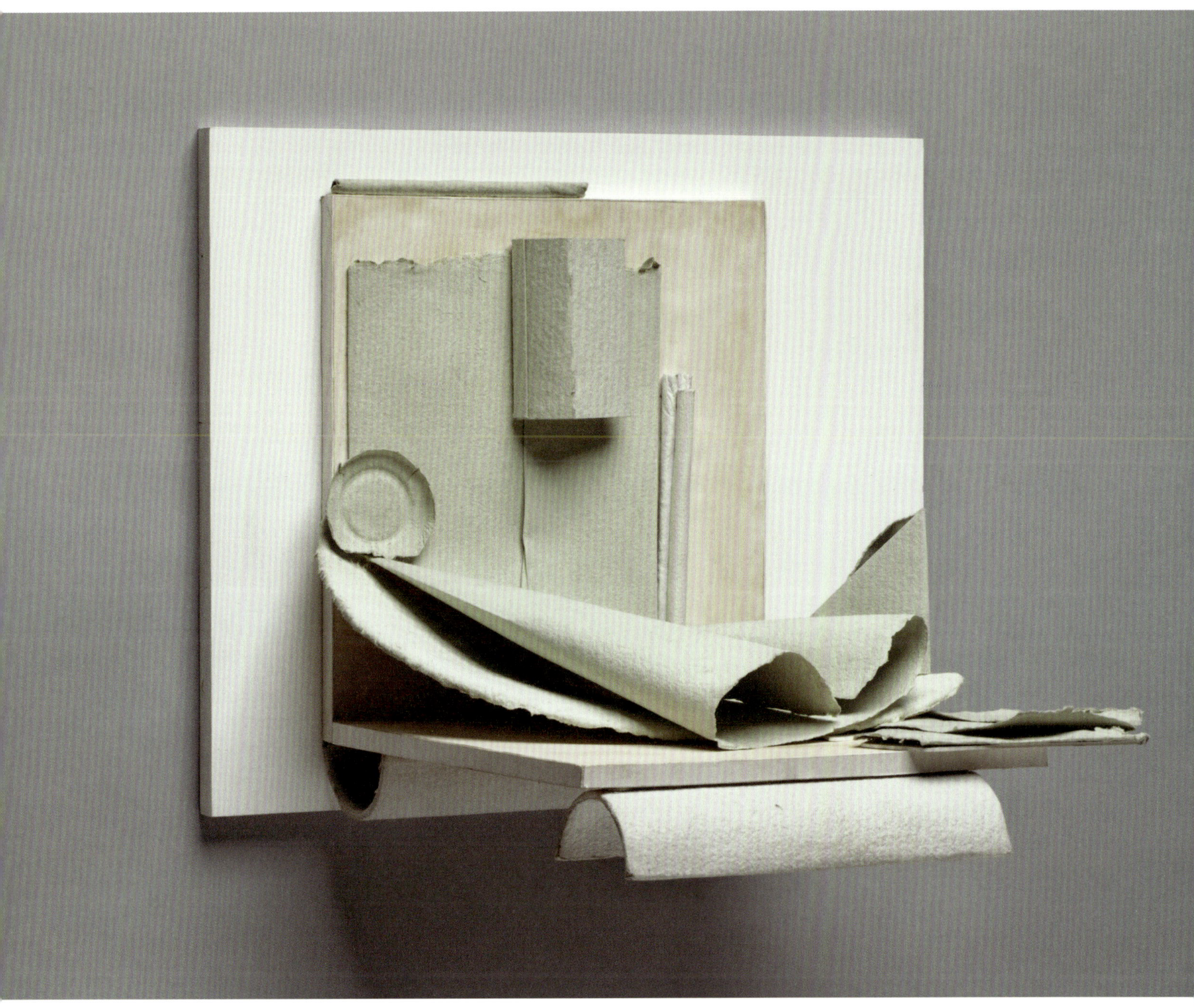

CAT. 48
Floor Paper Sculpture No. 51, 1981
Acrylic, handmade paper, and Tycore on cardboard tube feet, 19 x 21 x 19½ in. (48.3 x 53.3 x 49.5 cm)
B1420
Private collection

CAT. 49

Paper Sculpture No. 60, 1981

Pencil, chalk, acrylic, and handmade paper on Tycore, 30 x 19 x 5½ in. (76.2 x 47.6 x 14 cm)

B1429

Private collection

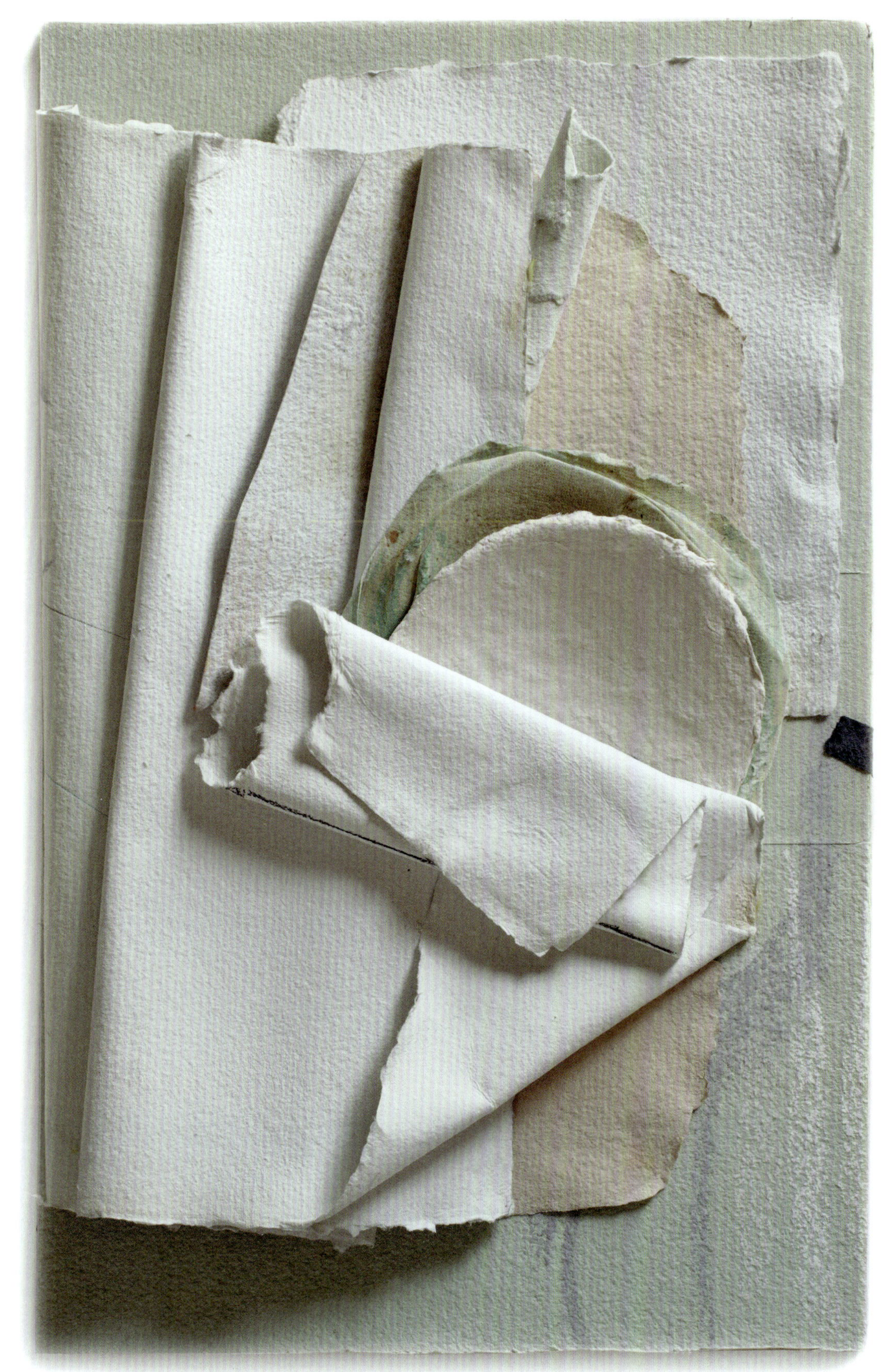

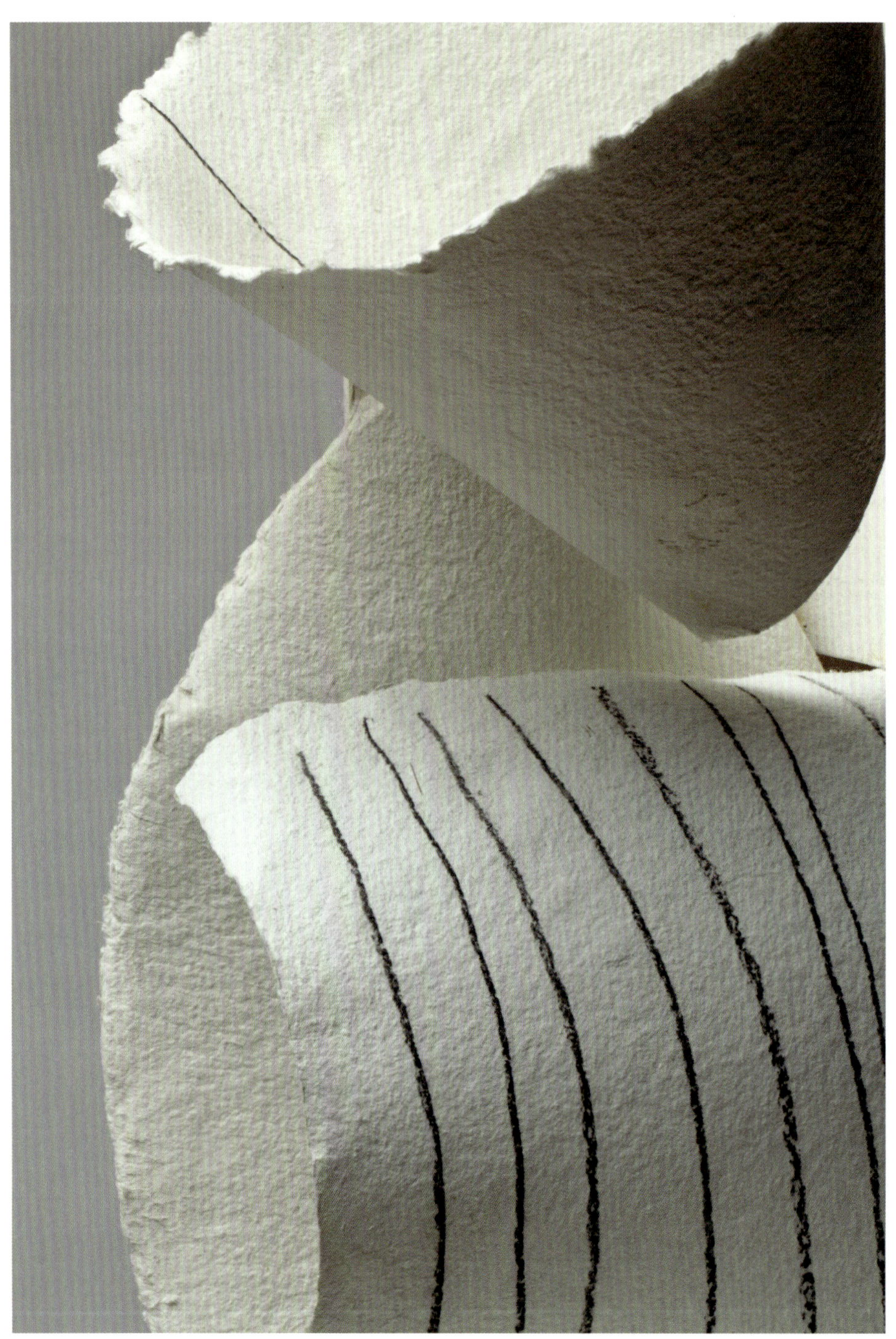

CAT. 50
Paper Sculpture No. 98, 1981
Pencil, chalk, acrylic, handmade paper, and Tycore on cardboard tubes filled with leadshot, 30 x 15 x 16 in. (76.2 x 38.1 x 40.6 cm)
B1466
Private collection, London

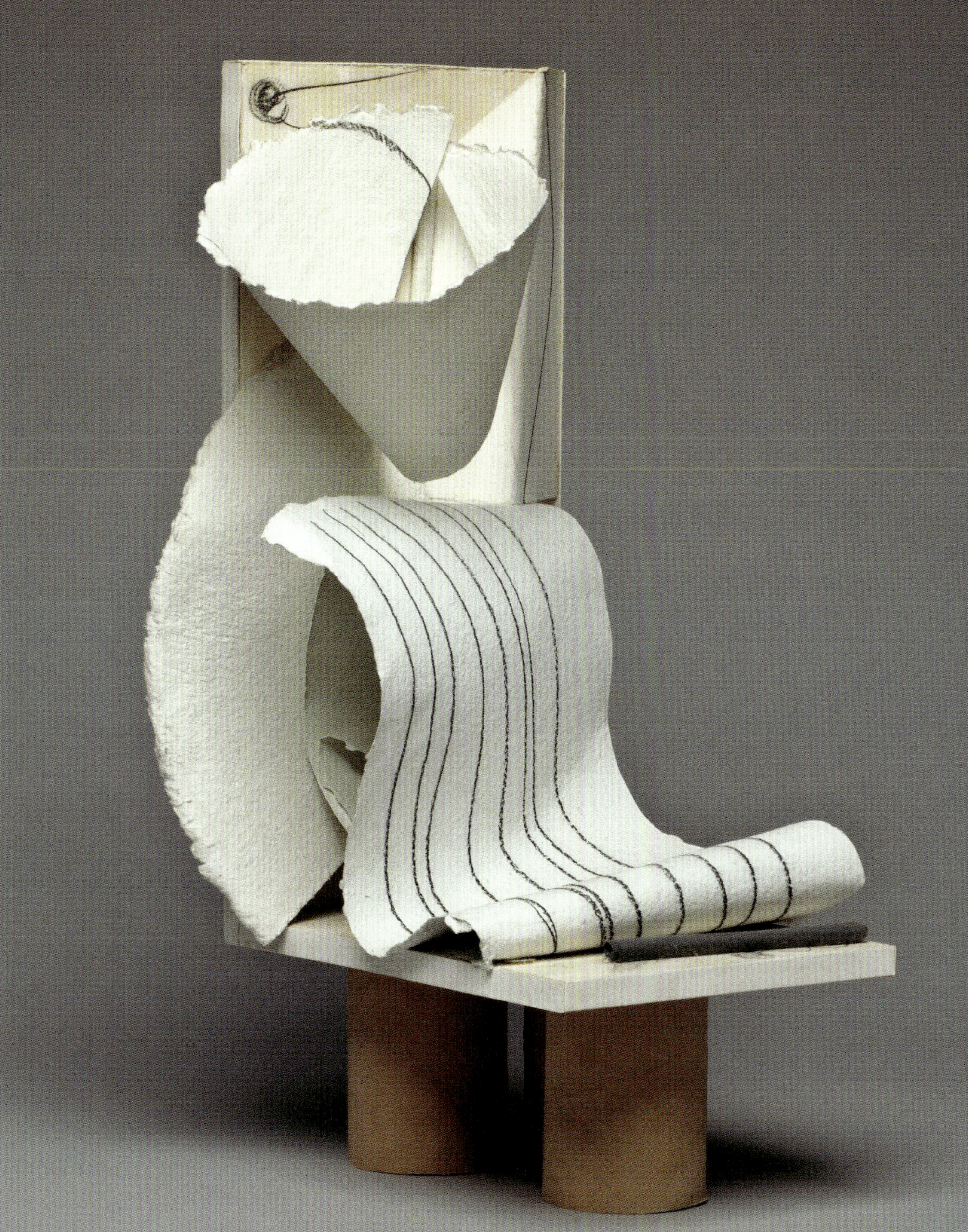

CAT. 51 (facing page)
Obama Parthenon, 1990/1992
Washi paper and crayon, 47½ x 38½ x 2 in. (120.5 x 97.5 x 5 cm)
B2127
Private collection, London

CAT. 52 (overleaf, left)
Obama Scatter, 1990/1992
Washi paper and gouache, 39 x 26 x 4 in. (99 x 66 x 10 cm)
B2135
Private collection, London

CAT. 53 (overleaf, right)
Obama Solitaire, 1991/1992
Washi paper, tissue paper, and gouache, 26½ x 16 x 4 in. (67.5 x 40.5 x 10 cm)
B2133
Private collection, London

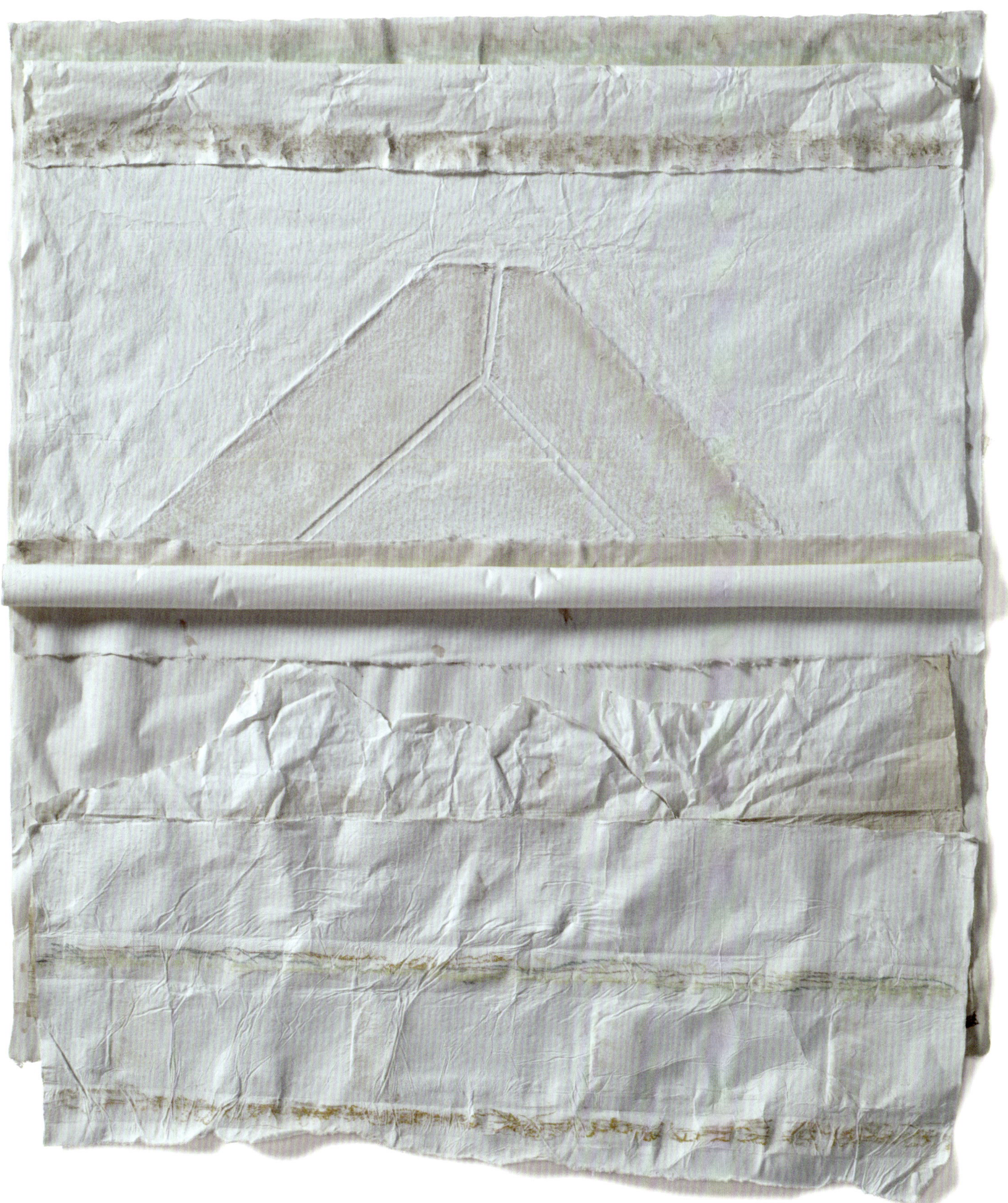

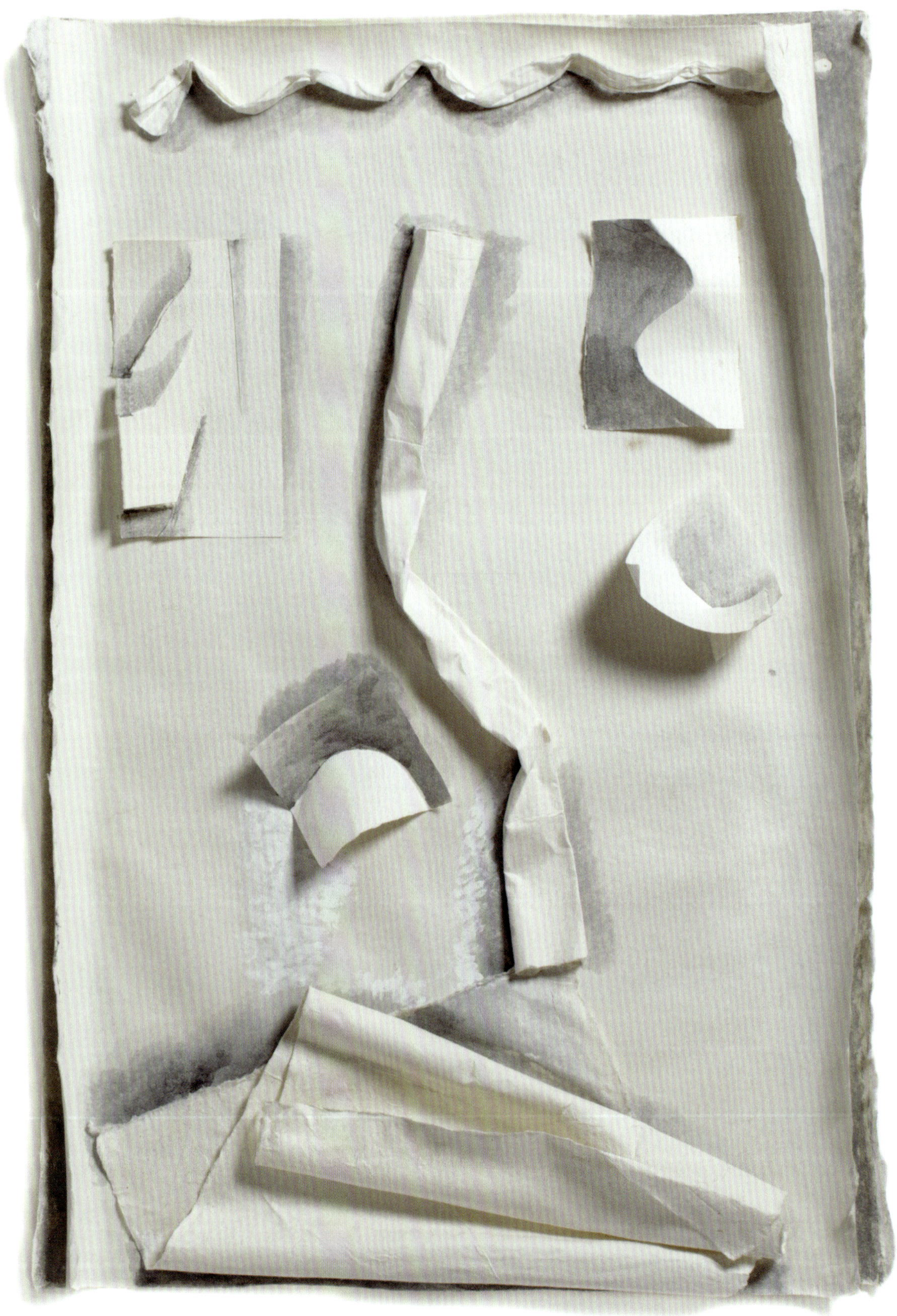

CAT. 52

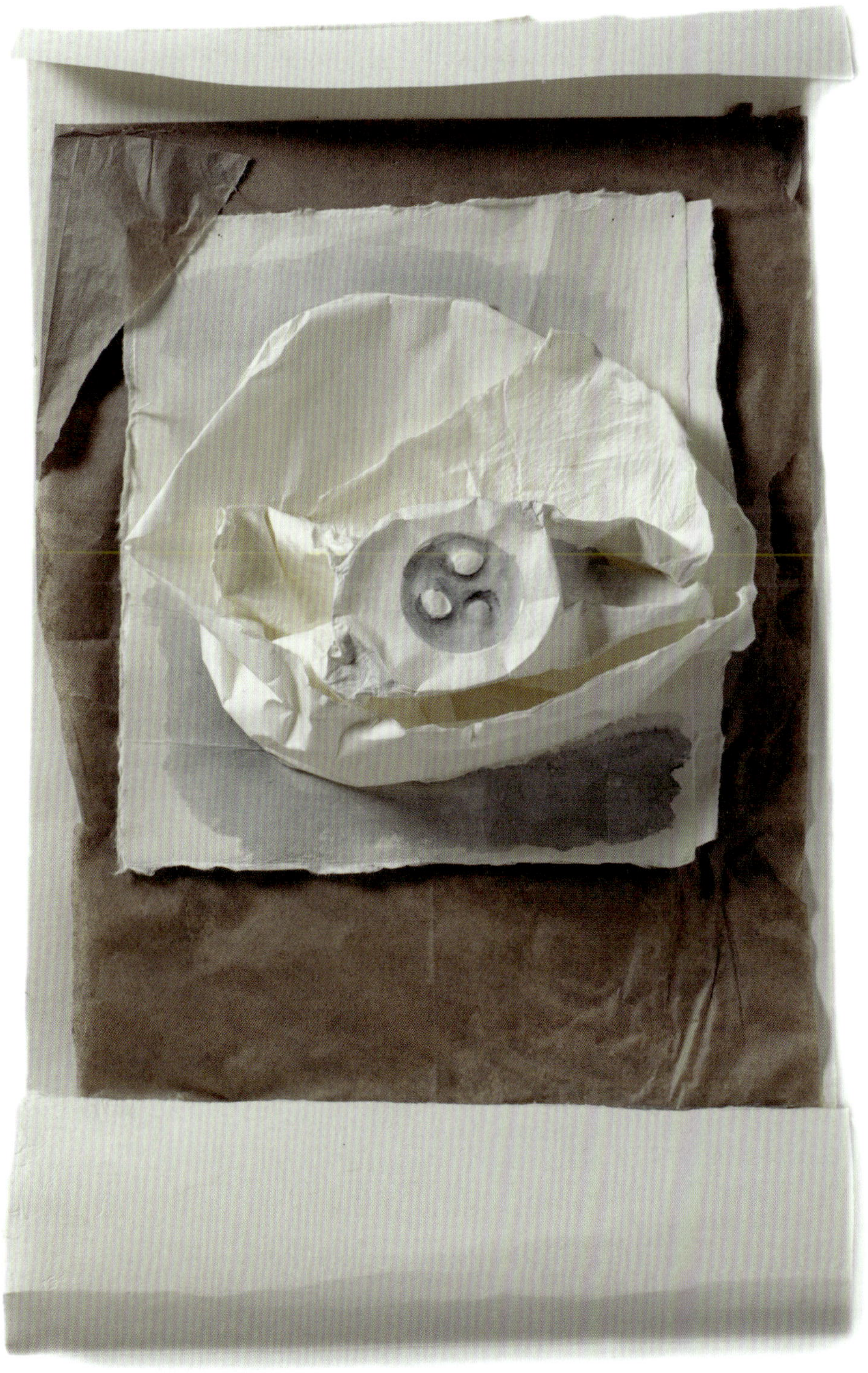

CAT. 53

CAT. 54 (facing page)
***Obama Lawyer*, 1990/1992**
Washi paper, tissue paper, and gouache, 38½ x 27½ x 4 in. (97.5 x 70 x 10 cm)
B2137
Private collection, London

CAT. 55 (overleaf, left)
***Obama Veil*, 1990/1991**
Washi paper, gouache, and pastel, 40 x 27½ x 2 in. (101.5 x 70 x 5 cm)
B2097
Private collection, London

CAT. 56 (overleaf, right)
***Obama Sky*, 1990/1991**
Washi paper and watercolor, 27 x 40 x 3½ in. (68.5 x 101.5 x 9 cm)
B2111
Private collection, London

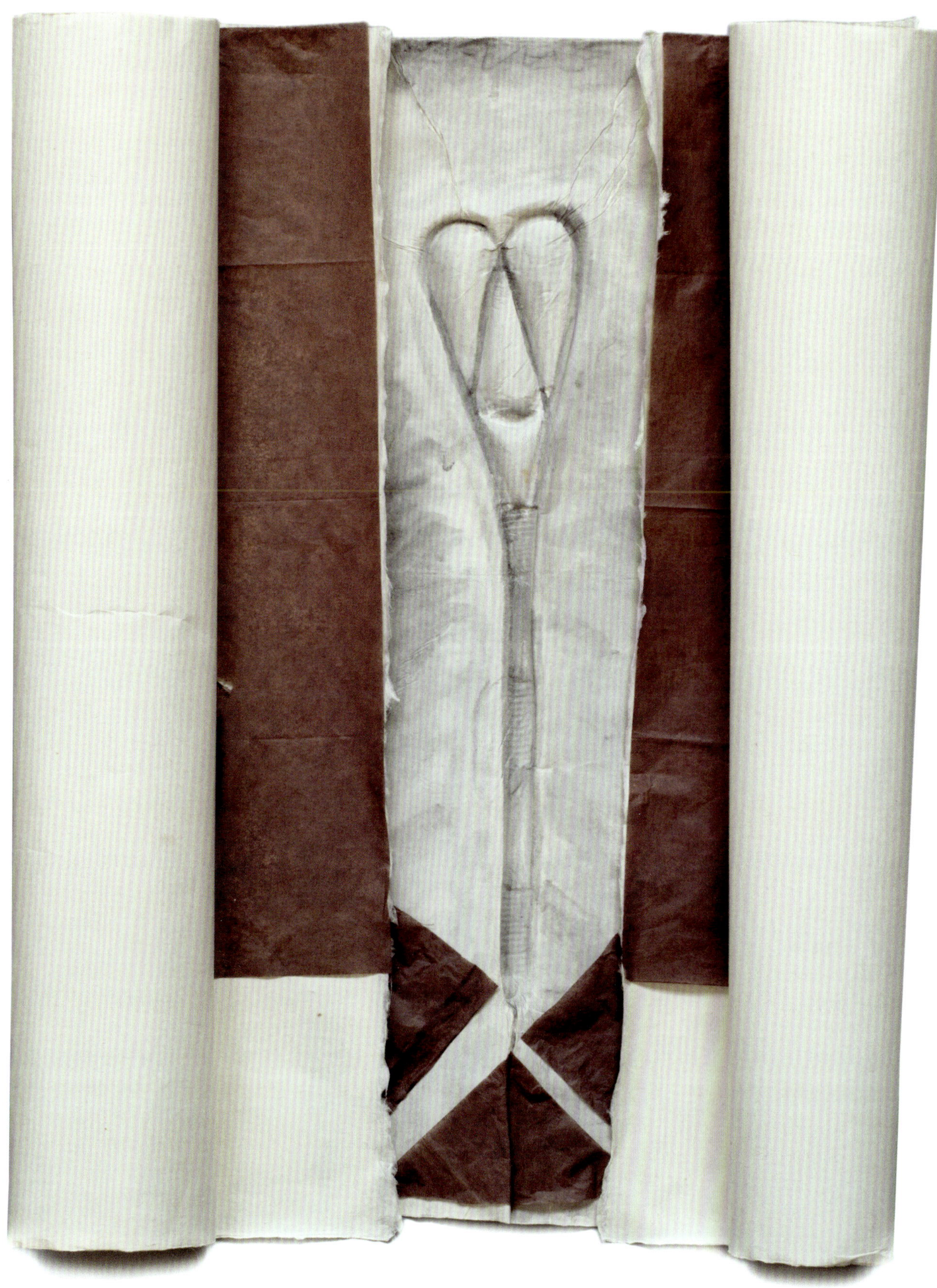

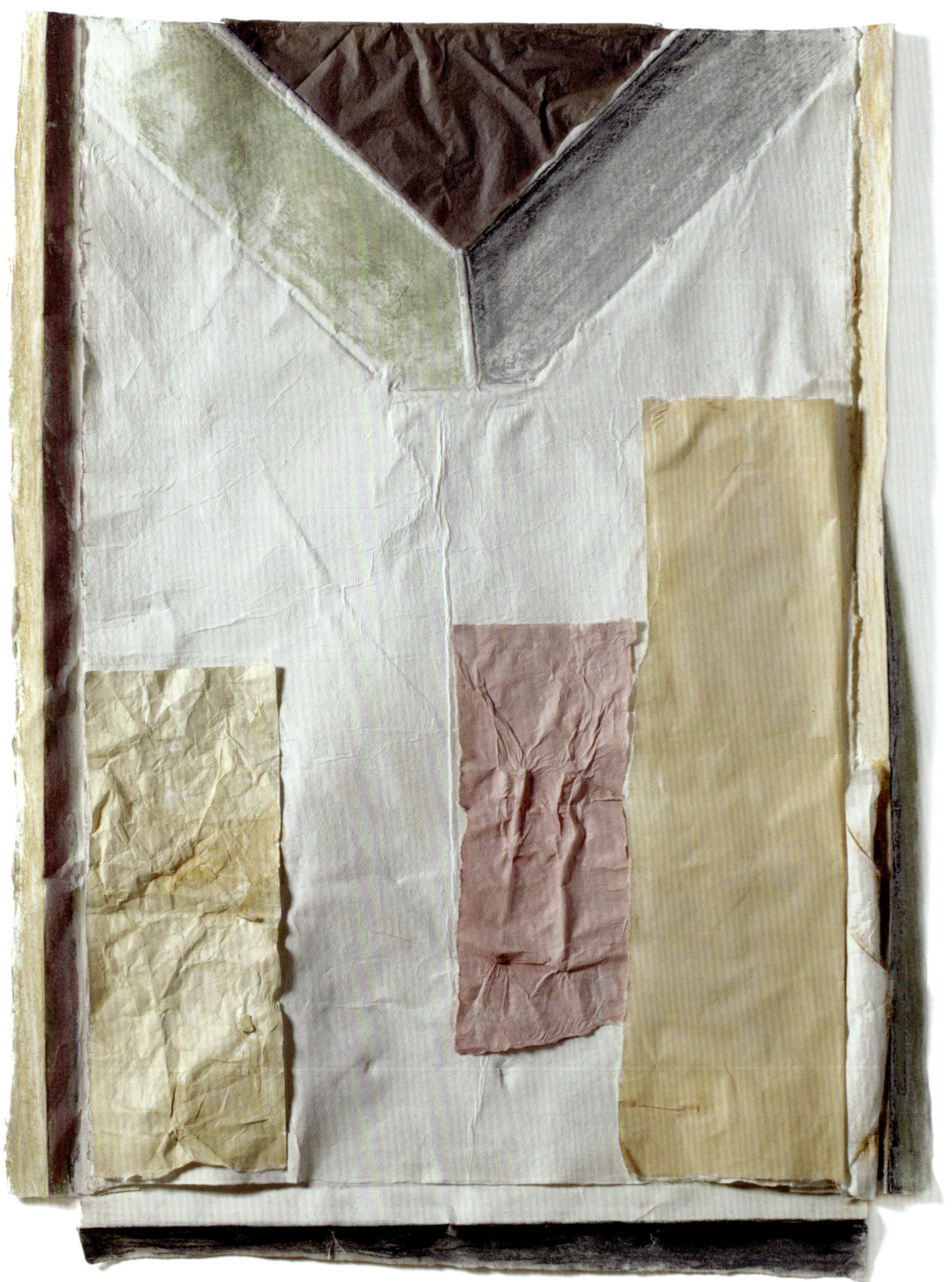

CAT. 55

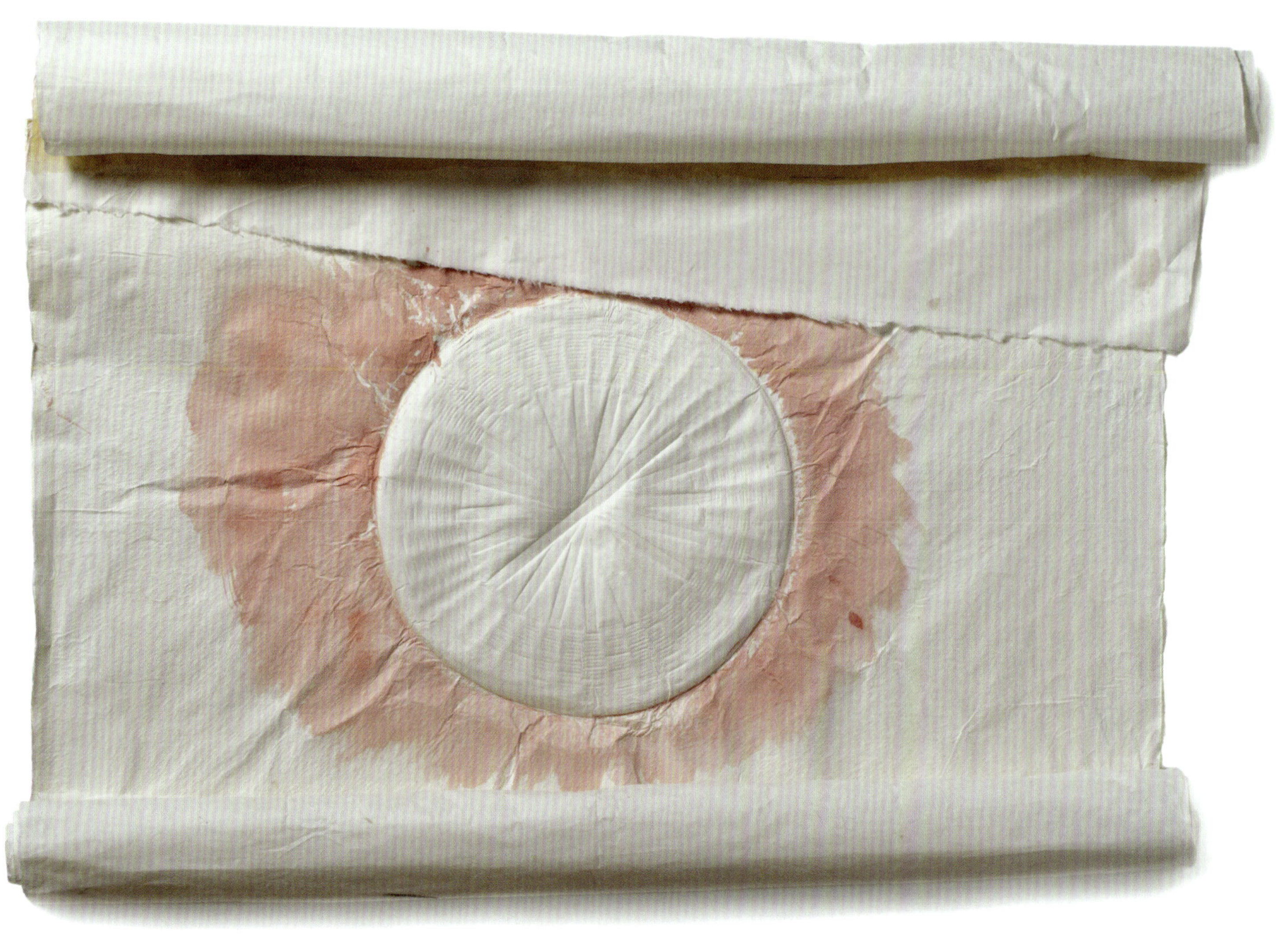

CAT. 56

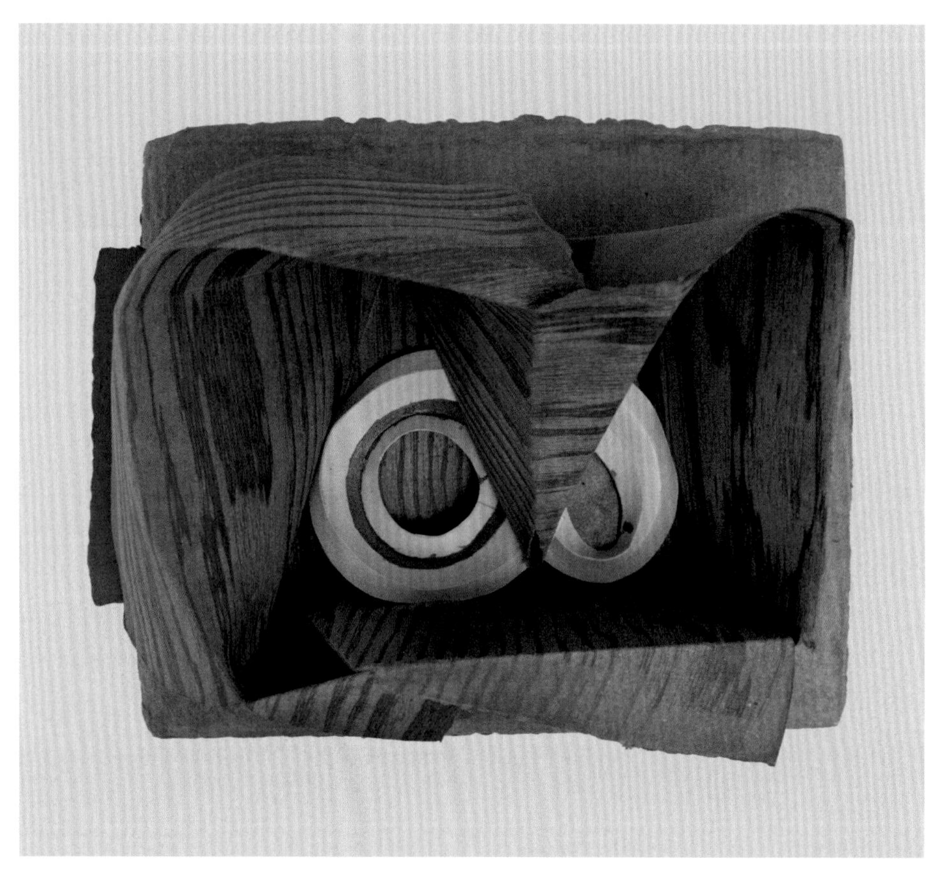

CAT. 57
Paper Sculpture No. 1 – Eyes, 1993
Paper, hand colored, 8½ x 16 x 14 in. (20.5 x 41 x 35 cm)
B2306
Collection of Karen Wilkin

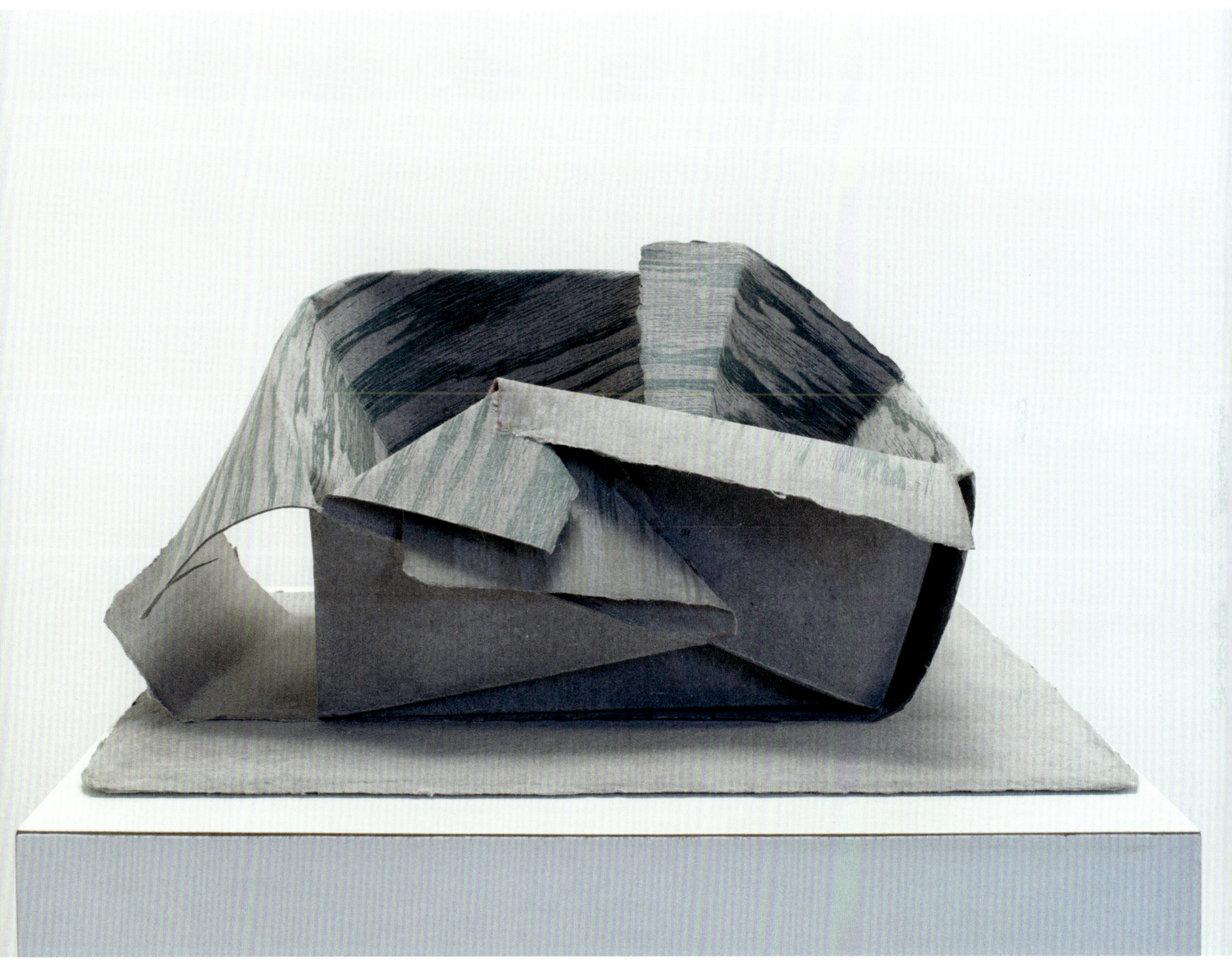

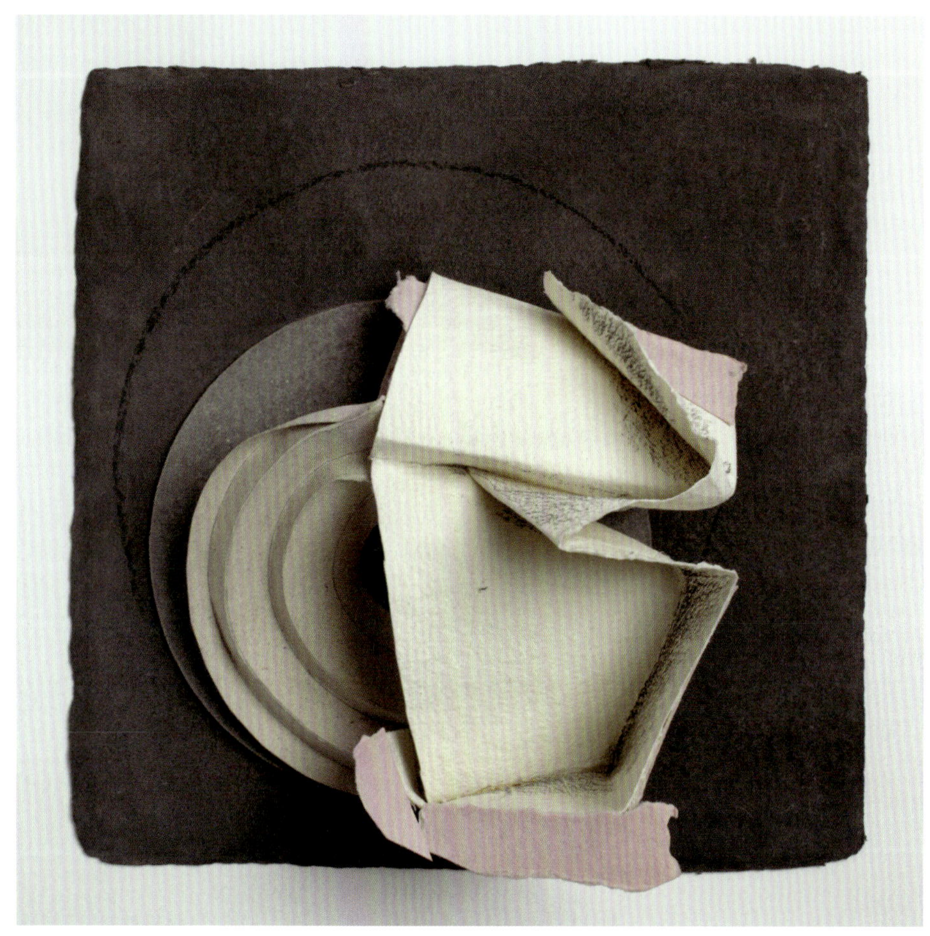

CAT. 58
Paper Sculpture No. 13 – Whirl, 1993
Paper, hand colored, 7½ x 16 x 16 in. (19 x 45.5 x 40 cm)
B2318
Private collection, London

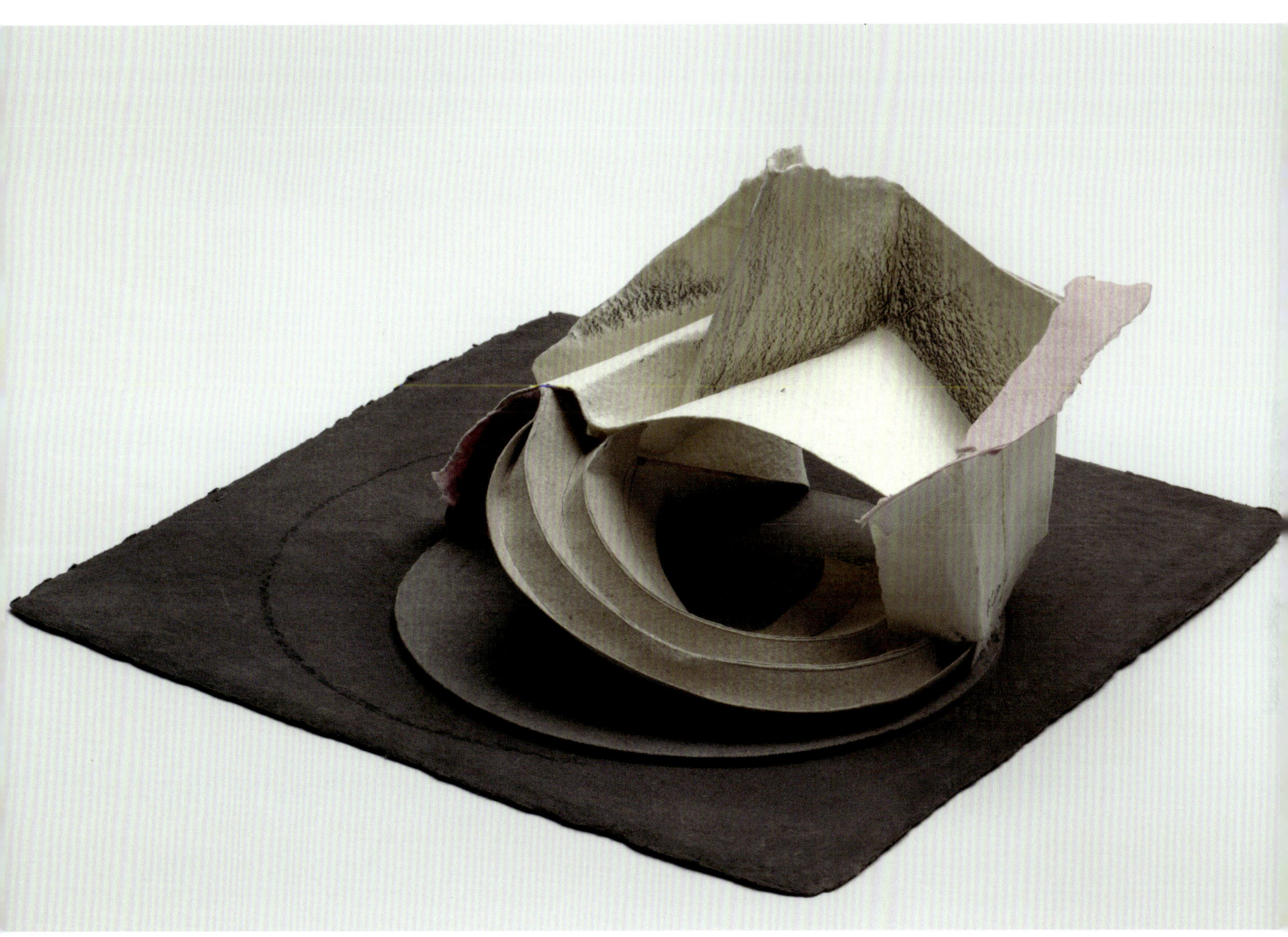

CAT. 59

Paper Sculpture No. 17 – Island, 1993

Paper, hand colored, 6 x 12½ x 15½ in. (14.5 x 31.5 x 40 cm)

B2322

Private collection, London

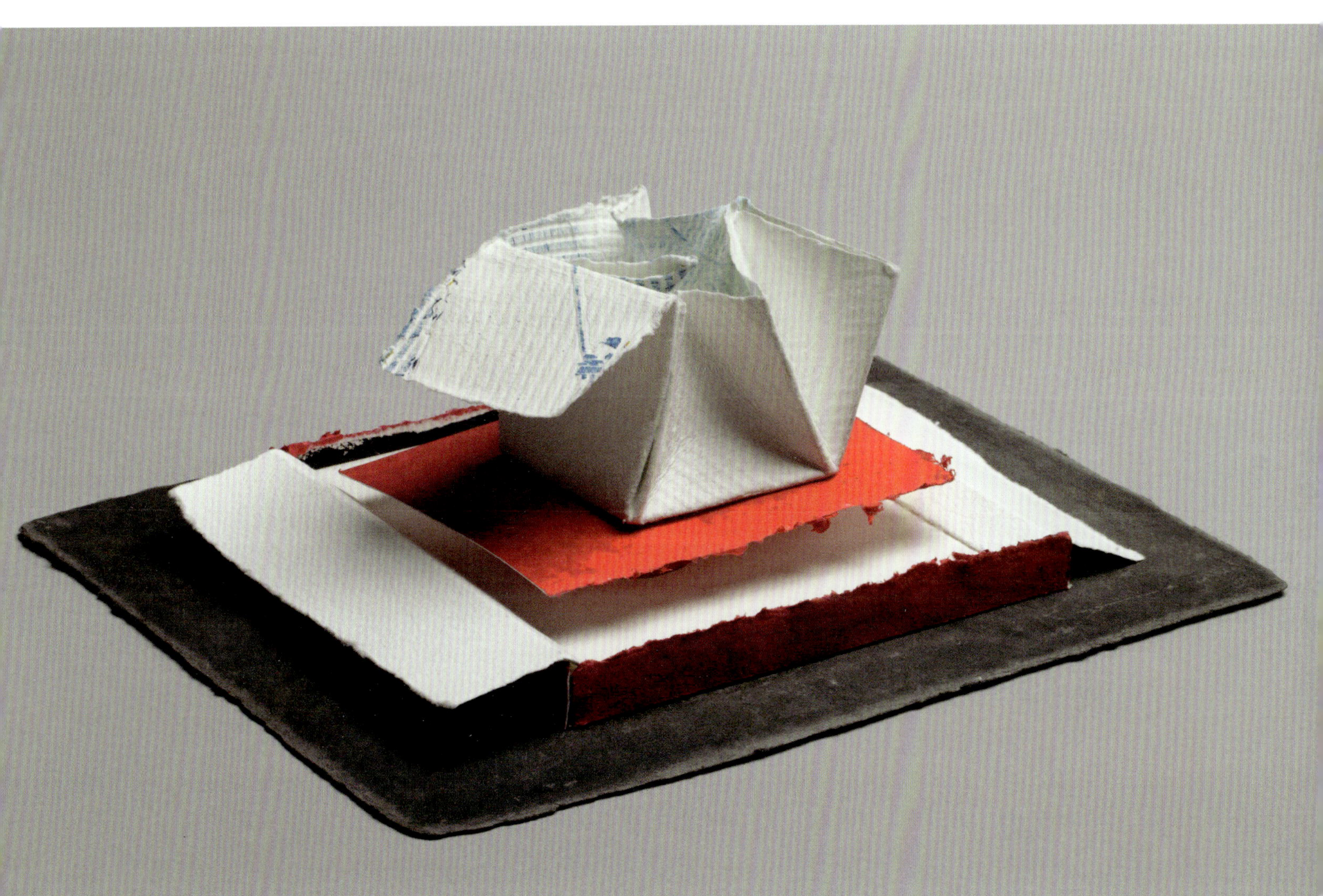

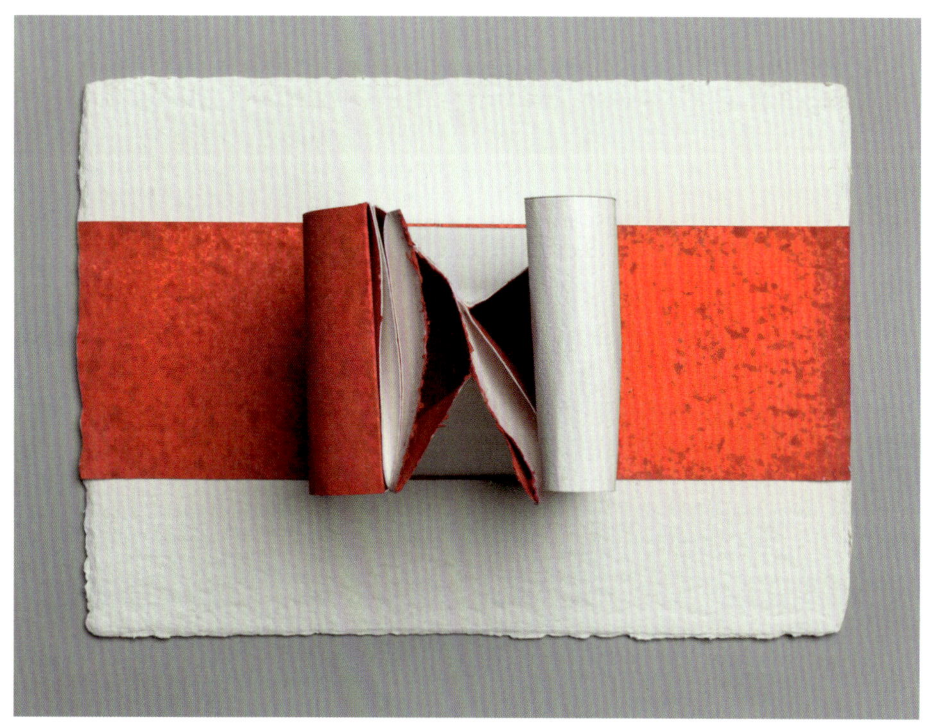

CAT. 60

***Paper Sculpture No. 34 – Red Carpet*, 1993**

Paper, hand colored, 9 x 22 x 16 in. (23 x 56 x 40.5 cm)

B2339

Private collection, London

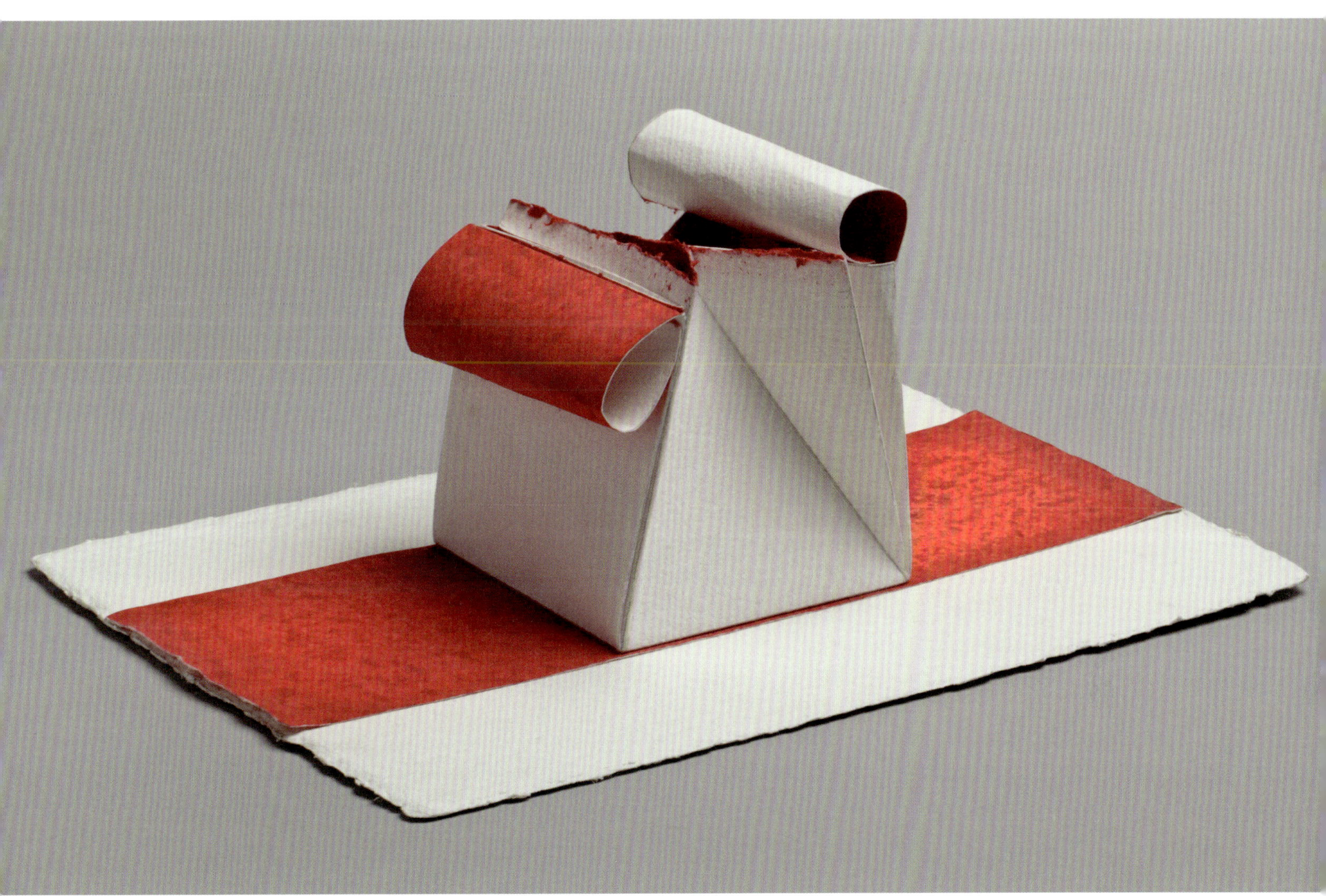

CAT. 61

Paper Slipper, 1999/2002

Handmade paper, rope, aluminum, and corrugated card base, 15 x 11½ x 13 in. (38 x 29 x 33 cm)

B2647

Private collection, London

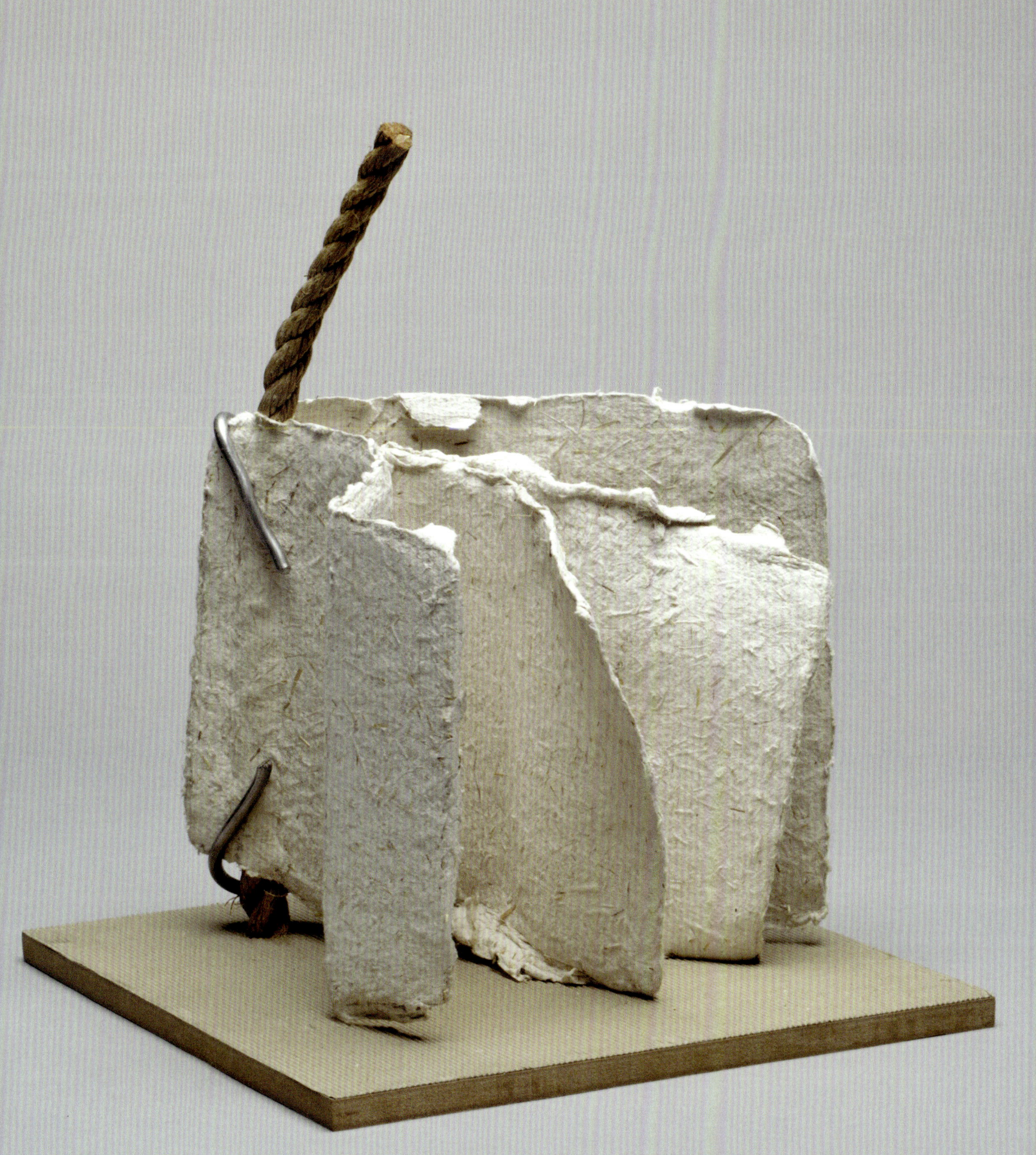

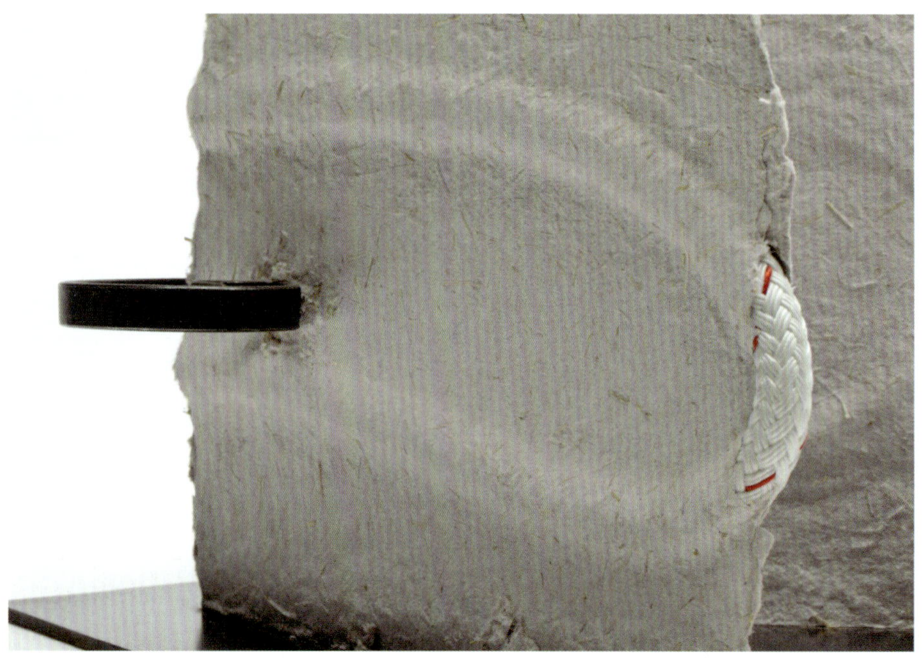

CAT. 62

Paperetto, 1999/2002

Handmade paper, rope, and steel on steel base, 10 x 13½ x 13 in. (25.5 x 34 x 33 cm)

B2651

Private collection, London

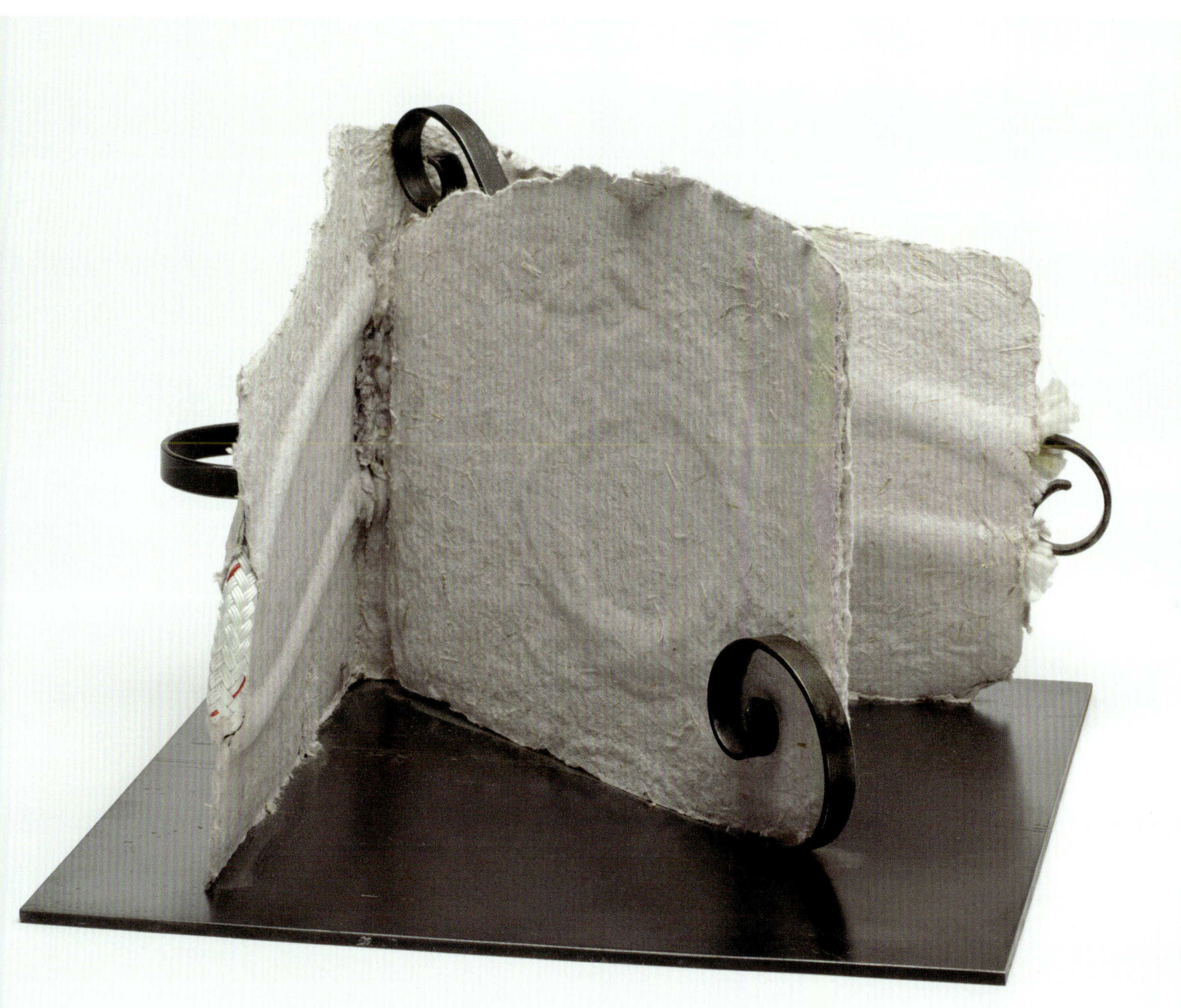

NOTES

1. Anthony Caro, "The Master Sculptor," *Observer Weekend Review,* Nov. 27, 1960.

2. Quoted in Diane Waldman, *Anthony Caro* (New York: Abbeville, 1982), 18–20.

3. Quoted in David Mitchinson, *Celebrating Moore: Works from the Henry Moore Foundation* (London: Lund Humphries, 1998), 120.

4. Herbert Read, "New Aspects of British Sculpture," in *The XXVI Venice Biennale, the British Pavilion* (London: The Westminster Press, 1952).

5. The other time when drawings and sculptures relate closely is Caro's study of the figure, for which see Julius Bryant and Rod Mengham, *Anthony Caro: The Figure* (London: Royal British Society of Sculptors, 2010).

6. David Sylvester, "Round the London Galleries," *The Listener,* Sept. 1, 1955.

7. Caro quoted in Phyllis Tuchman, "An Interview with Anthony Caro," *Artforum* 10 (June 1972): 56–58.

8. Waldman, *Anthony Caro,* 66.

9. Caro, quoted in Waldman, *Anthony Caro,* 68.

10. William Rubin, *Anthony Caro* (New York: The Museum of Modern Art, 1975), 178, n. 51, corrects the oft-repeated assumption that Caro had first seen the drawing, *Deluge,* 1510–11, Royal Collection, Windsor Castle, in an exhibition in the Queen's Gallery, London.

11. Smith's *Timeless Clock* (1957) is illustrated in Rubin, *Anthony Caro,* 142.

12. Anthony Caro, *Anthony Caro: Serie Barcelona y Serie Catalana* (Barcelona: Sala de Exposiciones del Banco Bilbao Vizcaya, 1989), 79.

13. Letter from Clement Greenberg to Anthony Caro, June 30, 1975, Barford Sculptures.

14. Compare, for example, the bronze *Variations on an Indian Theme* (1985–86), illustrated in Julius Bryant, *Anthony Caro. Figurative and Narrative Sculpture* (Farnham, Surrey: Lund Humphries, 2009), 56–57.

15. Kosme de Baranano, *Jewellery by Anthony Caro* (Madrid: Grassy Rotunda, 2006).

16. Caro did make some paintings, working in Helen Frankenthaler's studio in 1982, but the experiment was not deemed a success by the artist.

17. Martin Freedman et al., *Tyler Graphics, The Extended Image* (Minneapolis: Walker Art Center, 1987).

18. Fuji Television Gallery, Tokyo, *Caro—Paper Works, "OBAMA" Series,* texts by Shigeo Anzai and Ian Barker, 1992. For a fuller discussion of Caro's paper sculptures see Jean-Etienne Grislain, "From Sheet to Box. The Development of *Paper Sculptures,*" in Patrick Le Nouëne and Dominique Tonneau, eds., *Anthony Caro* (Montreuil: Gourcuff Gradenigo, 2008), 87–106.

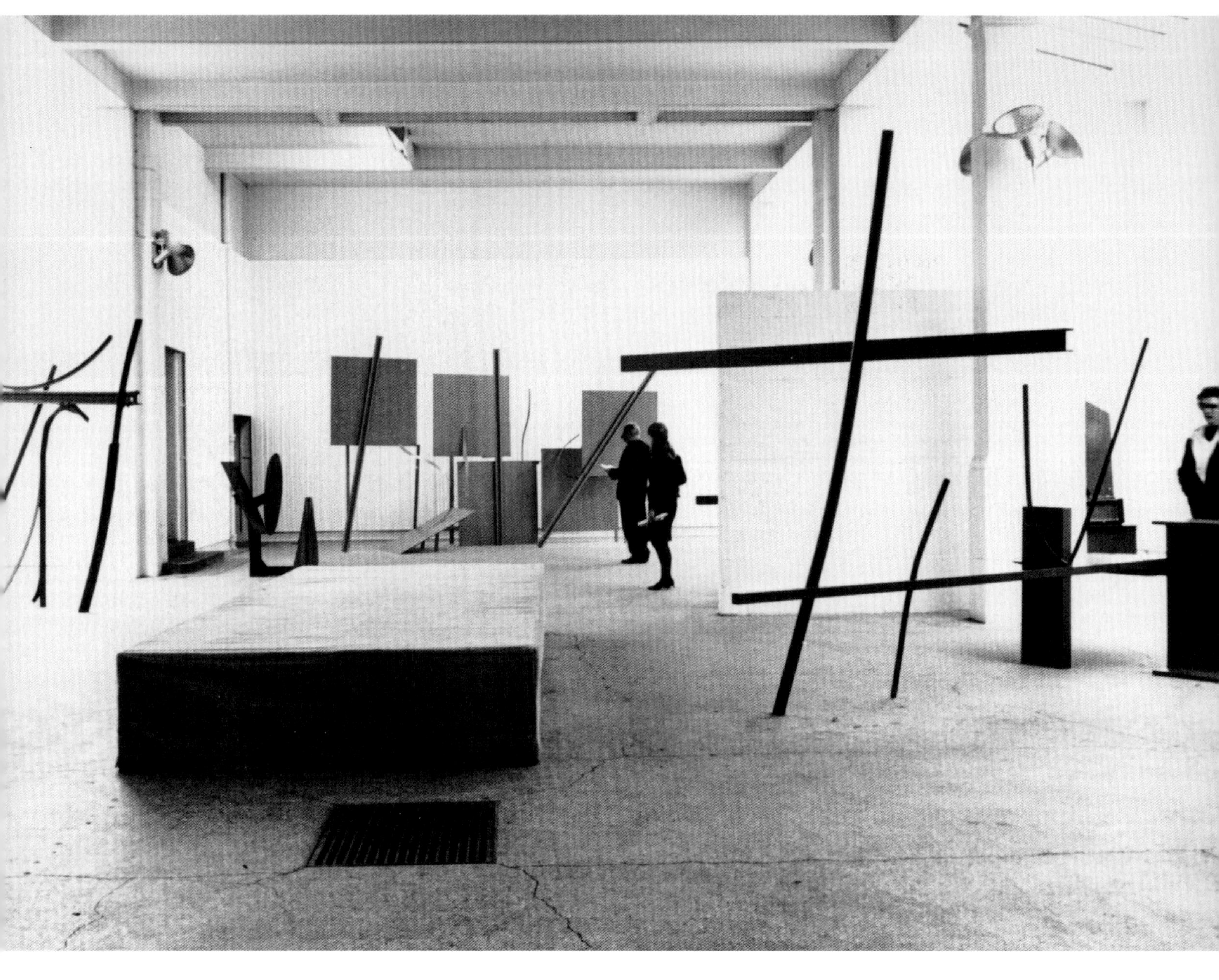

FIG. 7.1 Caro's exhibition at the Whitechapel Art Gallery, London, 1963

Select Biography

1924
Born, New Malden, Surrey, son of a City stockbroker

1937–42
Charterhouse School, Surrey. Works in studio of Charles Wheeler during school holidays

1942–44
Cambridge University, Christ's College, degree in mechanical sciences

1944–46
Royal Navy, Fleet Air Arm, as an engineer

1946–7
Regent Street Polytechnic, London, studying sculpture under Geoffrey Deeley

1947–52
Royal Academy Schools, London, training to be a sculptor of public monuments and portraits

1949
Marries Sheila Girling, a fellow student and painter. Two sons: Timothy (b. 1951) and Paul (b. 1958)

1951–53
Part-time assistant to Henry Moore at Much Hadham, Hertfordshire

1953–79
Teaches part-time at St. Martin's School of Art, London. Students include Richard Deacon, Barry Flanagan, Gilbert and George, Phillip King, Richard Long, Tim Scott, and William Tucker

1954
Moves to present home in Hampstead, with studio in the former one-car garage

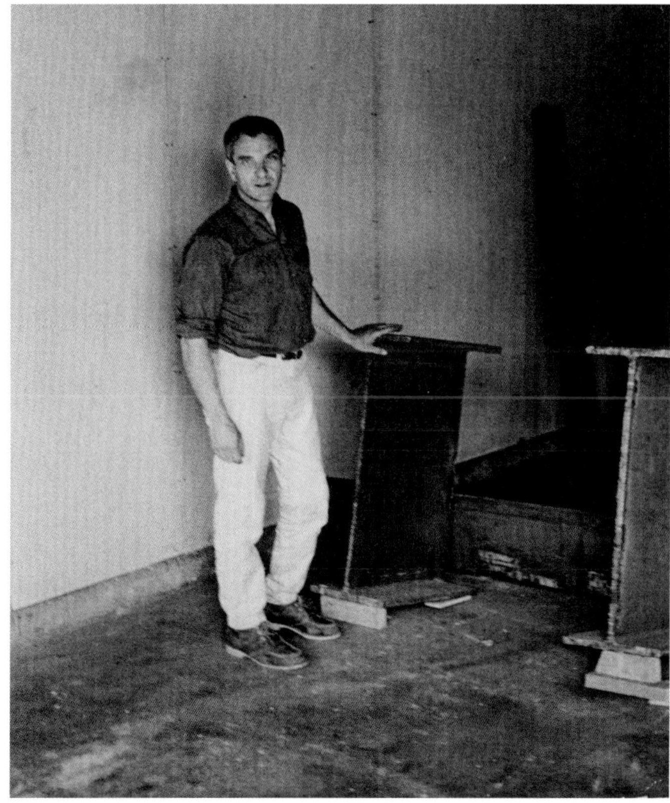

FIG. 7.2 Caro working in his garage studio, Hampstead, 1962

1955
Two figurative sculptures shown in group exhibition at Institute of Contemporary Arts, London, are singled out for praise by critics David Sylvester and Basil Taylor

1956
First solo exhibition, at Galleria del Naviglio, Milan, catalogue introduction by Lawrence Alloway

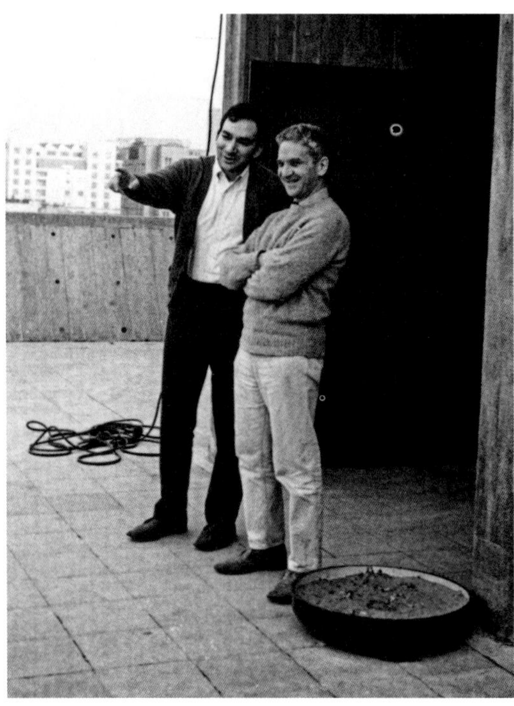

FIG. 7.3 **Caro with Michael Fried at the Hayward Gallery, 1969**

1957
First one-man exhibition in London at Gimpel Fils Gallery

1958
Works included in exhibitions in Brussels, Arnhem, Venice, and Pittsburgh

1959
Tate buys *Woman Waking Up* (1955). Clement Greenberg spends a day at Caro's home and studio. Visits the United States on a Ford Foundation English-Speaking Union grant; travels to New York, Los Angeles, and Mexico. Meets John Chamberlain, Richard Diebenkorn, Helen Frankenthaler, Jasper Johns, Ed Kienholtz, Robert Motherwell, Kenneth Noland, Robert Rauschenberg, and David Smith. Beginning of lifelong friendship with Kenneth Noland

1960
Makes first freestanding abstract sculpture from scrap steel: *Twenty-Four Hours* (Tate, purchased 1975). Establishes welding shop at St. Martin's and encourages experimentation, working with students rather than through formal teaching

1961
Michael Fried visits Caro's studio

1962
Makes *Early One Morning* (Tate, presented by the Contemporary Art Society, 1965)

1963
Solo exhibition of fifteen new abstract steel sculptures at the Whitechapel Art Gallery, London curated by Bryan Robertson. Appointed a visiting faculty member at Bennington College, Vermont, where he teaches (until 1965) with Jules Olitski and regularly visits Noland and Smith

1964
First solo exhibition in New York, at André Emmerich Gallery

1965
Begins visiting the United States regularly, up to four times a year. Clement Greenberg's "Breakthrough" article first published in *Arts Yearbook*

1966
First solo exhibition at David Mirvish Gallery, Toronto. Conversations with Michael Fried lead to the first table pieces

1967
Purchases steel from the estate of David Smith (d. 1965)

1968
Prairie (1967) on cover of *Artforum*

1969
Retrospective of fifty sculptures, curated by Michael Fried, at the Hayward Gallery, London. Acquires new studio in former piano factory in Camden Town, north London, where he is joined by new full-time studio assistant Patrick

Cunningham, but continues to work alone at home in evenings and at weekends. Makes *Table Piece LXXXVIII—Deluge* (1969–70), *Orangerie* (1969), and *Sun Feast* (1969–70). Begins to work at Noland's studio at Shaftsbury, Vermont.

1972
Works at Ripamonte Factory in Veduggio, Italy, using soft-end rolled steel

1973
Midday (1960) acquired by the Museum of Modern Art, New York

1974
A series of sculptures made in 1973 using rolled steel from a steelworks in Consett, Co. Durham, including table sculptures, is shown at André Emmerich Gallery, New York. Works at York Steel Company, Toronto, using mobile cranes to make large upright sculptures, known as the *Flats* series. Exhibition at Kenwood, London, of seventeen new table sculptures in rusted steel

1975
Retrospective at the Museum of Modern Art, New York, which travels to Walker Art Center, Minneapolis, Museum of Fine Arts, Houston, and to the Museum of Fine Arts, Boston. Works in clay with Margie Hughto at Syracuse University, New York

1976
Presented with the key to the City of New York

1977
British Council organizes retrospective exhibition of table sculptures for Tel Aviv Museum, Israel, which tours to Australia, New Zealand, and Germany. Artist in residence at summer workshop, Emma Lake, University of Saskatchewan, Canada

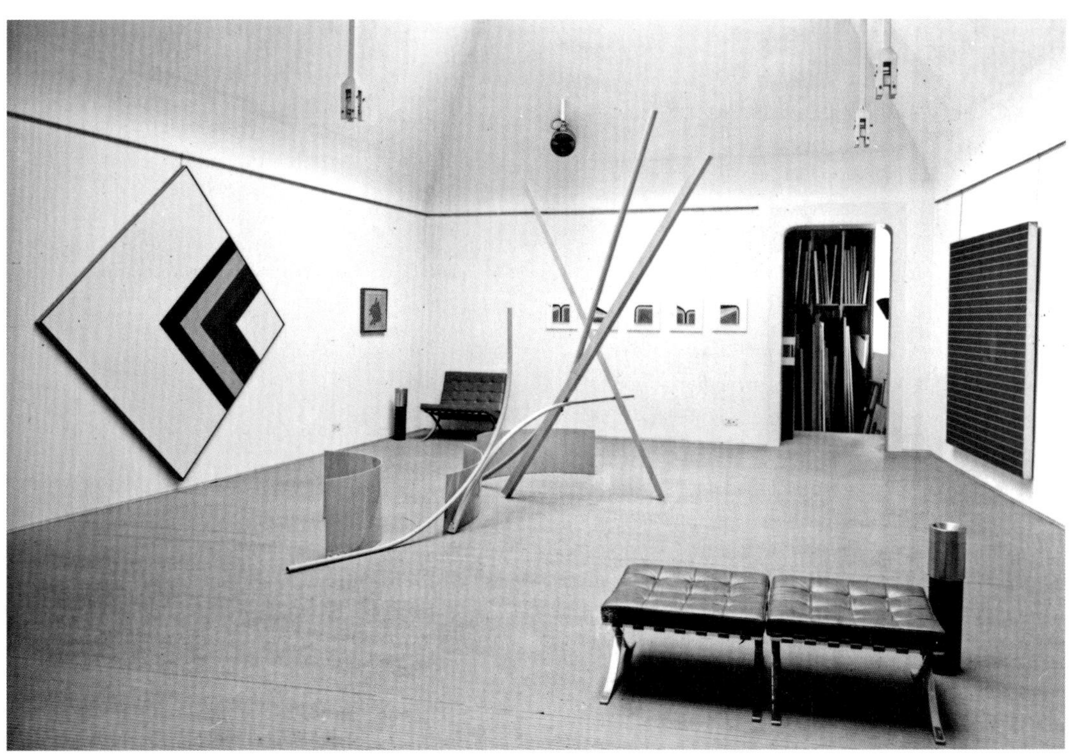

FIG. 7.4 Kasmin Gallery, London, 1966, showing *Crossing* (1965)

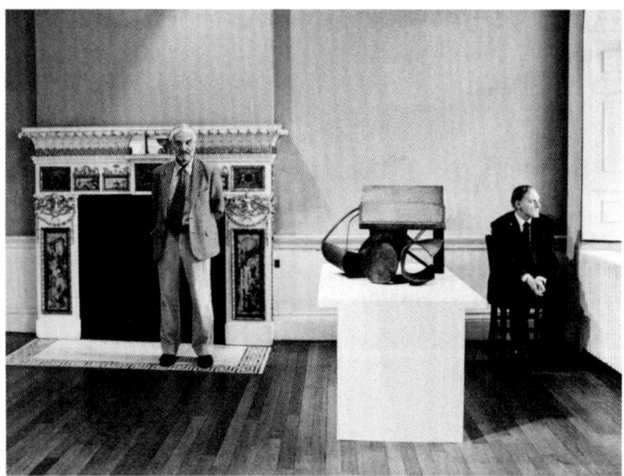

FIG. 7.5 Caro at Kenwood during his exhibition of table bronzes, 1981

1978
Makes *Writing Pieces*, series of calligraphic sculptures in steel. Makes *Ledge Piece* for East Building, National Gallery of Art, Washington, DC, at the invitation of architect I. M. Pei

1981
New bronze sculptures shown at Kenwood, London, and at Acquavella Gallery, New York. Makes wall sculptures in handmade paper with Ken Tyler, Bedford, New York

1982
Exhibition of bronzes inspired by Indian relief sculptures at André Emmerich Gallery, New York. First Triangle Workshop, a two-week summer studio for thirty artists from the United States, United Kingdom and Canada, held at Pine Plains, New York

1985
Builds a studio house at Ancram, New York (uses regularly until 1996). First visit to Greece. Awarded honorary doctorate, Cambridge University

1987
Triangle Workshop held in Barcelona

1988
After Olympia shown on roof terrace at the Metropolitan Museum of Art, New York. *Catalan* series of thirty-three table sculptures made from steel collected in Barcelona

1989
Cascades series of fourteen table sculptures. Awarded Honorary Doctor of Fine Arts by Yale University

1990
Visits Japan, makes paper sculptures with Mr. Ohé in village of Obama

1991
Sculpture Towards Architecture exhibition at Tate, London

1992
Retrospective in the Trajan Markets, Rome. Works with ceramist Hans Spinner near Grasse, France

1994
Trojan War shown at Kenwood, based on ceramics made with Spinner (British Council tours it to Thessaloniki and Athens in 1997). Workshop and exhibition *Caro, Noland, Olitski* held at Hartford Art School, Connecticut

1996
Promenade shown in Tuileries Gardens, Paris. Collaborates with architect Norman Foster and engineer Chris Wise on Millennium Bridge across the Thames (opens 2000)

1998
Book Sculptures based on ceramics made with Hans Spinner shown at Annely Juda Fine Art, London. *Caro—Sculpture from Painting* exhibition at National Gallery, London

1999
The Last Judgement (1995–99) shown at 48th Venice Biennale. Makes *Paper Book* series with Ken Tyler

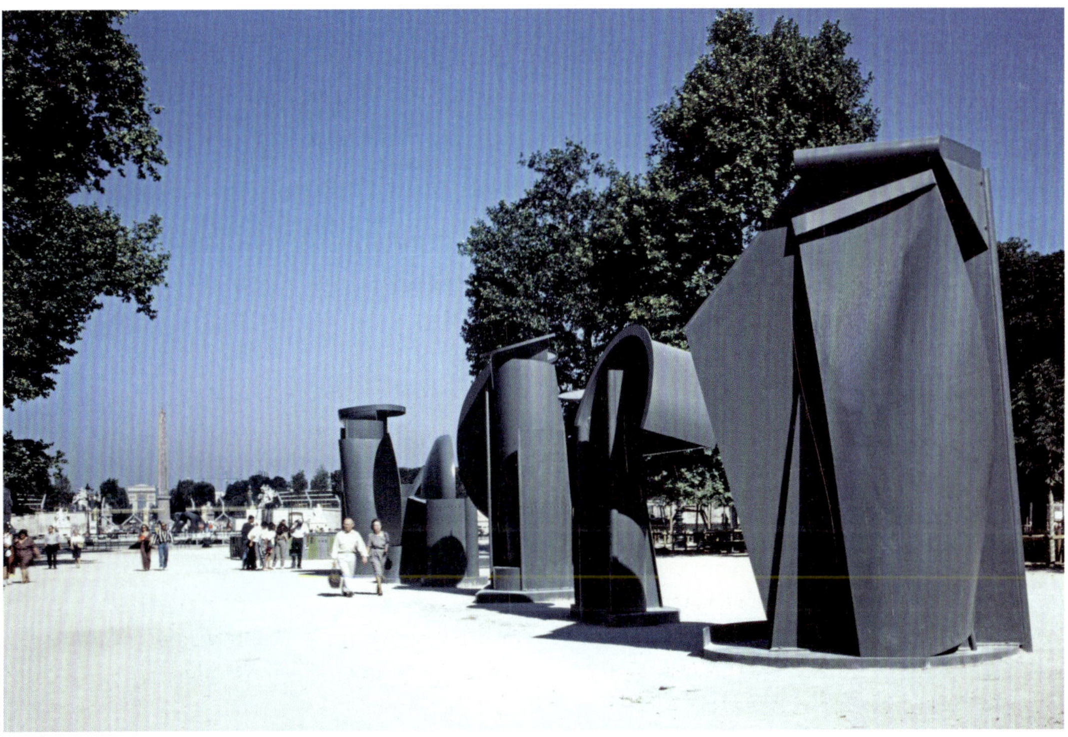

FIG. 7.6 *Promenade* at Tuileries Gardens, Paris, 1996

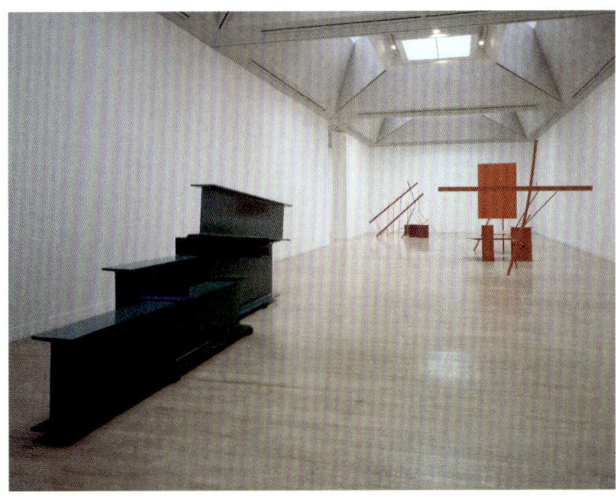

FIG. 7.7 Installation view of Caro's retrospective exhibition at Tate Britain, 2005

2003
Paper Book series shown at Annely Juda Fine Art, London

2004
80th birthday exhibition, including sixteen new works, at Kenwood (subsequently tours to California, Texas, and New York)

2005
Retrospective at Tate Britain

2007
New Galvanized Steel Sculptures at Annely Juda Fine Art, London (subsequently shown at Galerie Daniel Templon, Paris; Mitchell-Innes & Nash, New York)

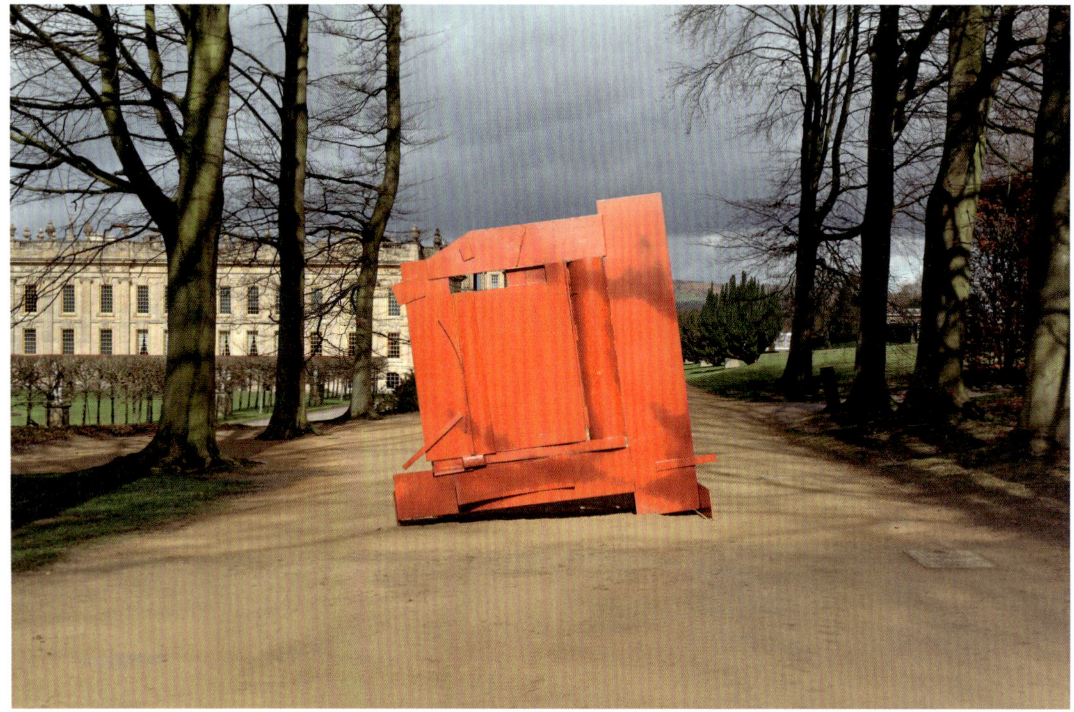

FIG. 7.8 *Vespers*, 1972–4, painted steel, as installed in Caro's exhibition at Chatsworth, 2012

2008
Chapel of Light inaugurated at the Church of St. John the Baptist, Bourbourg, France. Retrospective shown simultaneously at museums in Calais, Gravelines, and Dunkirk. Exhibition of portraits at the National Portrait Gallery, London. *Promenade* shown in the Courtyard of Burlington House, London

2010
The Figure exhibition of life studies at the Royal British Society of Sculptors, London. *Upright Sculptures* shown at Annely Juda Fine Art, London; Galerie Daniel Templon, Paris; Mitchell-Innes & Nash, New York

2011
Conceives temporary installation for Park Avenue, New York

2012
Exhibitions at Jubilee Park, Canary Wharf, London; Chatsworth, Derbyshire; and the Yale Center for British Art, New Haven. Prepares exhibitions for Museum Wurth, Künzelsau, Germany (2014) and Museo Correr (Venice Biennale, 2013)

Select Bibliography

Alberro, Alexander, and Stimson, eds. *Conceptual Art: A Critical Anthology*. Cambridge: MIT Press, 1999.

Alloway, Lawrence. *Anthony Caro: dal 19 al 28 Marzo 1956*. Milan: Galleria del Naviglio, 1956.

Annesley, David et. al. "Anthony Caro's Work: A Symposium by Four Sculptors." *Studio International* 177, no. 4 (January 1969): 14–20.

Armstrong, Elizabeth. *Tyler Graphics, the Extended Image*. Minneapolis: Walker Art Center, 1987.

Bachelard, Gaston. *The Poetics of Space*. Translated by Maria Jolas. New York: Orion, 1964.

Baranano, Kosme M. de. *Jewellery by Anthony Caro II*. Madrid: Grassy, 2008.

Barker, Ian. *Anthony Caro: Quest for the New Sculpture*. Künzelsau, Germany: Swiridoff, 2004.

Blume, Dieter, et al. *Anthony Caro: Catalogue Raisonné*. 15 vols. Cologne, Germany: Galerie Wentzel, 1981–2011.

Broodthaers, Marcel, and Michael Compton. *Marcel Broodthaers*. London: Tate Gallery, 1980.

Bryant, Julius. *Anthony Caro: A Life in Sculpture*. London: Merrell, 2004.

———. *Anthony Caro: Figurative and Narrative Sculpture*. Farnham, Surrey, UK: Lund Humphries, 2009.

Bryant, Julius, ed. *Art and Design for All: The Victoria and Albert Museum*. London: V&A, 2011.

Bryant, Julius, and Rod Mengham. *Anthony Caro: The Figure*. London: Royal Society of British Sculptors, 2010.

Bryant, Julius, and John Spurling. *The Trojan War. Sculptures by Anthony Caro*. London: Lund Humphries, 1994.

Caro, Anthony. "The Master Sculptor." *Observer*. London, November 27, 1960.

———. "Letter to Editor." *Art Monthly* 32 (December 1979): 27.

———. *Anthony Caro: Serie Barcelona y Serie Catalana*. Barcelona: Sala de Exposiciones del Banco Bilbao Vizcaya, 1989.

———. *Anthony Caro: Table Sculptures 1966–1977: [Catalogue of] a British Council Exhibition*. London: British Council, 1977.

Caro, Anthony, Robert Rosenblum, and David Sylvester. "On Picasso as a Sculptor." *Modern Painters* 7, no. 1 (Spring 1994): 35–39.

Clark, T. J. "Clement Greenberg's Theory of Art." *Critical Inquiry* 9, no. 1 (September 1982): 139–56.

Cohen, David. "The Last Modernist. Sir Anthony Caro." *Sculpture* 14:1 (January–February 1995): 20–27.

Compton, Ann. "Plastic Pleasures: Reconsidering the Practice of Modeling through Manuals of Sculpture Technique, c. 1880–1933." *Journal of Modern Craft* 3, no. 3 (November 2010): 309–24.

Curtis, Penelope. "How Direct Carving Stole the Idea of Modern British Sculpture." In *Sculpture and the Pursuit of a Modern Ideal in Britain, c. 1880–1930*, edited by David Getsy. London: Ashgate, 2004.

Curtis, Penelope, and Keith Wilson, eds. *Modern British Sculpture*. London: Royal Academy of Arts, 2011.

Dell, Christopher, ed. *What Makes a Masterpiece? Encounters with Great Works of Art*. London: Thames & Hudson, 2010.

Droth, Martina. "Anthony Caro at Chatsworth." In *Caro at Chatsworth*. Salisbury, UK, and Bakewell, UK: New Art Centre and the Chatsworth House Trust, 2012.

Eitner, Lorenz. "Art History and the Sense of Quality." *Art International* 14, no. 5 (May 1975): 75–80.

Fenton, Terry. *Anthony Caro*. London: Academy Editions, 1986.

Forge, Andrew. "Round the Galleries." *The Listener* (January 17, 1957): 102.

———. “Andrew Forge Interviews Anthony Caro.” *Studio International* 171, no. 873 (1966).

Fried, Michael. *Anthony Caro: Sculpture 1960–1963*. London: Whitechapel Art Gallery, 1963.

———. “Art and Objecthood.” *Artforum* 5, no. 10 (June 1967): 12–23.

———. *Anthony Caro.* London: Hayward Gallery, 1969.

———. “Caro’s Abstractness.” *Artforum* 9, no. 1 (September 1970): 32–34.

———. *Anthony Caro’s Table Sculptures, 1966–1977*. London: British Council, 1977.

———. *Art and Objecthood: Essays and Reviews.* Chicago: University of Chicago Press, 1998.

Fuller, Peter. “Anthony Caro: His Works and Views.” *Art Monthly*, 23 (1979): 6–15.

———. “Stockwell Depot.” *Art Monthly* 30 (October 1979): 14–17.

———. “Anthony Caro Talks About Henry Moore.” *Modern Painters* 1, no. 3 (1988).

Golding, John. *Caro at the National Gallery*. London: National Gallery, 1998.

Greenberg, Clement. “The Pasted-Paper Revolution.” *Art News* 57, no. 5 (September 1958): 46–49.

———. “Anthony Caro.” *Arts Yearbook 8: Contemporary Sculpture* (1965): 106–09.

———. *Art and Culture: Critical Essays.* Boston: Beacon, 1961.

———. *Clement Greenberg: The Collected Essays and Criticism*. Edited by John O’Brian. 4 vols. Chicago: University of Chicago Press, 1986.

Grieve, Alastair Ian. *Constructed Abstract Art in England. A Neglected Avante-Garde*. New Haven: Yale University Press, 2005.

Hall, James. “Clement Greenberg on English Sculpture and Englishness.” *The Sculpture Journal* 4 (2000): 172–77.

Haufschild, Lutz. “Conversations with Anthony Caro.” *Arts Magazine* 9, no. 38–39 (June 1978).

Hilton, Tim. “Obituary: Clement Greenberg.” *The Independent*. London, May 11, 1994.

———. “Still Reckless after All These Years: In 1960, Anthony Caro’s ‘Breakthrough’ Revolutionised Sculpture.” *The Independent*. London, March 13, 1994.

Hunt, Jeremy. *Flats*. Salisbury, UK: New Art Centre, 2007.

Jones, Caroline A. *Eyesight Alone: Clement Greenberg’s Modernism and the Bureaucratization of the Senses*. Chicago: University of Chicago Press, 2005.

Kahnweiler, Daniel-Henry. *The Sculpture of Picasso*. London: R. Phillips, 1949.

Krauss, Rosalind E. *Terminal Iron Works: The Sculpture of David Smith*. Cambridge, Mass.: MIT Press, 1971.

———. “Anthony Caro, André Emmerich Gallery.” *Artforum* 7, no. 5 (January 1969): 53–55.

———. *Passages in Modern Sculpture*. Cambridge, Mass.: MIT Press, 1977.

———. *A Voyage on the North Sea: Art in the Age of the Post-Medium Condition*. London: Thames & Hudson, 1999.

Lantéri, Edouard. *Modelling: A Guide for Teachers and Students*. 3 vols. London: Chapman and Hall, 1902.

Larson, Kay. “The Steel-Plated Theories of Anthony Caro.” *New York Magazine* 14, no. 35 (September 7, 1981): 58–59.

LeWitt, Sol. “Sentences on Conceptual Art.” *Art-Language* 1, no. 1 (May 1969).

Lovatt, Anna. “Rosalind Krauss’s ‘The Originality of the Avant-Garde and Other Modernist Myths,’ 1985.” *The Burlington Magazine* 153, no. 1302 (September 2011): 601–04.

Lynton, Norbert. *Caro: Five Sculptures by Anthony Caro: An Arts Council Exhibition*. London: Arts Council of Great Britain, 1982.

Mallgrave, Harry Francis. *Gottfried Semper: Architect of the Nineteenth Century: a Personal and Intellectual Biography*. New Haven: Yale University Press, 1996.

Martin, Barry. “New Work: Anthony Caro.” *Studio International* 187 (April 1974): 202–03.

———. “On the Occasion of Anthony Caro’s Retrospective Exhibition at MoMA.” *Studio International* 189 (May–June 1975): 233–35.

Masheck, Joseph. “Reflections on Caro’s Englishness.” *Studio International* 188 (September 1974): 93–96.

McAvera, Brian. "A Conversation with Sir Anthony Caro." *Sculpture* 21, no. 2 (March 2002): 25–31.

McLean, Bruce. "Not Even Crimble Crumble." *Studio International* 180, no. 926 (October 1970): 156–59.

McLean, Bruce, and Nena Dimitrijevic. *Bruce McLean*. London: Trustees of the Whitechapel Art Gallery, 1981.

Millard, Charles W. "The Reclining Figure and the Development of Modern Sculpture." *The Hudson Review* 27, no. 2 (Summer 1974): 234–44.

Mitchinson, David, and Julian Andrews. *Celebrating Moore: Works from the Collection of the Henry Moore Foundation*. London: Lund Humphries, 1998.

Moore, Henry. *Henry Moore On Sculpture: A Collection of the Sculptor's Writings and Spoken Words*. Edited by Philip James. London: Macdonald & Co, 1968.

Moorhouse, Paul. *Anthony Caro: Sculpture Towards Architecture*. London: Tate Gallery, 1991.

———. *Anthony Caro: Presence*. Farnham, Surrey, UK: Lund Humphries, 2010.

———, ed. *Anthony Caro*. London: Tate Publishing, 2005.

Murray, Peter. *Caro at Longside: Sculpture and Sculpitecture*. West Yorkshire, UK: Yorkshire Sculpture Park, 2001.

Nauman, Bruce. *Please Pay Attention Please: Bruce Nauman's Words, Writings and Interviews*. Edited by Janet Kraynak. Cambridge, Mass.: MIT Press, 2003.

Neff, Terry Ann R., and Graham William John Beal. *A Quiet Revolution, British Sculpture since 1965*. London: Thames and Hudson, 1987.

Nouëne, Patrick Le, Barbara Forest, and Aude Cordonnier. *Anthony Caro*. Montreuil: Gourcuff Gradenigo, 2008.

Pound, Ezra. *Gaudier-Brzeska: A Memoir*. London: Laidlaw & Laidlaw, 1939.

Prettejohn, Elizabeth. "From Aestheticism to Modernism, and Back Again." *Interdisciplinary Studies in the Long Nineteenth Century* 2 (2006): 1–16.

Read, Benedict, David Thistlewood, and Robert Burstow, eds. *Herbert Read : A British Vision of World Art*. Leeds, UK: Leeds City Art Galleries, 1993.

Read, Herbert. "New Aspects of British Sculpture." In *The XXVI Venice Biennale, the British Pavilion*. London: The Westminster Press, 1952.

———. *A Concise History of Modern Sculpture*. London: Thames & Hudson, 1964, reprinted 1974.

Reid, Mary. *Anthony Caro: Drawing in Space*. Farnham, Surrey, UK: Lund Humphries, 2009.

Richardson, John. "Early One Morning." *The New Statesman* (March 5, 1965).

Robertson, Bryan. *Anthony Caro: Sculpture through Five Decades 1955–1994: An Exhibition to Celebrate the Artist's Seventieth Birthday*. London: Annely Juda Fine Art, 1994.

Ross, Clifford, ed. *Abstract Expressionism: Creators and Critics: An Anthology*. New York: Abrams, 1990.

Rubenfeld, Florence. *Clement Greenberg: A Life*. New York: Scribner, 1997.

Rubin, William Stanley. *Anthony Caro*. New York: Museum of Modern Art, 1975.

———. *Frank Stella*. New York: Museum of Modern Art, 1970.

Russell, John. "Closing the Gaps: Anthony Caro's Elegant New Pieces." *Art News* 69 (May 1970): 37–39.

Smith, H. F. Westley. *Anthony Caro: Small Sculptures*. Farnham, Surrey, UK: Lund Humphries, 2010.

Stiles, Kristine, and Peter Howard Selz, eds. *Theories and Documents of Contemporary Art : A Sourcebook of Artists' Writings*. Berkeley: University of California Press, 1996.

Sylvester, David. "Round the London Galleries." *The Listener* 1 (September 1955).
Taylor, Basil. "Art." *The Spectator* 2 (September 1955).
Tuchman, Maurice. *American Sculpture of the Sixties*. Los Angeles County Museum of Art, 1967.
Tuchman, Phyllis. "An Interview with Anthony Caro." *Artforum* 10 (June 1972): 56–58.
———. "Anthony Caro: Sculpting Space." *Sculpture* 16, no. 8 (October 1997).
Vaizey, Marina. "Sailing Off into a Space of His Own." *Sunday Times*, October 1, 1989.
Varnedoe, Kirk. "Intellectual Subtlety in Constructed Steel." *Art News* 74 (Summer 1975): 38–40.
Wagner, Anne Middleton. *Mother Stone: The Vitality of Modern British Sculpture*. New Haven: Yale University Press, 2005.
———. "Scale in Sculpture: The Sixties and Henry Moore." *Tate Papers*, no. 15 (Spring 2011).
Waldman, Diane. *Robert Ryman*. New York: Solomon R. Guggenheim Foundation, 1972.
———. *Anthony Caro*. New York: Abbeville, 1982.
Wallis, Nevile. "At The Galleries: Different Worlds." *Observer*, January 13, 1958.
Wheeler, Charles. *High Relief: The Autobiography of Sir Charles Wheeler, Sculptor*. Feltham: Country Life Books, 1968.
Whelan, Richard. *Anthony Caro*. Harmondsworth, Middlesex: Penguin, 1974.
Wilkin, Karen. *Anthony Caro: Interior and Exterior*. Farnham, Surrey, UK: Lund Humphries, 2009.
Wilkin, Karen, and Bruce Guenther, eds. *Clement Greenberg: A Critic's Collection*. Portland Art Museum, 2001.

Index

Illustrations are indicated by italicized page numbers. Caro's works are listed by title.

Photography Credits

Every effort has been made to credit the photographers and sources of all illustrations in this volume; if there are any errors or omissions, please contact Yale University Press so that corrections can be made in any subsequent edition.

All illustrations are © Barford Sculptures Ltd, except for the images listed below.

© John Hammond: Figs. 0.1, 1.1, 1.5, 3.2, 3.7, 3.8, 3.9, 3.17, 3.18, 3.21, 4.7, 4.10, 4.17, 4.21, 4.26, Cats. 21, 22, 23, 24, 25, 26, 27, 28, 31, 36, 37, 39, 40, 41, 44, 45, 46, 47, 48, 49, 50, 51, 52, 53, 54, 55, 56, 58, 59, 60, 61, 62
© Tate, London, 2012: Figs. 1.2, 2.7, 2.8, 3.14, 4.6, 4.8
The Museum of Modern Art, New York. Mr. and Mrs. Arthur Wiesenberger Fund. © 2008, MoMA, New York: Fig. 2.10
Courtesy of the Artist and Mitchell-Innes & Nash: Fig. 2.12, Cat. 35
John Riddy: Fig. 2.14
From Charles Wheeler, *High Relief: The Autobiography of Sir Charles Wheeler, Sculptor*, Feltham, Country Life Books, 1968, plate 56: fig. 3.3
Photo: Anne Wagner. © The Henry Moore Foundation, All rights reserved, DACS 2011: Fig. 3.5
National Gallery of Art, Washington, D.C. Gift of Mrs. John W. Simpson: Fig. 3.6
Photo: David Smith. © Estate of David Smith/VAGA, New York: Fig. 3.10
Photo: Leo Lances. © Estate of David Smith/VAGA, New York: Fig. 3.12
Yale University Art Gallery, Charles B. Benenson, B.A. 1933, Collection: Fig. 3.13
EPW Studio/Maris Hutchinson, 2012: Figs. 3.20, Cats. 32, 33, 57
Photo: Carlos Granger: Fig. 3.22
Private Collection / Photo © Christie's Images / The Bridgeman Art Library: Fig. 4.1
Digital adaptation by Martin Shoesmith, 2012: Fig. 4.2
Photo: Sheldan C. Collins. © Charles Ray, Courtesy Matthew Marks Gallery: Fig. 4.3
The Museum of Modern Art, New York, Mrs. Simon Guggenheim Fund. © 2012 Artists Rights Society (ARS), New York / ADAGP, Paris: Fig. 4.9
© Centre Pompidou, MNAM-CCI, Dist. RMN / Droits reserves: Fig. 4.11
Yale Center for British Art, New Haven, Paul Mellon Collection. © Estate of the Artist: Fig. 4.12
Yale University Art Gallery, New Haven, anonymous gift. © 2004 Artists Rights Society (ARS), New York / ADAGP, Paris: Fig. 4.13
Photo: Michael Muller. Reproduced by permission of The Henry Moore Foundation: Fig. 4.14
The Museum of Modern Art, New York / Scala, Florence: Fig. 4.19
National Gallery of Art, Washington, D.C., Gift of the Collectors Committee: Fig. 4.20
© The Leach Pottery, St Ives / Victoria and Albert Museum, London: Fig. 4.22
© RMN / Béatrice Hatala: Fig. 4.23
Collection S.M.A.K. / Flemish Community, photography Dirk Pauwels, © DACS 2012: Fig 4.25
Peter Aaron / Esto Photographics Inc. 2007: Fig. 5.1
Yale Center for British Art: Cats. 1–20, 29
The Museum of Modern Art, New York, Gift of Guido Goldman in memory of Minda de Gunzberg. © 2012, MoMA, New York: Cat. 35
© The Metropolitan Museum of Art. Image source: Art Resource, NY: Cat. 38
© Mitro Hood: Cats. 42, 43